'This is a remarkable collection of essays on our relations with the dead and the mourning process. The authors are wide-ranging in their areas of expertise, drawing from social anthropology, history, philosophy, Jungian studies, and psychoanalysis, but together they provide both broad and penetrating insight into this most personal of our universally human concerns. Dr Brodersen is to be commended for this fine contribution to Thanatology studies.'

Dr Roger Brooke, *Emeritus Professor of Psychology, Jungian scholar, Duquesne University, author of* Jung and Phenomenology

'Like the vegetative nervous system that regulates digestion, heart rate and breathing without our having to think about them, many of our rituals of mourning operate beneath the surface to smooth the passages of life to death. This daring and complex volume explores those rituals and passages from many cultures intended to move us from this life to the next, although the transition is often seen to be anything but effortless for the living and the dead.'

Thomas Singer, MD, *Psychiatrist and Jungian Psychoanalyst, editor of the award-winning* Cultural Complexes and the Soul of America

'Jungian analysts and scholars have come together in this rich and creative collection to explore the universal facets of death, dying and the mourning processes that affect all of us. The content will appeal to therapists working with the archetypal in grief and dreams of the dead. Equally, those interested in the historic terrain of the land of the dead and burying rituals will find an anthropological sensibility to the topics. The collection is a significant contribution that expands collective psychoanalytic knowledge by assisting clients to traverse these experiences around death. This will inevitably become a seminal collection and resource in future for Jungians.'

Dr Stephani Stephens, *Psychotherapist and a lecturer in Counselling at the University of Canberra in Canberra, Australia, and author of* C.G. Jung and the Dead: Visions, Active Imagination and the Unconscious Terrain

'The wide-spread contents and different perspectives on death, mourning processes, burial rituals and intimations of immortality assembled in this book address various cross-cultural approaches to various aspects of death. As an archetypal experience, death has and will always raise many unanswered questions that challenge all of us. The present book is an attempt to address these issues from a Jungian point of view. Each author gives profound insight based on his or her personal field of interest and is written from the heart. This is indeed a courageous book that will help the reader to confront difficult issues and find a larger view on a life experience that is often feared, but inevitable.'

Evy Tausky, *Jungian Training Analyst and Supervisor, President of the Curatorium of the C.G. Jung-Institute, Zürich*

Jungian Dimensions of the Mourning Process, Burial Rituals and Access to the Land of the Dead

This innovative volume on the mourning process, burial rites and intimations of immortality offers diverse Jungian, cross-cultural, interdisciplinary and depth-psychological perspectives, written predominantly by graduates and candidates of the CG Jung Institute Zürich.

The themes of this book are particularly relevant as they relate to the COVID-19 pandemic and other environmental disasters, when so many people die without a proper burial and are, thus, not properly commemorated with their status value. The contributors cover a wide range of subjects from their clinical observations attached to grief and loss in the prolonged mourning process, the meaning behind burial rites in cyclical and linear temporalities and an analysis of why certain dead are excluded from becoming ancestors. Unconscious processes such as dreams, archetypes and cultural complexes from the personal and collective unconscious are also presented and explored.

This collection will be of great interest to interdisciplinary academic researchers, Jungian analysts and students, psychoanalysts, psychotherapists, anthropologists, cultural theorists and students interested in the mourning process, rites of passage, past and present burial practices and the imaginative, symbolic significance of the land of the dead.

Elizabeth Brodersen, PhD, is an accredited Jungian Training Analyst and Supervisor at the CGJI Zürich and currently a member of the Institute's Research Commission. Elizabeth received her doctorate in psycho-social psychoanalytic studies at the University of Essex, UK, and works as a Jungian analyst in a private practice in Germany and Switzerland.

Jungian Dimensions of the Mourning Process, Burial Rituals and Access to the Land of the Dead

Intimations of Immortality

Edited by Elizabeth Brodersen

Routledge
Taylor & Francis Group
LONDON AND NEW YORK

Designed cover image: © Nikpal as rendered as the owner
of the image on Getty Images.

First published 2024
by Routledge
4 Park Square, Milton Park, Abingdon, Oxon OX14 4RN

and by Routledge
605 Third Avenue, New York, NY 10158

*Routledge is an imprint of the Taylor & Francis Group, an informa
business*

© 2024 selection and editorial matter, Elizabeth Brodersen;
individual chapters, the contributors

British Library Cataloguing-in-Publication Data
A catalogue record for this book is available from the British
Library

Library of Congress Cataloging-in-Publication Data
Names: Brodersen, Elizabeth, editor.
Title: Jungian dimensions of the mourning process, burial rituals
    and access to the land of the dead : intimations of immortality /
    edited by Elizabeth Brodersen.
Description: Abingdon, Oxon ; New York, NY : Routledge, 2024. |
    Includes bibliographical references and index.
Identifiers: LCCN 2023004760 (print) | LCCN 2023004761 (ebook) |
    ISBN 9781032321950 (hardback) | ISBN 9781032321943 (paperback) |
    ISBN 9781003313304 (ebook)
Subjects: LCSH: Bereavement. | Burial. | Jungian psychology.
Classification: LCC BF575.G7 J86 2024 (print) | LCC BF575.G7
    (ebook) | DDC 155.9/37—dc23/eng/20230501
LC record available at https://lccn.loc.gov/2023004760
LC ebook record available at https://lccn.loc.gov/2023004761

ISBN: 978-1-032-32195-0 (hbk)
ISBN: 978-1-032-32194-3 (pbk)
ISBN: 978-1-003-31330-4 (ebk)

DOI: 10.4324/9781003313304

Typeset in Times New Roman
by Apex CoVantage, LLC

'The mourning process rises up raw and hard but that substance also forms the granite of our ancestral memories, aided by its access into the unconscious and the land of the dead.'

Elizabeth Brodersen

Contents

Contributors

Paul Attinello is a Jungian analyst in private practice and a retired senior lecturer at Newcastle University who has also taught at the University of Hong Kong and as a guest professor at UCLA. He received his PhD from UCLA and diploma as an analyst from the C.G. Jung Institute in Zürich. He has lived and worked on four continents, has been involved in creative and academic events and projects, HIV groups and programs, and is Co-Founder of the Psychosocial Wednesdays seminar series. He is published in a number of essay collections, journals and reference works, including the ground-breaking *Queering the Pitch: The New Lesbian & Gay Musicology*. He has written on contemporary music, the culture of AIDS and philosophical and psychological topics.

Elizabeth Brodersen, PhD, is an accredited Training Analyst, Supervisor and lecturer at the C.G. Jung Institute, Zürich. In 2008, she received her diploma in analytical psychology from CGJIZ and, in 2014, a doctorate in psychoanalytic studies from Essex University, UK. Elizabeth presently works as a Jungian analyst and supervisor in private practice in Germany and Switzerland and is a member of the English Research Commission at CGJIZ. She serves on the *International Journal of Jungian Studies* (IJJS) editorial board and is a member of the editorial board of Brill's Contemporary Psychoanalytic Studies series. Her latest publications include a monograph, *Taboo Personal and Collective Representations, Origin and Positioning within Cultural Complexes* (Routledge, 2019), and an edited book with Pilar Amezaga, *Jungian Perspectives on Indeterminate States, Betwixt and Between Borders* (Routledge, 2021).

Robin McCoy Brooks, MA, LMHC, TEP, is a Jungian analyst in private practice in Seattle/Bellingham, Washington, United States, and an international educator and consultant. She is Co-Editor-in-Chief of the *International Journal of Jungian Studies* and serves on the Board of Directors of the International Association for Jungian Studies. Robin is also a founding member of the New School for Analytical Psychology, an active analyst member of the Inter-Regional Society of Jungian Analysts and the International Association for Analytical Psychology. Further, she is a nationally certified trainer, educator and practitioner of Group Psychotherapy, Sociometry and Psychodrama. She is the author of

Psychoanalysis Catastrophe & Social Action (Routledge, 2022) and numerous chapters and articles. Her works focus on a variety of topics related to psychoanalysis, philosophy, catastrophic trauma, creative agency (sublimation) and collective individuation.

Cécile Buckenmeyer is a Jungian analyst in private practice in Lancaster, UK, and a member of IGAP (UK), AGAP and IAAP. She obtained an MSc in Jungian studies from Birkbeck (University of London) and trained at the C.G. Jung Institute Zürich. She has a long-term interest in the relationship between psyche, culture and place. Born in France, she has lived in Japan, the USA and, for the last 20 years, in the UK. Before her training, she worked as a cross-cultural consultant, primarily with Japanese organisations. At the 2019 IAAP Conference in Vienna, she presented a paper entitled 'The Hestia-Hermes Archetype and the Spirit of the Place.'

Vicente L. de Moura is a supervisor, lecturer, and training analyst at the C.G. Jung Institute Zürich. Former President of the Susan Bach Foundation, he is author of various articles and was curator of the picture archive of the C.G. Jung Institute Zürich between 1998 and 2015. He works as psychotherapist and analyst in his own practice. His website can be found at www.de-moura.ch

Erik Goodwyn, MD, is Clinical Faculty at the Billings Clinic, part of the WWAMI University of Washington School of Medicine–Billings, Montana, affiliate, Department of Psychiatry. He has authored numerous publications in the field of consciousness studies, Jungian psychology, neuroscience, mythology, philosophy, anthropology and the psychology of religion. He is Co-Editor-in-Chief of the International Journal of Jungian Studies, and his published books include: *The Neurobiology of the Gods: How the Brain Shapes the Recurrent Imagery of Myth and Dreams* (Routledge, 2012); *A Psychological Reading of the Anglo-Saxon Poem Beowulf: Understanding Everything as Story* (Mellen, 2014); *Healing Symbols in Psychotherapy: A Ritual Approach* (Routledge, 2016); *Magical Consciousness*, co-authored with anthropologist Susan Greenwood (Routledge, 2017); and *Understanding Dreams and Other Spontaneous Images: The Invisible Storyteller* (Routledge, 2018), winner of the 2019 International Association for Jungian Studies Book Award. He has delivered over 60 lectures, workshops and essays in peer-reviewed journals on the aforementioned topics, and has presented at conferences on these topics at sites in the United States, Switzerland and Ireland.

John Hill, MA, received his degrees in philosophy at the University of Dublin and the Catholic University of America. He trained at the C.G. Jung Institute Zürich, has practiced as a Jungian analyst since 1973, and is a training analyst at ISAP, Zürich. He is IAAP Liaison to Tbilisi, Georgia. He has taken on leading roles in theatre presentations on Jung in dialogue with his antagonists. His publications include: *The Association Experiment, Celtic Myth, James Joyce, Dreams, on The Red Book, Trauma* and *Christian Mysticism*. He published his first book in 2010: *At Home in the World: Sounds and Symmetries of Belonging.*

Verena Kast, Dr. Phil, psychologist and psychotherapist, was Professor of Anthropological Psychology at the University of Zürich. She is a teaching analyst and supervisor at the C.G. Jung Institute Zürich and a former President of the Curatorium of the Institute. She has numerous publications in the field of fairy tales, symbolism in general, relationship, mourning processes, emotions also in connection with complex theory and imagination.

Fernando Mendes is a clinical psychologist with practice in São Paulo, and a diploma candidate at C.G. Jung Institute in Zürich. He has a degree in law from the University of São Paulo and is a member of the Brazilian Bar Association. He also has an International Diploma on Public Administration from the École Nationale d'Administration (ENA) in France. He has worked in a number of key positions both in public administration and private corporation in human rights, cultural institutions and sustainable development.

Jon Mills, PsyD, PhD, ABPP, is a Canadian philosopher, psychoanalyst, and retired clinical psychologist. He is on faculty at the Postgraduate Programs in Psychoanalysis & Psychotherapy, Gordon F. Derner School of Psychology, Adelphi University, USA; Department of Psychosocial and Psychoanalytic Studies, University of Essex, UK; and Emeritus Professor of Psychology and Psychoanalysis at the Adler Graduate Professional School, Toronto, Canada. The recipient of numerous awards for his scholarship including four Gradiva Awards, he is the author and/or editor of 30 books in psychoanalysis, philosophy, psychology, and cultural studies including *Debating Relational Psychoanalysis: Jon Mills and His Critics* (Routledge, 2020). Mills was given the Otto Weininger Memorial Award for Lifetime Achievement by the Canadian Psychological Association in 2015

Valeria Céspedes Musso, PhD, is an independent researcher and is in private practice in Frankfurt am Main, Germany. She received her doctorate in psychoanalytic studies in 2017 from the University of Essex, UK. Valeria is currently a diploma candidate at the C.G. Jung Institute Zürich and a student member of the English Research Commission at CGJI Zürich. She has published an article in the *International Journal of Jungian Studies* and is the author of *Marian Apparitions in Cultural Contexts* (Routledge, 2018) and *The Mexican-American Cultural Complex: Accessing the Depth-Psychological Problems Due to Challenges of Assimilation in American Society* in *Jungian Perspectives on Indeterminate States: Betwixt and Between Borders* (Routledge, 2020).

Gerold Roth is a psychiatrist, psychoanalyst and psychotherapist and member of FMH. He is an accredited Jungian Training Analyst and Supervisor at the C.G. Jung Institute Zürich, Küsnacht, IAAP and honorary member of Psychodrama Helvetica (Swiss Association of Psychodrama). In 2022, he published with Isabelle Meier a book in German on depression entitled: *Depression-Verstehen und Behandeln aus Sicht der Analytischen Psychologie*, Kohlhammer Verlag.

Hiroko Sakata is a Jungian analyst in private practice in Japan, and a member of AJAJ (Japan) and IAAP. She is a certified clinical psychotherapist working mainly in educational settings and, since 2000, a lecturer at Mukogawa Women's University, teaching 'The Theory and Practice of Counselling in Schools' to students training to be teachers. She obtained an MA in child and adolescent psychology from Japan Women's University and trained at the C.G. Jung Institute Zürich where she wrote her thesis on Japanese mythology and the shadow side of Japanese society. She has an interest in sandplay therapy, expressive art therapy and dream work. She co-published a chapter entitled 'Eggs on a Tree and a Boy Who Eats a Peach,' in a book on sandplay edited by Hayao Kawai in 1987. She also contributed to the publication in Japanese of Natalie Rogers's books *Emerging Woman* and *The Creative Connection – Expressive Arts as Healing*.

Susan E. Schwartz, PhD, trained in Zürich, Switzerland as a Jungian analyst and is also a clinical psychologist and member of the International Association of Analytical Psychology. She teaches in numerous Jungian programs, workshops and lectures in the USA and worldwide. Susan has articles in several journals and chapters in books on Jungian analytical psychology. Her current book, *The Absent Father Effect on Daughters, Father Desire, Father Wounds* (Routledge, 2020), is translated into several languages. Her Jungian analytical practice is in Paradise Valley, Arizona, USA, and her website is www.susanschwartzphd.com.

Idalina Souza, PhD, is an accredited training analyst, lecturer and supervisor trainee at the C.G. Jung Institute Zürich and in the Instituto de Psicologia Analítica de Campinas (IPAC), affiliated with the Associação Junguiana do Brazil (AJB) and IAAP. She received her diploma in analytical psychology from CGJI in 2016. Her thesis topic was on *Three Temptations of Christ as a Model for the Highly Ethics Education including Children*. She previously received a doctorate in the São Paulo University (USP), working with Neuropharmacology in 1980. Idalina also received the diploma as a Jungian analyst from IPAC in 2018. There, she presented the thesis focusing on the theme *Shame, Humiliation and the Main Consequences of Depression, Criminality and Resilience*. She is currently the Director of the Instituto Ânima de Estudos Junguianos, dedicated to the post-graduation in Jungian Psychology and works as a Jungian analyst and supervisor in private practice for children, adults and the elderly.

Yasuhiro Suzuki is Professor in the Department of Clinical Psychology, Faculty of Education, Bukkyo University. Educated in the Faculty of Medicine in Kyoto University, and in clinical psychology at Bukkyo University where he gained his PhD in 2013. He received his diploma in analytical psychology from CGJI Zürich in 2008, where he trained to become a Jungian analyst. He also works as Teaching Member of the International Society for Sandplay Therapy (ISST), and as a psychiatrist in private practice. He is the editor and co-author of *Healing with Sand/Power of Expressing Images – Sandplay Therapy for Trauma, Developmental Disability, ADHD* (Nakanishiya Shuppan, 2021).

Acknowledgement

I am firstly indebted to the members of the English Research Commission, C.G. Jung Institute, Küsnacht, Zürich (CGJIZ) for giving me the initial space and support to formulate my ideas for this collection on the theme of the mourning process, burial rituals and access to the land of the dead: intimations of Immortality; in particular, Valeria Céspedes Musso, who contributed a chapter to this collection. Most of the contributors for this collection are international candidates, accredited analysts and teachers of the C.G. Jung Institute, Küsnacht, Zürich. We have all been affected by the recent global Covid pandemics and other environmental catastrophes, which means that we have often been unable to accompany the dead symbolically to their final resting place and reinstate their social status as valued ancestors.

I was fortunate to be able to present aspects of my research at the IAAP Congress in Buenos Aires, 2022, alongside two other panel participants: Jon Mills and Robin McCoy Brooks, both inspiring and erudite contributors to this collection. I also want to thank other international, scholarly and discerning members of the Jungian, Post-Jungian community, such as Andrew Samuels, Tom Singer, Verena Kast, Erik Goodwyn, Pilar Amezaga, Stephani Stephens, Marybeth Carter, Michael Glock, Isabelle Meier, Stephen Farah, Evangeline Rand, Roger Brooke, Susan E. Schwartz and others, for their deep curiosity and enlivening presence. Verena Kast, Erik Goodwyn and Susan E. Schwartz are also valuable contributors to this edited book.

The original inspiration for this collection came from a dream I had two years ago, which I relate here:

I dreamt that I received a white envelope in the post addressed to me in black copperplate handwriting similar in size and form to one that Harry Potter received to attend Hogwarts School of Magic. I opened the envelope and inside, to my surprise, was an invitation plus a brochure to visit the land of the dead. There were various routes I could take, all lit up and enticing, not at all depressing. I decided to take one route where I met a close, deceased research mentor of mine who was pleased to see me. I felt that he needed my help, as a living person, to explore and witness his surroundings and report back to the living.

When I awoke, I realised then that I would need to research this topic and look again at the various routes that were lit up and offered in the dream. The dream has subsequently led me to explore how differently each culture, depending on climate and topography, imaginatively configures the land of the dead and the journey undertaken to reach it.

The result is this collection from international contributors who each in their own way light up the interior landscape to give us imaginative signposts that carefully accompany the souls of the departed dead until they reach their final destination to become ancestors and impart wisdom to the living. Of particular interest are the qualitative cultural differences in creatively imagining the physicality of the land of the dead and the journey to arrive there. The rules to secure a safe arrival, and be accepted as ancestor, also govern how we live in any given socio-political structure. This collection thus reveals who are excluded as ancestors as the 'dangerous dead.' But, most of all, I want to thank the creative, inclusive, imaginative capacity of the psyche, particularly Jungian, to support, direct and sustain the deceased and their mourners through difficult times of separation, upheaval and loss.

Last, but certainly not least, I want to thank Christian for his steadfast help. I also give my heartfelt thanks to Katie Randall and the Routledge editorial team for their excellent support.

All client and interview material presented in this collection has been anonymised to protect their identity and privacy.

All references from Jung's Collected Works are translated by R. F. C. Hull and edited by H. Reed, M. Fordham, G. Adler and W. McGuire, published in the United Kingdom by Routledge and Kegan Paul and in the United States by Princeton University Press.

Copyright permissions and credits

Jungian dimensions on the mourning process, burial rituals and access to the land of the dead

Intimations of immortality

Elizabeth Brodersen

Introduction

This collection of comparative cross-cultural Jungian studies on mourning, burial rituals and intimations of immortality, imaginatively configured as the land of the dead, has great relevance today with the unprecedented, unexpected loss of lives due to COVID-19. Other pandemics, including AIDS and environmental and political acts of terror, are also presented. The mourning process and proper burial rituals to symbolically accompany the dead through their journey to become ancestors cannot be performed during these difficult events due to social distancing, migration, missing bodies and the collective fear of contamination. Unmarked mass graves means that the bodies of the dead, by necessity, become isolated and excluded, with their souls unaccompanied by the living through a ritual mourning process which gives meaning and identity to their social value as ancestors.

Each contributor in this collection attempts to offer signposts to the deceased in their journey to become ancestors. Pandemics, as arbiters of death, spotlight deeper psycho-social, psychoanalytical concerns that reflect cultural complexes attached to the mourning process, bringing them out of the shadows and more into focus (see Attinello, Chapter 4; Brooks, Chapter 5, Mendes, Chapter 7; Souza, Chapter 14; Sakata and Buckenmeyer, Chapter 15).

Contributed predominantly by Jungian analysts, scholars and candidates trained at the C.G. Jung Institute Zürich, and including three external international research experts on the mourning process, each chapter explores the multi-faceted, cross-cultural dimensions connected to death as a final rite of passage in life and explores the concept of immortality where the dead become ancestors to the living. The phrase first used by the poet William Wordsworth in his 1807 publication 'Ode: Intimations of Immortality from Recollections of Early Childhood' explores the themes of death and immortality of the child as the father. The concept that humans have an immortal soul, a manikin, a kin animal, a twin or a double as 'shadow' who transmigrates after death and is reborn finds expression in indigenous beliefs and in religions worldwide (Fraser, 1922; Van Gennep, 1960). All give guidance on how to achieve immortality through observing certain rules. The souls of the recent

DOI: 10.4324/9781003313304-1

dead must be carefully guarded and accompanied during the burial and mourning rituals so that they arrive safely in the land of the ancestors. The souls of the dead need the help of the living.

Problem of proof

The problem of proving the concept of immortality is left open by Jung (1939, paras. 741–745) and Hillman (1997, p. 66). Jung emphasises that such old and deep speculative concepts are 'golden vessels full of living feeling' and 'reason becomes unreason when separated from the heart' (para. 745). Clinically, Jung is more interested with transformation processes that lead to a rebirth/resuscitation in ego consciousness from working with dissociated, 'deadened' soul aspects of the psyche, particularly through dreams (1911–1912/1952, paras. 204–250). Jung (1934, paras. 798–815), however, also understands the idea of immortality as a deep unconscious psychic phenomenon that exists in its own right and is not created intentionally by the conscious mind. He suggests that the 'unobstructed universe' is a continuum extending beyond the time and space of the conscious ego, as evidenced through telepathy, the constellation of archetypes, and synchronicity, that all offer invaluable insights into the participation of the psyche in its deepest regions that could be described as eternal (cf. Mendes, Chapter 7, Mills, Chapter 12; de Moura, Chapter 13).

The emotional need to mourn

The continued emotional need for immortality where the dead reappear in life (cf. Stephens, 2020) and/or exist in the unconscious and appear in dreams (Olson, 2021; Kast, Chapter 10) stresses that the departure of a 'significant other' involves an often unbearable, deep and final loss which is enacted through the mourning process as a rite of passage. Van Gennep (1960, pp. 10–11) and Goodwyn (Chapter 8) explain that rites of passage include three stages: the first, as separation; the second, as the liminal, in-between stage; and third, the final aggregation phase where a new status value is given. Burial rituals describe the grief of separation and the beginning of a ritual, liminal passage into the unknown which the souls of the dead undertake to reach their final resting place in the land of the ancestors. Their success depends upon the action of the mourners, privately and collectively, who, through the courage and handling of their own grief, support and accompany the souls of the dead through their travails to find their final resting place. This resting place, however, is not always conceived as a permanent condition, but more as a rebirth linked to resurrection, whereby the body as a symbol of the cosmos, its destruction and rejuvenation, passes through a breakdown of old structures to initiate new beginnings (Hertz, 1905–1906/2018, pp. 19–33; Goodwyn, 2015, pp. 244–245).

The eternal return

Thus, the concept of an eternal return and a regeneration in cyclical time has played a crucial role in cosmological thought as far back as Palaeolithic-Neolithic times based on human observation of the cycles of the seasons, the rhythm of human life, the monthly cycles of the moon, menstruation, the daily cycle of the sun and the periodic near return of the planets to previous positions in the sky. As described by Eliade (1958, pp. 406–407; Mendes and de Moura, in Chapters 7 and 13 respectively), a belief that primordial time is cyclical, not linear, and the hope that a total regeneration of time is established by transforming successive time into a single eternal moment in the here and now, presupposes the precise return of all events, so that the individuals appear, disappear and reappear in every turn of the cycle seen by Eliade as the *lunar* perspective (Eliade, 1954, p. 88; Musso, Brodersen and Hill, Chapters 1, 2 and 3 respectively). Indigenous people believe that a contagious connection between themselves and parts of their body continues after that physical coaction has been broken (Fraser, 1922, pp. 45–47). They maintain that they will suffer after death from the same harm that might befall any severed parts of their body, such as hair, navel cord, bones, teeth and nail clippings that would still contain living aspects of their soul. Care is taken that these severed, marginalised portions of themselves or deceased family members are kept in safe places for resurrection purposes and not fall into the hands of those who might use them to their detriment. In some funeral rites, the orifices of the dead – nose, mouth, eyes, vagina, anus – are carefully closed or sown together because it is thought that the soul escapes through human orifices.

Behind these concerns are if the body of the deceased is moved, displaced or becomes unrecognisable, the soul cannot find her/his way back to the body. The soul becomes mislaid and lost, therefore losing its identity to become an ancestor. Care is thus taken in burial rituals that the soul remains close to the body through the help of mourners. Even if a mourner's presence in some cultures is considered unlucky because of her/his closeness to the departed whose soul may be hovering near them, the mourner's presence is still vital as she/he shares the grief of exclusion in the death process. In the *Mekeo* district of New Guinea, a widower loses all his civil rights and becomes a social outcast. I suggest that the mourning process itself is emotionally draining. The overwhelming emotions attached to death as the final departure of a loved one into unknown territory is dangerous, even contagious, hence the pollution rituals involved towards handling the process of dead bodies. The fear that a ghost takes over the body of the living could be interpreted as one's own longing to be reunited in death with the deceased, which must be contained in order to go on living.

For example, many funerary practices include lighting fires to keep demons at bay and warming the souls of the deceased. Lewis-Williams and Pearce (2005, p. 79) stress the emotional importance of the liminal transition period where mourners learn to carry on in new circumstances. The transition period is deemed over when the flesh of the deceased has decomposed and the bones can be buried without further taboo within the confines of house, signalling the reintegration into the community. Once their flesh has disintegrated and only bones remain, the dead have lost their personal identity and adopt an impersonal status as wise, collective ancestral spirits who guide the living. They pose no threat to the living because they would not be looking to possess the soul in a new body. Boyer (2001, p. 224) points out that the time between the funeral of separation and the funeral of incorporation allows anxiety and disassociation to subside (Haule, 2011, p. 232). Similar to puberty rituals, the dead are reintegrated into the community with new identities and new roles as ancestors.

Second burial

The period of mourning is over where the bones of the dead, after being initially separated from the world of the living, are reinstated as treasured relics and/or amulets that constitutes a renewal of social relations with the dead person identified as a valued ancestor. In Greek disinterment, bones are placed carefully in boxes and the time between the first burial and the second has lengthened, from two to three years to five and seven years (O'Rourke, 2007, p. 243). The numinous role of the second burial is important when the bones of the dead are exhumed and reburied within the family home as legitimate ancestors with renewed status value (see Suzuki and Goodwyn, Chapters 6 and 8). Some mourners re-enact these rites unconsciously through dreams in order to accompany their dead relatives to find their final resting place. One mourner dreamt of a second burial where she received the large, white leg bone of a close, deceased person. She had accompanied him as he died and through the mourning process by carefully tending to his grave as he made the transition to ancestor. The deceased had been a refugee without a specific homeland where his soul could find a resting place. The mourner dreamt that the large leg bone was placed in her grandparents' home and that two cleaning women were preparing space for it. The mourner related that the deceased had always given her a 'leg to stand on', and this value continues as part of her inherited, ancestral energy. In return, she has given him an ancestral home, as his had been displaced through war.

Social control and immortality: the excluded dead

The social status attached to a dead person has special significance for funerary rites. Those excluded from becoming ancestors are classified as the *dangerous dead*. They would like to be reincorporated into the world of the living as ancestors, but since they cannot be, because they are caught in-between social status values as anomalies, they behave like hostile strangers towards the living as vengeful ghosts. In Hindu belief, as in other cultures, violent and sudden deaths are believed to make the dead vengeful, and they torment the living through nightmares and accidents. Proper rituals are performed to prevent this happening such as *sharing in the deceased state* by becoming death-like themselves: not shaving, washing, wearing clothes, avoiding hot food and abstaining from sex in order to appease them.

Bodies that have transgressed social and religious taboos and bear evidence of execution or torture, such as corpses buried in peat bogs to preserve them from decay around 1600–2600 years ago, could have been kept in a permanent unresolved liminal state on purpose with their souls never allowed to rest. The anthropologist Taylor (2002, p. 16) suggests that these bodies could not be burned and sacrificed without offending the gods, but neither could they be properly buried without offending the ancestors or remain unburied, for their souls would wander and do harm to the living. The only solution was to keep them permanently marginal, their partially decomposed bodies kept recognisable to keep their souls near them. The bogs themselves were liminal places, watery, raised above dry land. The decomposition process was arrested and time effectively stopped. These ancient bog corpses bring to mind the tragic images of zombies as unforgiven, soulless, liminal beings in a permanent state of transgressed taboo. Composed of half-eaten flesh, but still recognisable and therefore most dangerous at the margins of society, they are the outsiders, doomed to wander the earth looking for peace.

Social control mechanisms, thus, play an important role politically behind the concept of immortality when certain souls of the dead are excluded from entering the land of the ancestors. Each culture may have different exclusions. It can be argued that the perception of exclusion reflects upon and underpins socio-cultural complexes (and their symptomatology) related to the 'immoral' or anomalous behaviour of 'others' imbued within monistic, authoritarian interpretations of original 'sin' as 'hubris,' 'dissent' and 'disobedience' as 'difference' and 'forgiveness' as the necessary meek subjugation and acquiescence to social norms. The New Testament (Bible, 1989 edn.) has an apocalyptic Day of Judgement where certain souls are saved and others damned and thrown into hell (Dante's *Inferno*) which is imagined as a fiery furnace, analogous to the earth's inner molten core. Historically, souls who remained, and in certain cultures still remain, unblessed without the prospect of immortality and entry into the land of the dead as ancestors are – for example, the homeless, paupers, suicides, same-sex relationships, unborn foetuses (through miscarriage or abortion), pregnant women, second-born twins, dissenters, illegitimate offspring, criminals, murdered victims and murderers – remain outside the realm of the ancestors and cannot be buried in consecrated soil. They are considered as liminal, unacknowledged beings, stuck in between social values.

The historian, Brown (2015, pp. 171–173), discusses the gradual emotional distancing from the early Church egalitarian practices between the poor and the rich in gaining absolution and entry into paradise. He highlights how financial wealth in church building as memorials played an increasingly pivotal role in the management of the Christian concept of resurrection and afterlife. Salvation became increasingly focused on financial assets, and the souls of the poor ignored. Russ (2005, pp. 129–147) stresses that, even today, it is through gifts and commodity exchange that souls are 'blessed' and 'absolved' at the threshold of death.

Prolonged mourning, war and displaced bodies

The mourning process attached to loss and bereavement is further complicated, prolonged and tabooed when a deceased close family member carries for the bereaved intense feelings of belonging, homeland and status attached to cultural roots, but lost through the trauma of war, forced migration and the shifting borders of cultural identity (cf. Debs, 2017, pp. 95–113). In such cases, the bereaved need to find ways to confront unprecedented experiences of destruction and loss that include not just the loss of a significant personal relationship but the loss of cultural roots and identity embedded within that person. Debs (ibid. p. 100) suggests that the mourning process conceptualised by Freud (1917, p. 150) as a repetition compulsion helps master distress caused by overwhelming loss and trauma. Repetitive play, for example, contributes to creating a new liminal space capable of transforming trauma by tempering its negativity through confronting the tabooed emotions associated with death and bereavement. Zeavin (2017, pp. 1–13) stresses the efficacy of war games and art work to codify, identify and contain trauma as *an active agency* in the self to comment upon and reinvent memory.

Another aspect of mourning for the dead concerns those whose death cannot be confirmed, because they are missing or forced to disappear by tyrannical force (Debs, 2017, pp. 106–107). When family members disappear without trace, their absence is transformed into a spectral presence that continues to haunt, considerably complicating the work of mourning. In the absence of the corpse or any material sign that gives form to absence, the disappeared becomes incorporated and encrypted within the self, perpetuating identification with the existence of the lost person. Efforts to shed light on the fate of the disappeared are the only ways to make such family losses of loved ones open to grieving (Abraham and Torok, 1972).

War and/or the displacement of identity means that the souls of those killed in battle away from home cannot always find their way to their final resting place or be commemorated. The mourning process is further prolonged when the dead personify valued soul aspects of the lost homeland to which the mourner is unable to return to bury that person properly. Natural disasters, war, changes in boundaries between countries, mean that the dead are caught between borders, as homeless souls, no longer belonging to a specific place (Auestad, 2017).

Each culture has its own unredeemed outsider spirits as ancestral *ghosts* or *phantoms* so moving portrayed by Kimbles (2021, pp. 31–53). Kimbles argues that black people's suffering in terms of murder and torture remains unseen, without social value, as an aspect of an intergenerational cultural complex attached to slavery and its inhumane practices that associates black people as a subspecies of humanness. Musso (Chapter 1) and Souza (Chapter 14) discuss how brown-skinned indigenous peoples in Mexico and Brazil have been equally devalued as 'non-white' in the collective consciousness of their respective cultures.

Kwon (2018, pp. 296–299) suggests that drastic changes in Vietnam's infrastructure due to political and economic crises has given rise to the development of two distinct burial commemorative structures that now co-exist: first, the restored ancestral temples holding the memorabilia of official family ancestors; and second, the external shrines for ghosts. These street shrines commemorate those spirits, who due to displacement and loss of their original homes, nevertheless receive the solidarity and hospitality of the villagers who acknowledge the ghosts' ontological status to exist.

Robben (2000, pp. 217–230) graphically recounts the abduction of Argentinian dissenters during the authoritarian regimes of terror, whereby guerrilla abductions were never publicly acknowledged and victims disappeared into pits or black holes. The political practice of obstructing funerary rites prevented people from coming to terms with their loss and grief. To reconcile such brutal losses, lost bodies were finally exhumed, identified and reburied in order to restore the torn fabric of society that also allows a commemoration of political dissent.

The journey to the land of the dead

The journey to the land of the dead and its entrance is envisaged in various physical forms (Van Gennep, 1960, pp. 150–155). The Northern *Ostyaks* locate the land of the dead beyond the mouth of the Ob, in the Arctic Ocean, illuminated only by the light of the moon. For the Irtysh *Ostyak*, the land of the dead is located in the sky, reached by ascending ladders or by climbing up a chain. For the ancient Britons, the other world of *Annwn* coincides with the swirling movement of the Atlantic Ocean surrounding Wales and features *Ceridwen*, the shapeshifting nature goddess of the Gulf Stream who brews inspiration in her magic cauldron, The Innuit sea goddess, Sedna, progenitor and caretaker of the sea mammals, is accessed through navigating under the icy yet volcanic Icelandic sea to the land of the dead, so graphically described by Rasmussen (1929, pp. 308–311; Brodersen, 2019, pp. 154–157). Other locations suggest citadels surrounded by walls or an underworld abode with bolted doors (the Sheol in Hebrew tradition) or situated high in a mountain or in its interior (Hindu, India). Since the deceased make this precarious voyage alone, families are careful to equip him/her with the necessary material objects they used in life to facilitate a safe passage. The land of the dead is perceived as a continuation of earthly life where members' status is protected through similar rules. Burial excavations show historically that women were buried with weapons and men with woven baskets that contradict the allocation of innate, fixed binary roles (cf. Hollimon, 2006). Ancient funerary rituals emphasise the daily revival of the sun god whose mythic, symbolic significance would be lost if not renewed through resurrection rites (Brodersen, Chapter 2). The Biblical NT, (Bible, 1989 edn) death and resurrection of Christ follows similar lines of overcoming death.

The land of the dead

The physical nature of the land of the dead varies depending on climate and topography. Each culture attaches its own descriptive and emotional value to the land of the dead, whether its arrival is perilous or relatively easy. Its physicality reflects a culture's own attitude to crossing borders and risk taking, whether it is interpreted as 'safe/pure' (heavenly) or 'risky/evil' (hellish). Heathen variations of the afterlife differ from monotheisms: for example, Valhalla is depicted as a boisterous place where competition, warfare and sex is allowed, similar to that of the Greek Mount of Olympus where their gods and goddesses abound with familial rivalry and murderous feuds. Old Pagan matrilineal Welsh myths place their paradise as the 'other world' in *Annwn* under the sea, comprised of crystal fortresses in the moving twilight of tidal currents where the ancestors give wisdom and courage to the living (Brodersen, 2012, p. 143; Chapter 2). Biblical heavenly paradise is depicted as platonic, without sexual relations. Traditionally, OT Genesis Myth, c 3000 BCE, excluded women and animals from entry because their 'profane' nature does not mirror the creationist purity of the male form.

Importance of ritual mourning

Goodwyn (2015, pp. 239–266; 2016, pp. 165–183; Chapter 8) and Roth (Chapter 9) correctly underline the importance of death rituals and their relationship to clinical studies of prolonged mourning and complicated grief. Mourning rituals help participants access and process their grief, which varies cross-culturally in its accepted expression. The emotional expression of the mourners tends to emphasise the needs of the deceased who require emotional strength to traverse the liminal passage to the land of the ancestor and not be hindered by an excess of sorrow. Tears would make the road too slippery to traverse (Goodwyn, 2016, p. 169). Goodwyn depicts the stoical emotional response in Brazil towards the death of babies who, as 'little angels,' have returned to the loving arms of the Virgin Mary in heaven, their death giving no cause for grief. In other ceremonies, among the Australian Aborigines, violent mourning rites are practised such as the burning of breasts, the slashing of thighs to give space to the painful emotional outpouring of grief within a confined space, transforming the violent scenes later into a jubilant celebration that emphasises that love conquers death.

Taylor (2002, p. 279) argues that modern cultures tend to insulate themselves emotionally from the reality of death and have lost connection with indigenous funerary rituals through industrialisation, two world wars and a growing disconnection with nature. Under the advance of science and medicine, fears about the human corpse as sacred as well as dangerous have been rationalised and sanitised. Experts, such as funerary undertakers, have taken over the process of mourning; taboo rites about purity, dirt and danger have been eliminated from the death process along with the active special relationship between the deceased and the mourner. Mannix (2017) equally stresses that actively preparing for death helps ease the transition for the dying and their bereaved families. Prohibitions about death need to be acknowledged with a renewed openness and positive structures that guide the painful process.

These sentiments have been supported by the work of Hockey et al. (2001). Small (2001, pp. 32–37) in a critical overview of how grief, mourning and death rituals are enacted, emphasises maintaining active, continuing bonds with the deceased as opposed to the Freudian linear model of disengaging and letting go of the past that no longer includes the deceased in the present. These new models of reflexivity are consistent with the characteristics of postmodernity where individuals recreate their own private identity and relationship to grief, freed up from collective labels attached to pathological disorders. Intimacy and emotions concerning bereavement and loss are engaged with in a different way, unrestrained by linear temporality and grand narratives about normalcy, being closer emotionally to pre-modern ideas of cyclical time. The poetics of grief is stressed over the need to theorise and make normative rules about how a 'healthy' grief 'should' look like.

Revival of mourning rituals

The modern revival of mourning rituals in therapeutic practice in response to global losses is redefining how we cope with grief. Patients with prolonged and complicated grieving have often lost their homeland, relatives, status and psychic roots, finding them difficult to transplant their cultural roots into new soil. The advantage of ritual in times of status transition can be well applied to death rituals and the mourning process. Ritual creates semi-permeable boundaries that help the bereaved formulate and express the new differences in status and relationship between the bereaved and the dead loved one. Rituals in liminal spaces allow the bereaved time to process their grief and loss in enactments of spatial, verbal and bodily experiences that lets the reality of death sink in (see Hill, Goodwyn, Roth and Kast, Chapters 3, 8, 9 and 10 respectively). The boundary between life and death is neither rigid nor absolute, but not too porous either, so that bereavement does not carry on indefinitely in a process that saps vital energy from life. However, if the deceased embodies important cultural, ancestral memories that empower the living, these memories need to be immortalised in some way so that they are not forgotten, but passed to the living. The symbolic concept of immortality gives comfort to mourners, because an afterlife guarantees that treasured values will live on eternally, regardless of time and space (Lifton and Olson, 1974, pp. 44–51).

Chapter parts

This collection of 15 chapters consists of seven parts, each describing aspects of the cross-cultural, psycho-social Jungian dimension of the mourning process, burial rituals and access to immortality through the land of the dead.

Part I describes the *cross-cultural, liminal relations with the dead* and features chapters by Valeria Céspedes Musso entitled '*Dia de los Muertos*: Day of the Dead in Los Angeles as *Numinosum*; Elizabeth Brodersen, 'A Comparative Ethnographic Study of the Journey to the Land of the Dead'; and John Hill, 'Crossing the Bridge to Uncertainty, a Life with Death and the Dead.' Musso examines the phenomenology behind the adoption of Mexican mourning rituals from the Mexican diaspora in the United States as well as the psychological need underpinning it.

Brodersen explores the symbolic journey to the land of the dead envisaged through two cultures: ancient Welsh cosmology and ancient Egyptian. She speculates that the physicality of the journey and the land of the dead itself is influenced by climate and topography. Hill suggests that the historical record witnesses the necessity of creating a transitional interlude to gain awareness of the interface between the living and the dead. He draws upon the Celtic/Irish Book of the Dead to illustrate Celtic intimations of life beyond death.

Part II addresses the theme of *pandemics and access to immortality* and features two chapters: Paul Attinello, 'Splintered Afterlives: AIDS, Death, and Beyond' and Robin McCoy Brooks 'C.G. Jung, Gloria Anzaldúa and Social Activism's Possibility.' Attinello movingly describes the history of HIV/AIDS that is still shrouded in incomplete narratives even after 40 years of songs, novels and films in the urban West. McCoy Brooks conducts an autoethnographic study of a community of care that arose during the early days of the AIDS pandemic, specifically describing the final year of the life of Lucas Harris, who died of AIDS, as seen through his wife, Gloria Anzaldúa.

Part III researches the theme of *burial rituals and crossing over* with two chapters, the first by Vasuhiro Suzuki entitled 'Bardo, Noh Play and Zeitgeist in Japan,' the second by Fernando Mendes called 'Pandemic, the Zenith of an Archetypal Disconnection.' Suzuki describes the Japanese burial practices that feature Bardo, who is excluded from immortality, and he also examines Noh Play as a symbolic contact between the living and the dead and its relevance for Jungian psychology. Mendes argues that the reality of death which had previously organised and structured societies is now disorganising them through their present lack. Using the example of Brazilian political structure during the Covid pandemic, he asks what will happen to our souls if there are no more mourning rituals or myths to validate them.

Part IV focuses on the theme of *grief, mourning and loss and their clinical dimensions* and features two chapters: Erik Goodwyn, 'The Problem of Death and Meaning for Depth Psychology,' and Gerold Roth, 'When the Mourning Process Needs Psychiatric Support.' Goodwyn examines the imaginative ways that humans deal with the universal consequences of death. He argues that the lack of symbolic archetypal rituals increases the clinical occurrence of complicated grief and prolonged mourning. Roth's chapter focuses on how to help vulnerable patients cope with an overwhelming loss and how that can depend on psychiatric support.

Part V concentrates on the theme of *eros, death and the unconscious* and introduces two chapters, the first by Verena Kast entitled 'Deceased Loved Ones in Dreams,' and the second by Susan E. Schwartz entitled 'Immortality, Mourning, and Ritual.' Kast draws on dream research that shows how dreams stimulate and promote the mourning process. When the deceased appear in dreams, they help with the process of bereavement by accompanying the bereaved through the mourning process. Schwartz explores the imaginative concept of immortality and loss in terms of an abortion, interpreted as the alchemical *nigredo* which, when differentiated, can promote a psychological rebirth.

Part VI addresses the theme *towards an archetypal ontology of death*, with chapters from Jon Mills, 'The Seduction of Immortality; Jung, Heidegger, and Hegel on Death,' and Vicente L. de Moura, 'Destiny and Personal Myth: The Analysis of Archetypal Constellations.' Mills discusses the ontology of death through the lenses of Jung, Heidegger and Hegel as a positive significance of the negative that sustains and transforms life. de Moura examines the cross-cultural concepts of destiny, fate and personal myth with the personal, collective and religions in their complex arenas.

Part VII explores the theme of *psycho-social dimensions of grief and the mourning process*. Two chapters illustrate aspects of this theme: Idalina Souza, 'Opening the Eyes to Invisible People,' and Hiroko Sakata and Cécile Buckenmeyer, 'The Katako Syndrome: Japan's Problem with Youth Suicide.' Souza's chapter aims to give a voice to Brazil's homeless people as *homo sacer* who became more visible during the Covid pandemic. Sakata and Buckenmeyer use the mythology, the fairy tale Katako, the popular manga *Demon Slayer* as well as clinical examples in attempting to understand what leads so many Japanese youths to commit suicide.

References

Abraham, N. and Torok, M. (1972). Mourning or Melancholia: Introjection Versus Incorporation. In Rand, N.T. (ed.), *The Shell and the Kernel*. Chicago: University of Chicago Press, 1994, pp. 125–137.

Auestad, L. (ed.) (2017). *Shared Traumas, Silent Loss, Public and Private Mourning*. London: Karnac.

Bible (1989 edn.). *The Revised English Bible*. Oxford and Cambridge: Oxford University Press.

Boyer, P. (2001). *Religion Explained: The Evolutionary Origins of Religious Thought*. New York: Basic Books.

Brodersen, E. (2012). In the Nature of Twins: A Study of the Archetypal Realm of Universal Duality, Opposition and Imitation between the First and Other in Creation Myths. In *IJJS*, Vol. 4, No. 2, September. London: Taylor and Francis, Routledge, pp. 133–149.

Brodersen, E. (2019). *Taboo, Personal and Collective Representations, Origin and Positioning within Cultural Complexes*. London and New York: Routledge.

Brown, P. (2015). *The Ransom of the Soul: Afterlife and Wealth in Early Western Christianity*. Harvard: Harvard University Press.

Debs, N. (2017). Ongoing Mourning as a Way to go Beyond Endless Grief: Considerations on the Lebanese Experience. In Auestad, L. (ed.), *Shared Traumas, Silent Loss, Public and Private Mourning*. London: Karnac.

Eliade, M. (1954). *The Myth of the Eternal Return. Cosmos and History*. Princeton and Oxford: Princeton University Press.

Eliade, M. (1958). *Patterns in Comparative Religion*. Lincoln and London: University of Nebraska Press.

Fraser, J.G. (1922). *The Golden Bough, a Study in Magic and Religion* (Abridged ed.). London: Penguin Books.

Freud, S. (1917). Mourning and Melancholia. In *Collected Works, Vol. 11. On Metapsychology* (Reddich, J. Trans.). London and New York: Penguin, 2003.

Goodwyn, E. (2015). The End of All Tears; A Dynamic Interdisciplinary Analysis of Mourning and Complicated Grief with Suggested Applications for Clinicians. In *Journal of Spirituality in Mental Health*, Vol. 17, No. 4. London: Taylor and Francis Group, Routledge, pp. 239–266.

Goodwyn, E. (2016). *Healing Symbols in Psychotherapy: A Ritual Approach*. London and New York: Routledge.

Haule, J.R. (2011). *Jung in the 21st Century, Vol. 1: Evolution and Archetype*. London and New York: Routledge.

Hertz, R. (1905–1906/2018). A Contribution to the Study of the Collective Representation of Death. In Robben, A.C.G.M. (ed.), *Death, Mourning and Burial: A Cross-Cultural Reader*. Malden, MA: Blackwell, pp. 19–33.

Hillman, J. (1997). *Suicide and the Soul* (2nd ed.). Woodstock, CT: Spring Books.

Hockey, J., Katz, J. and Small, N. (eds.) (2001). *Grief, Mourning and Death Rituals*. Maidenhead, UK: Open University Press.

Hollimon, S. (2006). The Archaeology of Nonbinary Genders in Native North America. In Nelson, S.M. (ed.), *Handbook of Gender in Archaeology*. Walnut Creek, CA and Oxford, UK: Altamira Press, pp. 435–450.

Jung, C.G. (1911–1912/1952). The Transformation of Libido. In *Collected Works, Vol. 5, Symbols of Transformation* (2nd ed.). London: Routledge and Kegan Paul, 1995.

Jung, C.G. (1934). The Soul and Death. In *Collected Works, Vol. 8, The Structure and Dynamics of the Psyche* (2nd ed.). London: Routledge and Kegan Paul, 1991.

Jung, C.G. (1939). Foreword to Jung; Phenomenes Occultes. In *Collected Works, Vol. 18, The Symbolic Life* (2nd ed.). London: Routledge and Kegan Paul, 1993.

Kimbles, S.L. (2021). *Intergenerational Complexes in Analytical Psychology, the Suffering of Ghosts*. London and New York: Routledge.

Kwon, H. (2018). The Ghosts of War and the Spirit of Cosmopolitanism. In Robben, A.C.G.M. (ed.), *Death, Mourning and Burial: A Cross-Cultural Reader*. Malden, MA: Blackwell.

Lewis-Williams, D. and Pearce, D. (2005). *Inside the Neolithic Mind*. London: Thames and Hudson.

Lifton, R.J. and Olson, E. (1974). Symbolic Immortality. In Robben, A.C.G.M. (ed.) (2018), *Death, Mourning and Burial: A Cross-Cultural Reader*. Malden, MA: Blackwell, pp. 44–51.

Mannix, K.M. (2017). *With the End in Mind: Dying, Death and Wisdom in the Age of Denial*. London: William Collins.

Olson, S. (2021). *Images of the Dead in Grief Dreams. A Jungian View of Mourning*. London and New York: Routledge.

O'Rourke, D. (2007). Mourning Becomes Eclectic: Death of Communal Practice in a Greek Cemetery. In Robben, A.C.G.M. (ed.) (2018), *Death, Mourning and Burial: A Cross-Cultural Reader*. Malden, MA: Blackwell, pp. 231–248.

Rasmussen, K. (1929). *A Shaman's Journey to the Sea Spirit. Report of the Fifth Thule Expedition 1921–1924, Vol. VII, No.1 Intellectual Culture of the Iglulik Eskimos*. Copenhagen: Gyldendalake Boghandel, Nordisk Forlag, pp. 123–129.

Robben, A.C.G.M. (2000). State Terror in the Netherworld: Disappearance and Reburial in Argentina. In Robben, A.C.G.M. (ed.) (2018), *Death, Mourning and Burial: A Cross-Cultural Reader*. Malden, MA: Blackwell, pp. 217–230.

Russ, J.R. (2005). Love's Labor Paid for: Gift and Commodity at Threshold of Death. In Robben, A.C.G.M. (ed.) (2018), *Death, Mourning and Burial: A Cross-Cultural Reader.* Malden, MA: Blackwell, pp. 129–147.

Small, N. (2001). Theories of Grief: A Critical Overview. In Hockey, J. Katz, J. and Small, N. (eds.), *Grief, Mourning and Death Rituals.* Maidenhead, UK: Open University Press, pp. 19–48.

Stephens, S.L. (2020). *C.G. Jung and the Dead, Visions, Active Imagination and the Unconscious Terrain.* London and New York: Routledge.

Taylor, T. (2002). *The Buried Soul: How Humans Invented Death.* Boston: Beacon.

Van Gennep, A. (1960). *Rites of Passage.* Chicago: University of Chicago Press.

Zeavin, H. (2017). War games-Mourning Loss through Play. In Auestad, L. (ed.), *Shared Traumas, Silent Loss, Public and Private Mourning.* London: Karnac, pp. 1–13.

Part I

Cross-cultural, liminal relations with the dead

Chapter 1

Day of the Dead in Los Angeles as numinosum

How honouring the dead reconnects Mexican Americans to their Aztec-Mexica ancestral roots

Valeria Céspedes Musso

Introduction

The aim of this chapter is to analyse the phenomenology of the Day of the Dead, or Día de los Muertos,[1] as observed in Los Angeles, California. While the Day of the Dead is nowadays widely observed in many parts of the United States, it was in Los Angeles that the first celebrations took place. Since its inception in the 1970s, participation to celebrate the Day of the Dead in the United States has grown in size amongst Americans of Latin American descent, but it has also attracted to its altars many Americans from diverse backgrounds. Against this background, I will concentrate on Mexican Americans' relationship to the Day of the Dead, which helped usher in a new conception of the dead based on its Mexica/Aztec[2] ancestral roots, which previously had been viewed from a European-centric and Spanish perspective. More precisely, I examine the Día de los Muertos as a *numinosum*, a force which I argue has seized the Mexican American community during a period of collective distress resulting from racial discrimination and marginalization. While Chicano artists and leaders utilized Mexican traditions and practices as a way to forge a new identity to embrace their indigenous heritage, I suggest here that this view should be complemented with a psychological perspective point-ing to additional forces pervading the cultural psyche of Mexican Americans and driving them to the deities associated to the realm of the dead of the Aztec world. Accordingly, in this short chapter, I offer a depth-psychological analysis aimed at exploring this phenomenon through the application of principles from my study of mass visions of the Virgin Mary (Musso, 2019) which in turn draws from Jung's theoretical approach found in *Flying Saucers* (1959).

Día de los Muertos in Los Angeles

It was during the Chicano movement of the 1960s, lasting until the mid-1970s, in which the *Día de los Muertos* was born. The Chicano movement was a social and political movement present in the United States which emerged during the unrest fomented by the Vietnam War and the African American rights movement led by

DOI: 10.4324/9781003313304-3

Martin Luther King Jr. (Novas, 2007, p. 110). It was a movement driven by people of Mexican descent with the aim of embracing Chicano identity, as historian F. Arturo Rosales writes, '[a] crucial part of mobilization revolved around the issue of identity and racial pride' (Rosales, 1996, p. xvii). As artist and activist Yreina D. Cervantes states,

> it was a time, especially in East Los Angeles in different Chicano and Chicana communities, [of] great political turmoil in Los Angeles. . . . Whether consciously we realized it or not, I believe that Día de los Muertos came in a very important time and was embraced in a very important time in a community that felt somewhat fragmented and most definitely marginalized . . . it came in a time in our community that really needed something that was really healing and unifying.
>
> ('Día de los Muertos,' 2019)

The Day of the Dead arose in Los Angeles in the early 1970s through Self Help Graphics & Art, a community-based organization formed by a group of artists who shared with the Mexican American community the cultural practices of Mexico, including those associated to the Día de los Muertos. Prior to the introduction of Día de los Muertos, such occurrence was not widely observed in the United States, and most 'Mexican Americans knew little about Mexico's Indigenous Día de los Muertos practices, observing, instead, popular Catholic All Saints' Day and All Souls' Day rituals' (Marchi, 2013, p. 272). In 1972, Self Help Graphics & Art organized the first Day of the Dead in the parking lot behind their building. They orchestrated a procession from a nearby cemetery to the site of Self Help Graphics & Art (ibid., 2019). What first began as a small and modest gathering has grown over time into massive celebrations taking place in Grand Park, Los Angeles, each year (ibid., 2019; Velasco, 2019). Self Help Graphics & Art has 'played a pivotal part in reinstituting the Day of the Dead in California' and the credit for its 'preservation and cultural impact' is in large part attributed to them (Velasco, 2019).

The observation of Day of the Dead takes place on 1 and 2 November annually. It is a syncretism of pre-Colombian indigenous traditions aimed at honouring the dead ancestors together with Roman Catholic All Souls' Day and All Saints' Day. From the perspective of Mesoamericans, it was important to maintain harmony between the living and the dead. As Regina Marchi (2013), who researched the Day of the Dead in the United States, writes,

> the dead were thought to have powers to enhance or thwart agricultural and reproductive fertility. It was believed that spirits of the dead and the deities were always present among the living and had to be cared for on a daily basis most especially during remembrance holidays, in order to ensure both family and community well-being.
>
> (Marchi, 2013, pp. 276–277)

Both in Latin America and in the United States, *ofrenda* (offering, in English) altars are built in preparation for Día de los Muertos, with preparations starting various months in advance. The ofrenda altars represent a sacred place and are intended to celebrate and honour loved ones who have died. A typical ofrenda altar is decorated with photographs of the deceased, candles to light the way for the dead, and marigolds whose aroma beckons the spirit to its ofrenda altar from the afterlife ('Día de los Muertos,' 2019). Mexicans who observed Día de los Muertos believe that, if you do not pray to the ancestors and offer an altar, their ancestors will not look favourably to the requests of the living who even have to pay a penalty and be punished by the dead (de Orellana et al., 2011, p. 71).

In the United States there is a continuous flow of immigrants from Mexico, and this immigrant replenishment allows Mexican Americans to 'not lose their identity as a distinctive ethnic group' (Vasquez, 2010, p. 48, italics in original). In recent years, there has been an increased influx of migration in the United States, particularly from the indigenous populations of Mexico. This immigration transplant has been instrumental for people from central and southern Mexico to replicate and practise their traditions in Los Angeles, including the Day of the Dead celebrations. According to Xóchitle Flores-Marcial,

> in reproducing Day of the Dead, Zapotecs have this responsibility to do it respectfully and as close to possible to the ways in which we celebrate this back at home in Oaxaca. So, we could become a reference . . . for other people.
>
> ('Día de los Muertos,' 2019)

The Day of the Dead has grown more popular amongst many groups of people outside the Mexican American and non–Latin American communities. Its imagery is widely found in popular culture in the United States, ranging from skulls, *papel picado* (traditional Mexican perforated paper) and Halloween costumes sold in shops to movies such as the 2017 Disney animated film *Coco* and the 2015 James Bond film *Spectre*. This increased popularity of the celebrations surrounding the Day of the Dead has different implications. On the one hand, these celebrations bring people together in the community. On the other hand, however, there is a concern that the tradition is becoming less respected and understood, with many people instead interpreting the Day of the Dead celebration mainly as a festive occasion about painting faces and wearing costumes without attributing any religious or spiritual significance to it, thereby diluting its authentic and original meaning.

The underworld of the Mexica

Día de los Muertos focuses on honouring deceased loved ones and welcoming souls back from the land of the dead for a brief reunion. Chicano Day of the Dead celebrates the reunion of their deceased loved ones, coming from a place where the dead most go to, called Mictlan. According to Aztec mythology, such place was ruled by the couple Mictlantecuhtli and Michlancíhuatl, god and goddess of the

Place of the Dead (de Orellana et al., 2009, p. 68). The underworld was also known by different names, such as Quenomamican, meaning 'Where One Somehow Finds Oneself,' or Ximoayan, meaning 'Place of the Fleshless' (ibid., p. 75). The fate of other souls and the place they went to was determined by their death. As prominent Mexican archaeologist Eduardo Matos Moctezuma states, 'unlike Catholic belief, in which the fate of the deceased is determined by moral factors . . . what defined the fate of the Mexica after death was the way the individual died' (ibid., 2009, p. 66). Moreover, for the Mexica, reward and punishment for good or evil actions and behaviours took place on earth (ibid., p. 75). In the religious worldview of the Aztecs, the dead journeyed to four possible realms after death. Warriors who died in battle or were captured for sacrifice accompanied the sun 'on his daily journey from sunrise in the east to noon,' and after four years they were transformed into birds (ibid., p. 66). Women who died in childbirth followed the fate of the warriors as their way of dying was equated with battle. The second place was called Tlalocan, where the water god, Tláloc, ruled. This place was reserved for people whose death was related to water, such as drowning, gout or dropsy. Tlalocan was thought to be an earthly paradise, eternally summer and green. According to Michel Graulich, 'the elect of Tlalcoc and the heroic women go through a short cycle from Mictlan to Tlalocan' (Graulich, 1981, p. 46). The third place in which the dead journeyed to was a place for children, called Xochatlapan or Chichicauhco. The deceased children were nursed from a tree yielding milk until they were ready to return to earth after four years.

The fourth after-death realm is represented by Mictlan. It was not a dark void inhabited by ancestors of any specific social rank or status; rather, it was a place where humans went to after they had died of natural causes on earth (Vento, 1995, p. 4). Scholar Arnold Carlos Vento (1995) argues that Mictlan should be viewed neither as an underworld similar to Western Christian doctrine nor as a final resting place, and that to the 'pre-Columbian peoples, the spirit was immoral; death was not a finality' (ibid., p. 4). Once the individual died, as part of the funeral rite, words were said to the corpse to the effect that everything comes to an end (de Orellana et al., 2009, p. 68). According to Fray Bernardino de Sahagún's *General History*, the corpse is told:

> that place is for everyone and it is very wide and there will be no other memory of you . . . you have already gone to the extremely dark place where there is not light, no openings, you do not have to be concerned about your life here and your past.
>
> (quoted in de Orellana et al., 2009, p. 68)

The corpse is then wrapped in a foetal position and mummified, and water is sprinkled on it. The deceased had to pass through nine dark and difficult places and overcome several tests before presenting herself or himself to Michlantecuhtli. It took the deceased four years and crossing nine rivers on the back of a dog to reach their destination, Mictlan (Ingham, 1971, p. 624). The mummified corpse was then recounted the places it had to cross to reach Mictlan:

between two crashing mountains; on a path guarded by a serpent; by the place of the green lizard; by eight barren lands and hills; by the place of the cold, obsidian-bladed wind; across the Río Chiconahuapan riding on the back of a small reddish-brown dog.

(de Orellana et al., 2009, p. 68)

A variant account of these trials is also recorded in the *Codex Vaticanus A*:

crossing a river; crossing between two hills or mountains; passing the obsidian hill, the place where banners wave; the place where people are shot with arrows; the site where hearts are devoured; the obsidian place of the dead; and the place without any smoke hole.

(ibid., p. 68)

Matos Moctezuma presents an interesting analysis of Mictlan. He envisions the nine steps of Mictlan to the duration of pregnancy (ibid., p. 68). Moreover, it was a womb receiving the dead, and the dead were to remain in Mictlan to be born (ibid., p. 68). As Matos Moctezuma states,

when an individual died, he had to undertake the return to the original womb, for which he had to overcome these dangers, just as to be born he had to face nine periods of suspension of the menstrual cycle and the vicissitudes of pregnancy to finally be given life.

(ibid., p. 68)

In fact, the Mexica had a concept of rebirth as chronicled by Spanish historians in the following stanzas: 'When we die, we really never do, because we live, we resurrect, we continue living, then we awaken. This fills us with joy' (quoted in Matos Moctezuma, 1971, p. 89).

The funeral rite was not the only ceremony in which the Aztecs honoured their deceased. Annually, they would have festivals to remember departed loved ones. Similar to Día de los Muertos, the Mexica would likewise make preparations for the Miccailhuitontli, or 'Little Festival of the Dead,' and Huey Miccailhuitl, or 'Great Festival of the Dead.' They were remembered on certain *veintenas* [20-day months] on the ritual calendar. Flowers were given to the deceased as well as offerings such as food and drink were taken to their tombs (Graulich, 1989, p. 53). The 'Little Festival of the Dead' may have been dedicated to dead children, but it may also be just a diminutive of the other one (ibid., p. 53). In the small commemoration, sad songs were sung in the temples and the tlamacazque or ministers dressed in black cloaks of henequen, people 'brought offerings of corn, squash and beans, and many other vegetables' (de Orellana et al., 2009, p. 77). As regards the large festival, chronicler Juan de Torquemada described it as follows:

> The people of Tlaxcala as well as others referred to it in this way because in this month they solemnly honored the memory of the dead with great clamor and cries and greater mourning than the first and they dyed their bodies black and they blacked their entire face. And so, the ceremonies were held day and night in all the temples and outside of them, there was great sadness, according to which each individual would express his feelings. And in this month, they referred to their dead kinds as gods and all of those individuals singled out for having died bravely in wars or in the power of their enemies and they made their idols for them and place them with their gods, saying that they had gone to the place of delight and gone in the company of other gods.
>
> (quoted in de Orellana et al., 2009, p. 77).

Other rituals were carried out, such as the 'relics of tears' in which elders removed the crusty bits from widows' faces formed after not washing their face or fixing their hair for 80 days. The priest then gathered the tears of the wailing widows, taking away their sadness, and in this way, 'the widows returned calm to their homes, for the pain in their tears had been removed from the city' (de Orellana et al., 2009, p. 71).

The religious thought and meaning of death diffused among the pre-Hispanic peoples, writes Carlos Serrano Sánchez, 'has contributed to how concepts and ideas have been shaped in modern-day Mexico' (Sánchez, 2012, p. 83). As more indigenous people of central and southern Mexico continue to migrate to Los Angeles, they bring with them their concept of death and the traditions in commemorating their dead. In the two-day celebrations of the Day of the Dead, similarities could be seen between the preparations of the ofrenda altar and the way in which the Mexica honoured certain groups of people. For example, ofrenda altars are made for the unsolved rape and murder of women working in transnational factories located between the US/Mexico border as well as for the activist and journalist 'warriors' who died defending Native lands and the environment (Marchi, 2022, pp. 90–93). I think that behind the phenomenology of the Los Angeles celebration of the Day of the Dead underlies a psychological need of the collective unconscious of Mexican Americans, as discussed in detail in the next section.

Psycho-social perspective

Prior to the Chicano movement, many middle-class Mexican Americans had adopted an assimilationist approach in integrating into American society. It was a time in American history when value was overtly placed on light skin colour, and Mexican Americans, whose phenotype did not fit into this category, faced prejudice and racial discrimination. Consequently, a new generation of Mexican Americans rejected the strategy of the previous generation and 'sought empowerment through "brownness"' (Foley, 1998, p. 65). The 1960s was a time of social, cultural and political upheaval. The Chicano movement was inspired and influenced by activists challenging old norms and ideas during this decade, particularly the Black Power movement. Such influence is exemplified by the initiatives of activists like Cesar Chavez advocating for the extension of labour rights to agricultural workers, many of whom were of Mexican origin, to stop their systematic exploitation. At the same time, activists also demonstrated and demanded that their Mexican identity and heritage be recognized and respected (Novas, 2007, p. 113). It was against this background that the Día de los Muertos was born, and it acted as a unifying symbol to bring together a fragmented community. Moreover, the phenomenology behind the Day of the Dead points to a religious need of the cultural unconscious of Mexican Americans to reconnect to its ancestral spiritual roots.

In my study on the Marian apparitional phenomenology (Musso, 2019), I found that an *emotional tension* formed prior to Marian apparitions, as Jung put it in his study on flying saucers, 'having its cause in a situation of collective distress or danger, or in a vital psychic need' (Jung, 1959, p. 7). In Jung's *Flying Saucers* (1959), compensation theory is used as a theoretical framework, and it also represents the main reference for the approach I adopted in my work on Marian apparitions (Musso, 2019) to interpret collective visions from a psychoanalytic perspective. In order to compensate for collective anxiety, such as war, religious persecution or nuclear threat, an image of the Virgin Mary appears as the healing unifying symbol. Jung's compensation theory asserts that the psyche is a self-regulating system working through a process of compensation according to which the unconscious aims to balance, adjust and supplement any tendency towards one-sidedness arising from consciousness (Jung, 1923, para. 693). Once the repressed unconscious has gathered enough energy charges, they break into consciousness forming dreams, beliefs, illusions, visions and so forth (Jung, 1959, p. 7; Samuels et al., 2007, p. 32). It can be argued that, after decades of racial discrimination and oppression endured by Mexican Americans, a one-sided constellation of repressed emotions formed in their cultural unconscious. Then, just like a war or religious persecution suffered by Marian seers, an event such as the civil rights movement triggered the numinosum. The Day of the Dead, a phenomenon in some respect similar to flying saucers and Marian apparitions, could be seen as a numinosum. Jung described the numinosum as

> a dynamic agency or effect not caused by an arbitrary act of will. On the contrary, it seizes and controls the human subject, who is rather its victim rather than creator. The *numinosum* . . . is either a quality belonging to an invisible object or the influence of an invisible presence.
>
> (Jung, 1938/40, para. 6, italics in original)

The Day of the Dead observation seemed to have taken a life of its own as the celebrations grew in size over the years. Similar to a numinosum, it has a mind of its own, and in addition, it is of a religious nature.

Jung's perspective on religion is something beyond creed or dogma; for Jung, religion is an 'immediate experience.' As Jung states in *Psychology and Religion* (1938/40),

> I want to make clear that by the term 'religion' I do not mean a creed. It is, how-ever, true that every creed is originally based on the one hand upon the experi-ence of the *numinosum* and on the other hand upon . . . trust or loyalty, faith and confidence in a certain experience of a numinous nature and in the change of consciousness that ensues. . . . We might say, then, that the term 'religion' designates the attitude peculiar to a consciousness which has been changed by experience of the *numinosum*.
>
> (Jung, 1938/40, para. 9, italics in original)

The religious and numinous experience arises from the autonomous level of the psyche (Corbett, 1996, p. 8). Under pervasive North American discriminatory atti-tudes and policies as observed during the 1960s and early 1970s against 'brown-ness,' a one-sided attitude prevails suppressing or denying the expression of the religious function; consequently, 'a general disturbance results' (Jung, 1957, para. 544). From this perspective, the Mexican American psyche reaches a point where it seeks synthesis, and to restore psychic balance, it needs to have an experience with the numinosum, thus projecting a symbol comprehensible to the individual, or in this case, the collective. It seems that a religious experience takes place as if there is a psychological need to break the tension of opposites created by cultural distress in an attempt to bring order and meaning in the midst of chaos. In *A Most Accursed Religion*, Greg Mogensen writes,

> as the pain increases so, too, does our sense of relationship to an omnipotent being. . . . As the persistence of our suffering mocks our ability to understand it within the categories of our usual existence, our sense of relationship to a wholly other will and purpose grows.
>
> (Mogenson, 2005, pp. 28–29)

While the Day of the Dead was used as a tool to gain political autonomy, regain specific cultural roots, and embrace the indigenous side, it could also be seen as an experience with the numinosum via the collective ritual allowing them to connect with something grander. As Edward Edinger states, 'understood psychologically, the central aim of all religious practices is to keep the individual (ego) related to the deity (Self)'; moreover, he argues that secular or political systems or movements 'are never an adequate container for religious meaning' (Edinger, 1972, pp. 63–64, 68).

From a depth-psychological perspective, the phenomenon behind the Day of the Dead could be seen as a return to the ancestral and to embracing the indig-enous side which was previously seen as shameful and impure. Moreover, the rejected indigenous side could be seen as the shadow of the Mexican American psyche. The shadow contains 'all the unpleasant things one wants to hide, the inferior worthless and the primitive side of man's nature' (Samuels et al., 2007, p. 138), but it also contains all sorts of positive qualities and potential. According to Walter Odajnyk (1976), 'members of shadow-bearing groups are usually demoralized and depressed' (Odajnyk, 1976, pp. 82–83). It is in the shadow in which we find the 'inner treasures' and integrate and heal feelings of shame and worthlessness, and Día de los Muertos grants one entry into the shadow world. As Eduardo Matos Moctezuma (1971) wrote, 'Death becomes the germ of life' (Matos Moctezuma, 1971, p. 87). In the underworld of Mictlan, seeds of a new life are hidden. Quetzalcoatl, the Plumed Serpent, turned himself into an ant and entered into the underworld in order to gather seeds for agriculture for the benefit of humanity. (del Castillo, 2020, p. 144). As Sandra Luz de Castillo points out, 'we get a hint of the hidden riches of the underworld as indicated by the Mountain of Sustenance. Located in the underworld, it exemplifies the life-death duality as personified by the underworld god and goddess' (ibid., 2020, p. 144). It is when we make our descent into the shadowy underworld that this death process introduces to us the possibility to become reborn.

In this context, it can be insightful to recall an interpretation of the so-called mestizo consciousness, moving away from Western rationalist epistemology. Prominent Chicana writer Gloria Anzaldúa proposes an original perspective on 'mestiza consciousness' which challenged enforced paradigms, thus freeing oneself from the colonized inner self (Anzaldúa, 1987). Anzaldúa grounded herself in Aztec cosmology, having a confrontation with the Serpent Skirt, Coatlicue. Coatlicue is one of the beings that dwell in the Region of the Dead. She, like Coyolzauhqui and Cihuateteo in the realm of the death, is referred to as liminal:

> they are women who are dead and at the same time very much alive. The underworld, the place of the dead, is also the place of creation, and therefore these half-dead deities or half-alive deities are in a process of decomposition and at the same in the process of returning to life.
>
> (de Orellana et al., 2009, p. 79)

There are other serpents in the Aztec religion and worldview linked to death, such as Cihuatéolt who was associated with snakes and represented the women who died in childbirth, and the fearful two-headed snake Maquizcóalt associated with death (ibid., p. 77). In one of the crossings in the underworld of Mictlan that the dead needs to overcome, a serpent also resides. In *Symbols of Transformation*, Jung associates the snake with the underworld and the guardian of treasures, as he states, 'that the snake really is a death-symbol is evident from the fact that the souls of the dead, like the chthonic gods, appear as serpents, as dwellers in the kingdom of the deadly mother' (Jung, 1952, paras. 577–578). When the Spanish conquistadores conquer the Aztec empire, the Spanish friars replaced the Mexican Serpent goddess with the Virgen de Guadalupe. Not only were the Mexican goddesses split, but after the Conquest, Anzaldúa says, they desexed Guadalupe, 'taking *Coatlalopeuh*, the serpent/sexuality, out of her' (Anzaldúa, 1987, p. 49, italics in original).

Guadalupe was made into a chaste virgin and Coatlicue and Tlazolteotl into *putas* or whores, and eventually, all indigenous deities and religious practices were associated with the work of the devil (ibid., pp. 49–50, italics in original). According to Aztec mythology, when Coatlicue becomes pregnant, her children, the moon and stars, become angry and decide to kill her. However, her Sun child Huitzilopochtli, who is still in the womb, emerges as an adult, and with the help of the serpent of fire, 'overcomes his brothers and puts them to flight' (Johnson, 1988, p. 164). Huitzilopochtli could be seen as part of Coatlicue and a source of serpentine power to draw on, a male snake god the likes of the youthful god Hermes and the Greek Saviour-Healer Asklepios. Moreover, he makes up the masculine component of the self-generated goddess or the ability of parthenogenesis. This male serpentine aspect makes Coatlicue even more powerful and a force to be reckoned with in the face of enemies of galactic strength. Additionally, the Serpent Skirt Coatlicue is a Kali-type deity of a raw, crude and instinctual passion which is needed to overcome destructive enemies, real or imagined.

The individual's descent into hell and sufferings allow her or him to better cope with internal complexes and anxieties created by the external world, such as racial discrimination and marginalization. In the struggle permeated with internal suffering and anxieties, the Serpent serves as a guide, or psychopomp, to help create new order out of the disorientation from the tension of opposites. In her confrontation with the serpent goddess of the underworld, Coatlicue, Anzaldúa's mestiza consciousness offers a way to recover the dead parts of oneself and transforming libido which had previously been stuck in the unconscious. It is a symbolic death of the previous one-sided rigid attitude towards embracing the Spanish 'whiteness' and recovering the rejected brown and indigenous ancestors via altar making and the annual observations of the dead.

By practicing the rituals and ceremonies such as the Day of the Dead, one connects to the ancestral spiritual realm which strengthens one when confronting outer world circumstances. Moreover, it connects us to community and a sense of belonging. This practice provides a container, as Edinger states, 'there is religious, metaphysical containment, for instance, in which a religious creed or a philosophical creed . . . is the containing agent' (Edinger, 1996, p. 33). In addition to being a container, the ancestral spiritual realm forms one part of the multi-level strata of the psyche, oscillating like a liminal being between the individual and collective realms. Jungian analyst Sandra Easter argues that Jung offered a 'strong perspective on working with our ancestors . . . particularly through his work in the *Red Book* which suggests "the dead" can have a significant effect on us' (Bright, 2016). In *Memories, Dreams, Reflections*, Jung wrote about his ideas on the dead:

> for the unconscious corresponds to the mythic land of the dead, the land of the ancestors. If, therefore, one has a fantasy of the soul vanishing, this means that it has withdrawn into the unconscious or into the land of the dead.
>
> (Jung, 1995, pp. 216–217)

For Jung, the dead were the 'voices of the Unanswered, Unresolved, and Unredeemed,' and he looked to them for answers which could not come from the outside world (Jung, 1995, pp. 216–217). Jung's relationship to his ancestral dead is similar to the relationship that the Mexica had with their own ancestors; that is, communicating with the land of the dead as a way to cope with the demands of the outside world.

Conclusion

In her book *Day of the Dead in the USA* (2022), Marchi seems to question the authenticity of the American observations of Day of the Dead as 'its material culture and rituals have become increasingly commoditized' (Marchi, 2022, p. 133). In addition to the commodification of Día de los Muertos, its celebration by several non-Latinos, most of whom arguably do not have an understanding of the tradition, inevitably has the effect of 'watering down' its original meaning. A connection to the ancestors is mostly missing in the United States, and Easter points to the many generations in the Western culture who have not tended to their ancestors as explaining why 'some many things seem out of balance' (Bright, 2016). Through the celebrations of the Day of the Dead, an archetype could have been activated, and the archetypal force behind the numinosum takes possession of those who are fascinated by it and unable to resist it. Americans are quite ripe for such a possession, through time having often been interested in metaphysical ideas and practices such as astrology, magic, hypnotism and spiritualism and fascinated with eastern religions and spiritualities and more recent practices and beliefs referred to as the New Age (Hendrickson, 2013, p. 623). It is as if the Mexican deities of the land of the dead are speaking to them, just like the Mexican Americans living in Los Angeles. Perhaps a new myth of the dead is being created not only in Los Angeles, but in other parts of the United States as well. As Edinger states in *The Creation of Consciousness*, '[a] noted feature of the new myth is its capacity to unify the current religions of the world . . . [it] will not be one more religious myth in competition with all the others for man's allegiance' (Edinger, 1984, p. 32).

Prior to the phenomenon of Día de los Muertos in Los Angeles, Mexican Americans had been mostly disconnected from their indigenous spiritual roots (Marchi, 2022, p. 44). The emergence of the Day of the Dead out of the Chicano movement of the 1960s gave birth to a new myth of the dead through which, every November for two days, many Mexican Americans honour their deceased loved ones arriving from their ancestral realm, Mictlan. While its conscious intention was to form a new identity based on indigenous pride, on an unconscious level, Día de los Muertos inspired Americans of Mexican descent to reconnect to their ancestral past, which is important in keeping rooted in one's own psyche. Using a Jungian depth-psychological approach, I have taken the theoretical framework from my work on Marian apparitions and applied it to the phenomenology of the Day of the Dead in Los Angeles. Accordingly, I argue that the basis for this phenomenon was an emotional tension having its cause in collective distress, for example, fragmentation of community and racial discrimination and marginalization. Moreover, I suggest that the phenomenology behind the Día de los Muertos represented a numinosum of a religious nature, breaking the rigid one-sided conscious attitude of identity via Spanish whiteness and ancestry. The numinosum helps restore the psychic imbalance of the cultural psyche of Mexican Americans. Out of the midst of chaos of the Chicano movement, a new attitude is created, one of identity rooted in brownness and Mexican ancestry, while at the same time a new myth of the dead emerged, consisting of a symbiotic relationship between the living and the dead in which every year the veil between the world of the living and the underworld of Mictlan is momentarily lifted, allowing people to reunite with their dead ancestors.

Notes

1 Both English and Spanish phases will be used interchangeably.
2 According to Mexican historian de Orellana, specialists are certain that the people inhabiting Mexico-Tenochitlan referred to themselves are Mexica (de Orellana et al., 2009, p. 65). In this chapter, the two terms are used synonymously.

References

Anzaldúa, Gloria. (1987). *Borderlands/La Frontera*. San Francisco, CA: Aunt Lute Books.
Bright, Bonnie. (2016). Working with the Ancestors: A Jungian Perspective with Sandra Easter, Ph.D. *Pacifica Post*, Pacific Graduate Institute, September 28. www.pacificapost.com/working-with-the-ancestors-a-jungian-perspective-sandra-easter.
Corbett, Lionel. (1996). *The Religious Function of the Psyche*. London and New York, NY: Routledge.
de Orellana, Margarita, et al. (2009). *The Aztecs-Mexica and Death: A Rebirth of Gods and Men*. Artes de México, 96, Muerte Azteca-Mexica. Mexico City: Renacer de Dioses y Hombres (Noviembre), pp. 65–80.
de Orellana, Margarita, et al. (2011). *Day of the Dead Ritual Serenity*. Artes de México, 62, Día de Muertos Serenidad Ritual. Mexico City: Segunda Edición, pp. 65–80.
del Castillo, Sandra Luz. (2020). *The Mexican Day of the Dead: A Jungian Inquiry*. [Doctoral dissertation, Pacifica Graduate Institute]. Proquest Dissertations and Theses Global.
Día de los Muertos/Day of the Day. *Artbound*. KCET. Season 10 episode 3. May 29, 2019.
Edinger, Edward F. (1972). *Ego and the Archetype: Individuation and the Religious Function of the Psyche*. Toronto, Canada: Shambhala Publications Inc.
Edinger, Edward F. (1984). *The Creation of Consciousness: Jung's Myth for Modern Man*. Boston and London: Inner City Books.
Edinger, Edward F. (1996). *The New God-Image: A Study of Jung's Key Letters Concerning the Evolution of the Western God-Image* (Cordic, Dianne D. and Charles Yates, M.D. Eds.). Asheville, NC: Chiron Publications.
Foley, Neil. (1998). Becoming Hispanic: Mexican-Americans and the Faustian Pact with Whiteness. In Foley, Neil (ed.), *New Directions in Mexican American Studies*. Austin, TX: University of Texas Press.
Graulich, Michel. (1981). The Metaphor of the Day in Ancient Mexican Myth and Ritual [and Comments and Reply]. *Current Anthropology*, 22(1) (February), pp. 45–60.

Graulich, Michel. (1989). Miccailhuitl: The Aztec Festivals of the Deceased. *Numen*, 36(1) (June), pp. 43–71.

Hendrickson, Brett. (2013). New Contexts for Curanderismo: Recasting Mexican American Folk Healing within American Metaphysical Religion. *Journal of the American Academy of Religion*, 81(3) (September), pp. 620–643.

Ingham, John M. (1971). Time and Space in Ancient Mexico: The Symbolic Dimensions of Clanship. *Man*, 6(4) (December), pp. 615–629.

Johnson, Buffie. (1988). *Lady of the Beasts: Ancient Images of the Goddess and Her Sacred Animals*. New York: HarperCollins.

Jung, C.G. (1923). Definitions. In *Collective Works, Vol. 6. Psychological Types*. Princeton, NJ: Princeton University Press, 1971.

Jung, C.G. (1938/40). Psychology and Religion. In *Collective Works, Vol. 11. Psychology and Religion*. New York, NY: Pantheon Books, 1958.

Jung, C.G. (1952). The Dual Mother. In *Collective Works, Vol. 5. Symbols of Transformation*. New York, NY: Pantheon Books, 1958.

Jung, C.G. (1957). *The Undiscovered Self*. Princeton, NJ: Princeton University Press, 2010.

Jung, C.G. (1959). *Flying Saucers: A Modern Myth of Things Seen in the Skies*. London and New York, NY: Routledge Classics.

Jung, C.G. (1995). *C.G. Jung: Memories, Dreams, Reflections* (Jaffe, Aniela Trans. and Richard and Winston, Clara Eds.). London: Fontana Press.

Marchi, Regina. (2013). Hybridity and Authenticity in US Day of the Dead Celebrations. *The Journal of American Folklore*, 126(501), pp. 87–89.

Marchi, Regina. (2022). *Day of the Dead in the USA: The Migration and Transformation of a Cultural Phenomenon* (2nd ed.). New Brunswick, Camden, and Newark, New Jersey, and London: Rutgers University Press.

Matos Moctezuma, Eduardo. (1971). *Conception of Death in Mexico the Spanish Conquest*. Artes de México, 145. Mexico City: Miccaihuitl El Culto a la Muerte, pp. 65–80.

Mogenson, Greg. (2005). *A Most Accused Religion: When a Trauma Becomes God*. Putnam, CT: Spring Publications, Inc.

Musso, Valeria Céspedes. (2019). *Marian Apparitions in Cultural Contexts: Applying Jungian Concepts to Mass Visions of the Virgin Mary*. London and New York: Routledge.

Novas, Himilce. (2007). *Everything You Need to Know about Latino History*. New York, NY: A Blume Book.

Odajnyk, Walter. (1976). *A Jung and Politics: The Political and Social Ideas of C.G. Jung*. New York, NY: New York University Press.

Rosales, F. Arturo. (1996). *Chicano! The History of the Mexican American Civil Rights Movement*. Mexico City: Arte Publico Press.

Samuels, Andrew, Shorter, Bani and Fred, Blaut. (2007). *A Critical Dictionary of Jungian Analysis*. London and New York, NY: Routledge.

Sánchez, Carlos Serrano. (2012). Funeral Rites in Pre-Hispanic Mexico. *Voices of Mexico*, 94, pp. 78–83.

Vasquez, Jessica M. (2010). Blurred Borders for Some But Not 'Others': Racialization, 'Flexible Ethnicity', Gender, and Third Generation Mexican American Identity. *Sociological Perspectives*, 53(1), pp. 45–71.

Velasco, Ana. (2019). Self Help Graphics & Art's Dia de los Muertos Legacy Told Through Prints. *Artbound*, May 30.

Vento, Arnold Carlos. (1995). Aztec Myths and Cosmology: Historical-Religious Misinterpretation and Bias. *Wicazo Sa Review*, 11(1) (Spring), pp. 1–23.

Chapter 2

A comparative ethnographic study of the journey to the land of the dead and the concept of immortality

Elizabeth Brodersen

Introduction

In this chapter, I speculate how mythical thinking imagines the physical nature of the land of the dead, the journey to arrive there, plus the creative interrelationship between the living and the dead imbued within the concept of immortality. Myth making is an archaic form of artistic activity, bringing relatively timeless images of the instinctual world into the realm of human history (Walker, 2002, p. 19). As Kerenyi (Jung and Kerenyi, 1948, p. 3) elaborates, a particular kind of subject matter determines the art of mythology: it contains immemorial tales about supernatural beings, heroic battles and journeys to the underworld. Mythology is the movement of that material: it is something solid yet mobile, substantial but not static and capable of transformation. Relating a myth is a form of contacting the cosmos by establishing and enclosing an area in which human actions and experience can be orientated. Mourning the dead and wondering where their souls disappear after death is one such experience, as it is analogous to imagining the experience of the sun when it sinks, separates and disappears at night-time to arise the next day as a collective regeneration of time through a repetition of the first cosmogonic act of creation (Eliade, 1954, p. 88).

I concentrate on two examples of the land of the dead, one from ancient Welsh/ Cymric sources about *Annwn* (the Otherworld) and the second from ancient Egypt (*Duat*), to show how their different topography and climate create both differences and similarities in their concept of an afterlife imbued within the concept of immortality. Myths are concerned with the cosmogony of kingship (the sun god) transmitted simultaneously into cratogonic genealogy, whereby humans partake in the constellation of deities and become one of them (Assmann, 2001, p. 100, p. 212).

In Cymric and Egyptian myths concerning the sun god, his relationship to the earth and the underworld, both are characterised by gods and goddesses who share relatable human emotions: *Ceridwen*, the mother nature goddess, is married to *Tegid Foel* of *Lyn Tegid*; she has a son, *Affagdu* (night-time), miserable with his ugly appearance, whom she wants to help through brewing a magic potion to dispel it. Isis, the Egyptian sky goddess, impatient for change, has numerous competitive siblings and is attributed to harming the ageing sun god Atum/Ra by creating

DOI: 10.4324/9781003313304-4

a poisonous snake from his dribbling spittle mixed with sand that bites him, in order to hasten the rebirth of her son, Horus/Ra (Budge, 1899, p. 137). In such ancient myths, before the advent of the OT Genesis myth, which robbed animals and women of their evolutionary creative agency, there is an easy transfer of affective qualities between animals and humans. It is not enough to speculate about the origin of creation; it is necessary to re-create that specific moment by returning to evolutionary, primordial sacred time to facilitate the complete renewal of the cosmos (Eliade, 1963, p. 37).

Where souls preside after death is mythically configured within ancient speculations about what happens to the sun (ego consciousness) when it sinks into the west and disappears. How does the sun survive the journey to the other side, arise the next day and be reborn? Each new birth represents a symbolic recapitulation of cosmogonic creation and that of a specific culture's mythical history (Eliade, 1963, p. 33). From ancient pre-Celtic Cymric/Welsh mythical perspective, the sun is imagined as the dragon's head, a fiery red ball that sinks into the west (pendragon) and forms the structure for the metamorphic quality of the nature goddess, *Ceridwen*'s cauldron of inspiration that revives the dead so that the sun/son is reborn as a cyclical return. The transmigration of souls after death that imaginatively shapeshift human into animal form and back again in a fluid interaction, depending on which affective qualities are needed, is a salient feature of both Welsh and Egyptian cosmogony.

Jung alludes to the ancient, paradoxical, alchemical dragon as Mercurius (see 1948a, para. 282–283), a symbol that combines the opposites (light/dark; life/death; male/female). Jung (1911–1912/1952a, paras. 351–354) also amplifies the Egyptian sun god Osiris, who undergoes death, dismemberment and resurrection to be reborn as a rising hawk (Horus/Ra). Spence (1945/1999, pp. 154–155) and Dames (2002, p. 30) suggest a strong similarity between the imaginative mythic death and resurrection of the Cymric/Welsh solar king, *Hu Gadern*, and the myth of the Egyptian Osiris/Ra and their respective journeys through the Otherworld. Both ancient cultures, which I shall explain in greater detail in this chapter, use the image of solar boats that carry the sun and the souls of the dead into the underworld for transmigration and resurrection purposes, pointing to similar doctrines of immortality (Rolleston, 1917, pp. 75–83). Differences between the two cultures lie in the physical nature of the other world which, in turn, reflects the physical topography, climatology and attitudes to chaos. Such differences influence whether the sun is transformed before it is resurrected, or whether it remains qualitatively unchanged (cf. Brodersen, 2012, pp. 133–149).

Welsh/Cymric cosmogony

The earliest description of *Annwn*, the Welsh/Cymric word for the Otherworld, is perceived as a place of Elysium where death transforms it into a place of delight. Ancient Britain is considered as a resort for the dead. Procopius, a Byzantine historian (500–665 BCE) relates how fishermen from Brittany ferry the souls of their dead across to the British coast where they disembark after having heard their names called by an eerie loud voice from the shore (Spence, 1915/1990a, p. 20). Once the souls disembark, the ferry boat rises up in the sea, as if unloaded of its burden.

Ancient Britons thus practice the Cult of the Dead which flourishes in North-West Africa and Spain 10,000 years ago and before Egypt has a definite culture. Spence (ibid., pp. 48–52) argues that Welsh/Cymric druidism is a branch of the Iberian/North African cult of the dead that predates the arrival of Celts in Britain c. 1000 BCE. The dead are perceived as the 'blessed dead' and possess a living, benign power to influence the living. Although the dead live in another world, the Cymru partake in their nature through blood ties, dreams and shared cultural experiences. The ancestors can be also contacted and appeased, and confer blessing and wisdom to the living through special portals (dolmens) that reconnect the sun rays at various equinoxes to the dead in reciprocal acts of warm nourishment (Stewart, 1986, pp. 151–152).

Cymric belief in immortality

The Celts and pre-Celtic megalithic cultures such as that found in Welsh/Cymric indigenous beliefs, based on literary and archaeological evidence, have a positive and profound attitude to death. Through exploring druidic-shamanic ideas (Green, 1993; Mathews, 1996; Rolleston, 1917; Spence, 1945), we ascertain that the soul is believed to be immortal and enshrined the very essence of a person who might resume her/his life in other bodies, or alternatively might dwell in the body after death in another region, or live on in the grave eating and drinking the food that bestows eternal life through contact with *Annwn*. Every culture has its symbol of the hero/warrior as a shaman: Jung (1911–1912/1952b, para. 580, emphasis in original) states: 'The treasure which the hero fetches from the dark cavern is *life*: it is himself, new born from the dark maternal cave of the unconscious where he was stranded by the introversion or regression of the libido.' Whoever travels to the underworld symbolically accompanying the sun as it falls from the sky into the darkness to find loss souls, seek advice and return, possesses shamanistic qualities (cf. Brodersen, 2019, pp. 147–164).

The nature of triads in druidic Welsh mysticism

Annwn belongs to an imaginative ancient druidic interconnected system of triads that have symbolic significance. Jung (1948b, para. 172–193) suggests that triads of gods are an early form of cosmological reflection, developmental differentiation and fractionation about birth, death and afterlife that expands consciousness by giving them forms and content within triadic familial dynamics (Brodersen, 2016, p. 35), The first triad depicts the origin and creation of the Cymru similar in symbolic structure to other creation myths: first, the sun god and originator, *Hu Gadern*, who travels from the land of *Hav* (summer) called *Defrobani*; the second, Prydain, son of *Aedd Mawr*, who first governs Britain; and third, *Dynwal-Moelmud*, who discriminates the laws, customs and privileges of the land. Another triad describes three devastating events that happened to the Isles of *Prydain* (Britain). The first is the flooding of lake *Llyn Llion*; all inhabitants perish except for *Dwyfan* and *Dwyfach*, who are preserved in a ship without a mask, similar to Noah's Ark in the OT Bible. The second is a great fire, when the earth splits and opens up *Annwn* (hell) as the earth's molten core. The third is the scorching summer, when vegetation and animal and human life are lost.

To rectify these events, three solutions are found: first, the ship of *Nefydd Naf Neifion* that carries the male and female of all living species when the lake bursts; secondly, the drawing of *Afanc* (the beaver) out of the lake in *Annwn* to the land by the branching oxen of *Hu Gadern* to stop the flooding and extinguish the fire; thirdly, the stones of *Gwyddon Ganehebon* that memorises all knowledge of the arts and sciences (Daniel, 1927; Davies, 1804/1996). It is the specific task of *Hu Gadern* to draw the souls of the dead out of *Annwn* into safety. By the strength of his strong emanation (his solar oxen), *Hu Gadern* draws the *Afanc* out of the underground lake as analogous of his ability to rescue life from the darkness of the abyss and regenerate it.

Taken symbolically, the triads represent the druidic/bardic shamanic mnemonics packed with vital significance: *Hu Gadern, Dyfnwl Moelmud* and *Tydain Awen* all represent differentiated aspects of the same life force. *Hu Gadern*, the mighty sun god personified by the Arch Druid, overseas, heals and instructs. *Dyfnwl Moelmud* personifies bardic poetic inspiration behind Cymric oral arts and ancestral memories, while the ovate, *Tydain Tad Awen*, is the central fire of the dragon's head (*Ceridwen's* cauldron) that sets creation in motion when it sinks in the west and arises reborn, to immortalise in stone the cycles of life, death and rebirth (Davies, 1804/1996, pp. 123–153)

Spence (1915/1990a, p. 200) argues that *Ceridwen*, the mother goddess of the underworld, embodies a cauldron as the uterus that contains the seeds (or eggs) of the not yet born. Cymric mysticism is based on the creation and the intermingling of two opposites: the divine principle in the form of the sun, and the other world *Cythrawl*. As an embodiment of chaos, *Cythrawl* is the great cauldron of unspecified soul-force.

According to Cymric mysticism, humans arise with the sun in the morning, traverse earth or *Abred*, the sphere of visible creative matter, and, at sunset, sink in the west into *Gywnffrydd* while still alive as the initiatory place of tried and tested spirits (ibid., p. 252). The unifying principle of these three spheres into the fourth, *Annwn*, is found in *Awen*, which refers to the first three letters of the Cymric alphabet. *Awen* reveals its relationship to trees and the secret name of their ancestor, representing the letters OIU: the O relates to the perfect circle of *Gywnffrydd*, the I to the mortal world of *Abred* and the U to the cauldron of *Annwn*. *Awen* is observed as the three rays of new light falling from the redhaired representative of the sun, *Celi*, warming the earth at the beginning of February at *Imbole*, the Cymric New Year (Brodersen, 2006, p. 12).

Ceridwen, *the shapeshifter*

The following Welsh/Cymric myth orally transmitted originates c. 6000 BCE and thought to be collected, written down and translated into English during the 12th century in the Mabinogion (Gantz, 1976), reveals how open sea, a moist, maritime climate on the north-western seaboard influences how the land of the dead is envisaged. This early Welsh/Cymric creation myth, still part of current oral folklore tradition in South Wales, features *Ceridwen*, nature moon goddess of creation and of the warm Gulf Stream, who, in the form of an old white sow (*Hen Wen*), swims around Wales giving form to its landscape as she passes by (Dames, 2002, p. 113; Stewart and Williamson, 1999, p. 42). *Ceridwen* is both the sea and land, combining images of both: she represents the dynamic, windy, tidal shoreline in Wales and its shifting physicality. As Sharkey (1975, p. 11) suggests, ancient Welsh mysteries take shape in the flux of in-between states, such as in twilight zones, or in the dew which is neither rain or sea water, using mistletoe as a symbol of fertility that is neither a plant or a tree (cf. *Poems from the Book of Taliesen, the Song of the Wind,* Evans, 1915/2018, pp. 3–6).

In this Welsh creation myth, *Ceridwen*, as *Hen Wen*, swims out of the sea in the morning of the world and transforms the landscape through metamorphosis. She swims ashore at Gwyneth in South Wales and shakes from her ear a grain of wheat, so this part of Wales called Gwent is renowned for its wheat. *Hen Wen* then swims around Dyfed and shakes from her ear a grain of barley and a bee, so that honey and beer are produced there. *Hen Wen* swims north and lands in Caernarfon. There, she frees from her ear a wolf cub and an eagle chick in order to reflect upon its craggy, mountainous terrain. *Hen Wen* swims on further north, past *Mon Mam* (the mother of Wales), the Island of Anglesey, where she shakes out a kitten into the sea. It becomes a whirlpool called *Palwg's* cat. *Ceridwen's* cauldron is thought to exist under this whirlpool in *Annwn*, Welsh for the 'Otherworld' (cf. Graves, 1948, pp. 215–216; Brodersen, 2012). Ancient Britons are as much influenced by the sea as by the land, fishing being an important food source. An easy explorative access to the sea opens up an imaginative concept of authority that undergoes a continual pushing of boundaries to establish new premises, including concepts about an afterlife and where the sun vanishes when it sinks into the Atlantic Ocean. Always fluid, resourceful but unpredictable, the sea demands an open-ended dialogue that pushes back fixed boundaries and opens up new terrain between the known and unknown.

Ceridwen *and* Hu Gadern

The mythical relationship of the sun god, *Hu Gadern*, and nature goddess, *Ceridwen*, is one of primal equality and cooperation. Both impulses seem to have existed equally and separately from the beginning in their individual roles of dispelling darkness (Graves, 1948, pp. 23–24; Ford, 1977). As *Hu Gadern's* presence is bright and temperate, but not dominant, *Ceridwen*, embodying the warm Gulf Stream, takes an active, regenerative role in transforming the landscape herself. *Hu*

Gadern's power is mitigated by all-year-round precipitation and wind that shield the earth from too much of his influence. The earth yields new growth more easily than in countries that suffer hotter summers or colder winters, where the earth is either scorched or ice bound for half the year. This cooperative relationship has led to more imaginative in-between possibilities, not found in countries that are dominated by a hot, strong sun.

The sun god *Hu Gadern*'s imaginative sovereign representative in ancient Britain is also tempered by his 'shadow' chief advisor and shaman, the druid Merlin, who has access to tribal memories in the collective unconscious. As personifications of light (fusion/safety) and dark (separation/risk), these same-sex personifications work well to transform the landscape by honouring both aspects (Dames, 2002). The druid is able to accompany the red sun as it/he sinks because, as a personification of mercury, he/she can withstand the sun's intense heat without drying up. As Jung (1952, paras. 88–90) points out, the personification of mercury as Mercurius with his/her quicksilver qualities is a suitable symbol for the fluid, mobile intellect required for creativity, encompassing both spirit and water. Jung (1948c, paras. 255–266) further emphasises the dual, androgynous nature of Mercurius as the primordial dragon and its alchemical relationship to unconscious processes: it is refractory like matter, mysterious and elusive, but confronts us as a living substance (ibid., paras. 286–289). Compared to the Christ symbol of unity and purity, Mercurius represents the hidden, 'shadow' ambiguity of all creative processes and is thoroughly pagan (ibid., paras, 286–289).

Hu Gadern's earthly symbolic representation takes the form of the dragon's head (Pendragon) as it sinks into the open sea in the west. The Welsh king, Arthur, as chief representation of the sun god, therefore, carries the flag of Pendragon, the image of the red dragon head breathing fire, accompanied by Merlin, the arch Druid as the dark, as it sinks into the darkness and arises the next day. These personifications of light and dark have a cooperative relationship. Their goal is not to facilitate the personal aggrandisement of 'one' over the 'other' but to encourage change and new ideas through renewed contact with the dead in *Annwn* whose courage inspires them.

King Arthur and Druid Merlin, thought to have existed in 5th-century Britain during the Saxon invasion, therefore, represent much earlier Neolithic symbolic roots as light and dark, order and chaos. *Annwn* is not a dark, judgmental place, but a twilight zone of mediation where the living sun (light/order/safety) dialogues with the ancestral dead (dark/chaos/risk) in a mixing of the two that promotes inspirational thinking and the renewal of the cultural landscape (Spence, 1945/1999, pp. 129–141). *Ceridwen*'s cauldron itself embodies the dragon's head as the sun/son penetrates into the unconscious at night, prophesising and giving advice combining the forces of chaos/unknown within a structured order. The liquid created and brewed by *Ceridwen* brings forth new life by reconnecting consciousness (light) with the presence of the ancestors (dark) who, having lived through death, engender active courage, psychic roots and tribal wisdom.

Annwn

Annwn as the land of the dead, mentioned in medieval Welsh literature (cf. Mabinogion, ca 12th century), lies imaginatively beneath the mortal world and is divided into several planes or kingdoms. Those who have the courage to travel through *Annwn* in dreams to dialogue with the dead can access its gifts and treasures, particularly *Cediwen*'s cauldron of inspiration that does not cook food for cowards.

Annwn is imagined as containing crystal fortresses, rotating portals and glass ships, giving images of a restless, watery expanse of sunken treasure, difficult to access in the moving, churning twilight of tidal currents and deep swirling caverns. It is a zone of shadowy radiance under the sea, where life force is stored and recreated in several stratospheres called *Caer* (a chair or castle), all qualitative, composite images of the ambivalent, unconscious, emotional, imaginative mourning structures that illustrate where the souls reside after physical death (Spence, 1945/1999, pp. 141–143). They also reflect the mediating, turbulent physicality of the Atlantic Ocean. *Caer Pedryvan*, the revolving four-cornered castle in the Isle of the Strong Door, where grey twilight merges into complete darkness, is lit only by the yellow flare of torches. It is difficult to find its entrance due to the churning nature of the open sea. *Caer Vedwit* is the Castle of Revelry, *Caer Golud* the Castle of Riches and *Caer Wydyr* the Glass Fortress populated by the dead, once resurrected, who cannot speak. This Glass Fortress is another image of the glassy expanse of the Atlantic Ocean. *Caer Wydyr* also appears in reference to Arthur's glass ship called elsewhere *Pryderi*, in which Arthur and Merlin Emrys, as representatives (day and night) of the sun god *Hu Gadern*, travels to *Annwn* to bring back the cauldron of inspiration, a prototype of the grail, amongst other treasures. Through their courageous endeavours to meet the dead, personal, cultural and collective consciousness is revitalized and reborn.

Dames (2002, p. 166) suggests that glass as a substance, similar to amber, acts like a supernatural lens able to bring past and future together in a combined focus that merges grief and loss with hope of renewal. A slight flaw in the crystal is thought to allow the departing soul of the dead entry into where ancestral memories are stored. The Druids believe the firmament is one vast wheel in a chair in which *Hu Gadern* (the sun) is seated, with his main representatives, *Celi* and *Ceridwen*. Embryonic matter is wafted across the ocean in a sacred boat like the crescent moon, the coracle of *Ceridwen*. In Druidism, all souls have their birth and rebirth from *Ceridwen* and *Awen*, and to come into the world, they must cross the Celtic Styx, traverse *Annwn* and descend into the train of the sun on its return on the morning. In this interpretation, *Annwn* becomes the imaginative source of spiritual inspiration rather than a land of the dead. It is an ambiguous place where the dead live again without pain or sorrow, aging or decay, but is a dangerous world to visit when one is still alive, except in dreams.

All these descriptions of *Annwn* with their diverse *Caers* describe the multifaceted, ambivalent emotions during the mourning process: the churning nature of grief, of not knowing which exit and entrance to take to avoid that loss is equated through *Caer Pefryyan*; the relief from pain equally experienced by mourners as revelry (*Caer Vedwit*); the protection from misery and the riches that the dead bring through inheritance is illustrated through *Caer Golud*. Although the dead cannot speak, their silent courage is felt through their ancestral memories that is stored in *Ceridwen*'s cauldron (*Caer Wydyr*), keeping them alive through the breath of nine maidens whose help is contacted through the unconscious in dreams and active imagination. Evans (1915/2018, pp. 117–119) vividly describes the virtues of each *Caer* of the dead as they become integrated as strongholds of ancestral memories and prophesies.

Ceridwen's cauldron

Ceridwen's potion transforms darkness into wisdom (Ford, 1977, pp. 159–181). Grigsby (2002, pp. 177–189) speculates that the later medieval version of the wounded fisher king and the search for the missing grail, also connected with Arthurian legend, attempts to re-establish this creative link to earlier, disassociated, Neolithic matrilineal kin care mythic structures. Night-time is personified by *Ceridwen*'s son, *Affagdu*, whom she describes as the 'ugliest boy in the world.' She brews a special potion in her cauldron to transform his ugliness. She gives a servant boy, *Gwion Bach*, the onerous task of stirring this potion for one year and a day, who accidentally spills three drops of the hot potion onto his thumb. He sucks his thumb and gains the immediate knowledge and wisdom meant for *Affagdu*. In her rage, *Ceridwen* pursues *Gwion*; both shape-shift; *Ceridwen* into a greyhound, *Gwion Bach* into a hare; then he becomes a bird and *Ceridwen* a hawk. *Gwion* then turns himself into a grain of wheat and she becomes a black hen and swallows him, both undergoing transformations that result in *Gwion* being reborn as Taleisen, the enlightened bard and druid (Rolleston, pp. 413–414, Graves, 1948, p. 24). When Taleisen is born, *Ceridwen* wants to destroy him, but his beauty (radiant brow, a rainbow of hope) hinders her. Instead, she wraps him in a leather bag and casts him into the sea where he survives and is saved by a fisherman. His unwanted birth and subsequent abandonment fit emotionally into the felt treachery and trickery of rebirth after death. As Jung explains (1951, paras. 287–291) concerning the child archetype: abandonment, exposure and danger are elaborations of the child's unexpected birth and describes the emergence of that new, unknown, risky nature.

For example, *Gwion Bach*, a lowly servant, through hard work (faithfully stirring the cauldron) is unexpectedly but justly rewarded and reborn as Taleisen. The 'child' also means evolving towards independence and separating from 'mother' as a necessary condition. Kerenyi points out (Jung and Kerenyi, 1948, p. 33) that, although the child at the beginning is a solitary figure, he/she is nevertheless at home in the primordial world that nourishes him/her. As a bringer of new light (or idea) that enlarges consciousness, the child overcomes darkness and the previous unconscious state. Taleisen is not only the son of *Ceridwen* but the mediator of earth and sun/sky because he is swallowed by *Ceridwen* at *Lugsassad*, the fire festival that imitates *Hu Gadern* at his strongest when the sun symbolically mates with the earth at mid-summer, the longest day.

Taliesin is another image for the rebirth of the druid, Merlin Emrys. He combines light and dark, young and old forces by mixing the 'good/safe' and 'bad/risky' opposites. Druids, as shamanic initiates of the dragon as the indigenous creative solar energy, embody the courage of their ancestors as their living dead, because they enter *Annwn*, to mediate with the dead, recollect the lost treasure (soul aspects) and bring them to consciousness for the revitalization of the collective consciousness (Evans, 1915/2018, p. 51; Merchant, 2012, pp. 8–22). Jung discusses the difficulty of dealing with the ancient, powerful, heathen, pre-Christian alchemical dragon and its ambivalent compensatory nature as Mercurius that requires real courage (Jung, 1948d, para. 267).

Depth-psychological aspects

Psychologically, the underworld/*Annwn* can be interpreted as the unconscious, that unknown area beyond the realm of the ego, that is uncultivated and undifferentiated and accessed mainly through dreams. The warrior/hero brings the sun (consciousness/knowledge) safely through the darkness as it reaches its lowest point, where all light seems to have gone in order to regenerate it into the next day as it rises again from its depth. Renewal does not take place without travelling symbolically through the abyss, assimilating what has been wasted, transforming it and bringing it to consciousness. Implicit in the idea of renewal is not just a repetition of the cycle but a widening of consciousness in the process which is brought to light. For Jung and Jungians, the unconscious is seen as a creative matrix; the abyss or wasteland can also be equated with the inferior or interior function, the fourth function in the unconscious that has been repressed to fit with collected norms. If too much vitality is sacrificed without the possibility of development, the unconscious becomes a graveyard, showing which aspect of the psyche has been repressed, wasted or killed. Perhaps it is a child who is dead or dying, perhaps the dream shows a female fighter with a sword in her hand, or a man tenderly holding a child in his arms. Confronting and entering into the wasteland through dreams can bring such 'deadened' or 'disallowed' aspects to life.

Afanc (Beaver) as symbol of transformation

Shapeshifting and the transformation of persons into other forms, particularly those of animals or trees, illustrates an imaginative fluidity arising from the lunar nature of spirit of *Annwn* that bridges instinct and culture by using his/her shape shifting talents. The *Afanc*, the ancient Welsh beaver, shows how unconscious energy is transformed into the service of human progress and enlightenment (see Dames, 2002, pp. 77–81).

Cymric druidic lore tells the story of a deep slit or cavern east of Dinas Emrys, in Snowdonia, an ancient beaver, blamed for damming up Welsh rivers, lives there sunk in an underworld hibernation in *Annwn*, causing floods and the formation of lakes such as *Llyn Dinas*. Druid Merlin, as representation of the sun god, *Hu Gadern*, attempts to tame the energy of this animal by using his sister, *Gwenddydd*, to entice the beaver out of his habitation and bind him into service with iron chains. She brings him food in the form of breast milk and lures him out of the underground. After breast feeding, the beaver sleeps peacefully on her lap until he realizes he has fallen into an iron trap. In his fury, he rips off one of *Gwenddydd*'s breasts that he has been holding while sleeping.

Once the beaver is caught, *Hu Gadern* attaches him to the plough along with the oxen. Indeed, *Hu Gadern* treats *Afanc* as if he were the plough himself, and in several aspects, this description is apt: the beaver's wide furrows are its stream valley habitat; its teeth are as sharp as the plough's coulter, while its conspicuously broad tail resembles the plough share, able to turn over the furrow slice, especially because the beaver's flattened tail is set horizontally. The *Afanc* is also associated with sexual potency which the sun god uses to transform some of the wildest regions in Wales into agricultural land as well as aiding him on his journey across the sky. Another main attribute of the beaver is its social cooperation and its great capacity for hard work against the normal, natural flow of water (unconscious libido). Its underside, thick, soft fur is utilized for keeping the head (thinking function) warm. The movement of *contra naturum* is the *liefmotiv* of the individuation process that prohibits, or dams, the flow of natural energy in order to create new upward structures for the common good.

The beaver is an animal of the watery depths, symbolising the vitality of the collective unconscious and linking it with the ancestors. Its evolutionary roots date back 35 to 40 million years. During the last Ice Age, giant beavers as large as small bears roamed the landscape, so by taming his energy, the sun god taps into the ancient creative potential reservoir of the unconscious and transforms it into concrete disposal energy. As a primordial amphibian, the beaver has both unconscious (water) and conscious (land) characteristics and acts as a perfect bridge to integrate both with its constructive architectural and engineering skills that create inland lakes, canals and dams through chewing away at trees, felling them and using branches as tools. Dams also create important water holes for other animal species and facilitate arable land for cultivation.

Through the image of the beaver with its intrapsychic relationship to the sun god and his sister/anima, we see how unconscious energy is first trapped, weaned and then civilised, through harnessing its creative drive. The painful weaning process requires sacrifice. But the beaver keeps his animal form which is mirrored as the plough in the night sky. There is no depreciation of its instinctual energy into a hybrid human form, only showing how it can symbolically transform the physical landscape and become immortalised through the act of consciousness by showing itself in the night sky.

Jung (1911–1912/1954c, para. 226) elucidates that whenever an instinct is checked or inhibited, it becomes blocked and regresses so that the energy changes its gradient and its form. However, this developmental process is accomplished only with difficulty, as the primary instinct is split into two; one 'breast' is sacrificed to become conscious. On being changed, it still carries something of the character of the instinct, although it is not an exclusive sexual act. From the pleasure of feeding through rhythmic sucking, after weaning, the mouth develops another significance, such as the organ of speech.

Hillman (1967, pp. 38–39) suggests that helplessness and thirsting is an open-mouthed, sucking condition which encourages the flow of milk as a process of mammalian nature, indicating that the prerequisite of rebirth is acceptance of dependency and the needs as a newborn. Milk, the *prima materia* as beginning, middle and end, restores the psychic connection with others and with oneself by feeding that primordial level.

Evaluation

Eliade (1958, p. 188) suggests that water symbolises the 'primal substance which exists at the beginning and returns at the end of each cosmic or historic cycle.' One could speculate that in countries where the sun sinks into the open sea at night rather than into a fixed, enclosed terrain, its inhabitants may experience greater long-term transformative possibilities. For maritime peoples on the western seaboard, following the sun's passage in boats as it sinks in the west not only encourages the discovery of new lands on the horizon but promotes the questioning of received knowledge. Their ontological pre-occupations differ from cultures that do not venture into that unknown territory (Sharkey, 1975, pp. 18–20). Following the sun as it sinks pushes the limit between the known (life/logos) and unknown (death/chaos), opening up new indeterminate spaces on the edge of existence. Ancient Britons developed an intense, ontological pre-occupation with these in-between realms involved with pushing back old boundaries, overstepping them and establishing new ones, still in evidence today.

Egyptian cosmogony concerning rebirth in the land of the dead

Similar to the Welsh Cymric imaginative journey of their sun god, *Hu Gadern* and his representatives, the mythic night-time journey of the Egyptian sun god Atum/Ra brings him into contact with the inhabitants of the underworld, the transfigured dead. From 1492 to 1072 BCE most pharaohs were buried in the royal necropolis on the West Bank of Thebes. The fertile imagination of ancient Egyptian speculation emphasises the ordered security of the sun god in his underworld journey, his transformation from the god who descends into the dark regions of the Duat and dismembered each night (Osiris/Ra) into a regenerated deity emerging each dawn, full of energy and life as Horus/Ra (Hart, 1990, p. 50). The Egyptians, similarly to the Cymru, believe that everyone has *ka* (a body) and *ba* (soul). After death, *ba* acquired the ability to move freely and independently of the body and could leave the tomb by day. It was required, however, to return each night to be reunited with the mummy (*ka*).

At death, the connection between *ka* and *ba* is temporarily severed, requiring numerous rituals and spells for them to be reunited. The dead have to be transformed through mummification, a process which purges the body of fluids contained within the most perishable organs, drying the body, anointing it with oils and resins, packing the cavities, wrapping limbs together in linen and being adorned with a gilded headpiece or mask. Styles of mummification vary according to their expense. Material needs, such as food, artefacts and magical objects, such as shabti figures to ensure that these figures undertake any hard work required in the afterlife by the deceased, are supplied, and they become endowed with supernatural attributes like those of the gods. If the rituals are correctly performed, the individual became akh, a transfigured spirit endowed with creative magical powers.

Mourning rituals

Behind the elaborate preparations for rebirth as seen through the papyrus texts and images collated in the *Ancient Egyptian Book of the Dead* (Taylor, 2010), death provokes a strong expression of grief and loss. Mummification for wealthy Egyptians marks the beginning of the liminal transition from the world of the living to the world of the dead, where specific spells for each stage in the journey through the Duat offers comfort, security and accompaniment to both the mourners and the mourned. Women as wives, mothers and daughters mourn dramatically for their dead, beating their hands against exposed breasts (papyrus of Ani; Taylor, 2010, pp. 92–93). After the completion of mummification, the opening of the mummy's mouth is performed so that *ba* can enjoy greater freedom to voice the different spells needed to ensure her/his eternal survival and to breathe better. An example of the instrument used to open the mummy's mouth is similar to that used at birth to cut the umbilical cord as well as cleaning the mucus from the newborn's mouth to make breathing easier (ibid., p. 99).

By such means, the dead seek to take part in the endless cycle of recurring life, and much of their funerary literature expresses their desire to gain admittance to the son god's company and travel with him. As with the Cymru, the process is differentiated as triadic: Manu comprises the western mountain where Ra begins his journey after setting; Duat, the underworld through which he travels at night; and Bakhu, the eastern mountain above which he rises in the morning. His light and speech awaken the dead and allow them to participate in his essence by giving order that emanates from his course. But in doing so, the god himself experiences the form of existence of the dead and sets an example for them by overcoming death and the dragon of chaos. In the depth of the night, he is united with Osiris/ Ra, the son with the deceased father, *ba* with the corpse, and from this union he receives the strength for the next life cycle.

For the Egyptians, the daytime is divided into three phases where the sun shapeshifts using hybrid form: Khepri, as the scarab beetle in the morning; Re, as the falcon headed man at midday; and Atum/Ra, the ram-headed man in the evening. In these triadic forms, he is simultaneously child, adult and old man. This activity is related to ideas of kingship and the dead in two ways: as an embrace by means of which the deceased father transmits *ka*, the vital dynamic force to his son; and, by uniting *ba* with the corpse, as the archetype of individual immortality. The myth of the son god's dismemberment and death expresses the inescapability of death, but that life's divine spark is imperishable, and continues in the Egyptian mind after death through the birth of Horus/Ra.

Egyptian cosmogony: fractionation into sibling and shapeshifting

Osiris/Ra and Atum/Ra are complementary pairing aspects revolving around the idea of eternal renewal centred on the sun god and his course. Osiris/Ra personifies finite time that has been realised and who remains the god of the dead, in the *duat*, as temporal time. The sun god, Atum/Ra embodies the virtuality of *neheh*, always in the process of infinite flux of his rising and setting in pulsating, rhythmic time. The Egyptians imagined a constellation whereby Osiris/Ra and Atum/Ra work together as embodiments of two antinomic aspects of time, as *ba* and the corpse (*ka*) in which the deceased lead an eternal life. *Ba* and the corpse would unite at night, *ba* alighting on the mummy in bird form, ensuring rebirth and immortality (Assmann, 2001, p. 79).

At the beginning of creation. Atum/Ra, as the active principal, gives birth to two offspring, Shu and Tefnut, in an act of separation, differentiation and fractionation. The wind god, Shu, is interpreted as the rising breath; Tefnut as his/her spit or glue. Shu performs the epic feat of division by separating heaven from earth. Quirke (2001, p. 32) interprets the first division in creation between moist and dry rather than cohesion and separation, but to my mind these emotional qualities include the latter description.

When Shu and Tefnut depart to explore the darkness, Atum/Ra creates a right eye, the sun, from his forehead, which he sends out as a ball of light to guide the offspring back safely. This right eye is personified by the lioness-headed goddess, Sekhmet, who embodies both breasts and a penis. Atum/Ra gives Sekhmet an active role of seeking out injustices and enacting punishment to those who transgress his authority.

In the absence of his right eye, Atum creates a second orb from the left side of his forehead, the cooler, reflective moon, personified by the moon-goddess Hathor. Through Atum's self-fractionation, the lion-headed Tefnut is differentiated into two further aspects of Atum/Ra: the fierce consciousness of the day-time sun and the gentler coolness of the moon's night-time vision (Pinch, 1994, pp. 23–25). Shu and Tefnut then replicate themselves in an interesting gender reversal order as personified by their offspring: Geb and Nut, Earth and Sky. The active Nut's body stretches over the passive Geb to procreate, giving birth to four children: Osiris, Isis, Seth and Nephthys. Shu separates Geb and Nut further to create space for Nut's ascendant function of protecting the sun god on his daily journey across the firmament. Each of Geb and Nut's four children acts as a bridge between cosmogony and the cratogonic transmission of kingship (Assmann, 1984, pp. 119–121). Each incestuously marries the equivalent contra-sexual 'other': Osiris, 'first-born' male heir, marries Isis, 'first-born' female, who are already together in the womb; 'second-born' twin, Seth, marries 'second-born' daughter, Nephthys, as elucidated by Florescano (1999, p. 213).

The ornate paintings of Nut in the sarcophagus hall of the tomb of Ramesses VI (1156–1148 BCE) in the Valley of the Kings show her ascendant function as a sky deity, revealing how the sun god Atum/Ra travels along her arched body (Hart, 1990, p. 14; Lamy, 1981, p. 42; Quirke, ibid. pp. 55–61). At the end of each 12-hour day, Atum/Ra is swallowed by Nut in the west where he travels along her underside in Duat to be reborn at dawn in the east as Horus/Ra. Redness, the colour of blood at dusk and dawn, symbolises the sun's cyclical death and rebirth.

The Duat

Competition between light/order and darkness/chaos is enacted between 'first-born' Osiris and 'second-born' Seth, as Seth challenges the legitimacy of Osiris as he completes his cycle as the Egyptian sun king. Once Osiris enters the Duat, he is dismembered and killed. In other words, the sun king (logos/consciousness) must enter the dark (chaos/unconscious) in an act, firstly, of separation from the known and, secondly, of assimilation with the dead to be daily reborn with them. The 'first' can keep her/his creative position only by interacting with the second 'shadow other.' Out of the overlapping, widening of their spheres, creativity is regenerated.

Archaeological evidence suggests that Seth is of greater antiquity than Osiris (Hart, 1990, p. 50). Traditional conjecture maintains that Seth ripped himself impatiently from Nut's womb in upper Egypt at Naqada where his major temple in the south was later erected. As violence and chaos became his major attributes, Seth incorporates images of King Scorpion and Apophis, the underworld snake of chaos. Such a ranking of Seth as 'first' intimates that chaos precedes order and consciousness in creativity and that chaos must be overcome in order to produce order and form (Quirke, 2001, p. 37), Seth is often portrayed as an 'unnatural' creature, a sort of anti-animal anomaly that expresses the violation of natural law: he has long ears like those of a donkey but straight cropped, a long tail but forked rather than tufted and a curving snout, quite unlike any part of a known animal. Such an unrecognisable animal form embodies the treacherous attack on perfect order when Seth entombs Osiris through trickery, pouring burning lead over the coffin to seal any openings (Spence, 1915/1990b, pp. 66–67).

Isis and Osiris

Creative intervention to save the sun/son appears in the form of Isis, as protective mother and overseer of the sun, who searches tirelessly for his body and regenerates him. Isis and Nephthys, 'first-born' and 'second-born' daughters of Nut, combine forces to mitigate the power of darkness/chaos personified by Seth. As Seth's wife, Nephthys unexpectedly mourns the loss of the sun, revealing an unconscious intra-psychic aspect of Seth in its important ambivalent, transformative aspect. The two women gather together the dead parts of Osiris/Ra so that Isis can incestuously mate with Osiris to create a new sun/son, Horus/Ra. Isis brings Osiris back to life to the point where a child is conceived in the form of Horus, the arisen son. After Horus is born, Isis flees with him to the inaccessible marshes of the Nile, a floating island called *Akhbit*, where she hides him until he is mature enough to challenge his uncle (Quirk, 2001, p. 38). The role of rebirth is given to Isis as mother/creator in the same way that it is given to *Ceridwen* through Talisen as *Awen*, as the new year/dawn in February.

Although Seth has been vanquished, as the last endurance test before sunrise, Horus/Ra must travel again through 'death' in the form of a snake (symbol of sexuality *and* separation) to be reborn within that knowledge (Taylor, 2010, pp. 186–187; Lamy, 1981, pp. 62–63; Spence, 1915/1990b, pp. 116–118), light and dark forces recombining to create a new dawn. The battle for primacy between the order/safety and chaos/risk continues in Egyptian cosmogony as a non-resolving dynamic.

This intense interplay between light/life and dark/chaos is amplified in the Egyptian Book of the Dead (Quirke, 2001, pp. 47–53; Taylor, 2010, pp. 146–147) where each of the 12 hours of the sun's underworld travel in the Duat is minutely controlled. Without this warring interplay and the divisive questioning of the sun's authority in the frightening challenge of Seth, there is no psychic renewal. All life is a totality of death and life; when the sun sinks, it does not die, but reaches the hidden fountain of life. As with Cymric mysticism, darkness is the cradle of life; in it the sun finds the courage to arise. Absolute life has its home in the realm of death (Hart, 1990, p. 53).

Khepri, the shapeshifter

One version of underworld journey of the sun god through the Duat is depicted in *The Book of Am-Duat* which illustrates how the sun god is reborn as Khepri the scarab beetle. On the psychic level, the Duat is the place of transformation symbolised by the metamorphosis of the scarab beetle (Lamy, 1981, p. 89). The scarab first exists as a worm or larva that can do nothing except eat; then a cocoon is woven within which the essences are broken down and redistributed during the metamorphosis into a winged insect. The cocoon is analogous to mummification and the transformation of the body inside the wrapped casings. The sacred scarab beetle, Khepri, is chosen as a symbol of the process of a vegetative metamorphosis. The beetle, having laid its eggs in the Egyptian sand, rolls them into a little ball of manure which it then propels across the sand with its hind legs to a hole that it has previously dug where the eggs are hatched by the rays of the sun. This action resembles the rolling of the sun across the heavens so that Khepri, as the rising luminary, is symbolised by it. Khepri is also a self-generated creator of the gods and looked upon as a type of resurrection: the symbol of the ball enclosing living germs and the sun stepping out of darkness as if arising from the debris and wasted matter embodied in the graves of the dead (Spence, 1915/1990a, pp. 136–137) underlines this imaginative feat. The scarab is imagined as pushing the sun as the world egg over the horizon to begin its daily journey across the sky.

Scarabs feed on dead animals, performing invaluable services of removing corpses, large and small, from fields and forests. Collectively, they clean up millions of tons of faeces each day, sanitizing surfaces as they add nitrogen (Caspari, 2003, p. 31). In Egyptian cosmology, rebirth is, thus, depicted in two forms: as Khepri, the scarab beetle in instinctual form; and as Horus the child archetype, son of Osiris and Isis, as the arising hawk god. Similarly, in Cymric myth, the beaver embodies an instinctual rebirth, and Taleisen emerges as the child reborn from *Hu Gadern* and *Ceridwen*.

Punishment

The Egyptian *Book of Caverns* shows darker depictions where punishments are enacted, such as decapitation and burning of victims. A number of cauldrons show burning of the bones of transgressors. Cauldrons do not possess the same inspirational rebirth properties as found in *Ceridwen*'s cauldron. Transformation occurs at the sixth cavern, where the scarab beetle head has amalgamated with the underworld image of Ra so that a combined creature emerges with the body of a scarab beetle and the head of a ram. The *Book of Gates* shows similar depictions of Ra executing enemies who question his authority. Similar to *Annwn*, life and death are a continuum, each engendering the other in complex forms that develop over time (Hart, 1990, p. 61)

The greatest challenge in the Duat is where the hearts of the dead are judged and weighed to see if they are worthy of immortality. Correct behaviour is equated with Maat as the divine twin principle of right and order (spell 125 of the *Book of the Dead*). If the procedure fails, the deceased is given to the devourer, an unnatural hybrid animal/monster with a crocodile's head, the forelegs of a lion and the rear of a hippopotamus. Its role is to eat the damned; some later text describes it as slaughtering and cutting out the heart, or throwing the damned decapitated and dismembered into fiery furnaces, prefiguring early Christian notions of hell and in the NT Apocalyptic Day of Judgement. An alternative version features the Lake of Fire located in the Duat, where the damned are burnt, but the blessed dead receive nourishment from it.

Afterlife

The ancient Egyptian nature of afterlife is an open-ended concept with different goals. The dead might dwell in the kingdom of Osiris/Ra, or travel through the Duat with Ra as he makes his nightly passage to the eastern horizon, or they may end their journey in the pastoral paradise called the Field of Reeds. The Field of Reeds is visualised as an earthly landscape of waterways leading past fields where abundant crops grow and where the gods and the blessed dead live in peace and contentment. Originally as described in the Pyramid texts, it is also part of the watery expense of the night sky on the surface of which celestial bodies voyage (Taylor, 2010, p. 242). A fundamental concept of the afterlife is to bring about a community between the two gods Ra and Osiris, who are regarded as complimentary as one divine being. As Osiris/Ra's eternal realm lies under the ground, one goal of the deceased's journey is to penetrate the many gates that lead to his domain through climbing ladders to enter a special relationship with him through funerary rituals and spells to become 'an Osiris' who triumphs over dismemberment and death. However, to achieve 'peace of mind and blessedness' offered to compensate the loss of earthly pleasures but considered by some dead as too static, it is regarded as important that the deceased could leave the inert body in the darkness and travel to the world above and enjoy earthly pleasures (spell 175 in the *Book of the Dead*), Thus, the corresponding spells (100 and 102) are concerned with gaining admittance to the sun god's boat and travelling in his company. In vignettes of the Field of Reeds appears the Great Ennead (a company of gods). Here, the deceased receive sustenance supplied by the Heron of Plenty. Surplus is given to *ka* spirits of the blessed dead. The deceased arrive at a place called *Oenqunet*, where they are united with their deceased parents. Afterwards, they join the Great Ennead at the end of their cyclical passage (Taylor, 2010, pp. 242–259)

Evaluation

Such creation myths show an intense symbolic preoccupation and investment in the sun god, particularly with his abandonment at night. Each of the 12 hours of his disappearance is imaginatively monitored so carefully that he never really goes out of sight. The myth developed out of topography where the river Nile and its delta is the single main source of water; the Nile has no tributaries. Its single, annual, cyclical inundation of the land has influenced and stylised Egyptian cultural consciousness, so when the sun sinks in the west, it sinks into a dry, western mountainous terrain. Little rain in a predominately desert landscape does little to mitigate the sun's intense power.

Von Franz (1972, pp. 74–80) specifically asks why Egyptian cosmogony features a sky goddess instead of a sky god as in other cultures and suggests that the Egyptians were more preoccupied with their symbolic existence as star gods in the afterlife than with their earthly existence. To become *Ba*, an immortal sky star, they need safe passage into the Duat and rebirth facilitated by mother Isis/Nun as sky goddess. I also suggest that the unconscious, fertile earthiness is limited in Egypt due to the lack of water. The original, inert, gluey nature of Nun, even when differentiated as Nut and transformed into Isis, is easily displaced by the king as strong (hot) as the Egyptian sun god and his same-sex brother as they battle it out for primacy. One could argue that Isis merely adjudicates this battle; she makes no direct claim herself, as reflected by her stylised, mediatory role as sky goddess, not as an earthly mother, such as *Ceridwen*, emotionally attached to and personally involved in the well-being of the physical land.

Conclusion

Comparing the ancient Cymric and Egyptian myths of the land of the dead and immortality, I notice that the sun god takes a different form. In the Cymric myth, the dragon, embodying chaos as a creative principle as the sun when it sinks into the unknown darkness, is more revered and less feared than in the Egyptian cosmogony, probably because the British sun is not as hot and requires less sacrifice to bring rain.

Both ancient cultures interpret the land of the dead as containing the seeds of future life and that life itself is inextricably linked with death. In *Annwn* and the Duat, there is an easy transfer of human to animal form that allows for a greater differentiation of emotions. Differentiation in both cultures takes the form of triadic fractionation. Spence (1915/1990b, p. 108) notes that both under/otherworlds are perceived as watery entities existing between matter and nonmatter, waiting for that spark of renewal that brings forth life. The Cymric, however, place more emphasis on the positive qualities offered by their dead as co-existing living entities rather than in their resurrection from the Otherworld. The Welsh dead accompany the living though their tribulations and offer courage and advice. In Egyptian cosmology, the underworld (Duat) is inhabited with fearful monsters who prey on the dead that gradually evolved into concrete, authoritarian punishment for earthly misdeeds of the dissenting 'others.'

Due to the different typography and climate, the Welsh mythological feminine is more active and autonomous than the Egyptian in creating the physical landscape. As Cymric myths show, the British feminine as *Hen Wen* embodies the muscles to actively push forth out of chaos and create new life. Without these muscles, creative life, literally and symbolically, stagnates and dies (Shearer, 1996, p. 272). The everchanging tides, open sea and shorelines around the British coast allows for a dynamic exploratory relationship with chaos. By contrast, the Egyptian sun sinks into a desert mountain and travels through a much drier, hotter, static underworld with little water available able to influence its longer-term transformative qualities.

The relationship between the 'first' and 'other(s)' in Egyptian cosmology reveals an essentially antagonistic power play between Osiris and Seth: 'one' personifying the good, visible aspects of creativity, the 'other' fearful of death attached to separation and unknown territory. Such a fear of chaos has resulted in an over-evaluation of the sun king's 'safe' authoritarian nature and a devaluation of unknown, unconscious processes as transient, chaotic and irrational (Brodersen, 2012). The Welsh concept of the dragon as the sun/son embodies more unifying, positive forces. Welsh cosmogony depicts a paradise on earth without the need to ascend into the heavens. The Other World of their living dead is a tangible, benign force where personal aggrandizement to become 'god' is not the goal: the courage to transform the cultural landscape and the resulting qualitative changes in the social infrastructure have primacy. Fear of separation and the courageous, imaginative overcoming of it transforms a culture into one capable of challenging authority and protecting the dead's status in afterlife.

Both these ancient cultures explore mourning rituals, the land of the dead and the concept of immortality from differing imaginative perspectives, but they share an equally intense concern for the well-being of their dead, as shown by the enriching details they offer to safeguard their security and status value as ancestors.

References

Assmann, J. (1984/2001). *The Search for God in Ancient Egypt*. Ithaca and London: Cornell University Press.

Bible. (1989 edn.). *The Revised English Bible*. Oxford and Cambridge: Oxford University Press.

Brodersen, E. (2006). *Warrior of the Wasteland: The British Cymric Druid as Symbol of Life, Death and Rebirth of the Welsh landscape*. Unpublished symbols paper, C.G. Jung Institute, Zürich.

Brodersen, E. (2012). In the Nature of Twins. A Study of the Archetypal Realm of Universal Duality, Opposition and Imitation between the First and the Other in Creation Myths. In *International Journal of Jungian Studies*, Vol. 4. London: Routledge, pp. 133–149.

Brodersen, E. (2016). *Laws of Inheritance, A Post-Jungian Study of Twins and the Relationship between the First and Other(s)*. London and New York: Routledge.

Brodersen, E. (2019). *Taboo, Personal and Collective Representations. Origins and Positioning within Cultural complexes*. London and New York: Routledge.

Budge, E.A.W. (1899/1988). *Egyptian Magic*. Harmondsworth, UK: Arkana, Penguin.

Caspari, E. (2003). *Animal Life in Nature, Myth and Dreams*. Wilmette, IL: Chiron Pubs.

Dames, M. (2002). *Merlin and Wales, a Magician's Landscape*. London: Thames and Hudson.

Daniel, J. (1927). The Druidic Church. In Mathews, J. (ed.) (1996), *The Druid Source Book*. London: Blandford Press, pp. 281–303.

Davies, E. (1804/1996). Celtic Researches. In Mathews, J. (ed.) (1996), *The Druid Source Book*. London: Blandford Press, pp. 123–153.

Eliade, M. (1954/2005). *The Myth of the Eternal Return*. Princeton: Princeton University Press.

Eliade, M. (1958/1995). *Rites and Symbols of Initiation* (Trash, W.S. Trans.). Woodstock, CT. Spring Publications.

Eliade, M. (1963/1975). *Myth and Reality*. New York: Harper Torchbooks.

Evans, J.G. (1915/2018). *Poems from the Book of Taliesin*. London: Forgotten Books.

Florescano, E. (1999). *The Myth of Quetzalcoatl* (Hochroth, L. Trans.). Baltimore and London: John Hopkins University Press.

Ford, P.K. (trans. and ed.) (1977). *Mabinogi and Other Medieval Welsh Tales*. Berkley, CA: University of California Press.

Franz, von M.L. (1972). *Creation Myths*. Boston and London: Shambhala.

Gantz, J. (trans. and ed.) (1976). *The Mabinogion*. London and New York: Penguin.

Graves, R. (1948). *The White Goddess. A Historical Grammar of Poetic Myth*. London: Faber.

Green, M.J. (1993). *Celtic Myths*. London: British Museum Press.

Grigsby, J. (2002). *Warriors of the Wasteland*. London: Watkins Press.

Hart, G. (1990). *Egyptian Myths*. London: British Museum Press.

Hillman, J. (1967). Senex and Puer. In Hillman, J. (ed.) (1994), *Puer Papers*. Dallas Texas: Spring Publications, pp. 3–53.

Jung, C.G. (1911–1912/1954a). Symbols of the Mother and of Rebirth. In *Collected Works, Vol. 5. Symbols of Transformation* (2nd ed.). London: Routledge and Kegan Paul, 1986.

Jung, C.G. (1911–1912/1954b). The Dual Mother. In *Collected Works, Vol. 5. Symbols of Transformation* (2nd ed.). London: Routledge and Kegan Paul, 1986.

Jung, C.G. (1911–1912/1954c). The Transformation of Libido. In *Collected Works, Vol. 5. Symbols of Transformation* (2nd ed.). London: Routledge and Kegan Paul, 1986.

Jung, C.G. (1948a). The Spirit Mercurius. In *Collected Works, Vol. 13, Alchemical Studies* (2nd ed.). London: Routledge and Kegan Paul, 1981.

Jung, C.G. (1948b). A Psychological Approach to the Trinity, Pre-Christian Parallels. In *Collected Works, Vol. 11, Psychology and Religion* (2nd ed.). London: Routledge and Kegan Paul, 1981.

Jung, C.G. (1948c). The Spirit Mercurius: As Quicksilver and/or Water; Mercurius as Fire, Mercurius as Spirt and Soul. In *Collected Works, Vol. 13. Alchemical Studies* (2nd ed.). London: Routledge and Kegan Paul, 1981.

Jung, C.G. (1948d). The Dual Nature of Mercurius. In *Collected Works, Vol. 13. Alchemical Studies* (2nd ed.). London: Routledge and Kegan Paul, 1981.

Jung, C.G. (1951). The Psychology of the Child Archetype. In *Collected Works, Vol. 9i. The Archetypes and the Collective Unconscious* (2nd ed.). London: Routledge and Kegan Paul, 1980.

Jung, C.G. (1952). The Initial Dreams. In *Collected Works, Vol. 12. Psychology and Alchemy* (2nd ed.). London: Routledge and Kegan Paul, 1981.

Jung, C.G. and Kerenyi, C. (1948). *Essays on a Science of Mythology, the Myth of the Divine Child and the Mysteries of Eleusis*. London and New York: Routledge.

Lamy, L. (1981/1997). *New Light on Ancient Knowledge: Egyptian Mysteries*. London: Thames and Hudson.

Mathews, J. (ed.) (1996). *The Druid Source Book*. London: Blandford Press.

Merchant, J. (2012). *Shamans and Analysts: New Insights on the Wounded Healer*. Hove and New York: Routledge.

Pinch, G. (1994). *Magic in Ancient Egypt*. London: British Museum Press.

Quirke, S. (2001). *The Cult of Ra: Sun Worship in Ancient Egypt*. London: Thames and Hudson.

Rolleston, T.W. (1917/1990). *Celtic Myths and Legends*. New York: Dover Press.

Sharkey, J. (1975). *Celtic Mysteries*. London: Thames and Hudson.

Shearer, A. (1996). *Athena, Image and Energy*. London: Thames and Hudson.

Spence, L. (1915/1990a). *The Mysteries of Celtic Britain*. Milton Keyes, UK: Lightening Source, Kessinger Pub.

Spence, L. (1915/1990b). *Ancient Egyptian Myths and Legends*. New York: Dover Press.

Spence, L. (1945/1999). *Magic Arts in Britain*. New York and London: Dover Press.

Stewart, R.J. (1986). *Merlin: The Prophetic Vision and Mystic Life*. London and New York: Arkana, Penguin Books.

Stewart, R.J. and Williamson, R. (1999). *Celtic Bards, Celtic Druids*. London: Blandford Press.

Taylor, J. (ed.) (2010). *Ancient Egyptian Book of the Dead*. London: British Museum Catalogue.

Walker, S.F. (2002). *Jung and Jungians on Myth*. London and New York: Routledge.

Chapter 3

Crossing the bridge of uncertainty

A life with death and the dead

John Hill

Opening questions

In this chapter, I will ask more questions than give answers concerning the dead and the afterlife. Without doubt there seems to be little continuity between life on earth and life after death. Yet the question remains: why have so many civilizations invested so much energy in creating edifices, myths, rituals and traditions in order to assure themselves that life continues beyond the grave? It is hardly possible to achieve any certainty on this subject through a process of discursive reasoning. I have had to conclude that a bridging spirituality cannot be created solely through conceptual reflection. Such a creation requires an all-embracing process which involves the whole person – body, soul and spirit. An attitude of this kind requires an existential leap into darkness, an appreciation of the age-old rituals of transitions, as well as attention to dreams, visions and synchronistic phenomena. They can initiate a change of attitude, embracing the living and the dead, here and now. Such a process awakens us to the possibility of passageways, connecting the living with the dead. In the spirit of Jung, I hope to bring this short chapter to a conclusion that is worthy of further reflection on an intangible subject:

> A man should be able to say he has done his best to form a conception of life after death, or to create some image of it – even if he must confess his failure. Not to have done so is a vital loss. For the question that is posed to him is the age-old heritage of humanity: an archetype, rich in secret life, which seeks to add itself to our own individual life in order to make it whole.[1]

Concerning our theme, I would like to address the following question. Can an ongoing meaning to life on earth be perceived, embodied, and preserved in an analogical lifestyle that resembles the way earlier man and woman reserved a large part of their energies for the care, devotion, and continued companionship with their dead ones? In erecting lasting monuments and participating in transitional rituals, humans have continually attempted to create links between the living and the dead. Through such means they gained an awareness of a renewal of life beyond death. These forms of consciousness contain the promise of immortality, not just as

DOI: 10.4324/9781003313304-5

a conceptual reality but as a living, physical and spiritual experience. Humanity's historical records witness the necessity of creating a transitional, transformative interlude, so that our ancestors could gain awareness of an interface between the living and the dead.

When we talk about the dead surviving beyond the grave, we imply many things that are not obvious. We suppose some form of a survival without the human body. We postulate a reality that appears to be intangible, invisible, hardly to be grasped by the five senses. Not to be grasped by the five senses? Does this mean that those who have passed on cannot be seen, heard or felt? Does it imply that we can only hypothetically postulate a life beyond physical death through a conceptual framework of the human intellect? After all, it is the human mind that creates invisible entities, as witnessed in our ideas, concepts, judgements. They have enabled us to understand the world around us. As the Greeks first discovered, our ability to create concepts and make universal judgements, that may or may not be verified, implies an activity of the intellect that recognizes order, seeks truth and is nourished by meaning in and through its interaction with existence. Philosophers of old have argued that the self-reflective capacity of the mind reveals a freedom and flexibility beyond the immediate reality of the senses and discloses the very nature of the human intellect as being transcendent and immaterial. Nevertheless, speculative activity does not prove the existence of a non-terrestrial realm of being, as inferred in the epistemology of Immanuel Kant.

When I studied philosophy at university, I felt the need to achieve an intellectual framework to confirm the immortality of the soul, which I had already believed in naively. I hoped for such a framework to communicate with others. Philosophical reflection, understood as a process of abstraction, provided a scaffolding to talk about this phenomenon. This approach, however, did not nourish my soul, which craved for the world of sense experience to animate and breathe life into the beliefs, rituals and traditions that I had known since childhood. It also did not account for the rich cultural diversity that humans have created through their understanding of life beyond the grave. An examination of the symbols and rituals that have evolved around death and survival reveal an enormous expenditure of energy that many diverse peoples of the world have invested to assure themselves that life can continue beyond physical death. A living spirituality cannot be created through a purely conceptual framework. As I have implied, such creations require an all-embracing process that involves the whole person, body, soul and spirit.

First answers

I would postulate that the earliest and most primitive human experience of a reality transcending the realm of immediacy happened in and through a symbolic understanding of the non-human environment. Paul Ricoeur contended that we first perceived the meaning of reality in a practical and functional way.[2] We used signs to reveal what the sun, moon, trees and waters could bestow on us. The sun gave us light and warmth, the moon guided our ways through the night, trees offered shade and food, in water we washed ourselves.

At some time, in some place, humans achieved what Ricoeur called a process of secondary intentionality.[3] Through this approach, humans perceived that the world around them might reflect another dimension that transcends its immediate usefulness, revealing the world's purposeful intentionality. The light of the sun was not just for sight and warmth, it became the centre of the universe on which all life depended. In the cycles of the moon, man and woman began to perceive the waxing and waning of life's energies. This movement within the human context was not just linear but followed a cyclic pattern. In the life of trees – their springtime flowers, their summer fruits, their autumn leaves and their winter bareness – humans perceived the stages of life; the joy and beauty of youth, the toils of mid-life, the fruits of mature life, the final radiance of life before death. The seasonal transformations of the trees symbolized the full cycle of human life. In washing our bodies in water, one day our ancestors perceived that we not only wash our bodies, we wash ourselves, our spirit, our innermost being. This act revealed a need to be cleansed, purified and renewed.

Gradually, the universe became sacred and imbued with spirit. In that process, humans perceived analogically the sacredness of themselves. Rituals were developed to maintain perception of that identity in the cosmos. Certain rituals, especially those worshiping sun gods and sun kings, entered human history. Their purpose was to uphold a sacred centre upon which all life depended. They represented the highest ideals of a people. There were rituals of agony and ecstasy, the mourning of the loss of life with the approach of winter and celebrating life's return in spring. There were rituals of purification to prevent defilement from death, corruption and sin. These symbolic perceptions and ritual enactments endowed the universe with meaning and kept alive a sense of the sacred that transcended the fleeting concerns of everyday life. Through symbols, humans became aware of their own transcendence, their own spiritual identity.

Further questions

I have appealed to the symbol-creating mind because through its perception of objects, we perceive the reality of the human spirit. However, as we approach our subject concerning death and the dead, we encounter anomalies in defining what kind of reality we are investigating. Does our search for a deeper understanding of death begin with an awareness of the finitude of life, with the visible and tangible realities of sickness, corpses or memories of lost loved ones? In this discussion, we must ask, have the dead survived the grave? Can they be our invisible partners in the investigation? Yet they are no longer with us. Do we have any way of verifying our experiences of the dead? Do they correspond with any reality? Have we any faculty of communicating with the dead? Do they still speak to us, hear us or understand us? Can our images, projections, fantasies, longings, hope and despair be answered, criticized or denied, as any dialogue in a partnership requires? Perhaps we will not be able to answer all these questions, but an appeal to a symbolic understanding is an attempt to evaluate experiences with the dead in terms of self-reflection, self-awareness and a search for meaning.

In our quest for continuity between the living and the dead, it is important not to idealize that continuity. There is always an element of uncertainty in moving across the bridge that links the living with the dead, particularly when considered from a moral point of view. This uncertainty finds expression in the famed Zoroastrian 'Bridge of Kinvat.' In the ancient religion of Persia, the dead who cross the bridge will meet a beautiful maiden if the soul is pure, but an ugly hag if not. The bridge is as narrow as a sharp sword, which remains flat for the good but rotates with its sharp edge pointing up to cut down those who are unworthy to pass into the next life.

The idea of a continuity between the living and the dead is an abstraction and, if understood in a linear way, can blend out polarity, disruption, pain and horror that accompanies us as we approach death and the end of human life on earth. If, however, we live with uncertainty, live in the full presence of suffering, the corruption of bodies and pain of loss, then continuity cannot be a flat ideology of sameness, but a process that arises out of individual experiences of a life that is continually broken up, out of joint and reassembled again. This is a process of strengthening the spirit, a living with death and the dead, and a gathering of all those signs and messages that seem to communicate something about life that is powerful enough to survive its disappearance from the human body. Not everyone can do this. Great care is required not to overwhelm the fragile psyche. There are sound reasons why many cultures have linked death with various taboos. The realm of the dead can be overwhelming. We need protection.

Once I heard of a teacher of Zen Buddhism who emphasized a shift in human values by outlining two distinct ways in understanding human nature. We understand humans to be either essentially earthly beings who undergo a spiritual experience or essentially spiritual beings who undergo an earthly experience. Unfortunately, the trend of contemporary lifestyles makes a process of understanding, nourishing and strengthening the human spirit a difficult undertaking. The continual influx of information about all the comforts that can alleviate pain, boredom and unhappiness may distract us from the truth of our spiritual identity. The ever-increasing isolation from nature, the cementing of environment, the advance of medicine, the building of vast monuments for the consumption of material wealth, the increasing obsession with productivity to satisfy or create new needs in a world that is becoming ever more virtual and artificial – all this puts pressure on us to live a lifestyle in which there is no time to stop, reflect and ask ourselves, what is the point to it after all?

What part do we play in a system in which we are but one tiny unit with a short life in a perishable body? The things themselves are made to last beyond an individual lifetime. But what about us, the most perishable of all, as Rilke so aptly expressed in his Ninth Duino Elegy?[4] What about our lasting? As members of the collective, we seem less inclined to erect visible monuments to remind us of our own passing, our dead ones, our ancestors. In this environment, soul and spirit remain undiscovered and undernourished. It is becoming increasingly difficult to find roots and be at home in a world, because the world as we know it no longer reflects our true selves, no longer reminds us that we are humans with an identity that may outlast physical death, no longer reflects the possibility of a continuous universe, both visible and invisible.

The response of civilization

A brief look at the history of civilization tells us that this was not always the case. An Australian woman once described the significance of the land for Aboriginal culture. In the 'Dreamtime' of the Aborigines, the ancestral heroes descended from the skies and became part of the land. A mountain range became the backbone of one ancestor, and a pool enshrined the weeping of another. Traces of ancestors, spread throughout the land, were respected in song, dance and ritual. Retaining ancestral memories is a way of keeping the land alive. The land is an embodiment of the ancestors. Through the ancestral link, descendants feel at home in their surroundings and in themselves. They gain an embodied understanding of ongoing being.

In the earliest cultures, humans created artefacts that indicated an increasing awareness of a spiritual identity surviving physical death. They erected visible signs of a continued presence of the dead among the living. The signs were caves, inhabited by the dead; standing stones, voicing the spirit of the dead; wooden stretchers upon which the dead were placed. Other cultures spared no means in creating monuments to honour their dead: the vast burial mounds of Neolithic culture, with codes linked with the movements of the heavenly bodies, the great pyramids and huge underground burial sites of Egypt, or the famed mausoleums of India, China and the classical world. The dead were laid to rest in burial sites with care and foresight. Enormously complicated embalming processes, favourite belongings, sacred objects, food and clothing were placed with the deceased, indicating a conviction that the dead continued to live and needed the support of the living to survive their departure from life on earth.

The abodes of the dead were often near at hand, visible and tangible embodiments of a continuous universe. The dead were not banished to intangible realms as in Christian conceptions of heaven and hell. Their presence was visible as they lay on the nearby stretchers of native Americans or rested in the stone necropolises close to the wooden villages of Etruscan civilization or felt in the otherworldly atmosphere of caves and offshore islands of Celtic Ireland. Wole Soyinka laments the effects of missionary activity on African culture. The book religions transposed the mythic cosmos into non-terrestrial realms, and thereby it lost its essence of 'the tangible, the immediate, the appeaseable.'[5] The African people were deprived of a means to communicate with their ancestral heritage, located in their natural environment. A tangible connection between the living and the dead was broken.

Not only did the land or burial sites testify to a continuity between the living and the dead, but countless rituals ensured that these traditions would be maintained and cultivated in the heart and body of the living. Anthropologists (Hertz, van Gennep, Turner) have understood these rituals as expressions of the rites of passage that otherwise appear at all transitional stages of human life: birth, puberty, marriage and death. In funeral rites, separation dominates, but other aspects of the passage rites, such as transition and integration, are also present. Initiation was an ongoing process, accounting for life's ever-changing seasons, for both the living and the dead.

A universal characteristic of funeral rites[6] evolved around the notion of a journey undertaken by the souls of the dead. They proceed on a path to be united with their ancestors or reincarnated among the living. Mourning rites provided a framework to ensure the continual support of the living for the dead as they progress to unite with the spirits of their ancestors or to return to a woman's womb. The rites entailed a suspension of social life and a living with the corpse, as in wakes and ritualistic wailings. Often there followed a washing, a painting, a dressing of the corpse, a period of fasting or a participating in ritual meals. In some cultures, the corpse was isolated during the time of decomposition of the flesh in the belief that it was sub-ject to evil influences, which could be overcome only through purifying rituals, as the burning of the deceased's belongings, thought to be impure.

The purpose of these practices was to prevent a return of the deceased to their home. In Ireland there was the custom to turn the chairs upside down, a clear mes-sage to the dead that they were not welcome in the family home. There were rituals designed to help the pining soul move from its old home on earth and gain sub-stance for its new home in the hereafter. In some cultures, particularly in Greece and Indonesia, the waiting period for the corpse to decompose was followed by a second burial of bones or ashes. Some believed that the dead could not enter the land of the ancestors until the corpse was without flesh. These rituals would have been performed by close relatives. When a chief died, the whole community became involved. The rituals of separation were ways of avoiding contamination with the dead. Today we might understand them as ways to prevent a blurring of boundaries or avoiding the risk of mental insanity.

Ritualistic images of a nocturnal voyage of the dead consisted in placing the deceased in a small boat, conceived as a journey to otherworldly islands, a passage-way through a labyrinth of bolted doors, an entrance to a cave or the crossing of a narrow bridge. The Arunta of Aboriginal Australia believed that the dead would lie in wait in stones, trees or bushes and from there leap into the womb of a passing woman who was young, fat and desirable. In many cultures, food, clothing, dolls or coins were used to help the dead continue their journey. The transition period of mourning might have lasted several months, gradually ending with a final burial of the corpse, a celebration of the deceased's union with the population of the under-world, an end of fasting, a ritualistic meal and a return to social life.

Celtic intimations of life beyond death

Until recent times the people of the west of Ireland believed that the souls of the dead would remain on offshore islands until the next stage of their journey was decided. In the famous *Navigatio* of early Irish literature, a pagan hero or Christian saint undergo an odyssey to various otherworldly islands. In an earlier paper I wrote:

> The islands they visit have little in common with the homeland they have forsaken. There are islands with just one animal species, an island with one vegetation, an island of one sex (the famed isles of women), islands of one human type (hermit, miller), of one human sentiment (laughter, sorrow) and islands of radical divisions (separation of youth and age).[7]

On their return home, the hero or saint discovers time has moved on, the land has become unfamiliar. The ringing of a church bell does not correspond with their memories of pre-Christian Ireland. The moment they touch land they are turned to ashes or, as with Brendan, have enough time to put things in order before they die.

These voyages seem to represent a preparation for what lies beyond the grave. The world that was familiar becomes disjointed, broken up and dissociated. We may ask, does this fragmentation of the world represent a form of madness, or does it indicate survival beyond the grave? The Rees brothers, comparing the *Navigatio* to the Tibetan Book of the Dead, contended that visits to otherworldly islands suggest 'the mysteries of the world beyond death had been at least partially explored . . . It is to teach the craft of dying and to pilot the departing spirit on a sea of perils and of wonders.'[8] No doubt this is powerful material. Not everyone can embrace it. Great care is needed not to overburden the weaker psyche. One needs to be grounded so as not to fall into a state of dissociation and activate a psychosis.

A similar heritage of Celtic Ireland is to be found in the famed illuminated manuscripts as the Book of Kells (see Figure 3.1) or the Book of Durrow. The structure of these works of art follows a similar pattern as the *Navigatio*. The familiar world that we know is broken up into separate entities and reassembled into a new form, creating a whole that links pagan and Christian heritages, nature and word, the inherent vitality of life and the transcendent power of spirit.

In an earlier work, I wrote:

> In this imaginary realm, God, angel, human, beast, plant are all interchangeable parts of a religious, poetic and artistic vision of the universe. . . . The metamorphoses of Creator and created, man, beast, plant, letter and image are made visible through the spirals, keys, letterings and zoomorphics. A human being may become part of an animal, appear as a plant, then be transformed into a letter. Animate beings become abstract forms, inanimate letters begin to devour each other. Following the ancient Celtic doctrine of metamorphosis, all parts of the universe become interchangeable. . . . Seen as a whole, these manuscripts reveal things not as they are, but as what they may become . . . not the actual unfolding of evolution but the multiple potentiality of creation . . . this world is perceived by imagination rather than through sensation and reasoning. It is no wonder that the main designs of these works – the interlacing's and spirals – reflect water and sun from which all living beings maintain their existence.[9]

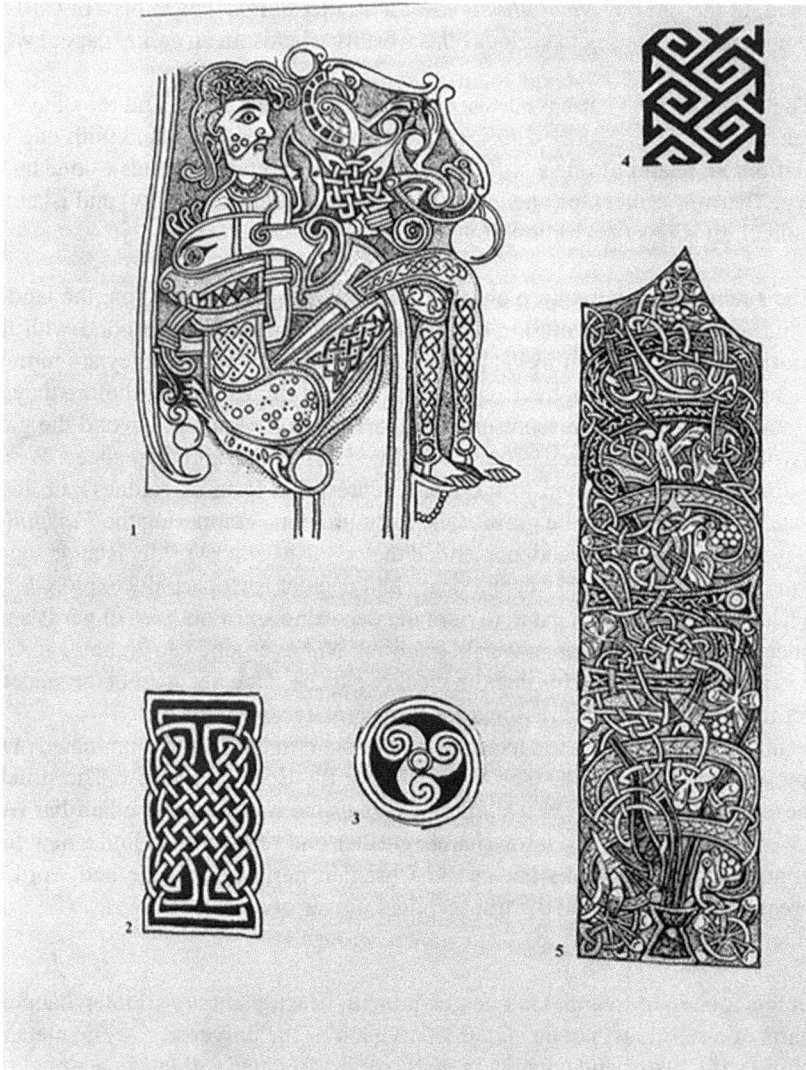

figure 2: interlacing as water;
figure 3: spirals as the sun;
figure 4: keys as fire,
figure 5: the tree of life

Figure 3.1 Book of Kells

Our Celtic ancestors saw no split between the visible and invisible. Through the visible world they perceived the invisible and could represent that synthesis in their legends and works of art. One scholar[10] contended that this union finds expression in their concept of 'Neart.' It expresses the presence of a universal divine energy in all being. The energy manifests in the changing seasons, the cycles of birth, decay and death as well as the movements of the sun and moon. 'Neart' is evident in the tales of shape-shifting that we find throughout Celtic literature, the most famed being that of Midir and Etain or *Ceridwen*'s and *Gwion Bach*'s metamorphoses as they try to out-wit each other. 'Neart' expresses a Celtic attitude of deep affiliation and kinship with all being. No one thing was absolutely separated from another. Similar to Jung's con-cept of libido, an underlying energy pervades the entirety of creation and expresses an inherent potentiality of one aspect of reality to be transformed into another. The Celts attempted to place themselves within that energy and thus feel at one with the universe. It was their source of inspiration for their creativity and poetic imagination.

What does this universal heritage say for us today? Why have the peoples of earlier cultures spent so much energy during their short lives in ensuring a continuity of life for their dead? We must ask ourselves if these countless symbols, legends and cus-toms express a pristine perception of human reality. In other words, can a lasting and deep meaning to life be perceived, embodied and preserved in an analogical lifestyle that resembles the way early man and woman reserved a large part of their energy for the care, devotion and continued companionship with their lost ones? Through the enormous expenditure of energy in the communal creation of a transitional space, creating links between the living and the dead, humans gained an awareness of a renewal of life and the immortality of the soul, not just as a conceptual reality but as a lived physical, psychological and spiritual journey. Without the creation of a tran-sitional interlude, there can hardly be any interface between the living and the dead.

Our present mourning ceremonies, which in some cases may only be limited to social obligation, can still help us to remember the loss of loved ones and give us a framework to express sadness and sorrow. These ceremonies usually consist of immediate burial followed by lesser anniversary ceremonies after 30 days or one year, allowing mourners to pay their final respects. Such impoverished ceremonies no longer permit survivors to participate in the condition of the deceased's soul, nor do they encourage the living to accompany the dead as they undertake the perilous journey through liminal spaces in search of a new existence, nor do they encourage mourners to participate in full celebrations necessary for a return to normal life. They hardly allow an experience of a liminal, continuous universe or a pattern of individuation that can bridge the realms of life and death.

The unbroken link of the night

Although the great monuments and rituals that link the living with the dead have been sorely reduced in our time, the ancestral lineage may still come alive in our dreams and visions of the night. Countless dreams and visions continue to remind us of the dead, at times preparing us to transit from life on earth to life in the here-after, linking us with a greater continuity between the living and the dead.

I have been working as a Jungian psychotherapist in Zürich for 50 years. This practical work has kept me rooted. My patients, with their troubled lives, their con-flicts, their sufferings, their rage and their love have formed much of my attitude to life. Inevitably, the theme of death and survival arose again and again. The dead have appeared in my patients' dreams, fantasies and active imaginations. Often such apparitions have helped patients survive critical periods of their lives.

Reviving the dead within

What comes to mind are those instances where the dead appear in dream or fantasy and represent repressed, split-off parts of the individual psyche. I remember the case of a woman who had been sexually abused as a child. After years of analysis, she suddenly began to draw pictures of a sarcophagus on which a petrified girl was placed. We both recognized that the girl was the client herself. Through the abuse, a whole section of her personality had been murdered, lost in the underworld of her psyche, thus not available to consciousness. Since then, she had never been aware that she possessed an identity as a woman in the presence of a man. Any thought or fantasies of this nature did not exist. The only signs that something was buried in the depth of her psyche were dreams of corpses and tortured animals, as well as tense moments of terrible irritability, fear and shame. After years of analysis, this person became convinced that therapy provided a safe context to talk about her gender. She began to draw pictures of herself as a woman. Although she had drawn hundreds of similar pictures, she had never done one as a mature woman, a sign that the stone figure on the sarcophagus had returned to life.

It seems that our dream life is constantly occupied with dead segments of our being that have long been denied, forgotten or repressed. Dreams do not follow physical laws. They remind us that wounded components of the soul do not die; they only disappear into the underworld. As we draw our attention to them, we can revive them, take care of them, transform them and make them worthy of life. Through a process of enduring pain and suffering, the dead return to life. These are moments of integration, great moments when you welcome them to participate in your lived life.

One female client had repeated dreams of the dead, which she could trace back to early trauma. Already as a small child she had to tolerate long absences from her mother. Many associations followed. Painful feelings of betrayal and abandonment began to emerge. Her cries of terror were not heard by the parents, and finally a core part of herself, which Winnicott understood to be the true self, gave up and withdrew. She lived a life of resignation and indifference. Almost in a state of emotional autism, she managed to preserve her contact with reality through forced adaptation to the expectations of others.

After several years of analysis, fragments of her deeper self returned to consciousness. She became aware of an inner child that had never lived its full life. A long struggle ensued to give voice to those silenced parts of herself. As she expressed rage and anger, she remembered how her jealous mother never allowed her to live her life as an adult woman. She did establish herself in the professional world, where she received support and respect, but a crucial part of her feminine identity could not voice itself. Relief came as her dreams began to reveal the dead parts of herself were still alive. She recognized the dead woman of her dreams to be an essential part of her femininity, which had not received support to live in the outer world. Although she welcomed the return of those lost lives, she was frightened that this energy might initiate loss of control. More work had to be done to provide a safe framework to voice the silenced woman in her. Only after she felt understood and respected as an adult within the analytic context, could she eventually express that same quality in the world outside.

Dreams prepare us to live and to die

As witnessed in the previous examples, dreams and fantasies draw our attention to the dead components of our inner life. This process is largely intrapsychic and concerns the search for psychological health and wholeness. Each time this happens, I stop and marvel at the incredible capacity of the psyche to bring back to life what was previously thought to be dead. I wonder if this natural process does not point to something deeper. In such examples, don't we witness the very foundations of the soul's immortality? Don't such experiences imply the soul's capacity to survive physical death? There are other kinds of dreams and visions, which possess qualities that point in that direction. They don't just contain symbols of lost parts of ourselves, but initiate us into the mystery of the inevitable end of life on earth. We may meet ancestors who help us to live or ancestors who help us to die. These dreams have an existential intention, informing us about survival after death, bearing significance not only for ourselves but for all humanity.

I have encountered many dreams of the dead that have been great support in the face of illness or death. One client, suffering from a relapse of cancer, was about to face more surgery. She was convinced her time had come. Just before the operation, her dead grandmother, whom she dearly loved, appeared in a dream, assuring her that all will be well. She did in fact get better with no sign that the cancer would return. She was convinced her beloved grandmother had come from the dead to help her overcome despair. The apparition brought tremendous relief; my patient lost her fear of death.

I have witnessed dreams that prepare the elderly to face the end of their life on earth. My mother-in-law was such a person. She was a wise woman, full of love and compassion for all whom she encountered. At 94 years of age and in good health, she had the following dream.

> I am in my room, and I feel very peaceful. I see a simple wooden coffin that radiates an atmosphere of peace. I think I should phone my eldest daughter to ask how she is and tell her how I feel. But then I think she is fine and can look after herself. I feel I should phone my youngest daughter, but I have the same feeling. She is fine and can look after herself.

This grand old lady knew the dream was foretelling her own death. She had two daughters with whom she had a close, warm relationship. She knew they could take care of themselves. She could begin to let go of her life on earth. She felt excited about the dream and was sure that it was preparing her for a peaceful death, but it would not happen immediately. She did not want to die at that moment, because she was looking forward to moving into her new apartment. She lived another six years and died shortly after her hundredth birthday.

One dream, presented to me while I was lecturing in Ireland, revealed in a startling and direct way the soul's capacity to prepare for physical death and for a future life beyond the grave:

> I am tugging and pulling at a rubber inflatable dinghy of a grey rubbery colour. I am trying to get it to fold up. I am making great efforts, but nothing is happening. Suddenly, the dinghy becomes a small silver vessel, and a voice says: 'This is the vessel of the spirit, treat it gently.' I am holding the vessel in my two hands and feel a great sense of peace.

The dreamer was not present at my talk, but we learnt that she was a 50-year-old woman dying from cancer in a nearby hospital. In the discussion that followed, we understood the dream as foretelling her death. We were informed that her body, through the illness, had become grey and rubber-like. The patient was hoping to die quickly so that she would not have to suffer. Jung once said that the unknown voice in a dream usually meant a voice from the Self, from the inner core of our being. The silver vessel was like those tiny boats of precious metal, discovered from ancient Egypt. The vessels were to carry the dead across the waters of the Underworld to be reborn with the new sun. The mysterious dream inspired the dying woman to prepare for life beyond the grave. Her perishable body was to be transformed into a spiritual body. The dreamer had to cross the dark waters that separate the living from the dead in a gentle and peaceful way. She would assume a spiritual identity that could survive the breaking up of her physical body. She began to participate in a continuity that was linking her present life with the afterlife.

The dead appeal to the living for support

In this chapter I have tried to give voice to the living as they approach death. I will now attempt to give voice to the dead as they appeal to the living for support. One client, who had suffered from major depression, had been in analyses with me for many years. One day, after several years of analysis, he relaxed into a trance-like state of consciousness. He began to wail and wail. He then became aware of an old woman from the past, who claimed she was a distant ancestor. She told him over many sessions that he held the key to redeem her sufferings and save 'the child' who seemed to symbolize the survival of the old woman's descendants, including my client. Speaking in local idioms from his ancestral heritage, which was by no means his accustomed way to express himself, she told him that all had been destroyed by the famine that ravished Ireland in the 19th century. She was still caught in that terrible vision of death and could not move on in the next world. My patient's suffering was her suffering. Only when he understood this and accepted responsibility for an ancestral chain, could the old woman let go and promised to no longer haunt her descendant. After several weeks, the strange dialogue ended and the woman informed him he had now accepted her suffering, which was part of his own history and the history of his people. She was redeemed and could go to heaven. The event and the working through of another traumatic incident in this man's life unexpectedly relieved him from continual periods of depression.

Sometimes I have the impression that the dead want the living to fulfil tasks that they could not do when alive on earth. I was reminded of this motif when a female client told the following dream:

> I heard a knocking at a door. My mother appeared, surrounded by a mysterious light. Her feet were wounded, full of cuts and sores. She spoke to me, saying: You must go on the path you have chosen to release me and yourself from suffering.

The mother of the dreamer had been dead for ten years. She had left her only daughter, the dreamer, a large house full of things that belonged to the family over generations. The dreamer felt burdened by this inheritance. She had no use for the big house and all the stuff in it. She continued to maintain it, only out of loyalty to her mother. The dream made her see her mother differently. She became aware of her mother's delicacy and fragility that she had hardly experienced when she was alive. She had known her mother as being hard, conservative and judgemental. Her mother moulded her life on outer values: politeness, duty and loyalty to family tradition. She seemed to have had little awareness of her own uniqueness as an individual. She could not move on in her new life, perhaps imaged in the 'wounded feet' of the dream.

Awakening from the dream, the dreamer felt a real presence of her mother. She also felt her own psychological and spiritual attitude to life received new confirmation from her mother who, when alive, discounted her daughter's chosen path. She now knew she had to continue her chosen way of life, not only for herself but also for her mother. Up to that point, she had kept the large family house as a link with the past. After the dream, she understood that the connection to family and ancestors was not to be understood in a concrete way, as, for example, holding on to the large family house, which had become a burden for mother and daughter. She understood the dream as pointing to a spiritual path, linking in a fuller way the living with the dead. Through the dream, my client realized that much of her family history could now be redeemed and transformed. From that moment on, she had enough energy to clear the house, choose what objects she wanted to keep, and finally sell it with the many things that had tied her to a material continuity of family tradition. She now understood how the world of objects had prevented the vision of a spiritual continuity that would transform and redeem an unhealthy family tradition.

Jung's answers

Anyone who has studied the phenomena of death and afterlife might call to mind research on death and dying by Raymond Moody and Elisabeth Kübler-Ross, which began in the latter quarter of the 20th century. Moody[11] examined 150 cases of people who had been declared clinically dead, but afterwards revived. He discovered a striking similarity among those accounts. He isolated 15 recurring components in them. No one person reported all of them, but very many reported most of them. Among the components were: hearing of themselves being pronounced dead, an experience of relief and peace, a hearing of noises, a passage through a void or dark tunnel, being alive in a body of energy and spirit, a meeting with one's loved ones or a figure of light and a reviewing of flashbacks from their life on earth. Most of these people came to a barrier – a body of water, a fence, a door, a grey mist – serving as a signal for them to return to life. These near-death experiences made a lasting impression on the lives of those concerned. They had no doubt about the importance and authenticity of the experience but would sometimes be humiliated by others who dismissed their accounts as hallucinations or wish-fulfilments. These people discovered that their attitude to life had changed. They were resolved to live better lives and to give more space to love and the seeking of knowledge. They had lost their fear of death and became convinced there truly is a life following death.

Jung was one of the few psychologists who was concerned about survival beyond death. One is reminded of his early interest in occult phenomena, of his conversations with the dead in the *Red Book*, of his dreams of the dead French soldiers who prowled around Bollingen, and the many dreams of his deceased family members and friends, as outlined in his biography.[12] Jung mentions a dream of his dead father who wished to talk to his son, the psychologist, about his failed marriage. Jung felt the dream referred to his mother's death, who would shortly meet her husband and resume their relationship in the afterlife. And there was the dream of Emma, Jung's deceased wife, who was continuing her work on the Grail Legend, which she had not finished while alive on earth.[13] Such dreams reassured Jung about an unbroken continuity of life on earth and in the hereafter.

In 1944 Jung suffered a heart attack. While still unconscious, he had a vision, in which he saw himself leaving the earth, rising above the Indian Ocean and standing before an Indian temple. He felt his life was being stripped of all earthly concerns; what remained consisted of all that he truly was and all that he had accomplished. Past, present and future were brought together into a new whole. He was certain that if he had entered the temple, he would at last have understood a larger historical nexus to which his life belonged. All the questions that were raised in this near-death experience could not yet be answered. The temple appeared as a barrier, familiar to those who have undergone similar experiences. Like many others, Jung was prevented from entering the deeper interiority of the afterlife. Much to his disappointment, he had to return to earth. It took weeks before he decided to live again. There followed further visions, including one of the *Hieros Gamos*, described as the marriage of Malchuth and Tifereth, and he had this to say:

> Although my belief in the world returned to me, I have never since entirely freed myself of the impression that this life is a segment of existence which is enacted in a three-dimensional boxlike universe especially set up for it. . . . We shy away from the word 'eternal,' but I can describe the experience only as the ecstasy of a non-temporal state in which the present, past, and future are one. Everything that happened in time had been brought together into a concrete whole.[14]

Jung went on to describe his vision after Emma's death in which she appeared as a young woman, dressed in the most beautiful thing she had ever worn. In this 'portrait' he saw 'the beginning of their relationship, the events of 53 years of marriage, and the end of her life also.'

Jung stood on the cusp between the pre-modern literal belief in an afterlife, modern scepticism and a post-modern attitude that is symbolic and mindful of the unique values and limits of personal experience. We have no direct knowledge of an afterlife, but we do have images, symbols and numinous experiences that point in that direction. Sometimes these images imply a psychological transformation, as described in Jung's notion of the transcendent function; other times they imply a metaphysical level of being that survives life on earth.

Concluding remarks: inclusive love

I began this chapter by outlining the many doubts concerning a possible afterlife. An intellectual approach to these questions could not give me sufficient satisfaction when approaching the perennial questions about life after death. Jung once implied that it seems healthier to believe in an afterlife than to succumb to disbelief. Without any conclusive proof about the existence of a trans-terrestrial world, I will end my reflections with an appeal to another reality that is not just about health but also about love, a subject that is often neglected in philosophical reflections on death and survival.

The following questions are not only to be understood as an endeavour to remember a life lived, but conceived as an attempt to rescue from oblivion certain questions that have been raised from a life that is open to the mystery of an ongoing creation. Love remains at the centre of that mystery, a mystery that is inclusive and embraces the unknown. With that attitude I can only continue to ask more questions than give answers.

I ask you, dear reader, can you still live a symbolic life that attempts to embrace what cannot be grasped by the five senses? Do you see those dark regions of your being reflected in the mysteries of nature? Do you still feel gratitude when you behold the golden radiance of the rising and setting sun? Do you appreciate the soft, gentle light of the moon, shining in the darkness of your night? Have you enjoyed the springtime flowers of youth and the autumn fruits of maturity? When you wash yourself in fresh waters, do you feel renewed and ready to start a new day?

Do you look back on your childhood and remember those special moments when everything seemed to fit together, and you thought they would last forever? Do you love your parents and siblings? Are you grateful for what they gave you? Or do you still harbour bitter memories? Have you continued to struggle with those dark moments of abandonment, abuse or betrayal? Have you sought help? Have you learnt to forgive? Can your soul breathe again, throw off the shackles of the past, and bring to fruition dreams of a world you never had? Have you found new friends, playmates and teachers?

Have you been satisfied with your adult life? Have you found your true love and created a new home? Have you fallen from grace, yet picked yourself up to start a new day? Can you forgive yourself and forgive others? Have you overcome the pain of rejection? Have you helped your children find their future? Have you served them well? Have you discovered your place in a profession, community or nation? Has your being blossomed in sharing your life with companions, colleagues and fellow citizens? Have you seen unwanted parts of yourself in enemies, rivals or foreigners? Have you built a palace and forgotten those who live in boxes? Have you chosen to be alone, contemplating the stars, connecting with all that is unseen? Have you been able to share your secrets with others and let them see the shine of the stars in your eyes?

Notes

1   Jung, *Memories, Dreams Reflections*, p. 329.
2   Ricoeur, *The Symbolism of Evil*, pp. 10–11.
3   Ibid., p. 15.
4   Rilke, Rainer Maria, *Selected Poems*, London, 1923/1942.
5   Soyinka, *Myth, Literature and the African World*, p. 4.
6   Hertz, *Death and the Right Hand,* London and New York, 1960. Some of the material appears in the following three paragraphs.
7   Hill, Archetypes of the Irish Soul, in *The Crane Bag*, vol. 2, p. 106.
8   Rees & Rees, *Celtic Heritage*, p. 325.
9   Hill, Archetypes of the Irish Soul, in *The Crane Bag*, vol. 2, pp. 108–109.
10 O Duinn, *Where Three Streams Meet*, p. 77.
11 Moody, *Life after Life*, New York, 1975, pp. 26–98.
12 Jung, *Memories, Dreams, Reflections*, London, 1961, p. 333ff.
13 Ibid., p. 341.
14 Jung, ibid., pp. 326–327.

References

Hertz, R. (1960). *Death and the Right Hand* (Needham, R.C. Trans.). London and New York: Routledge.

Hill, J. (1978). Archetypes of the Irish Soul. In *The Crane Bag*, Vol. 2. No. 1 & 2. Dublin: Folens.

Jung, C.G. (1961). *Memories, Dreams, Reflections*. Compiled and edited by A. Jaffe. London: Fontana Press.

Moody, R. (1975). *Life after Life*. New York: Bantam Press.

O Duinn, S. (2000). *Where Three Streams Meet*. Dublin: Columba Press.

Rees, A.D. and Rees, B. (1961). *Celtic Heritage*. London: Thames and Hudson.

Ricoeur, P. (1972). *The Symbolism of Evil*. New York: Beacon Press.

Rilke, Rainer Maria (1923/1942). *Selected Poems*, 9th Duino Elegy, translated by J. B. Leishman. London: Hogarth Press. Reprinted by Random.

Soyinka, W. (1992). *Myth, Literature and the African World*. Cambridge: Cambridge University Press.

Part II

Pandemics and access to immortality

Chapter 4

Splintered afterlives

AIDS, death and beyond

Paul Attinello

Getting into death

Responses to HIV/AIDS, a darkness that still shadows a large part of the world, have always focused largely on death – overlapping discussions around sex, drugs, politics, illness and treatment gain their heightened meanings from the expected result, the painful and premature death that invades the body through many systems.

Death is always the most difficult of confrontations, the archetypal image that never loses its charge. It may therefore seem strange that references to death from AIDS are often relatively diffuse, incomplete, and indeterminate, across 40 years of songs, memoirs, fiction, poems and films in the urban West. AIDS death narratives tend to shift abruptly between the terrifying and the trivial, the debased and the transcendent, and afterlives are unusually ambiguous – many works project a sense that there is some kind of continuation after death, but as one we are unable to see or understand.

Some of these afterlives include a longingly imagined release, as in the resurrection of those who have been lost at the end of *Longtime Companion* (1989/1995) or the unstable heaven in *Angels in America* (1991–1992). Some works that interlock death and the edge of existence suggest that we are not allowed to see what may be next, as in the novels *Unicorn Mountain* by Michael Bishop (1989) and *Was* by Geoff Ryman (1992), or the later film *Urbania* (2000). The instabilities of these afterlives can be viewed culturally, but I want to think of them in Jungian terms – the network of our discussions of religious thinking, fate and meaning, individuation and transformation, suggests a larger resonance for these choices.

Everything in these works is about death, everything moves endlessly towards death – yet there is a haze over each ending and, significantly, what might lie beyond. This haze has a metaphorical resonance, as though PWAs are caught between life and death, between good and evil, reflecting emotional and existential patterns familiar in psychological literature. Given the power of traditional archetypal discourses on death (Herzog, 2000), this suggests intense anxiety or imaginative fear – are the creators of these works worried that PWAs might not be welcome in an afterlife? – but they also show a willingness to imagine worlds beyond death

DOI: 10.4324/9781003313304-7

that are out of sight, out of reach – and more alive, more complex, more exciting, than traditional heavens.

Pedestals and frames

AIDS has been central to my own life for four decades – I was probably infected in the winter of 1981–1982, saw my first death in 1983, was diagnosed in April 1987 and have lived, been treated and worked with and in support systems on four continents. I should mention that I spent much of that time mesmerized by illness and death; even with a shift away from that spell over the past decade, I continue to focus on darker experiences and their roots. This subject position undoubtedly distorts my view and, though I am not religious, my hope for some understanding beyond the immediate practicalities of AIDS has left me alert to possibilities that could lead beyond the deathbed – though I also think that such fascinations are human, and likely to appear in anyone who is faced with heavy things.

It is worth reviewing the basic timeline of the understanding of AIDS in culture, as it has set up our responses. Cases are first noted in the media in the summer of 1981; because the condition seemed both deadly and chaotically incomprehensible, it took on intense projections between 1982 and 1985, generating a panic over the nearness of death that tells us how faint was our cultural awareness of it at the time. The early days of rapid decline and death shifted around 1986–1987 to something slower, though still inevitable and horrifying; a major change then came in 1996 with the first effective medications, at which point the cultural and existential anxiety around the virus substantially decreased. Of course, AIDS remains vast and terrible – more than 40 years, 40 million dead, and another 40 million living with the virus makes it one of the largest pandemics in world history.

Images, rituals, practices and other responses to death are manifold, and often imaginative, in the world of AIDS; early conflicts with institutional religion generated rites such as the releasing of white balloons, the transformation of a funeral chapel into a celebratory drag wake or political demonstration, and the crafting of colourful quilt panels – which are not only softer and more sensual than gravestones, but also more unexpected, more creative, more surprising. Such responses contrast with works wherein dying from AIDS is treated as an endless process, not only inevitable but extended in time (Howard, 1989) – a response that is hardly surprising as, after the appearance of medications that protected against pneumocystis pneumonia, people with AIDS could be extremely and variously ill over long periods of time. Of course, the religious imagination often constructs death as a springboard to an afterlife – and such a lengthy death, even one rejected by organized religions as proof of sinfulness, allows enough time for the person dying to imagine what might come next.

Most of the material I'm considering here – that is, AIDS-related stories that include afterlives – are relatively dense, with multiple characters, situations, levels: they are therefore different from most AIDS narratives, including major novels or plays or films, which tend to follow a more predictable line of individual tragedy. This points to another aspect of stories told, across cultures and situations, during the dark years: shock, recognition, inevitability, collapse – when those are the main points being made, the stories are linear, with unsurprising endings. Sociopolitical critics who have written about AIDS often see afterlives as wishful fantasies, though I would counter that death itself is sufficiently unimaginable that such fantasies ought to be seen, from a psychological point of view, as entirely reasonable. It's hard to say whether the ambiguous worlds of more tangled narratives that I'm considering allow for, or actually demand, a willingness to include afterlives, but that is where they appear.

Though I should say, more accurately: these narratives are where afterlives *almost* appear. It is as though we are issued an injunction: *you are not allowed to see what comes next.*

Longtime Companion (1989)

The film *Longtime Companion* (1995) explores the AIDS crisis in 1980s gay New York across a large ensemble of characters. The screenplay is by Craig Lucas, who often mixes realism and fantasy to focus on complex feelings and where they might lead. The film covers a great deal of ground – characters go through different problems, we see them at different stages – but it also connects them, not only by means of a meta-narrative continuity, but with final scenes that bring them together. It seems clear that Lucas, and the film's producers, saw this as an interlocking cluster of experiences, rather than as a single story.

The end is startling: Willy, Fuzzy and Lisa, who are among the last to survive a broad range of friends and acquaintances, walk along an empty beach on Fire Island at dusk. They talk, remembering with astonishment a time when they didn't wake each morning to wonder who might be sick or dead; they imagine what it might be like if there were a cure and compare it to the end of World War II; and they talk about an upcoming protest (*Longtime Companion*, 1995). There is a sense of accepting an ongoing battle, of planning the use of personal energy, and also of memory and reflection; this last moves from an expanded sense of the time they are occupying out to a time beyond that, into an imagined future.

And something strange happens: the light brightens to look like late morning, and the camera turns to the wooden walkways from the dunes down to the beach – but a lot of people are clattering down the walkways, and they are the dead returned to life. There are many of them, they are talking and laughing excitedly, as if in sheer joy at being together – the three living characters go up to them, amazed and happy, they hug the dead and talk to them. Finally, Willy sees the man he first loved and lost at what was for him the beginning of the disaster, and they hold each other. The dead man is casually, sexily fashionable in designer sunglasses and a tank top – he is from a time that was free from anxiety, sadness, loss . . .

Then the camera turns again, the light dims, we return to the three who are still in the world – and Willy says: 'I just wanna be there.'

Through all this, a folkish song for male voice and guitar with a warm, rough tone gives us a slightly different version. Song and film focus on the return of those who are lost, but leave technical questions of time and meaning unclear. The song (Campbell, 1989) focuses on different points in time and awareness, but jumps from one to another in no particular order – cleaning out someone's room, feeling a sense that they are still present, wondering about general expectations of life and time and survival, and imagining meeting in a 'post-mortem bar.' This alternation between dark and light emphasizes the instability of the scene, which is simple and ecstatic, a magical transformation that rejects explanation. It vanishes like magic, too – there is no way to ground the vision except in the feelings that generated it, and details remind us that it isn't reality, and so cannot stay, even as fantasy. The return to a darker sky and an emptier world is brief but inevitable; desire retreats into memory, the vision fades into the sound of waves.

This unclear afterlife could be seen as imagining an alternate reality where everyone has lived – though it doesn't suggest a timeline where AIDS never appeared (and even the idea of a 'timeline' belongs to the ordered constraints of science fiction, which this is not). I don't know many AIDS stories where alternative timelines appear, except the recent *The Fathers Project* (Herrera, 2018), which is specifically created by and for a post-AIDS generation. (I admit to imagining such timelines myself, though I don't recall imagining an AIDS-free past or present before perhaps 2000 – but I am not good at remembering the dates or sequence of my own charged emotional material). This is a mixed and thus more inconsistent fantasy – everyone comes back healthy, dressed as they were in memory, and they are all here at once; yet it is clear that they have come *back*, rather than being in 'our' world the whole time.

It may seem strange to dismantle this brief fantasy in such detail – the afterlives below, which more closely resemble familiar afterlives, expend more effort on why and how things happen, though their explanations are incomplete or conflicted. But there is a great emotional weight on this particular scene, and I suggest that that is not merely due to choices by the film's makers – a shared video representation of such a fantasy in the depths of the crisis might be merely a wish, not refined or fitted into a system, not concerned with implications or expectations, but still extraordinarily powerful. Do we share the vision – perhaps with the three on the beach, or with the filmmakers, or only with Willy – or with the friend sitting next to us, weeping, in the movie theatre – or even with the friend who died last year, before the film came out? Such sharing is also wishful: we are given what is wanted, what we think we need, and it is natural that we wish to share it – or, that we wish we *could have* shared it.

Unicorn Mountain (1988)

Two fantasy novels centred on gay men with AIDS, Michael Bishop's *Unicorn Mountain* (Bishop, 1989) and Geoff Ryman's *Was* (Ryman, 1992), offer incomplete, almost offstage afterlives; they were written in the midst of the crisis, when the basic science and symptomatic treatments were relatively clear, but long before the appearance of effective medications.

Bishop, a heterosexual Southerner who usually writes science fiction, wrote *Unicorn Mountain* on impulse, as it is outside his usual range of subjects. Libby owns a ranch in Colorado, but her ex-husband's brother Bo is dying of AIDS and has been rejected by his family. Libby allows Bo to stay with her while he is already quite ill – but she is concealing a secret: there are unicorns on the mountain, and they are also dying painfully. These stories interlock in unexpected, reflective ways, and there are other interlocking stories involving Native Americans and their traditions, ghosts and rituals, with layers of concrete and symbolic realities. The Native American materials offer more fluid meanings than Christian cosmologies, suggesting opening a wider space – those afterlives are often more flexible and fit better with Jungian ideas of transformation and individuation. This is, in fact, the kind of story most authors might resolve in a definite denouement – but Bishop does not: there are resolutions, the unicorns are partly saved as Bo dies, but the events and implications of the different threads remain varied and mysterious.

Many characters start out anxious or unhappy; clashes among strangers, genders, races keep arising, and negative projections simmer through much of the novel. Bo is a difficult burden whether he acts pleasantly or not, and often he does not; responsibility, especially for others, for those who suffer, is unwelcome but unavoidable, and we reach forgiveness and recovery only through long and winding paths. This world has more problems than AIDS, though it will be seen as the worst, the cruellest fate that can fall on anyone.

A major aspect of the book is the opposition between smaller anxieties and larger kinds of suffering – unicorns are seen in other stories as magical, beyond everyday concerns, but these unicorns have a miserable disease that pulls them down into our world, and the combination of wonder and empathetic sadness that they elicit pulls characters into wider awareness and increasing freedom from their projections. In parallel, Bo's physical miseries and erratic hostility challenge the other characters: he is not saintly, but he can recover enough to repair relationships. These chunks of suffering and recovery shift back and forth – we are repeatedly prevented from interpreting anything as purely symbolic or purely realistic, but are pulled from one aspect to another, reminded that responsibility on both levels demands attention and a willingness to acknowledge mistakes.

Bishop based his novel on his own 1985 interview with a gay man with AIDS, along with reading Nungesser's *Epidemic of Courage* (Nungesser, 1986), an early collection of personal and often deeply felt interviews. Though his research was not broad, it was astute – the characterization of Bo is complex but reasonable, as are the levels of personal and institutional care and rejection.

Bo's death is, finally, episodic and unpredictable: after many changes in and around him, he knows he will die the next day; friends and relatives are brought in or phoned, and Sam walks the healed unicorn through the yard to show all of those who hadn't known or believed. As Bo actually dies, characters in the same room, around the ranch and in other cities resolve or move forward in managing problems: joining and leaving, Bo's mother's rage, what will happen to ranch and business, the choice of the new shaman, and, of course, the unicorns.

Chapter 34 focuses entirely on Bo's death awareness – he knows he is dead, but his body has become too heavy to move. Sam's dead wife comes to him and insists he rise, finally grabs his hand, and pulls him out of his physical body. Though all that follows is a surprise to Bo, she acts as if it is all obvious – there is a comfort in her impatient commands, suggesting the implicitly orderly safety of the psychopomp, who always knows where she is going. They climb the mountain and go down into the mine, which was also the portal through which the unicorns arrived.

At this point, they enter a strange, vast desert, the red of sandstone, with dust and boulders everywhere: Bo feels the great weight fall from him, and he becomes in fact weightless. Dolores commands that he go forward, and he walks into a mysteriously other world (Bishop, 1989, p. 404).

To maintain the shifting interface between the everyday and the transcendent, between ideal and real, we are given two more glimpses of Bo – the black-and-white television in the ranch house sometimes shows otherworldly programs in the middle of the night, in colour. Shortly after Bo's death, the young woman who is becoming a new shaman watches a new episode of an American nature show that ended with the death of its host in 1985, three years before the book was published. Marlon Perkins is continuing his popular show in the afterlife, and Bo appears on a program about the unicorns – they discuss how the virus harming the unicorns is carried by living humans when they go to the world of the dead, and they talk about strategies for a cure, exactly as though the afterlife includes problems and panel discussions and searches for solutions. A night or two later, as the mine and its door to the other world is destroyed, they see Bo on the television one last time, in a nightclub, dancing with his dead ex-lover. In the final pages of the book, others find ways forward – even Dolores, who has been a tortured ghost for most of the story, passes 'through a spirit door into a territory of blissful hunting and happy dreams' (Bishop, 1989, p. 418).

Bishop has explained (Bishop, 2000, 'Author's Note – eBook Edition') that he saw AIDS as anachronistic, a horrifying plague from an earlier time – a time, we assume, when death was more evident, more ruthless. In our time, though, such ruthlessness seems to demand that we connect with those who suffer from it – if the unicorns, despite being beautiful creatures of fantasy, have a horrific disease that is destroying them, then we see Bo and others with AIDS as another kind of unicorn, carrying another kind of beauty.

In the world of *Unicorn Mountain*, there are a number of important cultural and transcendental structures operating, but none is treated as central: characters translate various afterlives and ways of being into their own terms. It is not like the synthesized polytheisms of, say, ancient Rome or Hinduism, or for that matter Gaiman's *Sandman* (Gaiman, 1989–96) – there is a sense that, in this narrative, everyone sees or knows a part but not all, and there is no point of view that integrates everything. Through the transformations and deaths that occur in the last chapters, each move and change follows its own logic – there are people, living and dead, who walk a particular path or set of expectations, but they pass others who seem to be on very different paths.

Was (1992)

Geoff Ryman's *Was* (Ryman, 1992) is also a kind of entangled AIDS novel. Ryman, a Canadian gay author, writes science fiction and fantasy, though across a more unusual range of worlds and subjects than Bishop; many of his works suggest painful processes of working through adolescence, sexuality and self-image. The three main stories in *Was*, intertwined across more than a century, are: the life of Jonathan, a gay actor who is dying of AIDS; the life of the 'real' (invented for this book) Dorothy, who was the inspiration for Baum's *Wizard of Oz* books (Baum, 1979); and Judy Garland across three points in her life. The synchronous interlocking of the characters' lives brings emotional material into intense focus – experiences that seem accidental in one life take on greater resonance when they are echoed across several lives.

The 'original' (fictional, though plausibly realistic) Dorothy Gale is seen as a child who is sent to a poor Kansas farmhouse in 1875–1876; we see her, after years of abuse, as a teen in 1881–1883, when she encounters a (fictionally transformed) Baum as a substitute teacher; and finally in 1956 in a home for the insane, where she sees the film that features a character that has her name (*The Wizard of Oz* (1939)), and later dies. Judy Garland is seen as a child in 1927, making the film in 1939, and as an adult star estranged from her mother in 1953. Jonathan, chronologically last but the focal point where the other stories will land, is a gay man with AIDS whom we see suffering, journeying and dying from 1987 to 1989, with a flashback to his difficult childhood in 1956–1957, when he sees the film for the first time. We also see pieces of other people's stories with synchronistic overlapping, notably Bill, a young assistant at the asylum who is kind to the 'real' Dorothy at the end of her life, who later becomes the psychiatrist in charge of a dying Jonathan.

All three main characters are trying to recover from childhood damage – Dorothy is maltreated and sexually abused for years, and when she tells her classmates, she is shunned by the town, then becomes delusional and intermittently homeless; Judy Garland is outlined in terms of her known biography, and so seen as manipulated and professionally successful but also addicted, alienated from the mother who made her what she is. Jonathan as an adult is unsettled, someone who has pushed himself through several careers; and as he goes through his illness, he generates a bitter humour that emphasizes his losses. We are shocked at his childhood, which appears relatively late in the book, where we see him as a strangely detached child who is deeply disoriented by the film *The Wizard of Oz*. His mother does not know what to do with his bizarre, self-harming behaviour; she distances herself from him, and he ends up endlessly unhealed – and then projects a vast (and not atypical) weight onto AIDS as tragic proof of his ruined nature. It is of course horrifying that even an imagined version of the Dorothy we know from the book and the film would be so grotesquely abused: and it feels horrifying in the book – Ryman is good at unpleasantly concrete physical realities, from the small, miserable farmhouse to her later disintegration. Jonathan's physical misery and mental disintegration as a man with AIDS is also horrifying – we are shocked at their suffering, which is ultimately, of course, the point.

The strangest part of the book is, however, the ending. Jonathan is travelling with Bill through small towns in Kansas, searching for the Dorothy of the film – though we already know from the story of the 'real' Dorothy that, soon after she (fictionally) meets Baum, she will be so abused and overcome that she will fall into her own psychotic world. Jonathan finds several houses that are not quite the right one, then is finally guided toward a field where the house had been – but, inexplicably, while Bill is a few yards away, Jonathan vanishes. The scene is written in a way that emphasizes absence, a completely unexplained and unexpected vanishing (Ryman, 1992, pp. 347–348) – Bill sees the car sitting with its door open, the engine running and the keys swaying back and forth but still stuck in the ignition, but as he runs across fields and tries to understand what has happened, he finds . . . nothing.

We know no more of Jonathan; this specific but incomprehensible disappearance is all we are given. The remaining pages of the book take us into a 'dreamtime' for Dorothy and others, while Jonathan's doctor helps the police search, unsuccessfully, and his partner receives a final letter of forgiveness. There is a suggestion of identifying with what is damaged, which is linked to identifying with what may not exist – Jonathan either passes into a world where the fantasies of the book, the film and the dreams of Dorothy, Judy and Jonathan might be real – or he accepts the reality of the damage that happened to him and the others, and thereby passes beyond the need to pretend that it didn't happen.

AIDS is often implied to be the external evidence, the justification, for the internal damage embedded in being gay – not only in right-wing ideology, but also by people with AIDS who are in therapy. This can be linked to the meanings in *Unicorn Mountain*, which works through a similar nexus of problems. Such afterlives could then be *releases* – they certainly work as releases from the stories, from pain and uncertainty, from a brutal and unsympathetic world – but they are also transformations: we want more, we want not only release but something that transcends, perhaps also in terms of kindness, this world.

Angels in America (1991–1992)

The most famous and most substantial fictional afterlife related to AIDS is the interlocking collection of connections, transformations and annunciations that appears in Tony Kushner's two-part play (and later television miniseries) *Angels in America* (1991–1992) (Kushner, 1993, 1994, 2004). The title points towards heaven; the play opens with a funeral and a monologue about different afterlives, and there is gradual and increasing interpenetration of worlds and voices from unseen beings. The first half of *Angels* is sprinkled with suggestions that the interlocking stories of very different characters are also linked through a fluid, approximately Judeo-Christian transcendence. At the end of the first part, something very strange happens: there is a great crash, the stage shudders, pieces of ceiling fall on Prior and his bed, and the stage directions indicate a brief blackout and the sound of the entire ceiling caving in. The lighting changes to an intense whiteness; the Angel, wings spread, flies down through the ceiling, calls Prior a prophet and says in a great voice, as though in an Old Testament passage, that the Great Work is beginning, the Messenger has arrived . . . and a final blackout comes down on the stage, the curtains close and the first part of the play is over.

The plot and materials of *Angels* are too complex to explain here, even focusing only on the 'otherworldly' parts; fortunately, the work is also widely known. Disembodied voices, shared visions, ghost heralds – then the angel's annunciations, building towards the visits to heaven – are all constructed as startling, balanced between realism, fantasy and afterlives. Details are dovetailed to make it impossible to decide whether phenomena are hallucinations by a sick man or by an addicted woman, or are things that are 'actually happening' within the frame of the play. Several distinct moments push this uncertainty towards its more fantastic end, including the shared hallucination between Prior and Harper, the implication that Hanna remembers her own meeting with the angel, and the late (often deleted) scene of Roy Cohn in hell – in a way that seems both comic and eldritch, the play threatens and encourages us by insisting that the limits of reality cannot be defined.

Despite the intense or ironic elaboration of images and meanings and their multi-levelled connections, the heaven of *Angels* is deeply unstable, not only in itself (quakes, the panicking angels, their desperate strategies and acknowledged incompetence) but in its presentation – it is both more and less than we think we need to be comforted and oriented in facing illness and death. Frames of reality and perception shift for individual characters in ways that make this 'heaven' impossible to entirely disbelieve; this is a heaven that is Jewish and Christian, comforting and alien, powerful and dilapidated, intensely charged and pathetically mundane.

The angel is at first in white, but in a later scene dressed in black, when they represent danger and death; then when Prior goes up to heaven to speak with the council of angel principalities, they all appear as hapless bureaucrats, human in their uncertainty, frightened and despairing in the face of loss and chaos: 'you have not *seen* what is to come' (Kushner, 1994, p. 134, emphasis in original). The central point will be, of course, that Prior chooses life rather than spreading a message of stasis, a super-conservatism designed to back away from apocalypse – he would rather be sick but alive than either dead or a transcendent prophet of the infinite. He chooses to remain human instead of either of the possibilities offered to him, because either would take away his humanity.

In understanding *Angels*, it is important to remember that it is designed as theatre: the extraordinary appearance of the angel at the end of the first part, the staged elements of transcendent worlds in the second – they are more real, and harder to see completely, in stage productions than they can possibly be in the television version. In the theatre, one looks sharply at the stage, at what may be a hazily bright light and the shaved head of what seems to be an angel, trying to understand just what one is seeing: we want to know what *is* this heaven that we are offered, or promised.

The television version, skilful as it is, unfortunately flattens this experience out a bit. I have told students that the original play is clearly designed as theatre: big lines, grand speeches – but of course television actors say their lines more lightly, in a more normal and naturalistic fashion. Some of the strangest speeches lose some of their power in such a context, and one misses some of the passionate hope that there is meaning beyond what we see every day. More importantly, video flattens out the experiential tangle of theatre: we can see everything clearly, or not at all; and now, of course. we can pause or slow any aspect of the video version. Satisfying as this may be in the short term, when one wants to catch details, it transforms something that may have seemed magic into mere artifice, even if surprising and beautifully made artifice; but perhaps it is always impossible to recapture the excited confusion of seeing such a work for the first time.

My Angels

I saw part one of *Angels in America* in its San Francisco premiere in a high, narrow old theatre, one soon to be torn down, in 1991. At the end of that part, when the angel appeared, it was an extraordinary shock of sound and light and voice – then the curtain fell, and all was dark. I still remember my intense feelings – the entire play was so exciting, wonderful and unknowable, it seemed to transform everything I had been experiencing for years – but it was also maddening: I remember thinking, in exaltation and frustration, part two isn't even finished, I might not live long enough to see it. An amplified voice, its strange intersexual tone, the shocking appearance of that figure . . . what *is* this, and will I ever know?

I then saw parts one and two together on a sunny afternoon and evening in Los Angeles, in the broad, open architecture of the Mark Taper Forum. The sheer excitement of seeing scenes set 'in' heaven, of seeing the elaboration and expansion of all the material of the first play far beyond anything I had expected, was exhilarating, and has stayed with me for three decades.

That may seem a bit strange as I remain, for a Jungian, unreligious (though I am not such a fool as to claim the certainty of atheism). Especially over the last decade, I have reoriented my connection to religion in line with Jung's suggestion that what is important in religion is not belief, but a willingness to relate to the experience (Jung, 1940, para. 10). As I've told friends, I don't expect anything after death, but I'd be pleased if there were more – and I know that I won't be around to be disappointed if there is not, and that is surprisingly comforting. Death is always bigger, always unexpected – and so, for me, the chaotic mystery of this play, its unknowable aspects, are vastly and incoherently comforting. That is, I think, what the appearance of the angel meant to me in 1991, in a year when I knew I would die soon – oh, look: someone is saying there will be something beyond this.

Perhaps that is one reason so many of the afterlives discussed here are fragmented but detailed, somehow *indicative* – they were rooted in the urban cultures of the disenfranchised but hopeful: we wanted to be offered some possible future and were willing not to know exactly what it might be.

As for this discussion: these materials on afterlives have been in my mind for years. I was confident that I knew what to say about these works – but that has not remained true through the process of writing it out. Of course, from an analytic angle where the immanence of a thing, even a symbolic work of art, is vastly more charged and layered than any conceptualization of it, I should have expected this.

It is also interesting how difficult it has been to finish this – as has been true with much of my writing about AIDS, which has finally become my central subject, my purpose, over the past decade. Difficulty doesn't arise because the material is sad, or simply because associated emotions are painful, but because it is all so *dense*: layered, multiple, every connection or idea leads down several paths, and they generate multiplying illuminations, memories, feelings. Even with material I had thought would be familiar, I find myself wanting to move away from it, to go and do anything else for a while.

As I've mentioned, the works examined here are each strangely fragmented and unstable. Perhaps this is not only because the intensity of our relation to AIDS and to the remembered dead, in combination with our inconsistent, still post-Nietzschean relationship to the idea of an afterlife, leave us endlessly disoriented and uncertain. I have realized, in the past decade, that death is always larger than anything we project onto it, any meaning we create for it; and death is of course so present in conversations around HIV/AIDS that its entire network of impacts can be touchily unbearable. But it is also true that my own tendency to go too far in the direction of the certainty of death, something that has characterized my experience of HIV/AIDS in contrast to many who have been more life-affirming, is challenged by all these works: it is not an exaggeration to say that the appearance of these films and novels over the years gave me room to imagine that my own story might not be one of endlessly falling into death.

Exeunt omnes

In 1984, most of the aforementioned works and their referents did not yet exist. I had seen Reid die the previous December, and the world seemed dark and dangerous; San Francisco is a small city, and it seemed as though AIDS was everywhere – more so I think than in New York, despite many of the histories and memoirs of that era. Theater Rhinoceros, a gay organization that is still in operation, advertised that it was creating an AIDS performance workshop. I sent in some scenes, and in September of that year became one of the ensemble of writers and actors for the first version of *The AIDS Show* (Blaney, 2011), which may be the second full-length play about AIDS.

Most of the scenes in *The AIDS Show* were realistic, fearful, angry or humorous; but I was fascinated by experimental theatre, and so I wrote a series of quasi-absurdist party scenes that connected the monologues and ensembles that made up the rest of the show. I also wrote a separate scene, not at a party – 'Hospital' is a death scene, and in the play we interleaved it with the final speech of Philip Real's clinic ensemble piece 'Stronger and Stronger', so that I was enacting the single onstage death in the show. As four actors spoke other fragments, I had this monologue:

> Wait –
> It'll be all right –
> I'll wait for you,
> if they let me.
> I want to . . .
> I saw the world end, it's bright,
> you can't see it,
> but I see it at night –
> so don't worry,
> but don't leave me.
> This can't be the last,
> I'll get through this one too,
> wake with another machine in my arm,
> my leg.
> Why me?
> Don't leave.
> When?
> Not now,
> not when I –
> no *time* . . .
> STOP!
>
> (Attinello et al., 1985, p. 73; copyright held by author)

So, an absolute identification with AIDS and death – it tells you something about me that I chose to write and act such a scene. It would be fair to say that, after Reid's death, I focused on death, and the fear of death, more than most of the other writers and performers; and that was still nearly three years before my own diagnosis. That monologue did, however, lead to the remainder of Real's monologue, which was originally about being semiconscious in a hospital – but, after my scene, it seemed to be about an afterlife: floating in a kind of unknown, not understanding, but not gone, either.

Years later, in Hong Kong, after the new medications had moved death and afterlives further away from our everyday lives, I took a boyfriend to see the film *Urbania* (2000). This brilliant film entangles a gay man, death and AIDS in a labyrinth of lies, corrections and imaginations too difficult to explain here; but it included a startling dream or vision where the central character speaks to his dead lover in a simple, pale room, one furnished with wood and white fabric. As he tries to tell his lover how much he misses him, how much he wants to avenge him, the dead man cuts him off, saying: you aren't supposed to be here, you can't stay. Another afterlife, but one that felt like an injunction: you are to be in the world, so go there.

There are, always, layers: layers in these works and their interleaving of possibilities, layers in memory and expectation, and in the way they mesh and change places over the years. I often point out in speaking about HIV/AIDS that the fact that so many have been affected by it means that there can never be any central or complete narrative for the crisis. I also accept that we are never certain what to think of death – most religions and philosophies attempt to frame death in particular beliefs or assumptions, and social psychologists have shown that much of our culture and activities are intended to fend off the fear of death. The works I am describing are trying to grapple with this vast instability, this endlessly inconclusive situation: that we do not know, cannot ever really know, what to do with this illness, or with the death that it pushes us towards.

So, I hope you forgive my foolish surprise that the difficulty, the unknowableness, of all these things still applies to me, after all these years. Writing about AIDS keeps including, over and over, the rediscovery that the waters are always already deeper than any place where our feet might find a foothold. But, like those who find themselves in these afterlives, if I know that that is what will happen, I discover that I can bear it, and continue.

References

Attinello, P., et al. (1985). The AIDS Show. In *West Coast Plays*, Vol. 17/18. Berkeley: California Theater Council.

Baum, L. (1979). *The Wizard of Oz*. New York: Ballantine.

Bishop, M. (1989). *Unicorn Mountain* [originally published 1988]. New York: Bantam.

Bishop, M. (2000). *Unicorn Mountain* [new eBook edition]. [N.p.]: ElectricStory.com.

Blaney, D. (2011). The AIDS Show Broke the Silence. *The Gay & Lesbian Review Worldwide*, Vol. XVIII(2), March–April, pp. 13–16.

Campbell, Z. (1989). Post Mortem Bar (music video). www.youtube.com/watch?v=eQ_6jEN5UPk.

Gaiman, N. (1989–1996). *The Sandman*. New York: DC Comics.

Herrera, L. (2018). The Fathers Project. www.iftheylived.org.

Herzog, E. (2000). *Psyche and Death: Death-Demons in Folklore, Myths and Modern Dreams* (New ed.). Woodstock, CT: Spring Publications.

Howard, B. (1989). *Epitaphs for the Living: Words and Images in the Time of AIDS*. Dallas: Southern Methodist University Press.

Jung, C.G. (1940). The Autonomy of the Unconscious. In *Collected Works, Vol. 11. Psychology and Religion* (2nd ed.). London: Routledge and Kegan Paul, 1991.

Kushner, T. (1993). *Angels in America, Part One: Millennium Approaches*. New York: Theater Communications Group.

Kushner, T. (1994). *Angels in America, Part Two: Perestroika*. New York: Theater Communications Group.

Kushner, T. (2004). *Angels in America* [DVD]. [N.p.]: Home Box Office.

Longtime Companion. (1989/1995) [DVD] [original release 1990]. Santa Monica, CA: MGM.

Nungesser, L. (1986). *Epidemic of Courage: Facing AIDS in America*. New York: St. Martin's Press.

Ryman, G. (1992). *Was*. New York: Penguin.

Urbania. (2000) [DVD]. [N.p.]: Commotion Pictures.

The Wizard of Oz. (1939) [film]. MGM.

Chapter 5

C.G. Jung, Gloria Anzaldúa and social activism's possibility[1]

Robin McCoy Brooks

Introduction

Threaded throughout Jung's *Red Book* is a reoccurring theme not readily digested in Western psychology that extolls the living power of the dead from our forgotten or repressed history (Jung, 2012; Hillman and Shamdasani, 2013; Ordóñez, 2021).[2] Sonu Shamdasani notes that in 1914, there was a shift in Jung's writing when he realized that his visionary figures were literally or symbolically imbricated with culture and what was currently happening in the world, most auspiciously the outbreak of the First World War on the European continent (2013, p. 130, RE p. 474).[3] Jung equated the loss of his soul with a loss of contact with a collective history in which he was complicit. The questions we grapple with, Jung implied, are handed down to us from a past immemorial arising from a part of our existence we are ignoring (Hillman and Shamdasani, 2013, pp. 24, 67). The presences of the dead are amplified by the real-world events of one's era, and it is our responsibility to apperceive their lament. Once apperceived, he stated, we need to 'turn to the dead, listen [to them] and accept them with love' (RE p. 344).[4] We must 'descend,' in other words, by looking inward and actively engaging what comes to us with a kind of courage and tenderness born from eros ('law of love') (RE pp. 346–347).

The dead demand atonement for unresolved violence, murder, wrongdoing, contempt or lives that were incomplete that reverberates with 'our present incompleteness' (RE p. 346). For example, in one vision entitled 'The Sacrificial Murder,' Jung is asked by a mysterious veiled figure to atone for the grisly death of a child by eating a piece of her liver that he must cut out of the corpse. (RB, *Liber Secundus*, p. 290). Aghast, Jung rebels, stating that he was *not the murderer* and demands to know *who is giving him such an order*. The figure responds: 'I am the soul of this child . . . and need atonement. . . . You must do this for my sake. . . . You share this guilt . . . because you are a man, and a man has committed this deed' (RB, p. 290). Upon hearing the reply, Jung surrenders. In this given moment, his whole being is called upon to enable the 'passing of a truth along its path' through a decisive action (Badiou, 2001, p. 40). The surrender opens him to another threshold, a horizon of being beyond the limits of personal identity *for the sake of someone*

DOI: 10.4324/9781003313304-8

else.[5] Jung gives himself over to this impossible demand in a field of pure horror described this way:

> I kneel down on the stone, cut off a piece of the liver and put it in my mouth. My gorge rises – tears burst from my eyes – cold sweat covers my brow – a dull sweet taste of blood – I swallow with desperate efforts – it is impossible – once again and once again – I almost faint – it is done (RB, p. 290).

Afterwards, the figure throws back their veil, revealing *she* is 'his soul.' In his next narrative breath, having performed a redemptive healing ritual that parallels the Catholic mass, Jung identifies the sacrificial child as the divine offspring of the mother of his soul (RB, p. 291f151).

In this scene, we can see how the individuation of one is inextricably bound to the individuation of a forgotten or unredeemed collective history accessed through the voices of the dead. I extend Jung's notion and put forward the idea that collective individuation in the public sphere is also an outcome of a profound healing work such as Jung extols. That is to say, *the individuation of a real-world collective depends on our living the truth of our self-engagements by bringing what is unredeemed in both our personal lives and past immemorial into the present through our works and with our communities.* Jung briefly ventures into the importance of community in the final section of *The Redbook*, entitled 'Scrutines.' 'Let us build the bond of community so that the living and the dead image will become one and the past will lie on in the present' (RE, p. 493). While the ideal of building such a healing community has virtue, Jung does not develop a methodological means that supports how we might actually build such a collective bond in the public sphere or with each other. Jungian psychology and indeed psychoanalysis in general is almost completely void of group theory or methodologies, even though we train, teach and commune in groups regularly.

While the basic conditions that foster *collective* individuation within today's catastrophic conditions are considered in the raw core of *The Red Book* and *Black Books* – Jung does not go far enough. What is missing in Jungian psychology is a flushed-out theory that explicates how the individual and collective co-influence each other towards an individuation of both and methodological means by which we may facilitate the mobilization of group individuation or coalition building in the public sphere (Brooks, 2022).[6] As James Hillman poignantly stated (just prior to his own death in 2011), Jung becomes 'one of the dead who is suddenly speaking' to us about *what is missing* or unfinished in *his* corpus (Hillman and Shamdasani, 2013, p. 141).

Jung's engagement with his 'personal cosmology' shares structural similarities with Gloria Anzaldúa's (1942–2004) self-writing practice. (Anzaldúa, 1987). Anzaldúa acknowledged the influence of Jung and James Hillman throughout her works, although she died before *The Red Book* (2009) was published.[7] She extended

Jung's notion of the transcendent function and enantiodromia into the 21st century by envisioning the individuation of a protean self to be inextricably bound to coalition building in the socio-political world that itself is animated by the unheard voices of the dead and one's ancestorial heritage from the past immemorial.[8]

Jung's vertices and Anzaldúa's distinct ontologies connect in the shared recognition that what has been estranged in human history is enigmatically lodged in the world's fabric today. Cultural distress thus becomes the outcome of what has become estranged in the self and the collective across time, emphasizing our collective responsibility to *listen to and actively respond to* the claims of the dead laid bare in moments of contemporary real-world danger. While the structure of this essay naturally compares and contrasts specific intersections of thought of these two thinkers, I am most interested in highlighting Anzaldúa's vision of personal and collective healing that incorporates aspects of Jung's theories but also extends them vividly towards social justice activism and coalition building.

Social justice was Anzaldúa's *razón de ser*. Her theoretical and aesthetic contributions have fundamentally shaped Chicanx, Latinx and women-of-colour feminism(s) by radically redefining feminism as a critique of structural power. Her notion of personhood not only confronted the self with its limitations but also provided necessary tools to participate in *social and personal transformation*. Anzaldúa's individuating self is capable of co-influencing the socio-cultural and/ or socio-political realms through a dialectical process that potentially individuates both. Her point of departure from Jungian psychology is in *how she roots social justice activism as a form of healing and transformation for the person and collective*.

I supplement this discussion by engaging my ancestor Lucas Harris in an autoethnographic illustration of the healing power of a mental health community from which an AIDS clinic would form from its grass roots. Lucas's story vividly conveys how the individuation of one reciprocally co-influences the individuation of a newly emerging off-the-grid community in response to the needs of the people it served within the horror of AIDS (Brooks, 2022, p. 51).

Eagle and serpent eyes – Lucas, and Anzaldúa

My fierce love for Lucas dragged me backwards into the hedges of AIDS opening me to the world's wound through my own. He was standing on the other side of the river beckoning me through his magnetism, his tragedy and love. At some point, it was no longer enough to yell at each other across the turbulence. I had to join him on the other shore so that we could be on 'both shores at once' (Anzaldúa, 1987, p. 101). Lucas was a spiritual activist – one who facilitates passages between shores (Anzaldúa, 2009, p. 248). He could see through the arbitrary nature of social categories and still take a stand – reject while accepting, exclude while including, live while dying. His laser wit could focus on the most benign aspect of life that simultaneously unearthed a painful truth. It was in the early 90s that

I called him out of desperation because something alive was clawing up my throat. We lived three hours away from each other. He was selling his worldly posses- sions in a garage sale getting ready to die. His body was wasting with AIDS. I was standing beside my underwear drawer putting laundry away when he picked up the phone. Suddenly, I blurted, 'Lucas . . . am I selling out?' Time stopped. 'Yes,' he simply said. In that moment, I was floating across the divide towards him in my shame, his hands reaching out so that he could catch me and soften my landing on the other shore beside him and them, deep in the ravaging realities of AIDS – invis- ible to a broader world that erased them. He could see that I was spiritually dying. Soon afterwards, my family and I moved to Portland in the whoosh of a baby's birth. Into the open wound of the world's shadow, I fell – joining the others who were there all along.

The metaphysics of *being on both shores at once* leads us to the work of Anza- ldúa. Anzaldúa was an author, poet, philosopher and queer feminist of colour who explored the aesthetics of knowledge production as they are shaped by identity- transformation, healing and social justice. She named the space in between shores *neptantla*, adopted from *Nahuatl* – the Aztec language from which she claimed indigenous ancestry as a sixth-generation mexicano from the Rio Grande Valley of South Texas (Anzaldúa, 2009, pp. 282, 303). '*The U.S. Mexican border* [it is a wound],' she said . . . '*where the Third World grates against the first and bleeds. And before a scab forms, it hemorrhages again, the lifeblood of two worlds merg- ing to form a third country – a border culture*' (Anzaldúa, 1987, p. 25).

Radical personal and collective transformation is possible, Anzaldúa claimed, only by grappling the opposing perspectives that *grate* against each other in between the borderlands. These opposing concrete and psychical realities arise at the intersection of life and death, living and dying, being and non-being, conscious and unconscious, differing geographies, cultures, ideologies, ethnicities, bodies, abilities, social class, belief systems, sexualities, gender and language, to name the obvious. On the transformational possibilities of bearing the tensions in *neptantla* space, Anzaldúa elaborated:

> At some point, on our way to new consciousness, we will have to leave the opposite between two mortal combatants somehow healed so that we are on both shores at once and, at once, *see through serpent and eagle eyes*. Or perhaps we will decide to disengage from the dominant culture, write it off altogether as a lost cause, and cross the border into a wholly new and separate territory. Or we might go another route. The possibilities are numerous once we decide to act and not react.
>
> (1987, pp. 100–101, emphasis added)

For Anzaldúa, the eagle and the serpent were symbols of 'heaven and the under- world, life and death, mobility and immobility beauty and horror' inspired by the Aztec goddess of mountain and earth, birth and death, Coatlicue.

She was three years old when the image of Coatlicue first entered her psyche throwing her into the 'underworld' (1987, p. 64). Anzaldúa's first exposure to a statue of Coatlicue was transformative. The statue was displayed at the Museum of Natural History in New York City, having been excavated in 1824 beneath Zocalo, the cathedral square in Mexico City, where it was buried since the destruction of the Aztec capital of Tenochititlán (Anzaldúa, 1987, p. 118n9). In the following extract, I relay her depiction of this statue in full because she highlights the symbolic significance of its parts:

> She has no head. In its place two spurts of blood gush up, transfiguring into enormous twin rattlesnakes facing each other, which symbolize the earth-bound character of human life. She has no hands. In their place are two more serpents in the form of eagle-like claws, which are repeated at her feet: claws which symbolize the digging of graves into the earth as well as the sky-bound eagle, the masculine force. Hanging from her neck is a necklace of open hands alternating with human hearts. The hands symbolize the act of giving life; the hearts, the pain for Mother Earth giving birth to all her children, as well as the pain that Humans suffer throughout life in their hard struggle for existence. The hearts also represent taking of life through sacrifice to the gods in exchange for their preservation of the world. In the center of the collar hangs a human skull with living eyes in its sockets. Another identical skull is attached to her belt. These symbolize life and death as parts of one process.
>
> (1987, p. 69)

Seeing through 'serpent and eagle eyes' is an outcome of newly acquired knowledge – what Anzaldúa calls *Mestiza consciousness* that is born from the 'synergistic fusion of the opposites' obtained by bearing the timeless and fierce energies of neptantla space that the symbol of Coatlicue embodies (1987, pp. 68–73). At any moment, something (one's health, external event, memory) pulls us from 'habitual grounding' and throws us into a free fall – opening us to our depths and radically shifting our perceptions (1987, p. 61).

Jung and the in-between man

I want to return to Jung for a moment to visit a remarkable passage in *The Red Book* where he also uses the allegory of the serpent and bird. Similarly, Jung describes the ways in which we may be transformed through love by engaging oppositional forces in the psychical and/or material realms that threaten to tear us apart.[9] Let's turn to the following passage:

> What is beyond the human that appears in love has the nature of the serpent and the bird, and the serpent often enchants the bird, and more rarely the bird bears off the serpent. Man stands in-between. What seems like a bird to you is a serpent to the other, and what seems like a serpent to you is a bird to the other.

Therefore, you will meet the other only in human form. If you want to become, then a battle between bird and serpent breaks out. And if you only want to be, you will be a man to yourself and to others.

(RB, p. 318)

The allegory of the serpent, bird and the man in between reverberates with Jung's encounter with his soul figure and the dead child described in the Introduction. Recall that his soul aspect appeared in human form as did the veiled red-headed woman and later the dead child of history. She (soul) specifically instructed him to 'man up,' so to speak, within the tension of present (World War I) and past horrors.[10] Take responsibility, in other words, for the destructive actions of *other men* then and now and do something about it in the real world (cf. Brooks, 2016). Witness, in other words the horrors of the disappeared from the spirit of the past and be guided (Jung, us) by the spirit of the present age in our present actions moving forward.

Shamdasani highlights that Jung recognized and differentiates a threefold nature of the soul throughout *The Red Book* appearing in multiple guises: serpent, human soul and celestial soul (RB, pp. 310f252, 311). The serpent or some other animal form dwells in nature and arouses fear and longing. The human soul lives forever within you. Celestial soul dwells in the Gods, is far and away accessible only in the form of a bird. Serpent (the raw ground of desire), Human (the sensual body), Bird (spirit). Self-agency (itself differentiated by Jung in the *Red Book*) is thus iteratively facilitated by recognizing and engaging the historically bound nature of individuation in order to live fully (authentically) in the present era *that* informs the forward moving *telos of the individual*. Anzaldúa departs from Jung here (as will be seen) in that her vision like Jung's involves going deep into the self, but unlike Jung's *expands out into the world in a simultaneous re-creation of the self and a reconstruction of society* (Anzaldúa, 1981, p. 208).

Healing as spiritual activism

Let us return to Anzaldúa's notion of Mestiza Consciousness described as the ability to see (with eagle and serpent eyes) what was before hidden *La Facultad. La Facultad*, she stated is the 'capacity to see in the surface phenomenon the meaning of deeper realities, to see the deep structure below the surface' (1987, p. 60). This part of the psyche, she furthered, is animated by images and symbols that are the 'faces of feelings . . . behind which feelings reside' (ibid.). Spiritual excavation becomes a tool for connecting the 'inner life of the mind and spirit to the outer worlds of action' (2000, p. 178). *La Facultad* opens one to excruciating aliveness more accessible for those who are 'pushed out . . . for being different therefore becoming more sensitized (when not brutalized into insensitivity)' (1987, p. 60). 'Those who are pounced on the most,' she further stated, 'have it the strongest – the females, the homosexuals of all races, the dark skinned, the outcast, the persecuted, the marginalized, the foreign' (1987, p. 60). Mestiza Consciousness is thus a kind of 'third eye vision' that transcends the fundamental split within the human experience that needs to be healed: the division between our animal bodies and 'in-spirited knowledge' (1987 p. 102; Fike, 2018).

Anzaldúa's engagements with Aztec creator goddesses was a means through which she could heal the denuding of these deities from their vibrant sexuality suppressed by male-dominated cultural influences.[11] She poignantly described how the biases in Westernized, Chicana culture sought to invisibilize her embodied experiences of soul this way:

> Like many Indians and Mexicans, I did not deem my psychic experiences real. I denied their occurrences and let my inner senses atrophy. I allowed white rationality to tell me that the existence of the 'other world' was mere pagan superstition. . . . Not only was the brain split into two functions but so was reality (p. 58). Thus, people inhabit both realities [and] are forced . . . to split between the body and the spirit and totally ignore the soul; to kill off parts of ourselves . . .
>
> (1987, p. 59)

The Azteca-Mexicana culture and the colonizing effects of Hernán Cortés and the Catholic Church in Mexico at the beginning of the 16th century drove the power of Coatlicue and other female deities underground by 'giving them monstrous attributes and by substituting male deities in their place . . . splitting the female Self and the female deities' (1987, p. 49).[12]

Healing from soul-loss for Anzaldúa required developing self-knowledge, building practices that were relational, social and attuned to cultural, ancestorial heritage and personal authenticity.[13] Her personal method was a self-writing practice that she named *Autohistoria-teoría. Auto historia-teoría* was a genre of writing that blended personal and cultural biography (2015, pp. 142–143, 147). A key insight into Anzaldúa's creative process behind how her writing came into being can be gained by examining how she formed and reformed new stories of healing that were carefully attuned to self and collective identity. This process was acquired by accessing ancestorial historical references, memoir, cultural myth, imaginal elaboration, metaphor, poetry and the linguistic movement between English, Castilian Spanish to North Mexican dialect to Tex-Mex and occasional Nahuad into an unfolding new language. Her writing intersects the geo/political/historic colonization of Mexico with psyche/social oppression of the female Chicano queer psyche that she sought to heal throughout her work.[14]

Her writing was a form of social activism because she de-invisibilizes herself *as a self-healing practice that is shared* – published, read out loud, discussed, critiqued. She bleeds all over her pages, pulling the reader into a somatic attunement. We can see how writers of *auto-historia-teoría* powerfully critique what is missing from the dominating discourse. By speaking from a raw authentic voice in her writing, she radically broke from what feminist Nadine Naber refers to as the 'academic industrial complex' – a pervasive structure that determines how and what kinds of knowledge may be produced within a power matrix that erases other ways of knowing.[15] Feminist philosopher Elena Flores Ruiz summarizes how Anzaldúa's very act of self-narrativizing challenges the epistemic imperialism that oppresses her by drawing on her corporeal intuitions and subaltern knowledges that are social and relational from the multiple interpretive and trans-historical traditions she inhabits (Ruiz, 2020, p. 240).

It was not enough for Anzaldúa to write down the 'stream' of engagements with the figures, images, fantasies and memories that haunted her. Her vision of healing incorporated personal work *and* dialectical engagement in the public sphere, with others building coalitional spaces through sharing and discourse. *The unifying ethos of such a diversified collective is a shared vision of ending multiple oppressions within the coexistence of shared concerns* (Pitts, 2021, p. 155). The embodied self, in Anzaldúa's view, is bound by linguistic, cultural and socio-historical meanings that confront the self with personal limitations and/or the permeations of what is unfinished and beaconing in a collective history. This is 'a path of two-way movement – a going deep into the self and expanding out into the world,' a simultaneous re-creation of the self and a reconstruction of society (Anzaldúa, 1981, p. 208). We develop new tools and practices whose goal, she claims, is to effect a spiritual 'shift' by 'acting as a bridge between political activism and spiritual activism' (Anzaldúa, 2015, pp. 19, 198). I will give you an example of the spawning of spiritual activism within the socio-political maelstrom of AIDS.

The shared dream that spawned an AIDS mind/body clinic

Lucas was a participant in Lusijah Marx's dissertation study in the mid-80s where they fatefully met. Lusijah, Graham Harriman and I (and others) co-lead many psychodrama retreats in the early years of the developing AIDS crisis as a means of building a community of healing for diverse and alienated persons living with HIV/AIDS. Psychodrama is a process where a protagonist elects to go into the centre of the room and the psychodrama director follows their emerging narrative by concretizing their story. Psychodrama is a living form of active imagination within the group as a whole often becoming psychoactive for those participating. This process is facilitated when the protagonist selects participants in the room to enact and amplify the narratives unfolding purpose.

During one fateful retreat, Linda's (not her real name) drama focused on her fear of dying, given that she was a breast cancer survivor having experienced horrific prolonged medical treatment with a poor prognosis. The omni-present viscerality of illness and terror of dying penetrated the room. Many of the participants in these retreats were in various stages of illness. The smell of disease hung in the air like raw sewage – flatulence, vomit, old sweat alongside of roasting turkey and brewing coffee. Linda's psychodrama opened a space for others to describe the concrete and surreal symptoms of their singular body's decline, relentless despair and terror about what was ahead, concerns about a lack of viable treatment or the horrific effects of the early treatments such as AZT, fears about terrible social alienation, rejection, dying alone and financial instability. Who will care for me, love me, fuck me . . . now?

The night following Linda's drama, Lucas and Lusijah each literally dreamed that they would build an AIDS healing centre together. Lusijah was a medical psychologist and a middle-aged mother of four living in a mansion with 12 couches, 25 exotic hand loomed rugs, five cars on a tree-lined boulevard with no street parking. Her husband was a heart surgeon. Lucas had given blow jobs on street corners for cash and later became a hair stylist before he became HIV positive. Lusijah was initially appalled. How could she trust this man with a 10th-grade education and 25 years her junior in such a major enterprise? She also knew that entering into such a collaboration with Lucas would split her heart so widely open that she was afraid. She knew she would be violently uprooted from the comforting distance of her everyday world in all of its securities. There would be no turning back. Lusijah and Lucas's dreams emerged within the coalitional space of an AIDS psychodrama retreat. They both surrendered to the calling of their depths. Lucas would dedicate his remaining short life with a sense of purpose he had not yet experienced and to what would become named as Project Quest, a non-profit AIDS clinic founded in 1989.[16]

We did not have the time to reflect on the relevance of Quest's emergence within the larger AIDS and gay rights movements that were simultaneously also emerging from grassroots communities across the United States and beyond. That would come later. 'Why didn't we write it down?" my colleague Graham Harriman poignantly asked me on a park bench in 2015.[17] Graham's question was a lightning bolt that cracked open our visceral memory of the unassimilable horror of AIDS and the healing power of community from those times through which the past could make a claim today. It was then that Lusijah, Graham and I began to engage the unanswered questions of the dead of AIDS in an autoethnographic study of *communitas* – an arts-based research project and book that continues today.[18]

Closing thoughts

My intention in writing this chapter is twofold. The first is to acknowledge the viability of Gloria Anzaldúa's underexposed work in Jungian psychology as it relates to envisioning the individuation of one to be inextricably bound to collective individuation. She is our ancestor. This I see as a corrective to what is missing in Jung's epistemological assumptions about how we *become* within groups and is an example of the possibilities we may generate within our field by considering interdisciplinary approaches as both Anzaldúa and Jung did.

Secondly, this chapter attempts to make the case that analytical psychology needs to continue embracing a broader vision 'of the people' where social justice is a core value beginning in our own house. While North American psychoanalysis and depth psychology informed practices have begun to incorporate multiculturalism into our discourse, there remains considerable concern about how we can actually integrate the lived experience of those who are on the margins within our profession and our communities at large (Gaztambide, 2019). We are challenged to seriously engage critiques that identify how psychoanalysis is infantalistic, decontextualizing, apolitical, universalizing, uses psychology of the individual to explain group phenomena, siloed, individualistically focused, hierarchical and reinforcing systemic oppressive systems we seek to eradicate (Brooks, 2022; Cushman, 1995; Gaztambide, 2019; Watkins, 2004, 2019; Wu, 2013). Embracing social justice as a core value within our discipline requires generating many forms of systemic change that create new conditions for liberation from our oppressive practices *within our own house*.

It is obvious that we are living in a state of sustained emergency, and how we practise and think about the psyche needs to adapt to our times. Analytical psychology has already begun to boldly think individuation beyond individual approaches by considering the socio-political realities in our discourse predominantly inaugurated by Andrew Samuels in the 1990s and others (Samuels, 2016; Saban, 2020; Oliveria et al., 2022).[19] With Lucas and others, I learned over 30 years ago that communities of care *can be formed* through grassroots coalition building practices known today as a 'mutual-aid' in activism circles (Spade, 2020). I believe our training institutes, academies, clinics and organizations can adopt mutual-aid coalitional spaces from the grassroots communities we are embedded in. We can create a wider vision of solidarity amidst diversity that can enable us to think together into new ways of understanding how to be with each other, our patients, our students and our world.

A mutual-aid culture attempts to meet each other's needs by recognizing how the systems that we have in place *are not*. Power is shared through forms of cooperative leadership towards an aim generated by the group. New tools are developed to deal with multiplicity and its messiness. Solidarity is laboriously formed from a shared vision of care – theorizing with an open heart – from eagle and serpent eyes. Changing the systems that maim, crush, avoid and disregard humanhood. This means learning from those who are not influential . . . empowering each other by sharing influence . . . softening the hierarchies, being curious about the material existence of others . . . leaning into conflict with care . . . bearing the heat of our ignorance with dignity . . . resisting taking an apologist stance . . . opening new valences of recognizing ourselves in another and when we cannot . . . noticing my body in relation to yours . . . orienting ourselves in how we do or do not relate . . . noticing who is invited and who is refused at the door . . . limiting ways that divide us and noticing what unites us. This is my work going forward.

Notes

1 Parts of this chapter were delivered in a plenary address at the International Association of Analytical Psychology (IAAP), 2 September 2022, Buenos Aires, Argentina.
2 Forthwith I denote the Illustrated Edition of *The Red Book* (2012) as RB, the Readers Edition of *The Redbook* (2009) as RE and the Black Books (2020) as BB.
3 See also Shamdasani and John Beebe's (2010) depiction the thematic relevance of World War I in *The Red Book*.

4 *Red* and *Black Book* Scholar Tommaso Priviero highlights the creative and transforming power of love (eros) depicted in Jung's psychic exploration with visionary accompaniment of the figures Salome representing Eros and Elijah – Logos. Salome would
  be interpreted as anima or soul in a later 1925 seminar representing the 'instinctive
  and erotic element that binds the mind of the individual to the force of the irrational.'
  Elijah would emerge as the compensating force and psychopomp in his own Danten-
  esque decent into Hell (Land of the Dead) without becoming Hell itself (2018, p. 41).
  Susan Rowland insightfully notes that the dead haunt because they have been cut out
  of the memory of history due to a collective loss of Eros (Rowland & Weishaus, 2021,
  pp. 94–95).

5 In *Psychoanalysis, Catastrophe & Social Action* (2022), I describe this moment of 'surrender' as the psyche-social nodal point through which the individual may move from
  personal concern to a form of political responsiveness in the public realm referred to as
  'trans-subjectivity.' Politicality is described in the *Introduction* as the struggle to articu-
  late the 'I' with the 'we' towards a fruitful individuation and an indeterminate future
  without dissolving the 'I' into the 'we' which is a regress to collective disindividuation
  (Introduction). In this case, the 'we' are psychical participants in the event.

6 Jung, similarly, held individuation (healing) is a 'process by which individual beings
  are formed and differentiated; in particular, it is the development of the psychological
  individual as a *being distinct from the general, collective psychology*' (Jung, 1971, para.
  757, my italics). Individual psychology, in other words, individuates separately from
  collective psychology. While this is the dominant position Jung maintained throughout
  his lifetime, there were moments when he intuited the importance of relatedness such
  as in 'Nietzsche's *Zarathustra*' lectures. Here he says: 'The self is relatedness . . . You
  can never come to yourself by building a meditation hut on top of Mt. Everest . . . Individuation is only possible with, through people' (Jung, 1988, p. 103). We must take the
  step Zarathursta could not take with the ugliest man (see Brooks, 2022, chap. 1). See
  footnote 10 in this chapter.

7 Anzaldúa's indebtedness to Jungian psychology is noted by her cited references to
  archetypes, mythology, shadow, collective unconscious, active imagination, imaginal
  psychology, dream work and her reimagining Jung's notion of the transcendent function with *neptantla* (2002, p. 548, 2009, pp. 92–93, 236, 2015, pp. 2, 28–29, 35–36, 45,
  127, 156, 176–177). Her master's thesis focused on 'an archetypal approach to literature using Jungian psychology' (2009, p. 93). James Hillman is referred to in at least
  three texts: *Revisioning Psychology* (1992), *Healing Fiction* (1983), *The Dream and the
  Underworld* (1979) (Anzaldúa, 2006, pp. 93, 108; 2015, p. 225n6).

8 It is well beyond the scope or focus of this essay to compare and contrast the ways in
  which Anzaldúa was or was not influenced by Jung or Hillman's thought. It is enough
  to say that she found epistemological support for the development of her own ontology.
  See Fike (2018) for a critique on her use of both. Fike reads in Anzaldúa a revisioning of
  Hillman's re-visioning psychology as she, he claims, provided a more inclusive vision
  of the psyche than Hillman puts forth.

9 Jung does not once use conceptual terms in *The Red Book* or *Black Books* tasked by his
  soul to devote his life to the realization and elaboration of what he learned in his self-
  investigation into life Jung (RB, pp. 211–213).

10 Bearing these unconscious opposing qualities is a signature process in Jungian psychology, elsewhere animated in Jung's engagement with the 'ugliest man,' a shadow figure
   from Nietzsche's *Zarathustra* that Jung comments on intermittently in his collective
   works. 'The man that makes for growth is the ugliest man, the inferior man, the instinctive collective being, and that is exactly what he loathes the most' (Jung, 1988, p. 164).
   Taking a step towards the ugliest man, the dead child from history, the soul figure of
   the snake (often found in *The Red Book*) is generated from a 'higher plane of love' that

allows us to break out of heretofore unconscious deadening social and psychological ideological restrains, as 'Saint Paul' had done (1927/1970, para. 265).

11 There isn't the space to describe further nuances within Anzaldúa's keen contextualization of the denuding of powerful female deities. See Pitt (2021) and Ortega (2016) for secondary source critiques on this important theme in her work.

12 In *Borderlands,* Anzaldúa powerfully describes the geo-political colonizing history of her people beginning with the 16th-century invasion of Mexico by the Spaniards led by Hernán Cortés into territory that was occupied by decedents of the Cochise people since 1000 BCE. The Cochise culture was the parent culture of the Aztecs (B 26). An enslaved indigenous girl would become Cortes's cultural translator, mistress and mother to his first-born son, thus founding a mixed-blood race (*la mezela*) of Spanish and indigenous people. She who is nameless becomes known by many names, including *La Malinche* and/or *La Chingada* (literally, 'the fucked one') each implying a tri-plex of contradictory socio-political significances including traitor (whore), survivor and icon (Lyall and Romo, 2022). The Anglos (white) migrated to Mexico in the 1800s colonizing what is now Texas, New Mexico, Arizona, Colorado and California.

13 In later works, Anzaldúa extends the notion of *la facultad* to into a post-*Borderlands* epistemology of self-development she called *conocimiento* (Spanish for knowledge) through which spiritual activism is an outcome. See her seminal article 'Now Let Us Shirt . . . Conocimiento . . . Inner Work, Public Acts,' chapter 6 in *Light in the Dark*:

Like love, pain might trigger compassion – if you're tender with yourself, you can be tender to others . . . Because most of you are wounded, negative emotions provide easier access to the sacred than positive emotions . . . The spiritual practice of conocimiento, such as praying, breathing deeply, meditating, writing – dropping down into yourself, through the skin and muscles and tendons, down deep into the bones' marrow where your soul is ballast – enabled you to defuse the negative . . . and other killers of the spirit. Spirituality became a port you moor to in all storms.

(2015, pp. 154–155)

It is beyond the scope if this chapter to elaborate these key theoretical concepts in depth.

14 Anzaldúa described historic layers of misogyny as 'man's nightmarish pieces' (1987, p. 39). Women 'are at the bottom of the class ladder, one rung above deviants (i. e. homosexuals and physically/mentally disabled) . . . valuing the welfare of the tribe above that of the individual' (1987, p. 40).

15 Nadine Naber, in the podcast *Liberation Pedagogy Project*, Episode 14 Liberate your research, March 2021. Naber is an academic and radical feminist scholar who teaches radical thinkers how to align their research goals and productions through authentic commitments to social transformation. See her website for more information on her published works and other works at https://nadinenaber.com/

16 Lusijah Marx, personal conversation, January 9, 2017. Quest exists today in a different form. As of this writing, Lusijah is a medical psychologist and clinical director of the Quest Center for Integrative Health, having expanded in 2000 to include all people affected by illness and chronic pain.

17 As of this writing, Graham Harriman is Director for the Treatment and Care Program for the Bureau of HIV at the New York City Department of Health and Mental Hygiene.

18 The title of the book Lusijah, Graham and I have written is *The Healing Power of Community in Mutual-Aid Cultures: Exploring Radicalized Mental Health through the AIDS Crisis* (Routledge, in process).

19 There are exceptions, of course. Andrew Samuels (2016) has since the 1990s written about, taught and organized conferences and collectives (with others) focusing on extending Jungian psychology into the socio-political realms of thought and practice. Tom Singer and Samuel Kimbles have together and separately extended a notion

of cultural complex adapted from the musing of Joseph Henderson in the 1940s that addresses collective psychology from a post-Jungian perspective (Singer, 2013; Kimbles, 2021). Note Kevin Lu's cogent critique of the theory of cultural complex's (2013) and Singer's reply (noted, 2013).

References

Anzaldúa, G. (1981). La Prieta. In Moraga, Cherrie and Anzaldúa, Gloria (eds.), *This Bridge Called My Back: Writings By Radical Women of Color*. Kitchen Table: Women of Color Press, pp. 198–209.

Anzaldúa, G. (1987). *Borderlands/La Frontera: The New Mestiza*. San Francisco: Aunt Lute Books.

Anzaldúa, G. (2000). *Interviews/Entrevistas/Gloria Anzaldúa*. New York: Routledge.

Anzaldúa, G. (2002). *This Bridge We Call Home Radical Visions for Transformation* (Keating, Ana Louise Ed.). New York: Routledge.

Anzaldúa, G. (2009). *Th Gloria Anzaldúa Reader* (Keating, Ana Louise Ed.). Durham, NC: Duke University Press.

Anzaldúa, G. (2015). *Light in the Dark Luz En Lo Oscuro Rewriting Identity, Spirituality, Reality* (Keating, Ana Louise Ed.). Durham, NC: Duke University Press.

Badiou, A. (2001). *Ethics an Essay on the Understanding of Evil*. London: Verso.

Brooks, R.M. (2016). The Intergenerational Transmission of the Catastrophic Effects of Real-World History Expressed Through the Analytic Subject. In Naso, Ronald C. and Mills, Jon (eds.), *Ethics of Evil Psychoanalytic Investigations*. New York: Karnac.

Brooks, R.M. (2022). *Psychoanalysis, Catastrophe & Social Action*. New York: Routledge.

Cushman, P. (1995). *Constructing the Self, Constructing America: A Cultural History of Psychotherapy*. Reading, MA: Addison-Wesley.

Fike, M.A. (2018). Depth Psychology in Gloria Anzaldúa *Borderlands/La Frontera: The New Mestiza. Journal of Jungian Scholarly Studies*, 13.

Gaztambide, D.J. (2019). *A People's History of Psychoanalysis from Freud to Liberation Psychology*. New York: Lexington Books.

Hillman, J. (1979). *The Dream and the Underworld*. New York: Harper Perennial.

Hillman, J. (1983). *Healing Fiction*. Woodstock, CT: Spring Publication.

Hillman, J. (1992). *Re-Visioning Psychology*. New York: Harper Perennial.

Hillman, J. and Shamdasani, S. (2013). *Lament of the Dead: Psychology after Jung's Redbook*. London, Great Britain: W.W. Norton & Company.

Jung, C.G. (1971). Definitions 29 Individuation. In *Collected Works, Vol. 6, Psychological Types*. Princeton, NJ: Princeton University Press.

Jung, C.G. (1988). *Nietzsche's Zarathustra, Notes on the Seminar Given in 1939* (Jarred, J.L. Ed.). Princeton, NJ: Princeton University Press.

Jung, C.G. (2009). *The Red Book Liber Novus a Readers Edition* (Shamdasani, S. Ed.). New York and London: W.W. Norton & Company.

Jung, C.G. (2012). *The Red Book: Liber Novus Illustrated Edition* (Shamdasani, S. Ed. and Liebscher, M., Peck, J. and Shamdasani, S. Trans.). New York and London: W.W. Norton & Company.

Jung, C.G. (2020). *The Black Books, 1913–1932: Notebooks of Transformation* (Shamdasani, S. Ed. and Liebscher, M., Peck, J. and Shamdasani, S. Trans.). 7 vols. New York and London: W.W. Norton & Company.

Kimbles, S. (2021). *Intergenerational Complexes in Analytical Psychology the Suffering of Ghosts*. London and New York: Routledge.

Lu, K. (2013). Can Individual Psychology Explain Social Phenomena? An Appraisal of the Theory of Cultural Complexes. *Psychoanalysis, Culture & Society*, 18, pp. 386–404.

Lyall, V.L. and Romo, T. (2022). *Traitor, Survivor, Icon. The Legacy of La Malinche*. New Haven, CT: Yale University Press.

Oliveira, H., Tadeu Gui, R. and Rubens, B. (2022). *The Insatiable Spirit of the Age Essays on Analytical Psychology and Politics*. Sao Paulo: Todos os Direitos Reservados.

Ordóñez, E. (2021). *Ancestry: The Deep Field of Reality*. Quechelah Publishing, http://www.quechelah.org.

Pitts, A.J. (2021). *Nos/Ostras Gloria E. Anzaldua, Multiplicitous Agency, and Resistance*. Albany, NY: Suny Press.

Priviero, T. (2018). On the Service of the Soul: C. G. Jung's Liber Novus and Dante's Commedia. *PHANES*, I, pp. 28–57.

Rowland, S. and Weishaus, J. (2021). *Jungian Arts-Based Research and 'The Nuclear Enchantment of New Mexico.'* London and New York: Routledge.

Ruiz, E.R. (2020). Between Hermeneutic Violence and Alphabets of Survival. In Pitts, Andrea J., Ortega, Mariana and Medina, José (eds.), *Theories of the Flesh Latinx and Latin American Feminisms, Transformation and Resistance*. New York: Oxford University Press.

Saban, M. (2020). Simondon and Jung: Rethinking Individuation. In McMillian, C., Main, R. and Henderson, D. (eds.), *Holism Possibilities and Problems*. London and New York: Routledge and Taylor & Francis Group, pp. 91–97.

Samuels, A. (2016). *The Political Psyche*. London and New York: Routledge.

Shamdasani, S. and Beebe, J. (2010). Jung Becomes Jung: A Dialogue on *Liber Novus* (*The Red Book*). *Psychological Perspectives*, 53(4), pp. 410–436.

Singer, T. (2013). Response to Kevin Lu's 'Can Individual Psychology Explain Social Phenomena? An Appraisal of the Theory of Cultural Complexes.' *Psychoanalysis, Culture & Society*, 18, pp. 405–415.

Spade, D. (2020). *Mutual Aid Building Solidarity During This Crisis (And The Next)*. London and New York: Verso.

Watkins, M. (2004). Seeding Liberation: A Dialogue between Depth Psychology and Liberation Psychology. In Slattery, D. and Corbet, L. (eds.), *Depth Psychology: Meditations in the Field*. Carpinteria, CA: Daimon.

Watkins, M. (2019). *Mutual Accompaniment and the Creation of the Commons*. New Haven, CT: Yale University Press.

Wu, K. (2013). Can Individual Psychology Explain Social Phenomena? An Appraisal of the Theory of Cultural Complexes. *Psychoanalysis, Culture & Society*, 18, pp. 386–404.

Part III

Burial rituals

Crossing over

Chapter 6

Bardo, Noh plays and Zeitgeist in Japan

Getting through the COVID-19 pandemic and the Ukraine crisis

Yasuhiro Suzuki

Introduction

This world is full and is occupied by the unseen dead. C.G. Jung names this situation the *Pleroma* (Jung, 2009, p. 347);[1] that is, nothingness or fullness. Jung also refers to it as the *Bardo* (ibid.).[2] We cannot see the dead as nothingness, but the dead surely exist behind us as fullness.

In 1916, Jung preached a sermon to the dead as follows:

> Now hear: I begin with nothingness. Nothingness is the same as the fullness. In infinity, full is as good as empty. Nothingness is empty and full. . . . That which is endless and eternal has no qualities, since it has all qualities. We call this nothingness or fullness the *Pleroma*.
>
> (ibid., pp. 346–347)

The COVID-19 pandemic and the Russian invasion of Ukraine have brought forth so many dead who suffer from grudges or tragedy, and who regret the unfinished tasks they have left behind in the land of the living. This is why we the living are forced to face these dead – but how do we do so? The current situation, Zeitgeist, forces us to confront this question seriously.

Jung states that his works are fundamentally nothing but attempts, ever renewed, to give an answer to the question of the interplay between the 'here' and the 'hereafter' (Life after Death) (1961/1963, p. 330). Jung seems to struggle, making great effort and repeated attempts to face the dead in his own way. We, too, must give an answer to the question of the dead in our own ways.

The souls of the dead who suffer with regret are wandering in the land of the living, not reaching the land of the dead. Their lives remain unfulfilled, and they cannot receive the spiritual release of 'Buddhahood,' that is, they cannot gain Liberation or *Nirdvandva* (*nirvana*). These souls therefore attempt to seek rebirth, the reincarnation through us the living because 'human life is the vehicle (of the

DOI: 10.4324/9781003313304-10

highest perfection it is possible to attain)' (Jung, 1952, para. 856). Addressing the soul, Jung writes,

> Man is a gateway, through which you pass from the outer world of Gods, dae-mons, and souls into the inner world, out of the greater into the smaller world. Small and inane is man, already he is behind you, and once again you find your-selves in endless space, in the smaller or inner infinity.
>
> (Jung, 2009, p. 354)

'Numberless Gods await the human state. Numberless Gods have been men. Man shares in the nature of the Gods. He comes from the Gods and goes unto the God' (ibid., p. 351).

The Tibetan Book of the Dead (*Bardo Thödol*) explains the aforementioned rein-carnation process as one unfolding beyond the concepts of space and time (that is, no space and no time: Jung, 1961/1963, p. 351), and is a set of Buddhist instruc-tions for the dead to find spiritual release during their time in the *Bardo* plane. 'The book is not a ceremonial burial, but a set of instructions for the dead, a guide through the changing phenomena of the *Bardo* realm, that state of existence which continues for 49 days after death until the next incarnation' (Jung, 1935, para. 837). In traditional Japanese Buddhism, this period of the soul's existence in the *Bardo* plane has been observed through rituals and customs of grieving and care meant to mourn the deceased (Ikui, 2012, p. 139). In contemporary Japan, the concept of *Bardo* remains available to people through Buddhist funeral rites.

If the dead are reincarnated through us the living, we are asked to fulfil the dead's unfulfilled tasks. This is why Jung (1961/1963, pp. 349–350) says as follows:

> Am I a combination of the lives of these ancestors and do I embody these lives again? Have I lived before in the past as a specific personality, and did I progress so far in that life I am now able to seek a solution? . . . I could well imagine that I might have lived in former centuries and there encountered questions I was not yet able to answer; that I had to be born again because I had not fulfilled the task that was given to me.
>
> (ibid., p. 351)

And further:

> Then turn to the dead, listen to their lament, and accept them with love. (We seek salvation and hence we need to revere what has become and to accept the dead. . . . their uncompleted work has followed them. A new salvation is always a restoring of the previous lost . . . besiege our ears with urgent laments . . . hear the dead.)
>
> (Jung, 2009, p. 297)

This is why 'we simply cannot live unless we come to terms with the dead, and that our life is dependent on finding answers to their unanswered questions' (Hillman and Shamdasani, 2013, p. 1).

To turn to the dead and listen to their lament, we the living engage in dialogue with the dead through mourning them. The work of mourning functions as mental care for the feelings of loss in the living, and, at the same time, functions the care for the laments (anger/wrath, hate, regret, sorry, pity, sadness, sorrow, agony, unfulfillment, incompleteness, etc.) of the dead. This latter care is also aimed at encouraging the dead to avoid reincarnation and achieve spiritual release, in which case the care might also be directed towards the *karma*, Archetypes, and Collective Unconscious which are repeated as trans-generational transmissions after reincarnation.

I would like to discuss this theme of the living's dialogue with, and responsibility to, the dead, utilizing the concepts of *Bardo* and Noh plays in Japan, and by focusing upon the following three points.

First, the concept of *Bardo* is represented in Buddhist funeral rites, as mentioned earlier. These rites are works of mourning for both the living and the dead at the *kiros* (reasonable timings and opportunities). They are aimed at care for the living, by enabling them to mourn their loss and, at the same time, at care for the dead, by encouraging them towards liberation after death.

Second, a Noh play is a symbolic contact/artistic dialogue between the living and the dead. The main character, the *shite*, is dead, a wandering soul who feels the burden of their unfinished human tasks. The living is the sub-character, the *waki*, who listens to the lament of the dead (their story of their grudge or tragedy). It seems to be a kind of analytical session between the living and the dead. The Japanese have thus not only cultivated rites for respecting the dead, but through Noh plays have engaged in dialogue with the dead, experiencing an artistic form of analytical psychology since the Muromachi era (about 600 years ago).

Third, I amplify the image of the epitome of all terrors, the all-destroying God of Death which appears in the *Bardo* in *The Tibetan Book of the Dead*, by using our Zeitgeist (the COVID-19 pandemic and the crisis in Ukraine). As regards Zeitgeist (Wotan), the images are overlapped and projected internally within us, and externally, constituting both internal and external reality.

Bardo

According to Buddhist teachings, it is said that there are four stages ('*shiu*' – 四有) in the process by which a being with consciousness is born, dies and then is reborn again. The four stages are birth ('*shōu*' – 生有), the period of life ('*honnu*' – 本有), death ('*shiu*' – 死有), and the *Bardo* ('*chuu*' – 中有), the period between death and the next rebirth (Ikui, 2012, p. 139).

On this model, as soon as the living being has died in this world, the soul enters into the matrix of the next phase (結生識), where it takes on a new body and wanders in the world of the *Bardo* for a period of 49 days until its next incarnation. During these days, the soul sustains its existence by imbibing the fragrance of foods, and also comes to observe the sexual intercourse between its future father and mother, which has produced a body that is suitable for the soul, based on the characteristics and tendencies that it has retained from its previous life. So, the soul chooses the matrix it will enter (ibid.). Wandering in this *Bardo* realm for 49 days, the soul is then drawn back to the physical world, having been unable to achieve its final spiritual release.

As mentioned earlier, the concept of *Bardo* is present in Japanese Buddhist funeral rites. After the corpse is cremated at the funeral rite, the bones are picked up and put into an urn by the family. This urn is kept at the family house for a period of 49 days, corresponding to the deceased's time in the *Bardo*, and then the bone box is placed in the grave as a second burial (満中陰).

The family, relatives, and friends gather to eat together and to mourn the deceased on several set occasions: the funeral day itself; and then again on the 7th, 49th, and 100th days after death; following this, they meet again on the first anniversary of the deceased's passing, and subsequently gather again on the 3rd, 7th, 13th, 17th, 23rd and 33rd anniversaries. On these occasions they talk about the deceased and share their memories along with their emotions of mourning. These rituals of mourning are formulated to provide many opportunities to assimilate the trauma of loss. According to Nakai and Yamaguchi (2001/2004, p. 148), the living gather to heal from the burden of two tasks: one is the task of grieving for the dead, and the other is the role of substituting for the dead in life. The times of the ritual opportunities are held to be in accord with the rhythms of the calendar and of our daily lives, such that patients may struggle safely to recover from the mental disturbances of loss, without becoming exhausted (ibid.).

There is a notable correspondence between the mourning schedule, which marks in ritual the process of the dead entering into liberation after death, and the process of a child growing in life. After the birthday itself, key Japanese rituals that celebrate the arrival of a new child include observations on the 7th day ('*oshichiya*' [お七夜]); the 100th day ('*okuisome*,' the weaning ceremony [お食初め]); and the 3rd and 7th birthdays (part of '*shichigosan*,' [七五三], ceremonies held to celebrate the child's growth at 3, 5, and 7 years of age). In the Buddhist notion of the four stages (四有), previously mentioned, a parallel is observed between the stages of the lifecycle between death and birth (*bardo –'chuu' –* 中有), and the period of life between birth and death ('*honnu*' – 本有), and this parallel is reflected in this correspondence of important dates in these two stages of the life cycle.

As people get through the work, struggles, and opportunities afforded by the rituals, their attachment (執着 – *upādāna/upadhi*) to the dead gradually fades away. At the same time, the dead's clinging to this world also fades away. Yet such work of mourning is held to require much effort and time.

The original title of *The Tibetan Book of the Dead* is *Bardo Thödol* (*bardo thos grol*), which means a set of Buddhist instructions for the dead during their time in the *Bardo* plane. It has a dual purpose: to help 'enlighten the dead on their journey through the regions of the *Bardo* and make the dead aware of the fact that they *are* dead' (Jung, 1935, para. 855). These two modes of the instructions are both chanted, one explaining the existence of *Bardo*, and the other leading the dead towards the possibility of spiritual liberation (Ikui, 2012, p. 139).

The Tibetan Book of the Dead assumes three distinct planes of the *Bardo*, which are encountered sequentially by souls after death: *Chikkai Bardo*, *Chönyid Bardo*, and *Sidpa Bardo*. In the first two planes, there is a possibility for souls to attain some form of spiritual liberation. Yet if they cannot achieve such a release during their time on the former two planes, then they will seek rebirth and reincarnate on the 49th day from the *Sidpa Bardo* (*The Bardo of Seeking Rebirth*). Such souls seek their next reincarnation from a region of no space and no time. As mentioned in the Introduction, it is in this sense that our world is 'full,' being occupied by the unseen dead.

It is through regrets over their unfinished tasks that the dead maintain attachments with this world, which prevent them from entering into liberation in either of the first two *Bardo* realms. As it were, the dead cannot receive insight from the Unconscious in this analytical context. In Buddhist psychology, the dead are instead swallowed by the darkness of Ignorance (*avijjā/avidyā* – 無明)[3] and cannot receive the wisdom (智慧 – *paññā*) of the enlightened mind (覚知-*buddhi*), which is necessary for liberation (*nirvana*) from reincarnation.

Noh plays

As mentioned in the Introduction, Noh plays constitute a kind of symbolic contact between the living and the dead. The main character (*shite*) is dead and haunts the world of the living under the burden of their unfulfilled tasks from life; the sub-character (*waki*) is living and listens to the laments of the *shite*.

During the performance, the ghostly *shite* reminisces on the glory days of their past life, experiences regret over past guilt, and re-experiences the sufferings and sights of hell. Finally, through the spiritual power of the priest-*waki*'s chanting from a Buddhist scroll, the *shite* can experience liberation and be released from its wandering, tormented state (Murakami, 1974, p. 333).

Murakami (1974, pp. 318–319) argues that the roots of Japanese entertainment originate in the dances and plays performed as part of possession rituals conducted in shrines, in which female mediums would enter trance states to utter the pronouncements of divinities. He further states that Noh plays also share this origin.

The experience of possession in prayer or other mental disciplines is known as 'Invocation Psychosis' (a kind of Catatonia) in Japanese psychiatry, and it is marked by symptoms such as acute personality changes, dream-like states and simultaneous possession (i.e. multiple possessing entities being present at the same time). These symptoms have been deemed sacred and awesome within their contexts of practice, in which belief in living and dead spirits has been normalized, and thus have not been seen as pathological (ibid., pp. 319–320).

From the viewpoint of possession, the roles of the *shite* in Noh plays are classified as follows: possession by a god, possession by a departed spirit, and possession by *shite* itself as the possessing spirit (ibid., pp. 321, 323–324). On the other hand, the roles of *waki* include invoking the departed spirit, as well as curing the state of possession. For example, the *waki* priest's chanting acts as an incantation to call the ghost (*shite*) to appear, or it may serve to help liberate the ghost, as in the play *Aoi no Ue* (葵の上).[4]

The ghost (*shite*) is an illusion which is reflected in the *waki*'s mind. But for the play's spectators, this illusion is encountered as a real character who evokes strong expressions of empathy. This identification with the *shite* helps to drive home the theme of the play, which is one of religious conversion, suggesting that when our distress is at its greatest pitch, the doorway to salvation opens (ibid., p. 334).

The Noh play thus seems to be a kind of analytical session between the living and the dead – both on the stage, as well as for the audience. For Japanese audience members, who cultivate respect for the dead through their long-lasting funerary rites, Noh plays both enable a symbolic form of dialogue with the dead, and also underscore the universal importance of such dialogue. This is perhaps one reason why Noh plays have survived as an art form for 600 years.

Learning from the dead is nothing but learning from the past – and from failures. 'No failures, no success': such learning contributes to our present and our future, empowering our lives. In this sense, the dead serve as case reporters or as patients participating in a self-help group. To appreciate a Noh play as an audience member is an opportunity to learn through participation in such a group.

Zeitgeist: getting through the COVID-19 pandemic and the Ukraine crisis

We are in the midst of the 'once-in-a-hundred-years' pandemic of COVID-19 as of this writing. Furthermore, the Russian invasion of Ukraine has poured oil on the flames, amplifying unrest and the insecure feeling of the current Zeitgeist. Images of the all-destroying God of Death, the epitome of all terrors, destruction, hell and torture seem to be prevailing all over the world. Yet such external images (of the all-destroying God of Death in the form of the COVID-19 pandemic and the Russian invasion) also threaten our internal reality.

Because of the global unrest and attendant feelings of entrapment, some suffer from depression and withdrawal from society, while others engage in self-harm or suicide attempts,[5] turning their impulsive aggression towards themselves instead of directing it externally towards others. Internally, people feel threatened, overwhelmed and engulfed by these images.

Although the COVID-19 pandemic and Ukraine crisis are external realities, the images of death, destruction, hell and torment originate in internal realities that get projected within ourselves. The images arise in the space where external and internal realities overlap.

Overwhelmed and threatened by such a harsh external reality, one's 'ego-strength,' the ability to face reality, can weaken, and *abissement du niveau mental* may occur: '[it is a] dangerous reversal of the aims and intentions of the conscious mind . . . a sacrifice of the ego's stability and a surrender to the extreme uncertainty of what must seem like a chaotic riot of phantasmal forms' (Jung, 1935, para. 849).

This allows images, such as of the all-destroying God of Death, to occur as hallucinations at the psychotic organization level,[6] and to occupy our internal reality.

This does not occur at the neurotic organization level, but at the psychotic organization level – that is, not at the level of the (personal) Unconscious, as in the case of a complex, but at the level of the Collective Unconscious. Jung points out that *karma* and Archetypes originate in the Collective Unconscious. The all-destroying God of Death, the epitome of all terrors and destruction, is one such archetypal image.

The true meaning of Jung's reading of *The Tibetan Book of the Dead* backwards seems to lie in the following: whereas the theme of reincarnation in the *Sidpa Bardo* represents the level of neurotic organization based upon witnessing the primal scene, the images of the Wrathful Deities (see Figure 6.1) and Peaceful Deities in the *Chönyid Bardo* represent the level of psychotic organization, with karma-based hallucinations from the Collective Unconscious[7] being projected as Archetypes.

For example, the terrible image of Wrathful Deities is as follows:

It is a meddling with fate, which strikes at the very roots of human existence and can let loose a flood of sufferings of which no sane person ever dreamed. These sufferings correspond to the hellish torment of the Chönyid state, described in the text as follows:
　　Then the Lord of Death will place round thy neck a rope and drag thee along; he will cut off thy head, tear out thy heart, pull out thy intestines, lick up thy brain, drink thy blood, eat thy flesh, and gnaw thy bones; but thou wilt be incapable of dying. Even when thy body is hacked to pieces, it will revive again. The repeated hacking will cause intense pain and torture.

(Jung, 1935, para. 847)

We have been threatened by pandemics, pestilence, cholera, smallpox, Spanish flu, and so on, repeatedly and collectively. We have been threatened by 'Wotan' (Jung, 1936/1964), the old Norse god of storm and frenzy, which Jung evoked in writings before and after the Second World War.

Although complex political issues should not be simplified or generalized about lightly, it seems that the Russian invasion of Ukraine is also a type of Wotan. The brutal battlefields seem to be the very image of the all-destroying God of Death. In the context of Wotan, huge inner reservoirs of energy suppressed by the COVID-19 crisis have burst forth and exploded outward. In this sense, the Covid disaster and the Ukraine crisis are not unrelated, but rather, are twinned expressions of the psychic forces of our present Zeitgeist. This corresponds to Jung's saying: 'the psychic conditions which breed demons are as actively at work as ever. The demons have not really disappeared but have merely taken on another form: they have become unconscious psychic forces' (1945, para. 431).[8]

The images are all shadow Archetypes in our Collective Unconscious and are projected inside ourselves. That is, they all emanate from within us (Jung, 1952,

念怒尊のマンダラ(ト ハ キルコル)

Figure 6.1 The Mandala chart of Wrathful Deities

Source: © Reproduced from Kawasaki, S. (Tr.) (1989/1993) by permission of Chikuma Shobo.

para. 851). All deities and demons, all heavens and hells are internal (Leary et al., 1964/1992/2007, p. 36).

While there is a risk of being overwhelmed by these internal and external images, if we face such shadows calmly and steadily, we might be able to restore a measure of supple, healthy ego-strength, and avoid being intimidated beyond necessity. Further, we might even recover a measure of the soul's divinity, in the sense that Jung proposes when he refers to the *Bardo Thödol* as an initiation process whose purpose is to restore to the soul the divinity it lost at birth (1935, para. 842). One approach to passing through this challenging time, and perhaps to regaining our soul's divinity, is to face these images through 'Gazing, Recognizing, and Letting Go' (see the next section).

Jung describes this process as a liberation of the self from its bondage to strife and suffering (1939/1954, para. 792). I believe that Jungian perspectives might contribute greatly to this difficult task, paving the way for many to deal with the current Zeitgeist.

Discussion

The Zeitgeist of the present time has forced us, the living, to face the fact that this world is full, and occupied by the unseen dead. The living are empowered by the dead, and therefore we must listen carefully to their lamentations, and enter into dialogue with them.

Jung's Psychological Commentary on *The Tibetan Book of the Dead* (1935) suggests that in more normal and peaceful times, problems stemming from the neurotic organization level can be managed with images drawn from the *Sidpa Bardo* plane; however, for our current era of extreme challenge and suffering, images of Wrathful Deities from the *Chönyid Bardo* plane, corresponding to the psychotic organization level, and occurring through *abaissement du niveau mental*, are required.

To liken this to Jung's near-death experience (1961/1963, p. 323), the *Sidpa Bardo* plane corresponds to his return to the earth, which he likened to entering a ' "box system" . . . in which each person sat by himself in a little box . . . a prison . . . hung up in a box by a thread,' while the *Chönyid Bardo* plane corresponds to his observation of being above the Earth in space: 'While I floated in space, I had been weightless, and there had been nothing tugging at me' – an impressive and overwhelming state.

To get through the state of *Chönyid Bardo*, we must secure a lifeline grounding us to the earth to ensure that we are not swallowed up by a black hole or the vastness of cosmic space. We must redevelop a supple and healthy ego-strength that can avoid being swallowed by overwhelming images, one that will not slip into *abaissement du niveau mental*. Jung argues (1935, para. 849) that no one who strives for selfhood (individuation) is spared this dangerous passage, for that which is feared also belongs to the wholeness of the self.

We must face these images, confronting them calmly and firmly, without trying to escape or avoid them. This is done through a process of 'Gazing' (*Virāga*),[9] 'Recognizing'[10] and 'Letting Go'[11] (Inoue, 2005, pp. 134, 139–141), in which the attachment (執着-*upādāna*) of both the living and the dead are released at the same time.[12] By gazing at them until they fade away on their own, we naturally let go of them (ibid., p. 134). The step of recognition enables the opening up of new space for the next step.

The dead person's attachment to this world is through the form of an unfulfilled desire; if this naturally fades, this soul may attain liberation.

The dialogue between the living and the dead must begin with each looking directly into each other's inner reality. Through mutual recognition, we may be able to let go of our attachment to each other and may thus finally achieve peace of mind.

In a sense, our present Zeitgeist might appear to be a path toward utter darkness (Jung, 1939/1954, para. 828), but it may actually lead toward illumination. This is the usual *enantiodromia per tenebras as lucem*, the union of opposites, which is the transcendent function. Since this function results in an increase of consciousness (since the previous condition is augmented by the addition of formerly unconscious contents), the new condition carries greater insight, which is symbolized by greater light (ibid.).

Whatever the Zeitgeist might be, each of us must begin by struggling to face our own internal realities one by one, before externalizing and projecting our inner problems onto the outside and blaming others.

Closing remarks

We the living are empowered by the dead. Life is empowered by Death. Life shines in Death like light shines in darkness. To make Life shine more brightly, we need to perform a 'Requiem for the Dead' (Yuasa, 1996; Suzuki, 2018).[13]

Jung (1952, para. 756) relates the encounter between light and darkness in the following passage. I have chosen to replace *light* with *Life* and *darkness* with *Death* to make for more fitting closing remarks:

The encounter between conscious and unconscious has to ensure that the *Life* which shines in *Death* is not only comprehended by *Death*, but comprehends it.

Notes

1 Jung used the term 'pleroma' to designate a state of pre-existence and potentiality, identifying it with the Tibetan *Bardo*: 'He must . . . accustom himself to the idea that "time" is a relative concept and needs to be complemented by that of the "simultaneous" existence, in the Bardo or pleroma, of all historical processes. What exists in the pleroma as an eternal process appears in time as aperiodic sequence, that is to say, it is repeated many times in an irregular pattern' (1952, para. 629, 2009, p. 347).

2 The reincarnation of the dead is repeated many times in an irregular patten. As regards reincarnation, Jung states as follows: 'the imperishable world erupted into this transitory one' (1961/1963, p. 18).

3 Ignorance (無明 – *avijjā/avidyā*) forces one to insist on pleasure and to refuse unpleasantness. The essence of ignorance consists of greed, wrath and attachment (貪瞋痴 – *lobha, dosa, moha*). Such ignorance compels the soul to seek rebirth.

4 The substitute *waki* makes an incantation (performing the *azusa* rite with a catalpa bow) and then the living spirit (六条御息所 – Lady Rokujo) appears and makes an attack on the new wife (Lady Aoi)'s house（後妻打ち）. The *shite* wears the face mask of a demon/ ogre (般若 - *Hannya*), and the evil spirit is quelled by the chanting of the Heart Sutra by the itinerant priest *waki*, which results in the *shite* receiving some spiritual release

(Murakami, 1974, p. 331). www.youtube.com/watch?v=zLPSdJHBKTk, accessed 10 May 2022.

5   In 2021, the rate of suicide in Japan increased.

6   The terminology of 'neurotic organization level' and 'psychotic organization level' are in accordance with Kernberg (1984)'s classification: NPO, BPO and PPO – that is, neurotic personality organization, borderline personality organization and psychotic personality organization.

7   The world of gods and spirits is truly 'nothing but' the collective unconscious inside me. Turning this sentence around, it reads, 'The collective unconscious is the world of gods and spirits outside me' (Jung, 1952, para. 857).

8   Wotan as Archetype (Jung, 1936, para. 395): Archetypes are like riverbeds which dry up when the water deserts them, but which it can find again at any time. An archetype is an old watercourse along which the water of life has flowed for centuries, digging a deep channel for itself. The longer it has flowed in this channel, the more likely it is that sooner or later the water will return to its old bed. The life of the individual as a member of society and particularly as part of the State may be regulated like a canal, but the life of nations is a great rushing river which is utterly beyond human control, in the hands of One who has always been stronger than men.

9   According to the *Paticca-samuppāda* sutra (縁起), the living's clinging/grasping/attachment (執着 – *upādāna*) unfolds as follows: the desire for love (渇愛 – *taṇhā*) is repeated and becomes customary, leading to attachment. This attachment takes on a patterned form and becomes a complex (有 – *bhava*). We must begin to gaze at (*Virāga*) and observe the complex, the constellation of scenes, Archetypes and Collective Unconscious in which the attachment is patterned (Inoue, 2022).

10 By reflection on the fact that ignorance (無明 – *avijjā/avidyā*) shaped our past actions (業/行 – *saṅkhāra*), we can see that our worldly existence (生存/有 – *bhava*) is created through the desire for love (渇愛), and through clinging, grasping and attachment (執着). We may then begin to witness ('gaze at' – *Virāga*) this desire and attachment vanishing. This is the stage of 'letting go,' note 11 in which wisdom (智慧 – *paññā*) paves the way for a new space of kind thoughtfulness (Inoue, 2005, p. 141).

11 This is the 'vanishing' mentioned above in note 10.

12 In other words, regarding notes 9–11, Jung (1939/1954, para. 797) describes the process as follows: 'the problem is not so much a withdrawal from the objects of desire, as a more detached attitude to desire as such, no matter what its object. We cannot compel unconscious compensation through the impetuousness of uncontrolled desire. We have to wait patiently to see whether it will come of its own accord, and put up with whatever form it takes. Hence, we are forced into a sort of contemplative attitude which, in itself, not rarely has a liberating and healing effect.'

13 At all stages of history, there are not only winners, but also losers. There are the shadow histories in contrast with the light histories – that is, the dark side behind the light side. Jung describes the spiritual importance of Requiem for the countless dead who have disappeared from the glorious light side to the dark shadow side with laments (Yuasa, 1996, p. 366; Suzuki, 2018, p. 317).

References

Hillman, J. and Shamdasani, S. (2013). *Lament of the Dead: Psychology after Jung's Red Book*. New York: W.W. Norton & Company.

Inoue, V. (2005). *Ānāpānasati-Sutta*. Tokyo: Kousei Shuppansha.

Inoue, V. (2022). Private letter.

Ikui, T. (2012). 65 Bardo. In Inoue, V., Kato, H. and Kasai, K. (eds.), *The Dictionary of Key Word about Buddhism Psychology*. Tokyo: Shunjusha.

Jung, C.G. (1935/1958). Psychological Commentary on *The Tibetan Book of the Dead*. In *Collected Works, Vol. 11, Psychology and Religion: West and East* (2nd ed.). Princeton, NJ: Princeton University Press.

Jung, C.G. (1936/1964). Wotan. In *Collected Works, Vol. 10, Civilization in Transition* (2nd ed.). Princeton, NJ: Princeton University Press.

Jung, C.G. (1939/1954/1958). Psychological Commentary on *the Tibetan Book of the Great Liberation*. In *Collected Works, Vol. 11, Psychology and Religion: West and East* (2nd ed.). Princeton, NJ: Princeton University Press.

Jung, C.G. (1945/1964). After the Catastrophe. In *Collected Works, Vol. 10, Civilization in Transition* (2nd ed.). Princeton, NJ: Princeton University Press.

Jung, C.G. (1952/1958). Answer to Job. In *Collected Works, Vol. 11, Psychology and Religion: West and East* (2nd ed.). Princeton, NJ: Princeton University Press.

Jung, C.G. (1961/1963/1995). *Memories, Dreams, Reflections*. London: Fontana Press.

Jung, C.G. (2009). *The Red Book* (Shamdasani, S. Ed.). New York: W.W. Norton & Company.

Kawasaki, S. (trans.) (1989/1993). *The Original Translation of the Tibetan Book of the Dead, or The After-Death Experience on the 'Bardo' Plane*, according to Lama Kazi Dawa-Samdup's English rendering, edited by W.Y. Evans-Wentz. Tokyo: Chikuma Gakugei Bunko.

Kernberg, O.F. (1984). *Severe Personality Disorders: Psychotherapeutic Strategies*. New Haven, CT: Yale University Press.

Leary, T., Metzner, R. and Alpert, R. (1964/1992/2007). *The Psychedelic Experience*. New York City: Citadel Press, Kensington Publishing Corp.

Murakami, M. (1974). Noh Play and Psychopathology. In Miyamoto, T. (ed.), *Psychopathology of Schizophrenia*, Vol. 2. Tokyo: Tokyo University Press.

Nakai, H. and Yamaguchi, N. (2001/2004). *Psychiatry for Nurse* (2nd ed.). Tokyo: Igaku Shoin.

NHK Special. (1993). *The Tibetan Book of the Dead*. www.youtube.com/watch?v=rWp YqnMWr0U (accessed 10 May 2022).

Suzuki, Y. (2018). *Individuation Process and Practice of Jungian Analysis*. Tokyo: Tohmi Shobo.

Yuasa, Y. (1996). *Jung and Christianity*. Tokyo: Kodansha Gakujutu Bunko.

Chapter 7

Pandemic, the zenith of an archetypal disconnection

Fernando Mendes

Introduction

When did we start to consider that some beings were human beings? In response to this question, theories are consolidated pointing to a certain period of human development in which converging factors indicate that it originates in what we call Humanity.

Some characteristics accepted as being sufficient to distinguish us from other animals, such as being bipedal, fashioning and using tools, having a larger brain, living in society and complying to learned behaviours, have emerged independently from one another throughout our evolutionary history. The one trait, however, that has been recognized as fundamental to characterize us as humans is our ability to assign meaning to certain phenomena, facts and life itself. Such ability has left archaeological findings, the most ancient of which being the sites with remains from ritualized burials.

At some point around 78,000 years ago, *homo sapiens* began burying their dead. A recent *National Geographic* (2021) article reports that the remains of a child have been found in what is considered to be the first grave, as the type of burial position shows intentionality in the act of burying. It is a glimpse of cognitive and emotional expressions that will continue to occur from that time on.

I am convinced that the practice of burying the dead is what marks the dawn of humanity, based on assertions found in disciplines as varied as philosophy, archaeology, ethnology, anthropology and the sciences of religion and psychology.

From this primordial behaviour we can observe the emergence of an archetype that I will call the archetype of an afterlife which has had a strong influence upon the shaping of all different human cultures, experienced as a living connection, a felt sense of immortality, since the beginning of our civilization.

On the significant importance of this moment for the development of culture, Spengler (1973) wrote of a 'Recognition of Death' as the initiating moment of every higher, mythologically inspired culture style; and here we already have it in the first awaking of consciousness to its powers at the stage of *Homo sapiens*. In this respect, Campbell (1988, p. 52) states: 'Whatever the specific myths may have

DOI: 10.4324/9781003313304-11

been that inspired these primeval burials, there is one general idea represented in all: that of a continuation of life beyond death, whether in this world or some other.'

Jung (1950, paras. 206–207), in turn, asserts that the mere fact that people talk about rebirth, or that such a concept even exists, means that there is also a psychic reality, one of the earliest propositions ever put forward by humankind. 'This kind of proposition is based on what I call an archetype.'

The idea of archetypes has been present in several thinkers of different times. Jung (1940, para. 89) says that mythological research calls them 'motifs.' In the psychology of the 'primitive' they correspond to Lévy-Bruhl's concept of 'representations collectives,' and in the field of comparative religion they have been defined by Hubert and Mauss as 'categories of the imagination.' Adolf Bastian long ago called them 'elementary' or 'primordial' thoughts. It is important to note that these theories point to an idea of the archaic, the primordial, the elementary and of being part of collective representations.

Jung (1954, para. 6), however, introduces the idea of the archetype as an organizer of both the psyche and the human behaviour. As part of the inherited structure of the brain, he affirms that 'the concept of the archetype, which is an indispensable correlate of the idea of the collective unconscious, indicates definite forms in the psyche, which seem to be present always and everywhere.'

The synchronic effects,[1] which also indicate the existence of an archetype at the base of this human behaviour, have led me to discuss two of these moments when death synchronously constellates over humanity, and a third one, where death is present, but in which we seem to have disconnected from this archetype, during the COVID-19 pandemic, with a special focus on Brazil.

1 The first takes place around 60,000 years ago[2] when *homo sapiens*, synchronously and across the planet, begins to bury their dead with clear indications that such practice was accompanied by rituals suggesting a firm belief in the afterlife. Those rituals are rites of passage, which, similarly to their counterparts such as birth, baptism, puberty and marriage, prepare the individuals to start a new phase in their lives, this time under a different status, and, at the same time, facilitate the entry of the deceased into the next realm and protect and comfort the living survivors.

2 A second period dates to around 5,000 years ago, when humans, again synchronously and across the planet, adopts the practice of building funerary monuments, majestic and sometimes gigantic testimonies of their belief in the afterlife, in the reality of the existence of other worlds, in the continuity of life after death and in rebirths. Such monuments appear in shapes and places as disparate as the Mastabas[3] in Egypt and the Sambaquis[4] in Brazil, among others found around the world.

3 The current period that was started with the COVID-19 pandemic, particularly focusing on the banalization of death and the effacement in meaning of life brought by its development, that seem to have caused a generalized melancholia, the pathological effect following the impossibility to live the grieving process, and the collective loss of a vital connection with the very archetype that made us humans.

The first burials: an archetype at the origin of art, religion, mythology and consciousness

The first burials and graves

Graves are the first material and symbolic evidence of an archetype related to the afterlife (see Figure 7.1). This alone would justify affirming that it is at the base of what we call humanity. Together with other archaeological findings of ceremonial remains from the Palaeolithic on, these sacred spaces that appear synchronously in the various regions of the world inhabited by our species allow us to conclude that there was a firm belief then in the existence of another world, a natural sequel to this one and part of one's existence. From then on, this archetype becomes tangible, manifest, and its existence is recognized by the then incipient collective consciousness of our species.

The first burials of the Palaeolithic are so important and meaningful in the history of humanity that they have been repeated, gaining new contours, for 60 millennia in Europe, Asia, Africa and the Americas. There is a lot of discussion about this moment, the dating of which goes further and further back. As it goes against the most accepted theories of occupation of the earth, it must be taken in account with great care, but must not be ignored.

The rites, the gestures and the work that the living dedicate to the dead are certainly signs of respect and affection, but they also demonstrate the belief in life in the beyond. In the first interments, the placing of food and ornamental objects, alongside the meaningful handling of the body, is noticeable, pointing to the idea of a post-mortem continuity. Through their funerary activities, all existent human

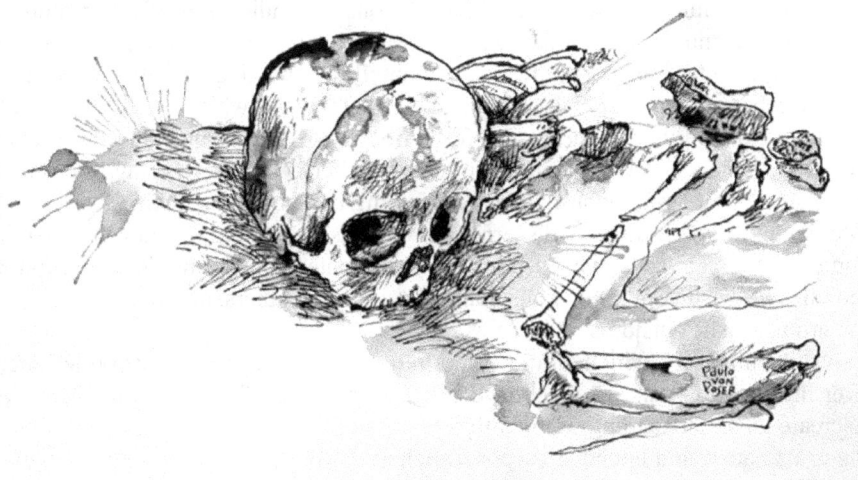

Figure 7.1 Line drawing by Paulo Von Poser, *The First Burial* (2022)

species since the Upper Palaeolithic have demonstrated a constant religious concern with the mystery of life after death (Ries, 2020, p. 400).

Eliade (1978, p. 28), referring to this period, clarifies that there are numerous archaeological findings such as human bones, mostly skulls, some dating from 50,000 to 70,000 years ago, stone tools and pigments, that allow us to confidently speak of graves. They witness the belief in a post-mortem life that seems, therefore, to have existed since the most remote times, whether using red ochre, a ritual substitute for blood, or other symbols.

Archaeological findings are not the only indicators that burials were the founding ceremonial of humanity, but they certainly contribute to affirming that this period is at the origin of consciousness, art, religion and mythology.

Evolutionary archaeology

Mithen (2003), from the so-called *evolutionary archaeology*, emphasizes the importance of death in the origin and development of human consciousness. It is one of the important approaches to return to this founding moment, among others, as we will see.

This branch of archaeology, based on fossil evidence, seeks to understand how the human mind evolved. He considers that over the last four million years, a function we now call intelligence or cognitive capacity has emerged in our minds. It is the possibility of becoming aware of what surrounds us, of what can be captured by sense organs. This ability is what will differentiate us from several other ancestors of our species when it reaches its zenith. What experts say is that about two million years ago, four modalities of intelligence gradually developed in hominids. When one modality was activated, the others were not simultaneously perceived.

One of them is the naturalistic intelligence that would have allowed, through the observation of the environment, the acquisition of knowledge related to the movement of animals, the passage of the seasons, the indications of water sources, the obtaining and processing of the resources necessary for survival, production of shelter, fire control, and so on. In short, an intelligent reading of the environment.

In another situation, social intelligence was activated, which allowed the creation of ways of living together, the formation of nomadic bands and the prediction of reactions and behaviours of others whether cooperative or aggressive, in addition to the possible consequence of sharing or not sharing their food. It is an intelligence that allows us to discern when there is collaboration and when there is competition, what adds, what separates, what creates bonds. That is, the origin of the rules of kinship, of group consciousness, as us and others, of those belonging to the group versus outsiders or enemies.

A third modality, which would come into operation separately from the others over millions of years, is a technical intelligence. One of its main functions was to create an understanding of the different possibilities of chipping a stone according to its nature and intended purpose, such as cutting, drilling, scraping, sanding, crushing, or to choose different materials, such as horns, animal teeth, bamboo and wood, suitable for the creation of the first instruments. The scientific study of these chipped or polished stones reveals habits, hunting and planting techniques, skills and inventiveness. Technical intelligence was fundamental for survival, it is what makes the *sapiens* sapiens, the one who knows that they are the author of their deeds. Material culture, in anthropological terms, derives from this modality of technical intelligence, just as kinship derives from social intelligence, and the knowledge of what is necessary to ensure survival comes from an ability to read the natural environment.

There is still a fourth modality, which produces something different from the other three because its object of knowledge and creation are immaterial values – linguistic intelligence. Brain development allowed sounds to be associated with meanings. Everything leads experts to believe that the first sounds were ono-matopoeias. They were the imitation of natural sounds, which time calibrated as vehicles for the collective transmission of shared meanings. One more step and articulations, inflections, syntaxes appear, and the ground is prepared for the birth of language, and with it, of distinguished and narrative communication. At the same time, linguistic intelligence allowed the symbolic perception of reality. In a true cultural revolution in the Upper Palaeolithic, the emergence of symbols, mythical stories, artistic expressions, rituals and religion, followed in a cascade.

When all four modalities of intelligence are combined, human culture is born. As Mithen says, our modern intelligence is strictly the same as that which emerged in the Upper Palaeolithic.

Funerary rites at the origin of consciousness

In the words of Gambini,[5]

> the fundamental mutations that affected and structured human intelligence at the end of the Upper Paleolithic and the first visible expressions that the early days of consciousness were emerging 60,000 years ago, are contemporaneous, both cause and effect, with the first funerary rituals ever known.[6]

That is to say, the oldest evidence available to evolutionary archaeology regard-ing the creation of symbols or the elaboration of meanings is the discovery of burial grounds. In these archaeological sites, it was found that alongside the bones, there are fragments of ochre painted skin, as well as small ornaments made of clay or bone fragments. This indicates that *homo sapiens* at that time, unlike any other animals, began to bury their dead and started to attribute meaning to death and to life, leading us to the all-important ascertainment that human consciousness begins with religion and art.

> The first painting support is the skin of a corpse, on which the ocher that comes from the earth is applied. It is the first canvas of a work of art conceived by a human. This is where we have the origin of art, religion and consciousness. It is

where we see the first evidence and proof that human intelligence was diversifying into specialized modalities for different purposes, such as technical efficiency to deal with the environment, life in society, language and symbolization.[7]

The contact with death was, therefore, fundamental for the birth of consciousness.

Despite being controversial, this theory of evolutionary ethnology reinforces the founding importance of the *afterlife archetype*, showing that this understanding has been present since the dawn of civilization.

Jung (1945, para. 804) suggests that it is not necessary to believe that death is a second birth capable of leading us to a survival in the afterlife, as the *consensus gentium* presents clear conceptions about it, which are expressed unequivocally in the great religions of the world that can be said to be a complicated system of preparations for the ending of life. Additionally, resorting to the psychological meaning of the idea and experience of rebirth, he reaffirms the psychic reality of the phenomenon: 'because it is ancestral, primordial and universal, the idea of rebirth is archetypal and, therefore, has psychic reality' (Stein, 2021, p. 89).

Human beings have an intense relationship with the future, unlike other animals, and here, the crux of the matter lies in that we know we are going to die. That leads us to infirm that the human being is the only metaphysical animal, the only one aware of their own death. 'Different systems of religion and metaphysics are thus other answers given throughout history to this question about the meaning of life, whose horizon is revealed by the experience of death' (Giacoia, 2005, p. 13).

This seems also to be present at the very beginning of mythology. Campbell (1988, p. 51) assumes that 'the earliest evidence we have of anything like mythological thinking is associated with grave burials.'

The way death was conceived was an important, if not a fundamental part in the conformation of who we are today, individually and collectively. And this first ritual that we are aware of, this founding rite, will be repeated in countless variations, in myths from all cultures around the planet, alive or revived in the different funeral rites. Death and its rites not only influenced the lives of the living, but they were also a determining factor in social, political and economic organization. In a bold way, we can say that death organizes the life of humans, including the structuring of the psyche itself.

Myths and rites of passage

Myths can be considered narratives of the archetypes, and rites, the enactment of the myths. Croatto (2001, p. 334), suggests that,

the rite appears as an analogy of the archetypal action shown in the myth. The myth says what the rite does. The rite and the word of the myth complement each other, without hegemony; the word alone, without anything else, leads to intellectualism or the ritualization of secondary things, and the rite alone, without anything else, degenerates into magic or loses its symbolic value.

The rite is born from the association of a practice with a belief. Funeral rites coincide with particular practices and reactions aroused by the death of others. Neolithic men and women multiplied the rites, attributing to them an increasingly rich symbolism: beautification of the body in preparation for ultra-terrestrial life, special care given to skulls, revived faces, a new ability to see proximity between the dead and the living. Such symbolism of life is yet another sign of a solid belief in a supra-earthly existence (Ries, 2020, p. 403).

I am thus calling the founding archetype of humanity that of an afterlife, mythologized and ritualized as a rite of passage, as a rite of transitioning from one status to another. However, unlike other rites of passage in which teenagers become adults, singles become married, pagans become Christians, here, we enter the unknown: the living becomes dead. In most cultures, after the rites of separation and transition are performed, the dead becomes an ancestor, a spirit, an ascendent reintroduced into society through the so-called rites of aggregation. In all cases, there is an underlying reintegration process, except for the dead who have not had their rites correctly performed.

In his seminal book *Rites of Passage*, anthropologist Arnold Van Gennep (2013) gives a special meaning to funerary rites, providing a clearer understanding of the acts that constitute them. He breaks them down into three stages: separation; margin or liminal (transition); and aggregation or reintegration. All rites of passage contain the three stages, but each emphasizes one specific aspect.

For example, birth rites emphasize aggregation, while funeral rites highlight separation. The marginal stage, specifically, will stand out in ceremonial performances, constituting an autonomous phase. The marginal stage assumes a central role in Van Gennep's ritual analysis, which, by examining the material rites of passage, reveals the importance of such an intermediate stage: rites linked to porticos, to the limits of the domestic world or to the borders between the profane and the sacred realms.

Those individuals for whom funeral rites have not been performed, as well as children who have not been baptized, whether christened or initiated, are destined to a sorrowful existence, unentitled to enter the world of the deceased. This makes them the most dangerous dead, for unable to enter the society there constituted, they wish to be reintegrated among the living, and, upon failure, they behave harshly. Together with those who leave no family and suicide victims, amongst others, they do not have the means of subsistence that the other dead find in their world, and therefore must seek them at the expense of the living. Furthermore, these homeless and uprooted dead often feel a bitter desire for revenge. In this way, funeral rites are simultaneously far-reaching utilitarian rites that help the survivors dispose of their eternal enemies.

On the importance and correct execution of the rites, Jung (1947, para. 214) is emphatic when he observes:

Insofar as earlier ages had in fact no knowledge of psychotherapy in our sense of the word, we cannot possibly expect to find in history any formulations similar to our own. But since the transformation of child into parent has been going on everywhere from time immemorial and, with the increase of consciousness being also experienced subjectively as a difficult process, we must conjecture the existence of various general psychotherapeutic systems which enabled man to accomplish the difficult transition-stages. And we do find, even at the most primitive level, certain drastic measures at all those moments in life when psychic transitions have to be effected. The most important of these are the initiations at puberty and the rite of marriage, birth and death. All these ceremonies . . . are observed with the utmost care and exactitude, are probably designed in the first place to avert the psychic injuries liable to occur at such times; but they are also intended to impart to the initiation and the preparation and teaching needed for life. The existence and prosperity of a primitive tribe are absolutely bound up with the scrupulous and traditional performance of the ceremonies. Wherever these customs fall into disuse . . . authentic tribal life ceases; the tribe loses its soul and disintegrates.

Additionally, let's remark that the dead were the first humans to have their abodes, to gather in the Necropolis, long before the living gathered in clans, tribes or cities. It is the dead and their cemeteries that have since the beginning been considered sacred. The so-called 'last abodes' of the first humans buried were actually the first ones, especially considering their status as nomads.

According to Mumford (1961/1973, p. 7),

mid the uneasy wanderings of Palaeolithic man, the dead were the first to have a permanent dwelling: a cavern, a mound market by a cairn, a collective barrow. These were landmarks to which the living probably returned at intervals, to commune with or placate the ancestral spirits. Though food-gathering and hunting do not encourage the permanent occupation of a single site, the dead at least claim that privilege. Long ago the Jews claimed as their patrimony the land where the graves of their forefathers were situated; and that well-attested claim seems to be a primordial one. The city of the dead antedates the city of the living. In one sense, indeed, the city of the dead is the forerunner, almost the core of every living city. Urban life spans the historic place between the earliest burial ground for dawn men and the final cemetery, the Necropolis, in which one civilization after another has met its end.

Wars have been unleashed for the right to have the land where the dead lie. Wars have been interrupted, as reported by the *Iliad* and the *Odyssey*, so that proper funeral rites could be carried out correctly. Rites are one of the most important collective expressions. It is said (Croatto, p. 343) that a group expresses its identity above all by their rites.

Therefore, the place where the ascendants lie, and the rites practised there have the power 'to couple.' Byung-Chul (2021) poetically describes rituals as coupling techniques.

They transform being-in-the-world into being-at-home. They make the world a reliable place. They are in time what a dwelling is in space. They make time habitable. Yes, they make it viable as a home. They put order in time, they furnish it.

The continuity of life expressed by the funerary monuments

During the Neolithic and Bronze Ages, the cult of the dead flourishes throughout the world and increases in geographically distant groups. The wide-scale transition of many human cultures during this period brings new symbolic elements, in addition to those already present in the early burial rituals.

Taking a leap of thousands of years, from the first burials, moving to 3,000–5,000 years ago, humans begin synchronously and across the planet to build funerary monuments, such as the mastabas and later the pyramids in Egypt and the sambaquis, among other monuments found around the world, an expression of the importance dedicated to death by all civilizations (see Figure 7.2).

Figure 7.2 Line drawing by Paulo Von Poser, *Funerary Monuments* (2022)

The funeral monuments

Funeral monuments that again and synchronically constellates in different parts of the world, when there is no possible communication among those peoples, once more show the correlation between synchronicity and the afterlife archetype.

> In addition to the underground mines . . . which were also a representation of the world of the dead, monumental temples and tombs spread everywhere. Firstly, mounds and then, with increasing enthusiasm, artificial mountains that had eminently funerary purposes, found in Egypt, in Mexico or in Peru.
>
> (Ribeiro, 2019, p. 49)

And then sambaquis in Brazil and dolmens in Europe.

In order to illustrate this, I'll turn to the detailed description by Ribeiro (2019). In Egypt, care for the dead begins with widespread construction of mastabas. The richest of them have rooms fully equipped for the afterlife, including tables with a funerary banquet, games, tools, weapons, vases, jars, decorated chests full of clothes and wigs, bathrooms with toilet utensils, cosmetics and washbasins, as well as miniatures and painted murals representing all of this.

In Ur,[8] a cemetery dating back 4,500 years ago and containing about 2,000 tombs has been found. Some of them have been attributed to the royalty due to the presence of abundant provisions as oxcarts, recreational games, musical instruments and cosmetics, beautifully and richly decorated sculpture and jewellery. There is also well-preserved evidence of a collective burial suggesting the presence of an entourage of soldiers and servants, supposedly necessary in the afterlife.

In southern Egypt, funerary pyramids spread up the Nile to Nubia, today Sudan. In the north, on the island of Malta, about 7,000 skeletons are deposited in an underground complex with interconnected chambers dug out of the rock 6,000 years ago. It is a necropolis built by a Mediterranean Neolithic culture characterized by huge tomb megaliths present in Crete and Troy, and similar to the dolmens and menhirs of northern Europe.

It is no different in the Americas. Between approximately 6000 and 1400 BCE, funerary mounds spread from the delta of the Amazon River to the delta of the La Plata River. They are structures up to 30 metres high, made of shells (sambaquis) or monticules (cerritos). At the archaeological site of Jabuticabeira II in the state of Santa Catarina, in Brazil, there is a huge sambaqui reaching 10 meters in width. It is estimated that more than 43,000 bodies were buried in it over a millennium of continuous occupation. Most of the sambaquis found are a hybrid of residence and cemetery. Here we see the dead and the living coexist. Necropolis and metropolis together, indicating death to be an essential part of life. In Canada and the United States, funerary mounds are prevalent, whereas on the Yucatan peninsula in Mexico, there is evidence of people sacrificed and thrown into caves called cenotes. In all cases mentioned, the offerings and the treatment given to the bodies constitutes further testimonies of the belief in rebirth, in another life or in a continuation of this one.

Afterlife, the ruling archetype

Later, the sacred books will strengthen this natural belief in life after death. In them, we have the thorough descriptions on how to enter the world of the dead. Tibetan, Mayan, Egyptian and archaeological remains show us the enormous importance given to death by successive civilizations in the following thousands of years, including Christianity and its Bible with premises of worthiness to enter or not the kingdom of heaven, of the beginning of another life after death, of rebirth in eternal life.

In the preface of *The Tibetan Book of the Dead* (Evans-Wentz, 2020, p. 54), Jung reaffirms his hypothesis that the archetype is an omnipresent but differentiated psychic structure that necessarily gives a certain shape and direction to each and every experience. It is the layer that contains those dynamic universal forms called the collective unconscious.

From the first burials, going through the funeral monuments and later, through the organization of the cities with the relevant role of cemeteries and funeral ceremonies, and considering the enormous amount of time, energy and resources used in these practices, we can consider that human societies were organized on a basis of a deep connection with the mystery of death and were deeply related to its corresponding myths, rites and symbols.

Under the influence of this afterlife archetype, millennia go by, and nothing changes much from this remote past until the age of rationalism, as Ariès (2014, p. 85) affirms:

> Until the age of scientific progress, human beings accepted the idea of a continued existence after death. One finds evidence of this belief in the first tombs of the Middle Palaeolithic period with burial offerings; and even today, in the midst of an age of scientific disbelief, one meets watered-down versions of the idea of continued existence or obstinate denials of immediate destruction.

In the few centuries that follow, with the arrival of rationalism in science, capitalism in the economy and materialism in philosophy, we start to slowly and inexorably disconnect from the past that made us human. From then on, we must prove that the unknown exists, that other worlds are possible. Furthermore, 'the society of production is dominated by the fear of death' (Byung-Chul, 2021, p. 92), whereas, as we have seen so far, archaic society does not acknowledge this separation between life and death.

Here we see an enormous difference from all previous civilizations, particularly in the newly invaded continents, where, at the dawn of modern Western society, the native inhabitants are not considered human, but rather soulless beings that need religious teachings to be worthy of eternal life. Since then, the original ancestors have been trying to warn us, through ways that include pacific resistance, rebellions and wars, of the possibilities of co-existence among different peoples and of respect towards diversity and nature. Also, their funerary rites are rich in teachings about the mythology that lies behind them and the belief that death is but an aspect of life, and not, as professed by our modern concept, something to be set apart from our minds while we just go on living our lives.

Covid pandemic in Brazil: aspects of a disconnection

A few centuries later, with the advent and development of information technology, the archetypal dimension present in the synchronic appearance of the first burials and, later, of the funerary monuments will give rise to the possibility for billions of people around the globe to receive the same information at the same time and in real time. Now, however, unlike at the two previously mentioned occasions, this fact no longer denotes the archetype of an afterlife as a synchronic expression of the collective unconscious.

The year 2020 starts with the Covid pandemic changing lives and lifestyles and making every inhabitant in the world face death (see Figure 7.3). In August 2021, an unknown woman expressed to me in a clinic that her mother died of Covid and when a person dies of Covid, they don't actually die, they disappear.

The passing of an individual has a distinctive, special meaning. When thousands of people are dying, however, losses seem to become nothing more than statistics. They nevertheless have a deep psychological impact in both the individual and the collective. Among other aspects of generalized extinction of all forms of gathering and sociability, pandemic-related restrictions include suppressing funeral rites as means of containing propagation of the virus: burials, services and other forms of

Figure 7.3 Line drawing by Paulo Von Poser, *Pandemic*, 2022

honouring the deceased and comforting the living are replaced by new, unusual formats, such as virtual funerals, online wakes and collective requiems, leaving millions of people worldwide grieving in solitude, confronting losses big and small. Pandemics, like wars, disorganize emotions.

In our practices and clinics, as well as in all other social, interpersonal or community relationships, meetings and reunions of all kinds instantly become unwelcome, dangerous, forbidden, deadly. Beyond the demise of individuals, the pandemic also causes the death of habits, of beliefs, of visions of the future and of representations of a shared world. So many losses that require mourning; mourning that does not take place.

> To have been plucked from a lot of things without having gone anywhere: this is a poignant description of the psychic state of the bereaved. The loss of the object is also the loss of the place that the survivor occupied in the life of the deceased [be it a person, a habit, a rite].
>
> (Khel, 2011, p. 18)

Beyond this individual trauma – the melancholic complex behaving like an open wound (Freud, 2011) – there is the collective one, the weakening and near extinction of rituals, especially those of passage, those related to death. We are now as far as it gets from the archetype that made us human.

In the first phase of the pandemic, with lockdowns and confinement, under the threat of deadly spread by contagion and a mortality unparalleled in history, we are faced with death in dramatic ways, each and every one of us. We see doctors having to choose which patients to let die without oxygen. We see piles of cadavers waiting to be buried, shortages of qualified morticians, a lack of coffins and tombs. The fear of dying, the death of loved ones, the radical changes in the ways of relating, the forced change of habits and routines, and so many other losses that go by without proper mourning.

Nonetheless, even in this most dreadful phase, we see positive repercussions around the world. Cleaner air, the return of birds to the cities, the regeneration of marine life and sightings of wild animals crossing our cities' avenues. Interpersonal relationships also benefit, with neighbours meeting and helping one another, a generalized drive for humanitarian aid and charity, increased social awareness and, in many cases, the strengthening of family ties.

In Brazil, however, we are not able to experience this positive aspect of the pandemic. Instead of the regeneration of the environment, what we see is an extreme devastation in all our rich and diverse biomes, such as the Pantanal and the Atlantic Forest, and particularly in the Amazon Forest that, according to scientists, may be getting to a point of no return.

Moreover, an indisputable disintegration of cultures can be observed, following the impossibility of proceeding with their rites. Distressing examples include the indigenous being deprived of their Kuarup,[9] or the ones who die in hospitals and are buried in mass graves in the city, far from their tribes. In all cases, what stands out is the pathology derived from the absence of mourning: melancholy and the collective disruption with their structural archetype.

Brazilian people, at this point, suffer the horrific consequences of destruction, extinction and genocide imposed by the disastrous actions or criminal omissions by the former president of the country and his supporters. How to understand this ruler who crosses all limits, who violates prohibitions, by acting as a somehow holder of death, practicing his power to kill on a daily basis, with no regard to the psychic dimension of his actions? How to measure the impact of this power held by the State on the life and death of populations? (Mbembe, 2018).

We watch, appalled, the secretary of the Private Insurance appointed by the government declare that the concentration of Covid-related deaths on the elderly means an improvement in public accounts, with the reduction of the pension deficit.[10]

We hear, alarmed, supporters of the government blasting their horns outside hospitals, in mistrust of their being in full capacity; eventually, these same supporters would physically invade health units, trying to prove themselves right,[11] bringing terror to the already-overwhelmed health workers and patients.[12]

We read about the violation of graves and coffins based on the denialist theory that they'd contain stones rather than bodies.[13]

We watch, incredulous and dumbfounded, the president of the Republic laughing and imitating Covid victims dying from asphyxiation, on national television.[14] We hear him downplay the threat posed by the virus, over and over: 'It is just a light flu.'[15] At the mark of 1,910 deaths per day, we hear him shout: 'Stop all this whining!'[16]

As we reach 10,000 deaths, with the entire health system on the verge of collapse, the president grunts, 'So what?' and goes jet skiing on the coast.[17]

At the 200,000 death count, we helplessly hear a maskless president say, before a devastated and traumatized nation who clamour for action: 'What do you want from me? I am not a mortician.'[18] This denialist president would later on pull the mask off a young kid's face during a ceremony.[19]

We witness the president of the Republic be convicted by the Permanent People's Tribunal for crimes against humanity and gross violation of human rights.[20]

We now reach the death count of 700,000 fellow countrymen, a world record in proportion to the number of inhabitants. Among them, the most vulnerable populations, the poor, Afro-Brazilians and the indigenous, are the ones who suffer the most.

What can be clearly observed at this point, not only in Brazil but also in other parts of the globe, is the complete banalization of death, which leads me to reaffirm the occurrence of an archetypal disconnection, related to humanity, to the collective unconscious, to the psychic reality, to the possibility to access, to believe in and to experience other worlds.

Jung stated that as our scientific knowledge increases, the degree of humanization of our world decreases (Jung, 1954, para. 585). Despite the record-breaking production of new vaccines against COVID-19, we see a deep psychic disorganization take place. 'Humans feel isolated in the cosmos since, no longer involved with nature, s/he has lost his/her unconscious emotional identification with natural phenomena. And these, in turn, have gradually lost their symbolic implications' (idem.).

Likewise, Von Franz, in an interview (1977, *The Urge of Life, the Urge of Death are the Same*) stated that 'This fear of death is the lack of ability to accept it. I think the non-acceptance of death is a neurotic symptom which goes with the entire neurosis of our civilization (. . .) We find ourselves disconnected from nature.'[21]

Recently, a Brazilian indigenous leader said:

> White people call us ignorant just because we are different from them. In fact, it is their thinking that is short and dark. They can't expand and elevate themselves because they want to ignore death. White people don't dream as far as we do. They sleep a lot and only dream about themselves.
>
> (Kopenawa and Albert, 2019).

Conclusion

For Hillman (2013, p. 105), we have a mistaken and unrefined view of death that goes no further than the physical. To this emphasis on physical death corresponds our emphasis on the physical body, not on the subtle body; in physical life, not in psychic life; literal rather than metaphorical. We have lost touch with the subtle forms of death, reflecting our unique ignorance of it, while the celebrations of many other cultures, Egyptian, Etruscan, ancient Greek and Tibetan, honour the world of darkness.

Hillman then asks, where does death go when it is no longer observed? According to him, psychology replies that it goes into the unconscious; the world of darkness has gone into the unconscious. To him, deep psychology is where today we find the initiatory mystery to the long journey of psychic learning, the worship of ancestors, the encounter with demons and shadows, the sufferings of hell.

And as for dreams, be it dreams of death, of the dead, or of the afterlife, as well as the experiences of those who went and returned, all point to the same paths: paths of eternity, the archetype that made us human.

Notes

1 'The synchronic effects are essentially linked to the appearance of archetypes' (Jafé, 1980, p. 54).
2 There are indications of graves since the Neanderthals, but no ritual remains. Surely, from 60,000 years ago, there were graves, and the oldest one is considered to be from 78,000 years ago. Cf. *National Geographic*, 2021.
3 Mastabas, a name that not by chance translates as *houses of eternity*, preceded the pyramids and were built for common people from the highest officials to very lowly servants.
4 Shell mounds with funerary purpose found along the coast of Brazil, which multiplied throughout the lake regions of the Americas, from southern Brazil to Canada. In Brazil, this civilization disappeared long before the Europeans' arrival.
5 Gambini, R. *Pássaro e Pedra*, 2023, in print.

6   When the text was written, the 78,000-year first grave had not yet been discovered.
7   Gambini, op cit.
8   Ur, an important Sumerian city-state, flourished from 3800 to 500 BCE.
9   A traditional funerary ceremony from the indigenous lands of Xingu, which brings together 16 ethnicities and more than 7,000 people, a ritual that resumes the creation of life through the resurrection rite, which synthesizes the eternal beginning while celebrating life. It represents the farewell of the dead and the end of the period of mourning.
10   Estadão, 28.05.2020
11   G1 – Paraná, 04.04.2021; São Paulo, in person.
12   UOL, São Paulo, 12.06.2020 – 'Presidente Bolsonaro pede para as pessoas arranjarem um jeito de invadirem hospitais para checar a ocupação de leitos.'
13   BBC News Brasil, 15.07.2020 – 'A farsa dos caixões vazios.'
14   BBC News Brasil, 27.11.2020
15   BBC News, 20.03.2020 e 27.03.2020
16   BBC News, 04.03.2021
17   CNN 28.04.2020
18   CNN 28.04.2020
19   G1, *Globo*, 24.06.2021
20   'The Permanent People's Court, meeting on September 1, 2022, considering the multiple witness and documentary evidence presented, in addition to information in the public domain, recognizes that the conduct of Jair Messias Bolsonaro: Consistent with having intentionally caused the death of several tens of thousands of people through his decisions taken as head of the Federal Executive Power, by rejecting the policy of isolation, prevention and vaccination in the face of the COVID-19 pandemic, constitutes a crime against the humanity. – Consistent in permanently inciting violence and publicly and continuously encouraging inhumane discrimination against a large part of the Brazilian people, it constitutes a threat to these groups that results in a reduction of their social space, configuring a serious violation of rights humans' (excerpt translated in, https://comissaoarns.org/documents/44/TPP-Sentenca-Bolsonaro-PORT-anexos.pdf).
21   Von Franz, YouTube, Interview Bollingen, 1977.

References

Ariès, P. (2014). *O Homem Diante da Morte* (Ribeiro, L. Trans.). São Paulo: Unesp.

Byung-Chul, H. (2021). *Capitalism and the Death Drive*. Cambridge and New York: Polity Press.

Campbell, J. (1988). *The Way of the Animal Powers*. Netherlands: Harper & Row.

Croatto, J.S. (2001). *As linguagens da experiência religiosa: uma introdução à fenomenologia da religião* (Gutiérrez, M.V. Trans.). São Paulo: Paulinas.

Eliade, M. (1978). *História das crenças e das ideias religiosas*. Rio de Janeiro: Zahar editores.

Evans-Wentz, W.Y. (2020). *O Livro Tibetano dos Mortos: Experiências Pós-morte no Plano do Bardo, Segundo a Versão do Lama Kazi Dawa-Samdup* (Oliveira, J.C.G. Trans.). São Paulo: Pensamento.

Freud, S. (2011). *Luto e Melancolia*. São Paulo: Cosac Naify.

Gambini, R. (2023). *Passaro e Pedra*, in print, to be published in 2023.

Gennep, A.V.G. (2013). *Ritos de Passagem*. Petrópolis: Vozes.

Geographic. (2021). May [Online]. www.nationalgeographic.com/science.

Giacoia, J.O. (2005). *A visão da morte ao longo do tempo*. Medicina (Ribeirão Preto). www.revistas.usp.br/rmrp/article/view/418.

Hillman, J. (2013). *O sonho e o mundo das trevas*. São Paulo: Vozes.

Jafé, A. (1980). *A Morte à Luz da Psicologia*. São Paulo: Cultrix.

Jung, C.G. (1940). Dogma and Natural Symbols. In *Collected Works Vol 11, Psychology and Religion. Psicologia e Religião*. São Paulo: Vozes.

Jung, C.G. (1945). The Soul and Death. In *Collected Works. Vol. 8. The Structure and Dynamics of the Psyche. Energia psíquica, a Dinâmica do Inconsciente*. São Paulo: Vozes.

Jung, C.G. (1947). Psychotherapy Today. In *Collected Works, Vol. 16. Practice of Psychotherapy*. São Paulo: Vozes.

Jung, C.G. (1950). Concerning Rebirth. In *Collected Works, Vol. 9i The Archetypes and the Collective Unconscious. Os Arquétipos e o Inconsciente Coletivo*. São Paulo: Vozes.

Jung, C.G. (1954). Archetypes of the Collective Unconscious. In *Collected Works, Vol 9i The Archetypes and Collective Unconscious*. São Paulo: Vozes.

Khel, M.R. (2011). Preface Melancolia e criação. In Freud, S. (ed.), *Luto e Melancolia*. São Paulo: Cosac Naify.

Kopenawa, D. and Albert, B. (2019). *A queda do céu: Palavras de um xamã yanomami*. São Paulo: Companhia das Letras.

Mbembe, A. (2018). *Necropolitica*, ed. São Paulo: N-1 Edicoes.

Mithen, S. (2003). *A pré-história da mente*. São Paulo: Unesp.

Mumford, L. (1961/1973). *The City in History. Its Origins, Its Transformations and Its Prospects*. London and New York: Penguin Books.

Ribeiro, S. (2019). *O oráculo da noite*. São Paulo: Companhia das Letras.

Ries, J. (2020). *Mito e rito: As constantes do sagrado* (Leite, S.C. Trans.). São Paulo: Vozes.

Shreeve, J. (2021). *Child's Grave Is the Oldest Human Burial Found in Africa*. Washington, DC: National Geographic.

Spengler, O. (1973). *A Decadência do Ocidente – Esboço de Uma Morfologia da História Universal* (4th ed.). Rio de Janeiro: Forense Universitária.

Stein, M. (2021). *Sincronizando tempo e eternidade: ensaios sobre psicologia junguiana* (Rosas, M. Trans.). São Paulo: Pensamento Cultrix.

Von Franz, M.L. (1977). YouTube Interview, Bollingen.

Part IV

Grief, mourning and loss

Clinical dimensions

Chapter 8

The problem of death and meaning for depth psychology

Erik Goodwyn

Introduction

Depth psychology has a challenge that I will call 'the problem of death': since what happens to us after we die is very mysterious, but high in stakes, our patients are often faced with trepidation about it. Not only does the inescapability of death create death anxiety within us, but it emerges again when we lose our loved ones. What happened to them? What will happen to me? These questions are of course universal. Since there is not a clear, agreed-upon answer to the problem of death, a modest, epistemologically cautious stance on this problem is quite reasonable for depth psychology.

Nevertheless, this very stance leads to a specific *problem of death for depth psychology*. The reason is the aforementioned epistemological stance has clinical consequences, as what our patients are craving most in these moments is an answer to this mystery. As I will show, this *lack* of a satisfying answer often feeds into their suffering. Thus, without some kind of technique or tools to handle the problem of death, we may be undermining our own therapeutic efforts.

At its core, the issue is that we have no agreed-upon set of *meanings* that we can offer our patients who are either going through a painful loss or facing death themselves to help them navigate this important and unavoidable event. This is probably why Jung emphasized the general importance of a 'religious' attitude and targeting one's overall sense of life's *meaningfulness*:

> About a third of my cases are not suffering from any clinically definable neurosis, but from the senselessness and aimlessness of their lives. I should not object if this were called the general neurosis of our age.
>
> (Jung, 1954, para. 83)

These issues are amplified many times over in patients facing death. Because of its nature, death forces us to tackle this issue of meaninglessness head on. Religions, however, unlike depth psychology, are not so timid about this issue. In contrast to depth psychology, religions boldly state what death means, in defiance of the evident mystery of it. Though cross-culturally the supposed meaning of death varies a

DOI: 10.4324/9781003313304-13

lot, there are a number of common features which I will explore in greater depth in this chapter. But the point is that for religion, death *always* has an available meaning within the religious/spiritual framework. Death is never meaningless. This is no accident.

The problem of death for depth psychology, then, is that depth psychology at present simply doesn't have such tools. In a desire to be religion-neutral, we have attempted to steer clear of placing any meaning like this onto death and broader questions of existence, and in its place we find what I shall call 'timid agnosticism,' a reluctance to ascribe any sort of meaning to death and spiritual/metaphysical matters, whatever the reason. Thus, despite good reasons for doing so, the avoidance of assertion about the mystery of death and the afterlife effectively robs us of an important opportunity to help our patients obtain what they so desperately are seeking: meaning.

Regardless of rationale, we should also recognize that psychiatry and depth psychology still have an element of Freud's staunch atheism as a guiding principle, though that appears to be changing (Freud, 1927/2010; Bienenfeld and Yager, 2007; Koenig and Larson, 2001). This is not to make any pejorative judgment against atheism, but rather simply to recognize that metaphysical stances on the problem of death have their own effects on treatment – if we are advocating for one or the other, we need to do it with awareness.

But why should this matter? What does a religious viewpoint actually do? Is it, in fact, merely dismissible wish-fulfilment, as Freud theorized? Or is there something more complex going on? To answer that, we must explore the primary *function* of the psyche, a subject that has not garnered nearly enough attention in the depth psychology literature. This question is fundamental to the problem of death. We cannot simply fold this question back onto our patients, and ask them, 'Well, what do YOU think it means?' Not only is that too easy, often if we do that, we just get 'I don't know.' We are the experts here, after all, not they. What we need is a reasonable, scientific and appropriate set of tools to *help* patients build meaning, for as we will see, it is primarily *the lack of meaning* that drives their suffering.

The primacy of meaning: a thought experiment

Recall or imagine the most painful loss in your life. Now, let's say psychiatry has become so advanced that we now have a pill that will erase any and all pain of the loss you are now feeling and it is 100% effective. Ask yourself: would you take this pill? Nearly everyone I have ever asked this question to or posed this thought experiment for has told me 'no.' But why? Isn't that counter-intuitive? Many popular forms of therapy and psychiatric practice focus heavily on 'symptom reduction.' Since pain is a symptom, psychotherapeutic techniques would therefore be measured in their ability to reduce pain. Yet here is an instance in which people are saying they would *choose to feel psychological pain!* Why?

To answer this question, we need to explore what psychological pain is. Psychological pain is related to physical pain in the fact that they have overlapping neural correlates (Chelnokova et al., 2014; Eisenberger and Lieberman, 2005; Kitayama and Park, 2010; Petrovic et al., 2008). It would appear that during the course of evolution, as greater complexity developed in the central nervous system, the existing pain system became utilized for more complex and sophisticated situations other than simple tissue damage detection and behaviour modification. This sort of 'exaptation' (modification of a neutral trait into an adaptive trait over time) is very common in evolution – nature always uses what it already has available. Thus, for example, it has been recognized in *homo sapiens* that *loneliness* feels extremely painful because it makes use of the same neural correlates as tissue damage (Chelnokova et al., 2014; Eisenberger and Lieberman, 2005; Kitayama and Park, 2010; Petrovic et al., 2008). The constant equation of lonely feelings with physical pain, therefore, is more than a mere poetic flourish or indulgence of songwriters. It is a precise description.

Using the example of loneliness helps us to understand how. Loneliness is a far more complex situation than tissue damage. It requires the perception of social isolation, which imports all the mechanisms involved in the organisms assessment of one's attachment status and vulnerability, along with a host of other very complex environmental and life-history situations. Loneliness, therefore, is an assessment of overall *meaning* for the organism. One might initially think this is the distinction of relevance between mental and physical pain, but in fact, this is not so. Tissue damage is itself an assessment of meaning as well. In this case, the pain is a non-verbal expression of meaning related to the relative and current toxicity of the immediate environment. The only difference, then, between loneliness and tissue damage is in the breadth and depth of environmental information that must be incorporated into the process in order for the system to register the subjective qualia of pain.[1] In both cases, the system informs the organism that something is wrong and that behavioural action should be modified to bring about a less painful environment, if possible. This meaning-making effort naturally applies to more than just pain and can be seen in the way memory is processed, the construction of confabulations in neurally impaired persons, and in the construction of dream content (Goodwyn, 2018).

This suggests, then, that the brain and psyche have an identifiable function. That function is the making of meaning. In other words, *the brain is a meaning-making organ, and the psyche aims toward the creation of meaning*. Put another way, the brain is a highly evolved organ designed to assess one's environment, as balanced against past events and future predictions, to wind up with a continually updating Gestalt of *how am I doing right now and what should I do?* This function is the same in all organisms with a central nervous system. Therefore, the difference between pain being caused by tissue damage and pain being caused by highly complex assessments of current social environment, coloured by key past events, is merely one of degree. In both instances, the brain and psyche are functioning toward the same goal: discerning what it all *means*, so that the organism may react appropriately toward pro-survival behaviours.

The meaning of pain

But (at the risk of sounding too clever by half) what does 'meaning' mean? In the model I am building in this chapter, 'meaning' has a precise definition: *meaning is an expression of context.* It is an array of relations between the subject and numerous environmental objects. This environmental configuration connects to that subjective qualia. This experience of this other person connects to those learned and innate emotional states. This most recent event of loss connects with those innately driven expressions of pain, as well as those culturally learned linguistic connotations, images and symbols.

Since humans have enormously elaborated brains and psyches, this meaning-making function can be quite complex and sophisticated – and of course, the drawback is that it can also go wrong in more ways, too. Snails, for example, do not seem to suffer from ennui. Nevertheless, the increase of complexity must have provided more benefit than drawbacks. And as the meaning-making became more complex and sophisticated, it makes sense that evolution would build a conscious ego as a secondary centre of the psyche designed to handle difficult problems handed to it by all the auxiliary systems, so that it can manage them in far greater depth of analysis, both rational and emotional. This became what we now call the conscious ego in *homo sapiens*. The primary method through which the ego accomplishes its aforementioned function is through its *recursivity*. In other words, in its effort to make meaning of the current-environment-as-coloured-by-the-past, it contains the older, more primitive tissue-damage assessments and integrates it with all the other input to obtain a higher-order meaning assessment that the simple tissue damage assessment cannot achieve. That is to say, with the evolution of the conscious ego, the psyche came to be able to assess meaning more comprehensively. The final outcome of an assessment of one's surroundings came to be able to incorporate pain *itself.*

Hence, we do not merely feel pain as perhaps a frog might, responding with primitive reflexes and evasion programs, but we higher-order mammals (and likely some birds) can ask ourselves, what does this pain *mean?* And with that ability came the ability to override and ignore the older, more instinctive proclivity to always flee from pain-causing stimuli. We know not only from experience but from the historical record that many people have been able to endure and even overcome tremendous physical pain for many reasons, *provided they had a significant meaning-based motivation to do so.*

In order for this behaviour to be possible, though, pain itself can no longer be the final arbiter of our motivations. It is possible for us to override it. But *toward what end* do we override it? In my opinion, we override physical and emotional pain the same way the central nervous system of any animal overrides any sensation it considers irrelevant. The guiding principle is *meaning.* If the brain and psyche determine that a given pain is an integral part of an overall more comprehensive meaning, the pain can be mitigated to a degree. Why, then, one might ask, is this ability to override pain not all-encompassing? Because, in general, I think the widespread ability to completely ignore pain would not likely be compatible with continued survival, as persons who are unable to feel pain for genetic reasons have shown (Indo et al., 1996). Nature has settled upon a middle ground, in which we can override pain *to a degree*, but cannot completely negate it except in extraordinary situations.

The point of all this is to emphasize the primacy of meaning over simple pain sensations – even that of grief itself, which likely evolved far earlier in our mammalian evolution (Panksepp, 2004). The modern human brain prioritizes meaning *over* pain. Moreover, this implies that the *absence* of meaning may actually *amplify* our pain to a degree. Evidence for this comes from the grief counselling literature itself (e.g., Wittouck et al., 2011). One of the most challenging aspects of helping one navigate painful loss is when the bereaved feel it was 'senseless.' If the death is seen as 'meaningless,' the grief is *amplified*. Part of the goal of grief counselling is to help patients 'make sense of' the death – this is, of course, an exercise in meaning construction. And because of the earlier assessment of the psyche as a meaning-making process, and the brain as a meaning-making organ, I believe this fact about grief has far wider implications for the psyche as a whole. For it means that even physical torture and the tragic loss of a loved one can be endured sometimes, provided there is meaning to mitigate it.

But what about meaninglessness? If the finding and construction of meaning is the primary function of our evolved psyche, then it makes sense that if the system fails to find any meaning, it would lead to an extremely dysphoric and defensive state. In order to drive this function, evolution would have needed to put a huge amount of emphasis on being able to find meaning via intense dysphoria designed to motivate meaning-seeking behaviour, and pleasure at meaning-*finding*. If no meaning can be found, it appears from the earlier assessment that the pain is heightened, and/or the meaninglessness *itself* becomes a source of pain. This pain-of-meaninglessness then generates a positive feedback loop of pain-meaninglessness-horror-more pain-etc., spiralling toward suicidal ideation. This means that meaning is the ultimate driver and pain is secondary to it. Thus, whereas pain can be tolerated if meaning can be found in it, *meaninglessness itself cannot be tolerated*.

So how do we tackle the problem of death?

Now that we have established that our primary goal to help individuals facing death and loss is one of meaning construction, we can see how humanity has already intuited ways to combat the problem of death through the use of mourning rituals (Goodwyn, 2017).

Early anthropologists: van Gennep and Hertz on mourning rituals

In the early part of the 20th century, anthropologist Arnold van Gennep (1960), in his *The Rites of Passage*, famously identified a tripartite structure in virtually all rituals which is still highly regarded today. The first of the three phases he identified is the *separation* phase, in which the target of the ritual is symbolically separated from the main social group in various ways such as hair cutting, body marking, isolation in the wilderness or physical removal to a sacred area and so forth. The second phase is the *transition* phase, in which ritual participants must stay for a while in a state of 'neither/nor,' where they are in neither the old state nor the new – for example, in rites of passage into adulthood, participants are neither child nor adult while in the transition phase. Military recruits in basic training are another example, which during the training the new recruits are not civilians any longer, but also they are not fully military members either. Finally, the third phase is *incorporation*, in which the participant is moved into the new social state. This is accomplished by body marking, hand-fasting, communal meals and many other acts.

Van Gennep demonstrates that this tripartite structure can be found in nearly all rituals worldwide, but mourning rituals are perhaps the most dramatic of all ritual events, with the deceased as the target of the ritual. Separation rites surrounding death (Van Gennep, 1960, pp. 164–165) include transporting the corpse in a special way, burning their possessions, killing slaves/spouses/animals, washing, purifying and various taboos. The grave site is itself separated through various ritual means. Sometimes there are mock battles for the corpse by various family members, which seems to involve fighting against losing a beloved member, and various physical methods for separating the components of the corpse into its various parts of body and/or soul. Incorporation rites usually involve stories about the journey to the dead and often involve a specialist reciting a vision or story of the deceased joining with the ancestors.

The double burial

Anthropologist Robert Hertz's classic essay on mortuary ritual (Hertz, 2009, pp. 197–212) complements van Gennep's analysis. Hertz reviews the variety of cultures that practice 'double burial'; a practice in which the newly dead corpse is buried (or exposed) for a time in a separate and special location (an example of the transitional state), then exhumed after a prescribed amount of time and buried again somewhere else. The practices on which Hertz based his analysis were observed in Indonesia predominantly, but they are by no means exclusive to that region and can be found in many areas around the globe. Here we can see evidence of van Gennep's tripartite structure, with the first burial representing a liminal state between newly dead and permanently buried. Further subdivisions are evident as well, between newly dead and quickly separated from the group, followed by a variable-length liminal state where relatives often keep vigil with the deceased, followed by burial.

One widespread belief during the time when the corpse is newly dead is that at certain times the corpse is *vulnerable to attack and must be defended* by various means, such as not only standing vigil but keeping a fire or incense burning, protecting orifices to keep spirits from entering the corpse and possessing it and so on (Hertz, 2009, p. 199). This particular cross-cultural theme, that of *helping the deceased*, is very prominent and will play a large part in our comparative analysis later. During this dangerous transitional state, the corpse not only needs help from the bereaved, but is also potentially dangerous itself when in this state living marginally in two worlds; the condition of being dead is in many places seen as a cause for suffering that the deceased want to share on the living. In many cultures, close relatives *share* this state and must abide by numerous taboos to symbolize the shared state of death, which are then lifted when the time of temporary burial is over. Variations on the practice of temporary burial and its symbolism are found all over the world, from Central Australia to Polynesia to North and South America, with temporary treatment ranging from burial to exposure under various conditions.

All these practices provide the bereaved, in physical, concrete terms, with a vivid picture of what is going on with the deceased's soul, as the body and its processional change is seen as a symbol of what the soul is going through. Note that all of these acts become highly potent *expressions of meaning* at a visceral, non-verbal and imagistic level. Viewed from an academic distance (i.e., reading about it but nothing more), it may be easy enough to dismiss all this as mere hokum, but participating in it is another matter, as the very acts in physical space necessarily incorporate not merely the cerebrum but the entire body. More on this later.

As in other cultures, Hertz notes that among the Indonesian peoples he observed, violent sudden death, death in childbirth, drownings, death by lightning and suicides are often given special treatment, as their bodies 'inspire the most intense horror and are got rid of precipitately . . . their bones are not laid with those of other deceased members of the group who have died a normal death' (p. 211). Later, we will see that, in Western psychological terms, such deaths are associated with higher rates of Complicated Grief (hereafter CG). Hertz argues that this distinction is made in many societies because of the intensity of the emotion impressed upon the survivors, in whom no rite can alleviate their suffering. This belief has parallels, contrasts and variations in other areas, such as in the Americas (Hultcrantz, 1979), where there are separate otherworlds and afterlife fates for those who die in such a manner. Note that it is unlikely to be a coincidence that these very kinds of deaths are the most likely to inspire feelings of 'senselessness,' and the intense quest to 'understand why' the death occurred. Not surprisingly, the response these cultures developed was *more* intense ritual activity and specially created rites to counteract the horror such events inspire.

In any case, the final resting place is not a permanent condition, but is frequently seen as a new birth – death/birth symbolism is seen in all kinds of rituals globally, and funerary rites are no exception. Comparing numerous mourning rituals, including Christian ones, Hertz concludes 'at whatever stage of religious evolution we place ourselves, the notion of death is linked with that of resurrection; exclusion is always followed by a new integration' (Hertz, 2009, p. 208). This is supported by the related cross-cultural link between death of the body and death of the cosmos, where the mourning ritual centres around the idea that the body is a symbol of the cosmos, so its death comes to be symbolized by the destruction and rejuvenation of the universe (Parry, 2009, pp. 266–268), providing an important *narrative restructuring mechanism*, which is another important theme. Note how all of these practices aid in the construction of meaning, and not merely through verbal discourse, but visceral blood-and-guts action in time and space. It would appear the importance of this activity was discovered by our most ancient ancestors and has been elaborated on endlessly throughout world ritual practice.

Cross-cultural theme: the dangerous dead

Mourning rituals have long contained two major elements: the first is the ritual containment of the fresh corpse with various methods used to keep the restless soul at bay, and the secondary rites, which occur some weeks to years later (depending on the status and power of the dead individual, as well as culture of origin), where the dead are firmly incorporated into the realm of the ancestors. Archaeologist Timothy Taylor recognizes these themes are extremely old and enduring (Taylor, 2002, p. 27). The second state – the transitional state – is recognized by the overwhelming majority of cultural data to be the most dangerous state, wherein the dead can wander and wreak havoc on the living (Taylor, 2002, p. 118). Other parallels exist in history. Evidence of rites of passage and second burial, for example, have been found in Natufian culture (Taylor, 2002, p. 226), and second burial has been observed in Central Asia, North and South America, Melanesia and Greece, among other places (Metcalf and Huntington, 1991, p. 35).

In Hindu belief, as in many others, violent and sudden death is believed to cause the deceased to be bitter and liable to torment the living either with nightmares or evil events (Parry, 2009, p. 271). Proper rituals must be performed to prevent this, and they usually involve the survivors *sharing in the deceased state symbolically* through not shaving, washing, wearing shoes or shirt, sleeping on the ground, avoiding hot food and abstaining from sex. Such a state is usually associated with an uncanny power for mourners and for ascetics who adopt such practices permanently (Parry, 2009, p. 277). It is difficult to imagine devising a more potent practice for the building of meaning than these.

Cross-cultural theme: ritually sculpting the emotionality of mourning

In many cultures, the closest survivors of the deceased share in his/her fate and are subject to quarantine and taboos (Metcalf and Huntington, 1991, pp. 90–95). As pointed out by anthropologists (Bloch and Parry, 1982), the two primary objectives apparently associated with cross-cultural death rites is to facilitate the transition of the dead from the world of the living to the Otherworld, however visualized, and to facilitate survivor's acceptance of the death and alteration of social life subsequent to it. The Wari, an Amazonian tribe, for example, for months after a death will go to all the places frequented by the deceased (favourite hunting, fishing or sitting spots, etc.), then cut the vegetation in a wide circle, burn it and sweep over the circle. As they do this they report thinking about the dead person, recalling and honouring their life, then afterward report that 'there is not much sadness there' (Conklin, 2009, p. 250). Again, these practices construct meaning not only through verbal and conceptual means, but through meaningful action in physical space. Such practices, since they are not merely verbal and conceptual, require a greater deal of commitment to them that makes it more difficult to equivocate about – one can either do such things or not do them, and doing them creates meaning, therefore, in a more tangible and lasting manner as a result, forcing one out of an ambivalent state.

In this manner, mourning rituals appear to serve grief processing. Grieving is a very natural process observed in numerous social animals (Panksepp, 2004), but in humans it is elaborated in a great number of different ways. These variations are numerous, but not arbitrary, and constrained by various biological and psychological universals that work in concert with surrounding cultural ideas (also so constrained) to produce the varieties of mourning rituals that exist. Though by no means limited to mourning, one commonly discussed purpose of funeral rites is to help participants express and process their grief in meaningful ways.

The example of the Tlingit, a North American coastal tribe documented in the 19th century onward by Western scholars, is illustrative. Like so many unrelated cultures, the practice of taking the body out a side door, mourners cutting their hair, fasting, painting themselves black, and singing death songs are also observed among the Tlingit (Kan, 2009, pp. 286–302). The Tlingit also invoke the ancestors by speaking their names and recalling their deeds (Kan, 2009, p. 289), and grief is expressed by mourners in sacred and highly treasured crying songs, by the sanctioned flow of tears during specific times, and by the male mourners striking the floor with their staffs four times, where they are instructed to 'pour all their grief' into the act of striking the ground (Kan, 2009, p. 291). Note the especially psychological advice *and symbolization of emotion in physical action here, as well as the culturally sanctioned, but strictly bounded expression of emotion.* These are common features of the ritual construction of meaning (Goodwyn, 2016).

Warmth and comfort are equated as the hosts adorn the mourners in various clothing during the ceremony as a way to symbolize and concretize providing comfort to them, and reinforced by the exchanging of gifts (sometimes accompanied by rubbing the gift on the forehead of the recipient). Funerals are, as in other places, associated with competitive games among families of the deceased as well as feasts, both of which emphasize the unity of them while allowing families to jockey for political position in a non-violent manner. Tlingit oratory is described as a great art form based on the idea that words had the power to heal or harm; thus, speeches were used to smooth out, strengthen and heal the mourner's 'inside' (Kan, 2009, p. 295), an idea quite similar to the principles of therapy based on depth psychology.

The Tlingit began such speeches with genealogical lists (not unlike those found in ancient European literature), which had the effect of connecting the speaker's ties with others present, and with culturally ideal typical emotions inherent in links such as a father's love for his children. Next, the speaker presented a story from his clan, of someone in great peril who is saved by some kind of mythical helper (god, animal spirit, etc.), with the host's sorrow equated with the hero's suffering, the guest's love with that of the mythical helper. Grief and non-grief are then pictured as opposites, compared with hunger/eating, light/dark, wet/dry, war/peace, and so on. Finally, the story is ended with the hero being saved by the mythical helper and the opposites reconciled. Love songs are then recited, bringing in images of reconciliation and fertility. This example is illustrative for a number of reasons. First, it shows us specifically how the meaning – i.e., the needed expression of context – is constructed for the Tlingit. The host's context is built with the elucidation and visuospatial depiction of her or his connections to the great ancestors of the past, the gods and the cultural narratives of heroes. Then, the host's grief *itself* is connected to cosmic opposites and mythical helpers, followed by music, poetry and dancing to express the context along channels other than mere verbal and cerebral. By the end, the host is connected to the entire universe in an ultimate expression of meaning.

This is but one example among many such rituals that appear to deal directly with the symbolization, enactment, visualization and concretization of grief and existential dread (among many other things) which solidify the context, and hence meaning, of the bereaved and deceased. Anthropologists Robert Jay Lifton and Eric Olson, for example, 'believe [the] influence of death on psychological life is due to the importance of symbolization in mental activity rather than to what Freud called a death instinct' (Lifton and Olson, 2009, p. 32). Lifton and Olson draw from Freud and Jung in their conception of the *meaning* of mourning ritual symbolism and argue that it aims toward 'symbolic immortality,' expressed in many ways.

Lifton and Olson recognized that ritual is therefore *highly analogous to psychotherapy*:

> The process of therapy in psychiatry involves a symbolic reordering analogous to that which occurs in experiential transcendence. When therapy is successful, a patient feels a widening of the space in which he lives. It is as if the narrow images through which he has seen reality have been reorganized so that the past appears more coherent and the future more inviting. Death imagery is reconceived, and life imagery of connection, integrity, and movement becomes dominant.
>
> (2009, p. 38).

This corresponds to the ever-recurrent linking of death to sexuality, fertility and vigorous assertions of continued life among the bereaved, and, in the end, the linking of the death to ultimate expressions of cosmic meaning for the individual. I would add, however, that Lifton and Olson neglect the important effect of focusing the bereaved on the needs of the *deceased* in deflecting the sting of death, as it becomes a restructuring of the relationship between the two in which such transcendence can be shared. This is an important difference, as cross-cultural death rites generally do *not* neglect this important piece of the process. I believe this commonly encountered attitude in depth psychology may worsen the problem of death; therefore, I do not think we should neglect the deceased. More on this later.

Cross-cultural theme: cultural beliefs and the emotional expression of mourning

The way participants in mourning rituals express emotion varies widely from dramatic outbursts of vehement emotional expression to self-consciously stoic non-expression. What is universal is that emotion *must* be dealt with in some manner or another; it is never ignored, and each culture over time develops a particular technique or belief system to 'sculpt' (if you will) the raw emotionality of mourning and loss. Several examples will suffice to illustrate the ways in which the emotion of loss is processed, constrained, enhanced, diminished and/or otherwise transformed via ritual expression.

The relationship between emotion and ritual is complex – it is not a simple matter of one causing the other. In studying various cultures, Metcalf and Huntington (1991) note that ritual weeping is closely and tightly structured within each culture at funeral rites. Many cultures have nearly on-cue weeping, but only at specifically outlined times, such as when the body is in a specific hut, just before the secondary burial, or when specialists recite highly poetic and/or theatrical lamentation performances. Amid all the variation, weeping occurs in carefully specified contexts and is a symbol with meaning and not necessarily a spontaneous show of emotion (1991, p. 47). Metcalf and Huntington summarize their assessment of the way grief and mourning rituals interact:

> It was and is our opinion that the psychic process of grieving only partially intersects with the performance of death rites. As we plainly say, it may be that ritual sometimes aids the process, but it could as easily be no help at all, or even an extra burden to bear.
>
> (Metcalf and Huntington, 1991, p. 5)

Among the Northern Cheyenne, grieving and weeping over the dead is expected to end in four days, lest mourners be given 'something else to cry about,' for death is seen as a release from a life of hard struggle, rewarded with reunion with the departed and a beautiful abode with the Creator god and the culture hero Sweet Medicine (Straus, 2009, p. 75). Here we see, again, that the actions and emotional behaviours of the bereaved are connected to the deceased in a spiritual manner, and the bereaved are called upon to *act in a manner which emphasizes the needs of the deceased*. Among the Andaman Islanders studied by A.R. Radcliffe-Brown, weeping has a strong ceremonial character to it that is, in relation to death, confined to certain events, including weeping over the corpse after death, over the bones of the dead man when they are recovered for purposes of second burial, at the end of the mourning period as joined by those who have not wept yet (2009, p. 151). Weeping accompanies other occasions such as the reunion of separated friends and weddings and is 'obligatory, a matter of duty' (p. 154). Here we see the expression of tears as having important spiritual consequences, for the deceased is a powerful cross-culturally resonant idea. This practice creates meaning by demanding *action* – an especially powerful means of creating meaning discussed earlier.

Mourning in the West: historical examples

A large number of the aforementioned themes found in widespread areas can be found in the ancient cultures of the West. Among medieval European cultures, for example, excessive weeping was believed to cause the deceased extreme discomfort in the next world and would result in the dead visiting the living in anger (LeCoutoux, 1996, p. 223). The idea of the journey to the land of the dead also existed among the ancient Germanic and Celtic tribes of northern Europe (Cunliffe, 1999; Davidson, 1968, 1988, 1993; Monaghan, 2006; Turville-Petre, 1964).

The belief that the newly dead were in an uncanny and dangerous (to the living) state, for example, was extremely widespread:

> a potentially vast number of revenants and ghosts existed: the deceased who sought vengeance or someone to avenge them or that aspired to ritual burial. They were discontented and envious – therefore evildoing dead. These beliefs can be found among all Indo-European peoples.
>
> (LeCouteux, 1996, p. 16)

The fact that the deaths which appear the most senseless and random are the ones which require the most ritual counterbalancing adds further credibility to the idea that such activities were developed to aid and enhance the psyche's meaning-making efforts, so as to stave off the existential horror loss can inspire. Often rituals used to quiet the dead involve decapitation or dismemberment of the corpse, pinning or staking the corpse in place (to prevent it from walking around on its own), or cremation (1996, pp. 19–31). Additional ritual effort was often done (as in cases cross-culturally) in situations of uncanny or emotionally intense deaths (LeCouteux, 1996, p. 29, n.23). Also prevalent in Western historical examples are the folkloric themes of the helpful bereaved and a focus on the needs of the deceased.

Other common beliefs that we have seen reported in other cultures appear in European folklore, saga, and folk practice across many centuries (collected by LeCouteux, 1996, pp. 32–44; see also Jaffe, 1964) and include the following:

Practices that seek to help the spirit of the deceased in their confused newly dead state:

- The corpse's eyes and mouth had to be closed, in order to prevent the spirit from leaving the corpse prematurely, as this occurred at common orifices.
- The dead body needed to leave the house where death occurred through an unusual opening (like the side of the house) that was rapidly closed up. This was done to confuse the corpse's spirit to keep it from returning.
- The dead are often bound either in a pinned or stitched shroud, or their limbs corded together with various sacred or profane ties to keep the spirit from reanimating the corpse. Stakes were often used to pin the corpse in place.

Practices that seek to soothe the spirit of the deceased and aid their journey to the Otherworld:

- Vigils for the recently dead are common, often including singing, games, and dancing.
- Food, tokens, favourite objects and tools are buried with the corpse, also with money, along with slaughtered animals and/or sometimes a slave or spouse ritually killed beforehand, in the case of high-ranking dead. Subsequent dead could be given any forgotten items with the idea that they would be given to the formerly dead in the next world (LeCouteux, 1996, p. 159).
- Means of transportation, from boat to new shoes, are provided to the corpse to ensure safe travel to the Otherworld.

Beliefs that emphasize the occult powers of the deceased, which encouraged proper treatment of the corpse with spiritual rewards or punishments (i.e. restructure the relationship of the bereaved to the deceased):

- Honouring the dead is a duty that brings with it blessings of good harvest, luck in battle, etc., and maledictions when breached or ignored.
- The dead have power over animals and local vegetation, and local weather patterns.
- The dead can take animal form – often marked by characteristic colour (often grey or red).
- Could cause madness in the living if displeased.

In Western industrialized nations, of course, such practices and beliefs are encountered very rarely, though they often crop up in spontaneous fantasies and dream material clinically. Such instances should not be taken likely, as they may be manifestations of the psyche's inherent meaning-making efforts. If we allow these eruptions of the unconscious to pass uncommented on, we may miss valuable meaning-making material.

Death ways in modern nations

Historian Claude LeCouteux argues that much of the aforementioned kinds of beliefs and practices about the dead such as the dangerous transitional period, the ability of the dead to affect the land and the many needs of the dead from the bereaved are eroded by industrialization and disconnection of humans from the land. Such practices typically 'exist wherever a human community lives closely connected to nature. . . . The farmer, the mountain-dweller, and the sailor have experienced ghosts and tend to believe in them' (LeCouteux, 1996, pp. 226–227). This is no doubt part of the picture. The massive economic, cultural, and technological changes undergirding modern industrial society likely have their part as well.

It is interesting, however, that in the United States, despite the vast number of cultural backgrounds present, there is remarkable uniformity in the method of death rite, and though exceptions exist, they are rare and limited to small, tight-knit, isolated communities. For the rest of us, generally a dying person is sequestered in a sterile environment such as a hospital or nursing home, in which the rest of the bereaved are removed from the dying process. Then, a doctor pronounces a person dead at an agreed-upon time, whereupon the corpse is rapidly removed to a funeral parlour, where embalming, institutionalized 'viewing' and disposal by burial occurs (Metcalf and Huntington, 1991, p. 194). This commonality of practice exists despite widely disparate cosmology and beliefs about the afterlife, and very commonly no beliefs or extremely vague beliefs are all that are held among participants: 'Just how Americans conceive of death [is] a thorny issue. Few seem able to adopt a thoroughgoing agnosticism, and yet the majority seem shaky in their faith in a Christian afterlife' (1991, p. 196). Since afterlife beliefs appear to be such an integral part of what is helpful in the grieving process, this high level of agnosticism is of deep concern regarding the problem of death – it appears to be culturally and historically driven, rather than driven by wider scholarship and clinical practice. But such influences may actually be in need of overturning.

Archaeologist Timothy Taylor argues furthermore that the sheer level of insulation from death experienced by the typical modern is excessive, unprecedented and probably unhealthy psychologically (2002, p. 277). 'This is a reversal of the common practice in tribal societies, where the care of the corpse is specifically the duty of the nearest relatives and the idea of a stranger being involved would be deeply offensive' (p. 279). While perhaps not going this far, Metcalf and Huntington do observe that:

> In contrast to medieval Europe, the nuclear family in America has been invested with enormous sentiment that was formerly dispersed over a wider group. Yet in a country where 'togetherness' is a national fetish, no phase of the most severe crisis of the family's existence takes place at home. The oddest feature is that a society that provided harsh living conditions and little chance of mobility for its members stressed a positive role for them in death, whereas a country that emphasizes individual achievement allows only a passive role to the dying.
>
> (1991, p. 208)

The aforementioned 'togetherness,' moreover, is an obvious example of protesting too much. Western nations are among the most disconnected ever encountered in all history. Moreover, this approach to death is not unique to America and can be observed in the non-identical but heavily overlapping situation observed in other rapidly industrialized nations, which suggest economic factors are behind them. Traditional Japanese beliefs, for example (Lock, 2009, pp. 103–106), were that proper ritual separation of soul and body was necessary at death and that harsh treatment of a corpse is repulsive and disrespectful – beliefs that have survived a considerable amount of Western influence, judging by surveys done in the 1980s, which showed the majority of Japanese still performed daily rituals at their homes and graves of their deceased parents and grandparents (Lock, 2009, p. 104).

Hence, these practices contain a number of typical and universal thematic elements. In modern commercialized settings, however, this situation is interpreted differently by participants than in the more rural communities from which it evolved. In older communities, reports anthropologist H. Suzuki (2009), mourning rituals such as washing the corpse were done to ensure the purity of the corpse, and to protect it from the evil spirit *onryo*. In modern settings, however, the ritual is explained by the funeral industry as something far more vague and diluted, designed simply to 'bring family members together in the ceremony.' Without any sort of explanation of the purpose of this gathering, however, this purpose lacks substance and hence leads to rapid erosion. For example, as in many cultures, an all-night vigil is carried out with the body, though this practice was dwindling in urban communities when Suzuki reported it in 2000 because the beliefs surrounding the practice changed. In rural communities, the vigil was believed *essential* to protect the deceased's soul from evil spirits from entering the body. In modern urban settings, this belief has dwindled, and the deceased is felt to be 'taken care of by professionals.' Thus, the absence of beliefs about impurity, death pollution and evil spirits make such practices 'optional,' which typically leads to people opting out of the practice. Thus, the example of Japanese mourning rituals provides further evidence, in comparison with old and new, that (again) the role of *helpful bereaved* has eroded completely, giving way to a more passive role of the bereaved as 'experts' take over the process, separating the bereaved from the deceased and cutting off critical modalities through which meaning-making efforts have traditionally been accomplished. When the traditional meaning is gradually disintegrated and dismissed as 'ancient superstition,' the need for such rituals disappears, but the problem is that *nothing replaces it* but timid agnosticism, which leaves urbans highly vulnerable to meaninglessness.

Comparing cross-cultural analysis with the clinical study of mourning and Complicated Grief (CG)

Normal mourning and Complicated Grief (CG) are related phenomena. In general, many researchers recognize that CG results from a failure of normal mourning. In other words, CG can be viewed as abnormal mourning, rather than as an unrelated phenomenon. I think that inadequate ritualization of the normal mourning process, along with a stifling and timid agnosticism, probably contributes to the occurrence of CG. I think that examination of strongly recurrent themes may help us understand what elements of mourning rituals and beliefs may minimize the development of CG. As we will see, the critical process required to prevent CG is *meaning-making*, and the practices (or lack thereof) of modern Western nations undermine our ability to deal with the problem of death.

The clinical manifestations of CG, as outlined by various researchers on the subject (Maercker and Lalor, 2012; Simon, 2013; Nakajima et al., 2012; Alves et al., 2014; Eisma et al., 2013; Bogensperger and Leuger-Schuster, 2014), gravitate around a number of common features. These include preoccupation with the deceased, a paradoxical denial of or refusal to accept the death combined with avoidance of reminders of the death, persistent yearning for the lost loved one, detachment from others, feelings of emptiness or meaninglessness, and inadequate adaptation to the loss. All of these symptoms must persist longer than six months to one year after the death to qualify as CG. Prevalence of CG is estimated to be 4.8% for the general US population, with an incidence of between 8% and 25.4% among those currently experiencing grief (Newson et al., 2011; Simon, 2013).

Much of the presumed psychological potency of these ritual acts is likely enhanced by their public nature, as they force participants to perform and utter the prescribed actions before an assembly of the like-minded. Like all rituals, these communications reinforce pervasive myths and beliefs, create a sacred space and time and connect the abstract and ineffable to the concrete and physical, all of which helps to facilitate the transition in the minds of the bereaved in a visceral and material manner, connecting inner feelings with outward objects and materials. These practices create meaning, which, as we have seen, is capable of great power over the pain and horror of death. For example, in many rites, the decay of the body signals in an unambiguous way that the deceased has travelled to the Otherworld, which is both an event in whatever spiritual dimension believers acknowledge, and also an event intra-psychically in the bereaved. In any case, something sensorily concrete and not generated by the individual is interpreted as a sign from the physical world that the intrapsychic event has occurred, making the crucial connection between inner world and outer world. Meanwhile, variably circumscribed expressions of emotion accompany such rituals, providing for either a controlled explosion of emotionality, or a heavily transformed expression of a conspicuous *lack* thereof (which may be entirely the point). Both kinds of practice appear to be capable of actually up- or down-modulating such emotion, and the mechanism through which this works is through the manipulation of meaning, and the recruitment of the participants (and the deceased) into a cosmic narrative with high stakes and urgency. Through these practices, passive, private agony becomes public, heroic action.

Tools to handle the problem of death

So where does this lead us in our quest to find tools to face the problem of death? Inspired by Jung's exploration of cross-culturally appearing myths and rituals – the most persistent motifs of which can be accurately labelled 'archetypal' – we find extremely rich material to prevent us from needing to reinvent the wheel. Reviewing cross-cultural rituals reveals that most death rites contain some or all of the following features:

1 Provide a cultural container for the raw emotionality of grief that puts it firmly into a culturally defined context.
2 Force acceptance through intense, extended close contact between the deceased and the bereaved.

3 Contain a collection of important tasks for the bereaved to accomplish to help the deceased transition into the next world.
4 Recognize the especially vulnerable state of the bereaved and the community closely following a death.
5 Recognize the even more vulnerable state following a violent/unexpected death.
6 Create a framework to destroy and then reframe and reorganize the relationship between bereaved and deceased.
7 Employ methods to physically enact (symbolically and otherwise) the new meaning structure that also commonly channels emotional expression in culturally specific ways.
8 Employ methods to integrate the death into a coherent narrative that is compatible with surrounding belief systems.

It is highly notable and concerning, however, that the most commonly encountered death ways in the United States and other industrialized societies *do not have* many of the above elements. US death ways, for example, do not have clearly defined beliefs or traditions that circumscribe and define the 'proper' emotional expression of the bereaved. One possible exception to this is the *clinical definition of CG itself*, which is under continual debate and is primarily limited to health care professionals. It should be noted that theme 5 (extraordinary death) *is* a noted and identified risk factor for CG (Simon, 2013), but in this case it is not seen as 'spiritually dangerous,' but rather only more potentially emotionally upsetting. As mentioned, the stance of timid agnosticism that inspires eschewing spiritual interpretation may reduce the overall impact on the bereaved since it goes unaddressed and/or undefined.

Furthermore, while wake traditions bring the bereaved near the deceased for a brief period of time in Westernized nations, this amount of time is miniscule compared to other cultures and continues to shrink with industrialization and modernization, as evidenced by the changes occurring in Japan and in America. Appalachian all-night vigil and wake traditions, for example, have dwindled within even just the last few decades. With few exceptions, there are no tasks for the bereaved to accomplish that are believed to help the deceased in Westernized nations, and there is no recognition of any sort of vulnerable state for the deceased or the bereaved that must be addressed ritually. Furthermore, violent/unexpected deaths do not receive any sort of special treatment in general. There are moreover very few methods specifically aimed at physically enacting/channelling emotional expression. And, as mentioned by Metcalf and Huntington (1991), coherent narrative systems are also commonly lacking or excessively vague, so integration with them is impossible. Put simply, all the cultural tools most of humanity has developed over the ages to construct meaning have disintegrated to a mere shadow of previous practices and beliefs in Westernized nations. These activities by their nature make meaning, as they establish connections of context between the bereaved and everything else, including the deceased, the world, the spiritual plane and the Eternal. We therefore ignore them at our peril.

Conclusions

What does clinical work in analytical psychology tell us regarding the problem of death in depth psychology and CG? There is some empirical and theoretical work that suggests that the cultural themes described in this chapter, nearly all of which are integrated into most traditional mourning rituals, have been independently dis-covered/invented by therapists in an attempt to deal with CG after the fact, rather than preventatively, as traditional rituals appear to do. Reinventing the wheel, it seems, has become our only recourse. In a widely recognized approach to treat-ing CG, M. Katherine Shear advocates using imaginal and in vivo techniques that involve confronting the deceased and 'revisiting' the deceased, as well as various interventions that aim toward redeveloping a psycho-spiritual connection with the deceased (Shear et al., 2005). These interventions are clearly variants on the afore-mentioned processes found in many world rituals, including themes 2, 6 and 8 (forcing acceptance, reorganizing relationship with deceased, narrative-forming). Another approach advocates not only confrontation but the creation of new rituals to commemorate the deceased (Wagner et al., 2006), in which one can see themes 2, 6 and 7 (forcing acceptance, reorganizing relationship with deceased and physi-cal enactment of emotion), but with the non-spiritual 'commemorate' connota-tion instead of a spiritual interpretation. Though motivated by the aforementioned agnosticism, I believe 'commemoration' is considerably de-fanged from what it could be if it were full-blooded in a spiritual sense. I justify this claim because spiritual explanations incorporate a cosmic/mythic meaning that 'commemoration' cannot possibly achieve. Commemoration, noble as it is, is still simply too confined to the individual to be as powerful, as meaning-making by necessity requires us to go beyond ourselves into the wider universe of past, world, future and gods, not to mention the world of the deceased. If we do not accept a spiritual reality behind such activities, they run the risk of being too weak to create meaning in the sense needed when facing the problem of death.

The concept of 'sense-making' has been recognized by some investigators (Nakajima et al., 2012) particularly in the case of violent/unexpected death, which addresses themes 5 and 8 (extraordinary death and narrative-forming). But again, the manner in which these concepts are explored are deliberately de-spiritualized in order to accommodate our ethos of timid agnosticism. Some inves-tigators (Bogensperger and Leuger-Schuster, 2014; Neimeyer, 2000) propose that an important aspect of recovery from CG is 'meaning reconstruction' and 'sense making' processes, which reflects theme 8 (narrative-forming) and this chapter as a whole. It is stated by these researchers to be important for reorganizing the bereaved's relationship with the deceased in a positive manner, which seems to support the importance of theme 6 (reorganizing relationship with the deceased). Again, though, if we are unwilling to 'go all in' with a spiritual reality behind these ideas, our efforts may lack sufficient power.

Support for the importance of theme 3 (the bereaved helping the deceased) is difficult to find, but hints can be found in the study of rumination and CG (for example, Eisma et al., 2013). In this work, recurrent self-focused negative thinking is commonly identified as a risk factor for CG, presumably because it interrupts problem-solving, blocks instrumental behaviour and drives away social support. The excessively self-absorbed nature of such thinking furthermore can be seen as a way of avoiding painful aspects of the loss. I can see in this, also, as a failure of meaning-making, in that the connections of the bereaved with her or his social, spiritual and natural environment are cut off in a state of excessive introversion. This relentlessly self-focused dwelling on the bereaved's feelings and reasons why the loss occurred increases and perpetuates psychopathic grief responses, not only because it distracts from confronting the loss, but also because feeling better makes ruminators feel disloyal to the deceased (Stroebe et al., 2007). I argue that theme 3 (the bereaved helping the deceased) specifically addresses these concerns and may be a very powerful protective factor that can reduce the risk of ruminative thinking because such practices force the bereaved to spend a great deal of time and activity *focusing on the deceased and initiating physical action toward that end*. Such ritual acts may assuage the grief because they concretize the emotions and structure the guilt, providing solid ways in which it can be dealt with that alleviate doubts that what you have done is 'enough.' Having provided spiritual services for the deceased – which reinforces, reconstitutes and perpetuates their continued bond – the bereaved can reassure themselves that they have done and are doing what has been agreed upon *a priori* by the culture (i.e., outside of oneself) for the deceased and helped them achieve their final destination and any other ongoing needs. To feel that one is not needed, after all, is to feel alone. It also prevents ruminative avoidance of the reality of the death in the same manner that close proximity does, by occupying the bereaved in continual activity that registers on multiple (self) communicative channels (Rappaport, 1999).

Finally, support for the importance of theme 8 (narrative-forming) may be found in the study of narrative reconstruction in CG (for example, Alves et al., 2014). In this framework, the normal transitioning of acute grief to integrated grief is seen as a process of continual self-narrative formation that is interrupted if the bereaved is unable to reconceptualize their own life narrative in light of the new death. Since death often temporarily makes the bereaved's self-narrative incoherent and unstable, increased mental resources are required to create a new self-narrative; but in CG this process is interrupted and stagnates, so that the bereaved is in an incoherent self-narrative state that allows psychopathology to continue. Alves et al. (2014) found empirically that changing self-narrative co-occurred with therapeutic change, supporting the theory as well as the principles I have outlined in this chapter. These results suggest that ritual mechanisms aiming toward that end, such as the elaborate integration of the death into established cultural narratives, cosmology and mythology, may achieve the same results.

These observations raise many concerns regarding the adequacy of American death ways to handle the stress of mourning and help prevent CG and show us the severity of the problem of death we are facing in analytical psychology. Unfortunately, there are no rigorous cross-cultural studies to my knowledge that compare the rates of CG in cultures that have the aforementioned factors incorporated in their death ways. Such studies would be challenging to perform for a variety of logistical and conceptual reasons. Nevertheless, the foregoing theoretical considerations certainly raise concern that the present death ways may be inadequate and may require additional cultural intervention (which in our culture will typically manifest as psychotherapy which, unfortunately, occurs *after* the mourning ritual has already been performed).

These various findings provide preliminary support for the idea that traditional mourning rituals may help prevent CG through highly concentrated non-verbal and verbal acts of symbolism, belief and spirituality, in the service of meaning-making. By comparison, the best studied treatment for CG in the United States is a targeted cognitive behaviour therapy modality (Wittouck et al., 2011) that involves 'loss processing and restoration of life without the deceased' (Simon, 2013, p. 420) and hence presumably only addressing themes 2, 8 and possibly 6 (forcing acceptance, narrative-forming and reorganizing relationship), and not the other themes. This leads one to suspect such methods may be less than optimal since they lack substantive cultural consensus on the 'proper' parameters/boundaries of emotional expression (theme 1), they lack significant tasks for the bereaved to accomplish in the name of the deceased due to their vulnerable/dangerous state (3–5), and they lack non-verbal, symbolic and/or physical means to enact grief and other emotional or intangible expressions (7). I believe the motivation to exclude these other themes is generated by the ethos of timid agnosticism and a desire to separate spirituality from psychology in an artificial and potentially even harmful manner.

Psychiatrists and other mental health professionals as well as pastoral counsellors should, therefore, consider the aforementioned factors in developing interventions when helping patients who are struggling with mourning. In the frequently encountered setting that has no established traditional psycho-spiritual meaning-making tools, depth psychology will continue to struggle with the problem of death. As it stands, I suggest that therapists may benefit from working with their patients to attempt to *co-create* these factors when addressing CG in a non-invasive manner that honours a patient's personal autonomy. This will avoid timid agnosticism by entertaining bolder statements regarding the meaning of death in its full-blooded and spiritual form. We will need to gently probe the patient's own intuitions on such issues and work toward ritualizing the meaning-making process, emphasizing the importance of finding meaning. Whether or not this, frankly, 'reinvention of the wheel' technique will be as good as what can be provided in a more culturally/traditionally rich context remains an open question, but it may help considerably nonetheless. In any case, finding some kind of meaning and encouraging fuller commitment to it, rather than asserting that such meanings are 'wish fulfilment,' may lead to more positive outcomes. In these instances, it may be more important to assess not so much the truth value of a given belief system, but ask, 'What does having such a belief system *do*?'

All cultures have developed (with varying degrees of self-awareness) ways to handle the universal problem of death. While not all cultures have all eight of the themes in their mourning rituals, many cultures have most of them. In the rapidly expanding world of the modern Westernized nation, however, these themes have disintegrated, likely because the forces that shaped them have not had enough time to 'catch up' with the technological, cultural and political changes of the last 150 years. The foregoing represents some hints as to what directions we may need to go to help alleviate this gap and answer the inextricably psycho-spiritual problem of death in an effective way that meshes with modern life.

If either therapist or patient is a professed or enthusiastic atheist or agnostic, however, this process will be challenging. In those situations, it is important to recognize that rigid adherence to that framework may itself stifle the meaning-making process in an unavoidable way and need to be set aside for the good of the patient to whatever extent is possible. My recommendation here is to draw from Jung, who noted that regardless of the truth of the afterlife, 'Life behaves as if it were going on.' That is, the unconscious does not seem to care if we don't believe. When asked if he himself believed death is the end, he replied that we can't know, but clinically, 'nevertheless there is something within us that doesn't believe it, apparently' (Jung, 2008). To this I would add that given our knowledge about how meaning-making is so critical to mitigating the problem of death, we may have to suspend our disbelief and act *as if* some kind of spiritual framework were true in order to navigate the problem of death. In such a case, such individuals may be able to stomach such a stance because it is not intended as a true commitment to any belief system, but a commitment toward psychological health. After all, the mystery goes both ways: we don't know if any religions are true, but we also don't know that they are false. If one decides to act as if one was true for the sake of self-care and/or patient care, that is a worthy goal.

Finally, there is the case when patient and therapist adhere to wildly different religious beliefs. In this case, it is most important to recognize the importance of the common ground that even the most seemingly opposing religious beliefs have, and downplaying the differences, no matter how stark. Even though, for such 'opponents,' the meaning of death may be quite different, I believe focusing on common ground paves the way forward. This is because regardless of what the meanings are proposed to be, the worst enemy of psychological health and integrated grief is not the meaning of the other system. No, the true enemy is meaninglessness.

Note

1 I am ignoring the issues related to the mind-body problem, as they do not impact on what I am analyzing here. For a full discussion of my views on that subject, see Goodwyn (2021).

References

Alves, D., Fernandez-Navarro, P., Baptista, J., Ribeiro, E., Sousa, I. and Goncalves, M. (2014). Innovative Moments in Grief Therapy: The Meaning Reconstruction Approach and the Processes of Self-Narrative Transformation. *Psychotherapy Research*, pp. 25–41.
Bell, C. (2009). *Ritual*. London: Oxford University Press.
Bienenfeld, D. and Yager, J. (2007). Issues of Spirituality and Religion in Psychotherapy Supervision. *Israel Journal of Psychiatry and Related Sciences*, 3, pp. 178–186.

Bloch, M. and Parry, J. (1982). *Death and the Regeneration of Life*. New York: Cambridge University Press.

Bogensperger, J. and Leuger-Schuster, B. (2014). Losing a Child: Finding Meaning in Bereavement. *European Journal of Psychotraumatology*, pp. 1–9.

Bowlby, J. (1982). *Loss: Sadness and Depression*. New York: Basic Books.

Chelnokova, O., Laeng, B., Eikemo, M., et al. (2014). Rewards of Beauty: The Opioid System Mediates Social Motivation in Humans. *Molecular Psychiatry*, 19, pp. 746–747.

Conklin, B. (2009). Thus Was Our Bodies, Thus Was Our Custom: Mortuary Cannibalism in an Amazonian Society. In Robben, A. (ed.), *Death, Mourning and Burial*. New York: Blackwell.

Cunliffe, B. (1999). *The Ancient Celts*. New York: Penguin.

Davidson, H. (1968). *The Road to Hel*. New York: Praeger.

Davidson, H. (1988). *Myths and Symbols of Pagan Europe*. New York: Syracuse University Press.

Davidson, H. (1993). *The Lost Beliefs of Northern Europe*. New York: Routledge.

Eisenberger, N.I. and Lieberman, M.D. (2005). Why it Hurts to Be Left Out: The Neurocognitive Overlap between Physical and Social Pain. In Williams, Kipling D., Forgas, Joseph P. and Hippel, William Von (eds.), *The Social Outcast: Ostracism, Social Exclusion, Rejection, and Bullying*. London: Williams_RT424X_C07.indd 110.

Eisma, M., Stroebe, M., Schut, H., Stroebe, W., Boelen, P. and Bout, J.V. (2013). Avoidance Processes Mediate the Relationship between Rumination and Symptoms of Complicated Grief and Depression Following Loss. *Journal of Abnormal Psychology*, pp. 961–970.

Freud, S. (1914–1916). Mourning and Melancholia. In Freud, S. (ed.), *On the History of the Psycho-Analytic Movement Papers on Metapsychology and Other Works*. London: The Hogarth Press, pp. 239–258.

Freud, S. (1927/2010). *The Future of an Illusion*. New York: Martino Fine Books.

Gennep, A.V. (1960). *The Rites of Passage*. Chicago: Chicago University Press.

Goodwyn, E. (2016). *Healing Symbols in Psychotherapy: A Ritual Approach*. London and New York: Routledge.

Goodwyn, E. (2017). Rediscovering the Ritual Technology of the Placebo Effect in Analytical Psychology. *Journal of Analytical Psychology*, 62(3), pp. 395–414.

Goodwyn, E. (2018). *Understanding Dreams and Other Spontaneous Images: The Invisible Storyteller*. New York: Routledge.

Goodwyn, E. (2021). Bodies and Minds, Heaps and Syllables. In *Synthese, Vol. 199*. Heidelberg: Springer Verlag, pp. 8831–8855.

Hertz, R. (2009). A Contribution to the Study of the Collective Prepresentation of Death. In Robben, A. (ed.), *Death, Mourning and Burial*. New York: Blackwell, pp. 197–212.

Hultcrantz, Å. (1979). *The Religions of the American Indians*. Los Angeles: University of California Press.

Indo, Y., Tsuruta, M., Hayashida, Y., Karim, M.A., Ohta, K., Kawano, T., Mitsubuchi, H., Tonoki, H., Awaya, Y. and Matsuda, I. (1996). Mutations in the TRKA/NGF Receptor Gene in Patients with Congenital Insensitivity to Pain with Anhidrosis. *Nature Genetics*, 13(4) (August), pp. 485–488.

Jaffe, A. (1964). Symbolism in the Visual Arts. In Jung, F. (ed.), *Man and His Symbols*. Garden City, NY: Doubleday and Co, pp. 230–271.

Jung, C.G. (1954). The Aims of Psychotherapy. In *Collected Works, Vol. 16. The Practice of Psychotherapy*. Princeton, NJ: Princeton University Press.

Jung, C.G. (2008). YouTube: 'Jung: Death Is Not the End.' www.youtube.com/watch?v=T-Ab3tlpvYA.

Kan, S. (2009). The Nineteenth-Century Tlingit Potlatch: A New Perspective. In Robben, A. (ed.), *Death, Mourning and Burial*. New York: Blackwell.

Kitayama, S. and Park, J. (2010). Cultural Neuroscience of the Self: Understanding the Social Grounding of the Brain. *SCAN*, 5, pp. 111–129.

Koenig, H.G. and Larson, D.B. (2001). Religion and Mental Health: Evidence for an Association. *International Review of Psychiatry*, 13, pp. 67–78.

LeCouteux, C. (1996). *The Return of the Dead*. Rochester: Inner Traditions.

Lifton, R., & Olson, E. (2009). Symbolic immortality. In Robben, A. (ed.), *Death, Mourning and Burial*. New York: Blackwell.

Lock, M. (2009). Displacing Suffering: The Reconstruction of Death in North America and Japan. In Robben, A. (ed.), *Death, Mourning and Burial*. New York: Blackwell.

Lunde, P. and Stone, C. (2012). *Ibn Fadlan and the Land of Darkness*. New York: Penguin.

Maercker, A. and Lalor, J. (2012). Diagnostic and Clinical Considerations in Prolonged Grief Disorder. *Dialogues in Clinical Neuroscience*, pp. 167–176.

Metcalf, P. and Huntington, R. (1991). *Celebrations of Death* (2nd ed.). London: Cambridge University Press.

Monaghan, P. (2006). *The Encyclopedia of Celtic Mythology and Folklore*. New York: Checkmark Books.

Nakajima, S., Masaya, I. and Takako, K. (2012). Complicated Grief in Those Bereaved by Violent Death: The Effects of Post-Traumatic Stress Disorder on Complicated Grief. *Dialogues in Clinical Neuroscience*, pp. 210–214.

Neimeyer, R. (2000). Searching for the Meaning of Meaning: Grief Therapy and the Process of Reconstruction. *Death Studies*, pp. 541–558.

Newson, R., Boelen, P., Hek, K., Hofman, A. and Tiemeier, H. (2011). The Prevalence and Characteristics of Complicated Grief in Older Adults. *Journal of Affective Disorders*, pp. 231–238.

Panksepp, J. (2004). *Affective Neuroscience*. New York: Oxford University Press.

Parry, J. (2009). Sacrificial Death and the Necrophageous Ascetic. In Robben, A. (ed.), *Death, Mourning and Burial*. New York: Blackwell, pp. 205–206.

Petrovic, P., Pleger, B., Seymour, B., et al. (2008). Blocking Central Opiate Function Modulates Hedonic Impact and Anterior Cingulate Response to Rewards and Losses. *Journal of Neuroscience*, 28, pp. 10509–10516.

Radcliffe-Brown, A. (2009). The Andaman Islanders. In Robben, A. (ed.), *Death, Mourning and Burial*. New York: Blackwell.

Rappaport, R. (1999). *Ritual and Religion in the Making of Humanity*. New York: Cambridge University Press.

Robben, A. (2009). *Death, Mourning and Burial*. New York: Blackwell.

Shear, K., Frank, E., Houck, P. and Reynolds, C. (2005). Treatment of Complicated Grief: A Randomized Controlled Trial. *JAMA*, pp. 2601–2608.

Simon, N. (2013). Treating Complicated Grief. *JAMA*, pp. 416–423.

Straus, A. (2009). The Meaning of Death in Northern Cheyenne Culture. In Robben, A. (ed.), *Death, Mourning and Burial*. New York: Blackwell.

Stroebe, M., Boelen, P., Hout, M.V., Stroebe, W., Salemink, E. and Bout, J.V. (2007). Ruminative Coping as Avoidance: A Reinterpretation of its Function in Adjustment to Bereavement. *European Archives of Psychiatry and Clinical Neuroscience*, pp. 462–472.

Suzuki, H. (2009). The Phase of Negated Death. In Robben, A. (ed.), *Death, Mourning and Burial*. New York: Blackwell.

Taylor, T. (2002). *The Buried Soul*. Boston: Beacon Press.

Turville-Petre, E. (1964). *Myth and Religion of the North*. Westport: Holt, Rinehart and Winston.

Wagner, B., Knaevelsrud, C. and Maercker, A. (2006). Internet-Based Cognitive-Behavioral Therapy for Complicated Grief: A Randomized Controlled Trial. *Death Studies*, pp. 109–128.

Wittouck, C., Autreve, S.V., Jaegere, E.D., Portzky, G. and Heeringen, K.V. (2011). The Prevention and Treatment of Complicated Grief: A Meta-Analysis. *Clinical Psychological Review*, pp. 69–78.

Chapter 9

When the mourning process needs psychiatric support

Gerold Roth

Introduction

Following a severe loss, mourning is a normal and important process. The process hurts as the person in mourning is full of longing and sadness and frequently battles with an ambivalence between painful and positive memories, the feeling to have lost a part of one's own personality, on the one hand, and feelings of gratitude for what the deceased person meant personally, on the other. Loss can be the death of a close person, but also the death of a loved animal, of an important personal object or of a physical or mental ability.

It is only natural that clinical literature describes mourning reactions in connection with the loss of a close person; from the view of Jungian psychodynamics; however, it is useful to extend the triggering events in the aforementioned sense. The symptoms are usually quite similar and, above all, the soul should find ways to integrate the loss into its own personality. This is all the more so as frequently the loss was also a partial loss of one's own personality.

In such cases, it is not recommended to commence clinical psychotherapy. A person in mourning is vulnerable, and s/he can demonstrate individual symptoms which point to a psychic problem. Any psychic problem with illness characteristics consists of several symptoms, and the symptoms have to have a certain intensity. If the therapist now enters into an intensive analytical effort, there is the danger that the symptoms become fixed, and in the worst-case scenario, the result is the image of an illness which is *iatrogenic*, caused by medical intervention. In case someone suffers from an incomplete image of an illness, the word *patient* is derived from the Latin *patior* (= suffering); our attitude has to be primarily psycho-educational, in that the patient learns that such suffering in the mourning process is normal and, at best, we support members of the family and friends who are already helping the patient, or at least should be helping. Problems of non-support within familial dynamics could point to deeper psychic familial disturbances that Jung uncovered in the Word Association Experiment (WAE) relating to unconscious parental complexes that block psychic development, growth and vitality if they remain unaddressed and undifferentiated (see Jung, 1904–1906, paras. 7–497, 1914, paras. 438–465).

DOI: 10.4324/9781003313304-14

Clinically relevant problems

Sometimes, however, there is a reasonable suspicion of a clinically relevant problem. The patient refers to us for our therapeutic support. Our attitude is one of calming the patient, and we begin to explore at two levels: on the one hand, there could still be a normal mourning reaction, and it is with this attitude that we communicate and we listen; but, on the other hand, we look for symptoms which extend beyond the framework of a simple mourning reaction. In case the findings point to a serious clinically relevant problem, we change the level and prepare for a psychic evaluation. In such cases, we are alarmed by the patient's multitude of symptoms, but also by his/her rigidity which can also cover up a suicidal tendency. The patient in mourning requires professional help.

In such cases, it is important to have good initial differential diagnostic skills where I apply the vulnerability-stress model. This presupposes that, in case of a psychiatric evaluation, the combination of biology, life history and social factors can lead to vulnerability and that in cases when extra stress is added, an illness can be triggered. For example, the stress of a loss can tip the vulnerability or predisposition balance into an acute psychiatric illness which is more than a mourning reaction loss with illness elements. Patients with long-term processes of psychiatric problems have suffered severe loss and, for this reason, we sometimes have to handle two separate psychiatric diagnoses. However, it can also be the case that in a family with a long-term psychiatric patient, it is s/he who in case of a mourning process has the most ability; above all, if s/he has learnt as patient how to handle her/his structural vulnerability, assuming that the learned therapeutic structures in therapy are made conscious enough. More frequently, we find the symptoms of a mourning reaction that extend deeper and have lasted for more than six months. In this case, two diagnoses are possible: firstly, for the DSM5 (APA, 2020), a continued complex mourning disturbance (309.89); or secondly, for the ICD11 (World Health Organisation, 2022), continued mourning reaction (6B42). Analysed precisely, these diagnoses apply only to mourning cases concerning the death of friends and relatives; if they concern animals, important objects or physical abilities, one would rather tend to diagnose a simple adjustment disorder.

But what are the symptoms in the case of the mourning process that turn into a psychiatric problem? Of course, the limits between normal and illness are fluid and strongly dependent on the individual suffering of the person in mourning. Generally, there is:

- a continued occupation with the lost person, the lost animal, object or the lost personal ability
- feelings of guilt, fury, denial, self-blame
- difficulty to accept the loss
- feeling of having lost a part of one's own personality
- inability to express positive feelings
- lack of feeling
- difficulty with being socially active – withdrawal
- tendency to suffer physical illnesses

Why are these considerations so important, despite the undeniable danger of stig-matisation through a psychiatric diagnosis?

1 When we enter into psychotherapy, it is always important to take the psycho-logical structure of the patient into consideration. This helps us not to overex-tend the patient, so that she does not succumb to rigid resistance or even become psychotic. We can apply the structure axis of OPDII – a precise diagnostic on point is normally not necessary, and/or we enter into considerations regarding the stability of the ego–self axis. Additionally, of course, there is a close connec-tion between the structural considerations and the psychiatric diagnoses.
2 But there are also financial aspects: the psychotherapy of a mourning patient will be covered by insurance only if there is a problem with illness character, and this is why we should, in case of doubt, possibly also in cooperation with a psychiatrist, prepare a diagnosis and discuss that with the patient. And, last but not least, in the absence of therapy, a mourning reaction can develop into a severe psychiatric disorder.

Psychotherapy

Therapeutic attitude

As Jungians we perceive of our relationship with the patient as marriage qua-ternion, thus as a system of transference and countertransference from the ego and the unconsciousness of the therapist to the ego and unconsciousness of the patient (Jung, 1946, paras. 353–539). The weaker the structure of the patient, the more aware the therapist needs to be concerning the dynamic of the problem, and the more s/he has to adjust interpretations against the background of this consciousness. The stronger the consciousness of the patient, the more openly the transference-countertransference dynamics can be discussed with possible implications for an individuation process. Basically, the dynamic of a mourning reaction is similar, and it is important that the therapist understands this, also in connection with other specific personal dynamics (dual diagnoses) as best as pos-sible (see Figure 9.1).

As Jung elucidates, (ibid., para. 364) the therapist by 'consciously taken over the psychic suffering of the patient, exposes her/himself to the overpowering contents of the unconscious and hence their inductive power.' However uncomfortable such mutual unconscious infections are, they bring with them unique alchemical thera-peutic possibilities (para. 365).

When commencing therapy, a number of aspects of the problem confront the therapist. The patient offloaded her symptoms and there could be something like a transference healing. In case the patient is more or less stable, this would thus be a purely reactive problem with the result that the therapist will interpret and mirror what s/he saw and understood and thus provide the patient with new autonomy with integrated loss experience. In case the patient is less stable, this processing will be possible only slowly and perhaps only to a limited extent, and the therapist remains, to an extent, a container of the sadness which could not be processed.

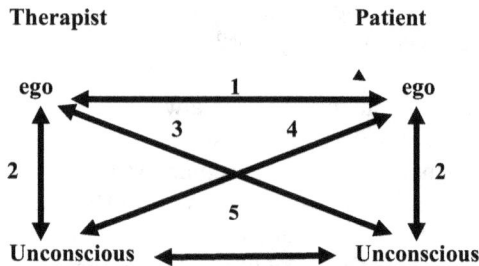

1 T and P have a mutual conscious relationship.
2 T and P each have a relationship to their unconscious.
3 Ego of T and unconscious of P have a mutual relationship.
4 Unconscious of T and ego of P have a mutual relationship.
5 Unconscious of T and unconsciousness of P have a mutual relationship.

Figure 9.1 Marriage quaternion

Less structured patients have a clear tendency to enter into at least a partial sym-biosis with the therapist, and as a result, the transfers are suddenly complicated by topics beyond the mourning process. This means that the therapist has to intervene in a clearly structured manner in a well-intended relationship, in which uncon-scious aspects play a role. Or, put differently: for the patient, the boundary between inside and outside is fluid; s/he perceives the therapist as part of her/himself, and objects of the therapist (for example, the consultation card) can turn into transfer-ence objects. These are dynamics, which simply have to be accepted. The therapist should be aware that s/he speaks as the voice of the partial personality of the patient.

Here is an illustrative example:

I cared for a then 35-year-old man with whom in late adolescent, a schizo-phrenic illness broke out in connection with cannabis consumption. He took the prescribed medications, and I saw him for longer conversations where we also spoke about his very colourful dreams and pictures and where, above all, we were putting these in order. One day his father called me that the mother had, in connection with tinnitus, committed suicide, and I was supposed to contact the client and give him the news. I refused and proposed instead that the family should tell him in a moment when I would be sure to be available so that I could, depending on the reaction of the patient, intervene immediately. This is exactly what we did. Emergency intervention was not necessary, and at the next routine consultation I was able to discuss his sadness in all peacefulness.

I am sure the reader is interested in whether this partial symbiotic therapist–patient relationship could be dissolved. In certain cases, this is certainly possible. How-ever, in an acute mourning situation, this is not the right moment, since acute mourning is also stressful. Added stress, in particular with long-term patients, can always trigger a latent vulnerability into an acute problem.

The importance of burial rituals in the mourning process

The close relationship with the therapist, or generally with another person, is part of the structure for long-term psychiatric patients, and for this reason, rituals are particularly important for them in order to cope with any loss. It is also the case that people with stable personality structures require rituals, but they become independent more quickly from the constant object relationship. Two examples of long-term patients illustrate this problem:

> In a long-term department of a psychiatric clinic, patients are permitted to look after small animals, which are of course of great importance for them. An almost 70-year-old schizophrenic patient had a guinea pig which fell ill and suddenly died. We were all concerned whether it would be possible to stabilise the patient to such an extent that he would continue to live in the department where he was comparatively free. The clinic priest arranged for a burial ritual with the patient and, following this, the patient very quickly stabilised.
>
> A young, mentally impaired patient is brought to me, since he became more and more uneasy and aggressive. The anamnesis showed that recently his stepfather, with whom he had a good relationship, had died and that the family had concerns to take him along for the burial. I quickly remembered that he needs the ritual of a burial and discussed this with him and his relational persons in the sheltered home, where he lived. They agreed with an attempt, and I was also able to motivate the priest to conduct a brief sermon for the patient and the clinic personnel, and this turned out to be quite a relief for the patient.

These examples make me arrive at an important point: we should never make a taboo of death in our work as carers and therapists, and the family needs to have the feeling that we have enough time available, when we inform them about a death. This is particularly relevant in cases of a sudden death, in particular in cases of suicide. In psychiatric clinics it is additionally important that co-patients be informed; otherwise, there is the considerable risk that other patients imitate the behaviour of the suicide victim (of a Werther-effect) This is illustrated by the following two examples:

> In case of an emergency hospital ward (my experiences relate to small country hospitals) there are always sudden cases of death, and it is the task of the doctor in charge to inform family relations. This should take place at a moment where I am likely to have enough time available. In this case it is important to be available like a rock in the storm for the family relations and I've never experienced that this offer was abused. And there was no one reaction like another; indeed, there are probably as many reactions to tragic losses as there are people in these situations.
>
> In an open psychotherapy ward in a psychiatric clinic, I learnt that a patient who had left three or four weeks ago had committed suicide. Since many patients had known this woman, we informed the entire patient group. The reaction was as expected; many patients doubted the purpose of having to work on their

improvement, and the group felt like an open wound. Time and time again, we had conversations, until towards midnight it slowly became quieter. Such interventions are very burdensome, but at least we managed to avoid subsequent suicides.

In the case of patients with better structures, it is, of course, easier not to taboo death. The therapist will hardly turn into an introject; he accompanies the patient with a sense of orderliness and explanation, and, in this way, helps him/her find a place for the deceased in his/her soul and to return to the normal flow of life. This is illustrated by three examples:

I looked after an elderly woman with an incurable neurological illness until her death. Her husband was very engaged and facilitated, also with private care, that she could be at home until death, while I visited the patient every fortnight. Following her death, the husband requested that he could now attend therapy. He suffered a heart attack which he was able, following a brief hospitalisation treatment, to have treated in an internist day clinic. He started, as a pensioner, to study at university which, of course, I very much supported, made the acquaintance of an older woman whom he married before long and the therapy could be concluded.

Another patient was treated because of light recidivist depressive episodes in my ambulant psychodrama group. As her mother was dying, she was assailed by considerable feelings of shame and guilt that everything could have run differently, with fewer conflicts, more harmoniously. In a game at the deathbed of her mother, she was able to carry the conflict from a fear-inspiring fantasy to a real level: a co-patient played the mother and in between times, she could also experience the side of the mother during a change of roles while she herself was played by the co-patient. A week later, she reported that the mother had peacefully passed away. She was able to spend much more time at the deathbed and some of what we had practised, she was also able to speak about.

Another patient was on a journey in South America with her partner when her mother died. The family was not able to reach her in time and, as a result, the burial took place without her. She and her partner felt guilty in view of their independence, they withdrew and became fixated in working with this loss. In conversations with the couple, we worked intensively on this obviously ambivalent relationship, but it was particularly important that, again, there was a parting burial ritual: both requested the priest to repeat the parting sermon and, luckily, the priest agreed to do so.

I think that it is important in the treatment of mourning reactions, as with most mental health conditions, that we do no more than is necessary; the danger of iatrogenic damage is otherwise too extensive. The reason is that a mourning case could, similar to the trauma resulting from a post-traumatic exposure, result in a violation of the patient's personality which reaches into pre-conscious elements that can also reveal psychotic symptoms. Different from psychotic patients, mourning patients have a much better self-healing capacity and we can place much greater trust in stabilisations. There is no sense in opening an unconscious complex which the patient has been able to live with; otherwise, we end up in the situation of the magic apprentice of Goethe. In this poem ('Der Zauberlehrling'), the magic apprentice tries to practise magic while the magician is absent, but he cannot stop the process he has initiated and ends with complete chaos in the atelier. Obviously, it would be appropriate for young and trained therapists to work also with dreams, images in art and active imagination. Mostly, as the examples show, I do without this in the cases that I have personally helped.

In some international cases, however, where the deceased person represents and embodies the loss of a homeland and cultural roots, due to war, pandemics, forced migration and environmental tragedies that have led to the difficulty of performing burial rituals, I understand that there would be more complicated and prolonged grief attached to the mourning process and finding an adequate closure.

Mourning reactions as archetypal phenomena

I refer back to the marriage quaternion which, above all, means that I am at eye-to-eye level with my patients, who at times can also be very close and, at the same time, I need a clearly structured and delimited identity; with one foot in the unconscious of the patient and the other on safe ground, as this was formulated by Dörner and Plog (1996), 'To Err Is to Be Human.'

We can understand our relationships with other people, and, in particular, people with mental health issues against a background of the collective and cultural unconscious, specifically the background of fairy tales and myths as 'unfinished business.' Jung recognised the efficacy of indirect thinking (Jung, 1911–1912/1952, paras. 4–46) through dreams, myths and fairy tales that have the capacity to dialogue with tabooed, dissociated emotions attached to grief and loss and transform them by bringing them into a legitimate dialogue with the ego.

I think that at least some psychic disturbances have archetypal dimensions. and recognising that reduces the need to 'shadow' scapegoat 'others' in search of guilty parties to blame. When personal loss and suffering are placed within the objective psyche, personal problems take on a wider significance as being meaningful to humanity as a whole. Definitions of psychical problems, as in psychiatric disorders, are superficial and necessarily simplified. Although these factors illuminate an illness, they can never offer an in-depth explanation.

When thinking of the mourning reactions as the topic of discussion, I remember the fairy-tale 'Aschenbrödel' of the Brothers Grimm (2002) and the saga of Orpheus of the Greek mythology (Trip, 1974). I shall follow up by summarising both stories, while focusing on what is important for our topic.

Aschenbrödel is a single child and loses her birth mother. The father remarries and the stepmother brings two daughters into the marriage. They all neglect

Aschenbrödel, who has to sleep in the ashes. One day, her father leaves for a business trip and he promises to bring something for his three daughters in accordance with their wishes. The stepsisters wish for beautiful dresses, respectively pearls and diamonds: Aschenbrödel, however, wishes – 'Father, the first branch which on your way home touches on your hat please break it off for me.' The father brings all that was wished and Aschenbrödel places the twig on the grave of her mother. where it soon turns into a beautiful tree and Aschenbrödel regularly visits the grave. One day the prince in a nearby castle sends out invitations to a ball because he wants to choose his future wife. Aschenbrödel also wants to go but her stepmother imposes impossible conditions. Due to the relationship with her deceased mother, however, Aschenbrödel is able to meet these conditions and she goes to the ball. This is where she attracts the interest of the prince, but she disappears without being recognised. This is repeated three times. At the third time, she loses a shoe and the prince looks for the woman who fits with the shoe. He finds her and marries her.

The singer and talented lyre player Orpheus marries Eurydike, a Naiadnymphe. Shortly after the wedding she is bitten by a snake and dies. Orpheus resolves to bring her back from Hades and climbs into the underworld. Once there he sings so beautifully that the ghosts permit him to retrieve his wife, but on the condition that he promise not to look back until he reaches home. He leads his wife up to the entrance of the underworld, but suddenly he becomes afraid that she would not follow him and he turns around – and immediately Eurydike disappears and again becomes a shadow. Orpheus tries another time to enter Hades, but the path is blocked for him. He returns to his home where he himself soon dies, he is torn to pieces by Kikonierins, who move about as Mänades.

In this archetypal material, we thus find two forms of handling the loss of a close person. Aschenbrödel places the twig which her father brought with him on the grave of her mother and cares for the plant. This sprouts roots and soon turns into a proud hazel bush which Aschenbrödel regularly visits. When she is in need, the hazel bush helps because she receives the necessary dresses and also help for the completion of the senseless tasks of her stepmother. Aschenbrödel has processed the death of her mother, and with the hazel bush she has a living, helpful relationship. In this case, death does not mean that there is nothing left, but it becomes a transitional phenomenon, symbolically viewed, as a lively and very helpful memory that serves as a positive, intrapsychic aspect of herself.

For Orpheus, his Eurydike is simply dead when she is supposed to become alive again. Everything should be as before the deadly snake bite, but Orpheus lacks trust in the creative transformative unconscious processes offered to him symbolically in the underworld. The snake as an ambivalent symbol of change (shedding of its skin for a new one) is not transformed, but remains the cause of a concrete death. There is no assistance to be expected, either with rituals or with an extensive symbolic understanding. Orpheus would probably not have accepted such an offer. The whole event turns into a concrete brutal act, and it is hardly surprising that he is torn into pieces.

I think that our handling of clinically ill mourning patients, and probably also that of mourning friends and family, generally moves between those above two scenarios of hope and/or despair. In most cases, there is first a reaction which I would now characterise as an Orpheus reaction: allocations of blame to others, but also to the self, are frequent. People are in bottomless sadness, and in particular for older spouses, there is the not insubstantial risk that the remaining partner will also become ill and die. However, given time, there can be positive transforming memories, although a relapse into bottomless sadness always remains possible.

Conclusion

Before we commence in supporting the mourning process as psychotherapists, we need to be informed about the deeper psychodynamics of the mourning process and to establish whether there is a psychiatric disorder with illness elements that involves an ongoing complex mourning reaction with or without a second diagnosis. On this basis, I have discussed the type of mourning support that the patient should be neither underwhelmed nor overwhelmed: both normally result in a blockage, and the mourning support is broken off or, even worse, results in a psychosis. In this context, we rely on the healing efficacy of Jung's creative and imaginative concept of the psychology of the transference and, in particular, the term of marriage quaternion. We also depend on the stability of the patient to work with such phenomenology and interpretation that optimally contains the seeds to healing unconscious complexes imbued within the mourning process that encourages the patient towards self-reliance and independence. The chapter concludes with a reference to the archetypal basis of the processes as discussed with excerpts from 'Aschenbrödel' and the Orpheus myth to help guide the patient towards a wider understanding of his/her processes and life choices.

References

American Psychiatric Association. (2020). *Diagnostische Kriterien DSM-5*. Göttingen: Hogrefe-Verlag.

Dörner, K. and Plog, U. (1996). *Irren Ist Menschlich*. Bonn: Psychiatrie Verlag.

Grimm, Brüder. (2002). *Kinder- und Hausmärchen*. Zürich: Manesse Verlag.

Jung, C.G. (1904–1906). Studies in Word Association; Associations of Normal Subjects. In *Collected Works, Vol. 2. Experimental Researches* (2nd ed.). London: Routledge and Kegan Paul, 1992.

Jung, C.G. (1911–1912/1952). Two Kinds of Thinking. In *Collected Works, Vol. 5. Symbols of Transformation* (2nd ed.). London: Routledge and Kegan Paul, 1995.

Jung, C.G. (1914). On the Importance of the Unconscious in Psychopathology. In *Collected Works, Vol. 3, The Psychogenesis of Mental Disease* (2nd ed.). London: Routledge and Kegan Paul, 2000.

Jung, C.G. (1946). The Psychology of the Transference. In *Collected Works, Vol. 16. The Practice of Psychotherapy* (2nd ed.). London: Routledge and Kegan Paul, 1993.

Trip, E. (1974). *Reclams Lexikon der antiken Mythologie*. Stuttgart: Philipp Reclam jun.

World Health Organisation. (2022). ICD11. www.findacode.com (accessed 15 November 2022).

Part V

Eros, death and the unconscious

Chapter 10

Deceased loved one in dreams

Verena Kast

Introduction

Death is the ultimate existential confrontation with life for us as humans; the final disappearance of a beloved, important person from our lives is a tragedy, and one not easy to understand. That's why we need our imagination and dreams to help us form a mental picture, to endure the uncanniness of this existential experience, the frightening thing about it, and to bring us into a bearable adjustment to this loss. Dreams with the deceased seem to be important in all cultures, and we are not surprised. Dreams in the grieving process are helpful, first, because they comfort: there is not just the loss, of course there is, but in a way that is hard to define, the deceased is still there. Second, dreams help to change the relationship with the deceased in such a way that one can continue to live with that loss and not just feel like a deprived person. (Kast, 1988, 2013)

Since the loss of a person close to us is emotionally very upsetting, it is also the dreams in the mourning process, especially dreams where deceased people reappear, that the mourners give great importance to: some are accompanied by feelings of great astonishment and emotion; mourners can feel overwhelmed and have the impression of experiencing something completely extraordinary. These dreams are often remembered for a long time.

Other dreams of the deceased are more every-day; their experience is accompanied by a quiet joy and gratitude that the deceased is still there and still occupies an important place in their psyche. What these dreams have in common is that they feel so real because the deceased is so physically present in the dream.

Most dreams with the deceased arouse positive emotions, even if at first, for example, the grief over the illness of the now-deceased once again dominates, or the feeling of loss is revived by the dream. Nevertheless, the dream not only emphasizes the loss but also conveys the feeling that the deceased is still present. To be distinguished from this are dreams in which the deceased still reproaches the person left behind, in which it is clearly expressed that a psychological problem, which existed even before the loss, must be solved. But these dreams feel different: they are more every-day and not overwhelming. I'll leave those kinds of dreams aside in this chapter.

DOI: 10.4324/9781003313304-16

A deeply moving dream with the deceased father

I'm in my garden, tending to weeds. As I rise from my stooped position, I see my father standing at the garden gate, quite alive. I wonder if he doesn't know he is dead. But he raises his hand in greeting and wishes 'Good luck to you!' – 'Good luck to you, too,' I say – and I feel how much we love each other. He turns away.

The dreamer, a 60-year-old woman, is overwhelmed by the fact that her father, who died a few months ago, has appeared so real, so present, so clearly in the dream. She is deeply touched by the dream.

I feel alive again, somehow I felt like I was under a glass bell for the last few months, now I'm breathing properly again. Now I have made peace with my father's death – we assured each other that we were important to each other. I still had to experience that. He turns away – he leaves. I am very sad – and very much with myself. But I know that I can always remember this dream, the essence of our relationship was once again experienced. The dream is deeply touching, very special. When I imagine it again, I feel connected to something greater.

There are experiences that seize us emotionally, grab us, leave us breathless, give us the impression of having experienced something fascinating – or terrifying – something that goes beyond our everyday experience and that we cannot grasp at first. It is strange, alienating, astonishing, completely unusual what one experiences there: a wonderful, or frightened, astonishment about something overpowering, which we do not really understand at first, seizes us; we are seized by awe. We feel one with the world around us, one with the great whole, and that gives us an experience of meaning, of belonging to a great whole. But these are also moments when we humans find ourselves in a context quite different from everyday life. It is as if a gap opened up in the clouds, and for a certain time we can see ourselves, life and others as a whole.

If the deceased appear to the mourners in this way, then they feel connected to something greater, connected to the deceased, but also connected to life as a whole, life and death. This is comfort – and it is much more than comfort, it is an experience that connects to a wholeness. Such dreams are gifts. They also have an impact on our values and worldview.

Dreams of the deceased – how we deal with them

If we dream of deceased people, then these are emotionally significant dreams, which we remember, but which we also memorize well by visualizing them again and again with all senses. This is especially true shortly after the experience of loss, while we are processing the loss. But even years later, if a person appears in our dreams who has long since passed away, this dream touches us particularly. We marvel at the fact that deceased people are still alive in the dreams, sometimes very much so. And we understand these dreams as a 'sign from over there.' Marie Louise von Franz (1984), following C.G. Jung, speaks of the deceased initially still having a 'presence' in the dreams of the bereaved, which they would gradually lose. In the course of a year, the dreams with the deceased do become less, that is, they are present in our inner space, and we have adapted somewhat to the new life situation. But this does not mean that deceased people cannot reappear in dreams after years in a tremendous presence. How present the dreams are with the deceased also depends on how the mourners deal with them.

Mourners visualize dreams with deceased people when they are not frightening. They imagine the dream over and over again, connected to the emotions it triggered. Similar to a beautiful love experience, we want to preserve it in our imagination for as long as possible. And what are the emotions? Love, relief that the person, who is no longer there, is still 'there' in some way, is present and one can connect with him/her. A new form of bonding, of being connected, is possible.

By enriching the dream with his/her imagination, especially by visualizing the relationship to the deceased in the dream again and again, the mourner accepts – and at the same time does not accept – that the deceased person is no longer there. The emotional energy that was contained in the relationship revives the relationship with this being in the dream, making the deceased increasingly alive and more present. At the same time, this is a psychological way to internalize the deceased person. The more the figures in the dream are sensually visualized, the more alive they become, and the more likely further dreams will follow. Through imagination an inner life is created. By intensively imaginatively remembering the deceased from our dreams, they get a permanent place in our inner life. The emotionally very impressive dreams with the deceased especially stimulate the mourning process to deal emotionally with the memories in an imaginative way.

Some aspects of research on the subject

Meanwhile, there is much research dealing with deceased in dreams – also in the context of the mourning process – with questions of how these dreams influence the mourning process, but also how they change the understanding of the mourning process (Black et al., 2014, 2016, 2020; Owczarski, 2021).

The literature indicates that 50%–80% of people report at least one dream with a deceased person in the period following a loss. For people who are in a therapeutically guided grieving process, it is about 70%, and it is usually several dreams. Most people dream about deceased people – even years after the loss. And it is always a special situation that is talked about.

Just as people grieve differently, they have different dreams (Black et al., 2016). Garfield wrote a typology of such dreams in 1996 that have revised these themes. These typologies can be understood by psychotherapists working in practice. There are typical dreams in a grieving process.

In dreams, the deceased may be ill, suffering, and the dreamer suffers with them. In other dreams, the deceased appears healthy and full of life, often 'in their prime' as the dreamer puts it, sometimes young and healthy. Sexual and romantic situations can be experienced, experiences of great closeness. Sometimes the deceased gives indications that are taken seriously; this is often also in connection with dreams that indicate that too great a closeness to the deceased still exists, that a phase of separation is called for.

The mourning process

From love we promise ourselves the abolition of existential loneliness, the death of a loved one throws us back again into this loneliness. We have temporarily lost a fundamental security in life. Through the process of mourning, we are able to bring a new sense of security back into our lives.

We are seized by the feeling of grief when we have lost a person or an asset that has represented a special value to our lives. Associated with this feeling of grief are feelings of sorrow, fear, anger, guilt, etc. Allowing and experiencing these feelings causes us to enter a process of mourning, but also a process of development, through which we slowly – and very painfully – learn to accept the loss and to engage in life anew without the person we have lost, without the good we have lost, but with everything that this person awakened in us, what this good enlivened in us, and what we do not have to give up. And increasingly, we meet the deceased person in our imagination and in our dreams.

The loss of an important relationship

The mourning process has to be seen in the context of the relationship from which we have to detach ourselves because of the loss that has occurred. When we build an intense relationship with a person, we grow together with him/her, but together with him/her, we also grow. This is why mourners say they now feel torn apart, feel like a bleeding wound and feel uprooted. The process of this growing together is abruptly interrupted by death and changes the whole life; one no longer understands oneself, one no longer understands the world, one feels strange, towards oneself, but also towards the world. We enter into an identity crisis; we have to define our identity anew. In the course of the mourning process, we reorganize ourselves from a relational self to our individual self, i.e. we have to reflect again on ourselves as individuals, to find an own relation to the world again, without losing the memory of the deceased.

The detachment of the individual self from the relational self

When we lose a person, we lose a relationship that is important to us, a relationship that has a history that we both hoped would continue to develop into the future, a history that we can relate to each other in memories, a future that we can imagine together and realize together, or so we think. If we lose a person with whom we had a close relationship, we lose the relational self.

The relational self is a self that emerges between the two: it is the internalization of the dynamics of a lived, committed relationship. Associated with this is a reciprocal revitalization of personality parts over time. This relational self is dynamic, changing with time and with the relationship. Each of the two experiences this relational self from their own perspective, even if it is experienced as 'shared.' Of course, even in a close relationship, there are parts of the self that are little affected or unaffected by the relationship.

This relational self is formed by the lived I-Thou relationship, especially by the mutual being perceived and the associated barely perceptible but significant assurance of the respective identity of the individual in development: The way the deceased person saw us, concretely also looked at us, lovingly, kindly, critically, knowingly, as no other looks at us anymore. The I-Thou relationship also includes the everyday life that is created together, the shared interests, the works that one has accomplished, is accomplishing and still wants to accomplish. These 'works' can be children, undertakings that we have created with each other by stimulating, exciting, challenging each other and, as a result, realizing something. In most relationships, things become possible that would not have been possible alone – on the other hand, certain possibilities also lie fallow. Of course, there are also undertakings, creations, which originate much more from one's own self, in which the partner has hardly any part. This is the case, for example, when one has a great interest in something that does not interest the partner. Her share then consists in the fact that she does not inhibit these interests, but perhaps she accompanies them benevolently.

The relational self allows projections to be maintained for years and not to have to be taken back: the man, 78, who is convinced that his wife is stingy, and who after her death, triggered by a dream, realizes that he himself is downright grotesquely stingy, and that it is quite a different attitude to life to be patronizing to others and to oneself.

Dream

'I receive a parcel. The sender is my deceased wife. I open the package and unwrap a small wooden man with a label around his neck. It reads: The puny, miserly little man back.'

The dreamer is happy to have received a package from his deceased wife. However, he spends a lot of time complaining – and also taking it as evidence of her stinginess – that the woman didn't write a real return address, just her name. He goes on about how he will die soon and would like to know where the woman is now, whether there is an afterlife, how one can still pack parcels there. The therapy session is coming to an end: I ask about the puny, stingy little man. And he answers: 'You already know that I am stingy, too.' I point out to him that it's important that he knows that – that he can consider whether he wants to spend the rest of his life as a stingy man or/and a begrudging one.

This is an example of how a dream initiates a detachment from the relational self and calls attention to one's self.

However, the relational self on a more unconscious level includes not only projection and delegation, but also personal idiosyncrasies and developments that have been awakened, loved out of one, by the relationship in each other (Kast, 1986, p. 5). This aspect of the relationship self is rooted in infatuation, in the phase in which one sees the ideal life possibilities in each other and in a possible future – the vision for the relationship self has its origin. Even if many things are idealized, possibilities for development are also glimpsed, which can also be partially realized through the joint relationship. Of course, in the course of the relationship, idiosyncrasies are also enlivened, 'forced out,' which are seen as less positive: the woman who loses her trust because she has been lied to repeatedly, and who has become profoundly distrustful through the lived relationship. In the relationship itself, of course, difficult interactions are also reflected.

Dream

A young woman, 29, has lost her husband in a motorcycle accident. She was already 'disillusioned' with him and the relationship before the loss experience. Thus, she thought she was not actually sad, and she did not understand why she felt so drained and powerless, barely able to care for her young children.

She dreamed:

> I'm much younger, wearing a colorful summer dress, I'm full of energy, and I'm dancing with Heinz (her late husband's name) devotedly and very wildly. We are totally in love – a wonderful feeling.
>
> When I woke up, I was very disappointed – and then again I wasn't: I completely forgot how in love we were, how vital my husband was, what a good feeling of life he gave me. All I've been thinking about lately is the man who, instead of helping me, went biking . . . I shouldn't forget that: he could give me so much joy in life.

An aspect of the community self was experienced – and with that, she also found access to the better aspects of the relationship again, and also more to herself. In particular, she remembered how much he had always stimulated her as well, and wondered if she could pursue some of those suggestions as well, even in the absence of her husband.

When we lose someone close to us, we not only lose that person, but we also lose the relational self in the sense that it can no longer develop. We now have to plan for the future on our own, and we can no longer share memories with each other. That stimulating 'Do you remember . . .?' is absent. Having to remember alone is remembering without the stimulation of a partner. But even new experiences we have can no longer be shared. Thus, the recently widowed woman says in the face of a wonderful mountain landscape:

> Walter (the name of the late husband): Look how beautiful the glacier is in the evening sun and then I knew very painfully that I will never again be able to share this beauty with him. And that he will never be able to see this beauty.

We need to reorganize from the relational self to our own self in such a way that what has grown in the relationship can be taken over into our own life and experience. The natural process of mourning enables us to reorganize ourselves from the relational self, back to the individual self in a long-lasting, emotionally significant process of transformation, in such a way that much of what was experienced in the relational self can be integrated into our own life in a changed form. This is accompanied by the acceptance of the loss; what remains is a grateful melancholy, always interspersed with a longing for the deceased person, which, however, does not interfere with the joy of living and creating, and perhaps even the other way around; because one is alive, one wants to be as alive as possible.

The loss of the attachment person

When we lose a person, not only has the relational self reached a conclusion, but we are also very likely to lose the or an 'attachment person,' that is, the person to whom we turned with trust in situations that were stressful for us, with whom we shared difficult experiences, by whom we felt supported. It may be that there are different 'attachment figures' in our lives; if not, we not only experience a loss, but we can no longer talk about this difficult experience with the person with whom we have otherwise shared our deepest needs.

Thus, then, the process of mourning is a very painful process of a peculiar vitality, which takes a lot of strength and time and forces us to confront ourselves and the relationship that has been broken off, and which opens the possibility for us to get in touch with ourselves anew, to step out of the habit and also to learn anew many things about our relationship behaviour, but also to enter into a new relationship with the deceased. Grieving takes time with different lengths of time for individual people, depending also on who you have lost, what age you are, etc. The process of mourning is a process of development, and development takes time.

Remembering dreams trigger the memory

When we have lost someone, we are still left with memories. We can largely dispose of the memories, as fate has no access to the memories. The memories are safe from fate as long as our brain still enables the memories. What will be tomorrow, that is in many ways unavailable – over our memories, over our lived life, we can dispose.

When we imagine past situations vividly again, they can be experienced emotionally. We do not wallow in the past; we visualize past situations and experience them 'now.' We experience the situation, as if the deceased person would be present in reality. 'As if . . .' is very powerful. We imagine how it was back then – and experience the situation again vividly – maybe we even change it a bit, so that we like it even better. Our memory is creative and constructive depending on the mood and situation, but also on the intention to create – our memories can also change a bit, but above all, the evaluation of these memories changes.

For this memory work, dreams have great importance, all dreams, but especially the dreams that bring back the deceased, speak of her/him, speak of the relationship one had with her/him. Dreams are about what is also bothering us in everyday life, but they bring these problems into a wider context, so that new, creative solutions become possible – or they show us something that we have forgotten or neglected. Not infrequently, dreams trigger this memory work. (Kast, 2019)

Mourners remember, tell of life with the deceased; family and friends tell, and so there is in memory an ever more complex picture of the deceased that we want to preserve. And these memories are also miraculously stimulated by dreams – and we value the memories stimulated by dreams more highly than those from every-day narratives. They belong more clearly and essentially to our inner life.

Sometimes impulses come through short dream fragments: The already mentioned 29-year-old woman dreams: 'My husband writes me a card from Schwä-galp.' I don't know what it says. But when I was awake, I remembered how much the Schwägalp (place in the Alpstein, Switzerland) meant to us – and that I never went there again. Dreams that awaken nostalgic feelings, awaken feelings of the eroticism associated with these places – and that simply do the dreamer good. She does not have to give up these feelings, even if she has lost the man.

For mourners, this process of remembering, in which many nostalgic feelings arise, is precisely paradigmatic for dealing with loss: you have lost someone, you have lost a lot, no doubt, but the memory of the life lived remains and can fill you with vitality.

For these memories, which simply resurface, or which one allows to resurface figuratively and emotionally, one needs attention, which one is more likely to mus-ter if one has experienced that they animate. If one can also share them with other people by telling them, they become even more vivid. For mourners, it is indispen-sably important to recall many of these situations – even banal ones – in memory, to experience what was common, but also what was one's own in these situations, also to find out what one would have liked to have done differently in this situation. Thus, one detaches oneself from a relationship self, back to one's own self and detaches – but one has not only lost, one also has inner living images, also ideas, what would still belong to life, what one has not yet lived enough. There are also ideas moving forward. Once this space of memories is accessible, many memories come to life, of course not only those that please you. And there are also images for the future: illusory expectations of the future, concrete expectations of the future – at least for the near future – can also be experienced.

Internalized versus externalized continuing bonds

In the grief literature in the last decade, also in the context of the question of 'post-traumatic growth,' the question has been raised after a loss experience whether continuous bonds to the deceased tends to facilitate or impede acceptance of the loss (Black et al., 2020; Calhoun and Tedeschi, 2006) While it was once thought that continuous attachment to the deceased tended to make grief more difficult, it is now thought that the opposite may also be true. Various researchers have suggested that there are different forms of continuous attachment to the deceased: An internalized bond that refers to experiences that primarily stimulate contemplation, memory, reflection, thus making the deceased an 'internalized secure base' (Black et al., 2020, p. 1), while externalized continuous bonds refers to experiences in which the deceased is still experienced as present in one's life – one hears him, one still sees him. The data tend to indicate that internalized bonds, which are associated with a secure attachment style of the mourner, lead to the connection to the deceased being experienced as a secure internal base, while the externalized attachment tends to lead to anxiety, to intrusive thoughts that the deceased wants to harm one, and this does not give relief as we know it from the internalized bonds. However, it is also possible that externalized attachments prevail at the beginning of mourning, which are later replaced by internalized ones. In complicated grief, however, it seems that these externalized bonds persist.

How does this fit with my theory, which sees mourning as an adjustment to loss by reorganizing from the relational self to one's own self, so that thereby also the internal representations of the deceased change? This also results in a new relationship with the 'inner deceased,' which continues to change over time. Also, in my concept, a relationship, a bond to the deceased remains, but one has nevertheless detached oneself in such a way that one can also turn to living people again. If this internalized bond is idealized, if it is partly described as pure love, then this does not seem to me to be appropriate to the loss.

Both seem to me to be very important: the detachment from the deceased, the reorganization to one's own self, to ask oneself anew the question of identity – and to integrate consciously and gratefully into one's own life what has grown through the relationship. Now this does not mean that one gives up the connection to the deceased – but it does mean that it is allowed to change. The detachment of children from their parents seems to me to be the paradigm: children become more and more autonomous, find more and more their own identity, take with them much that has grown in them through the relationship with the parents – and also retain a bond. The relationship with parents is an internalized secure base. This is also how I see the detachment from and attachment to the deceased. To emphasize only the changed attachment as something that establishes continuity with the deceased would be one-sided, would not do justice to the existential significance of the loss.

C.G. Jung (1928, para. 598) pointed out that a 'persistent attachment to the dead makes life seem less worth living, and may even be the cause of psychic illnesses.'

Separation dreams

The fact that detachment is also necessary, that the continuous bond must change, is shown by the typical dreams with deceased persons in which separation is called for (Black et al., 2016). They are dreams in which the deceased travels to a place where one is not allowed to follow him/her, sometimes the mourner is told with gestures to stay behind, or the deceased disappears in the mist, and the figure dissolves.

The dream of a 52-year-old man, nine months after the death of his beloved daughter in a mountain accident:

> I am in Finisterre, by the sea. A big ship is ready to leave. I see only one person on this ship – my daughter, healthy and young. Full of joy, I want to board this ship too, but it is really leaving, my daughter shows me with her gestures that I should stay away from her and the ship. And then she says, 'Don't forget that you are married.' I am very sad and remember that I don't even know where my wife lives anymore.

The dreamer has awakened sad and very thoughtful, next to his wife. He understands the dream to mean that he should really let go of his daughter and turn back to the living. Finisterre is for him the westernmost point of Europe. He knows from old funeral rites that the dead in the west were handed over to the sea in a dugout canoe – in their journey to the sunset and then again to the hoped-for sunrise. Emotionally, for me, it means that he needs more distance from his deceased daughter, that he must not die with her, either. He has been so preoccupied in memory work with what all came into his life in contact with his daughter that he has neglected his relationship with his wife. 'I really don't know where she is inside.'

The experience of loss changes – the mourner becomes involved in life again, the tapestry of life weaves on, good experiences can be had again. In the same way, dreams change – dreams with the deceased become fewer, but do not stop. The connection to the deceased as inner figures also changes, but they are a basis to which one can still refer if necessary. But this intensive empathy, thinking, identifying with deceased figures from the dreams decreases, the most important relationship is no longer that to an inner figure. One turns more to life again, to the outside, to other people, inward to new creative ideas, new plans, new challenges.

Cultural differences in the meaning of the deceased in dreams

The way people deal with the deceased in their dreams is also related to their worldview. Hinton et al. (2013) presented a study on normal and complicated grief among Cambodian refugees. He and his team studied mourning processes in traumatized Cambodian refugees. They found that dreams with the deceased have a central place in the mourning processes. They further demonstrated how grief and PTSD interact with each other, thus developing a model in which dreams with the deceased play a central role. They draw attention to the fact that in complicated grief, the activation of PTSD should be noted.

The deceased in the dream gives the Cambodian an indication of their spiritual state. In the first year after the loss, dreams of the deceased are usually comforting, but not if they appear poorly dressed, dirty and hungry. Then donations to the dead are necessary: one must give them what they need. However, if one dreams of a deceased person a year after death, it is very disturbing: it means that the deceased has not been reborn and so is wandering on this earth as a ghost and therefore potentially dangerous. Again, merits must be made, especially on special days memorial to the dead.

Hinton distinguishes three different dream types (Hinton et al., 2013, p. 9): visiting dreams, nostalgia dreams and dreams that reactivate trauma. Under visiting dreams fall friendly greeting dreams, then also dreams in which help is asked for and especially those feared are soul-calling dreams. In these, the deceased asks the dreamer to accompany him/her. Feared consequence of them are displacement, illness and death. Of these visitation dreams, 62% are categorized as 'disturbing.'

Nostalgia dreams (13%) concern scenes from the time before Pol Pot, eating together, being happy or dreams about the Pol Pot time, but about peaceful working in the rice field.

In dreams in which the trauma is reactivated, the situation that originally triggered the trauma or an imagined trauma is dreamed about. These dreams call for merits in order for the rebirth of the deceased to occur.

Hinton et al. (2013) develop a model of how dreams, understanding of dreams, and somatic symptoms are related:

A dream in which the deceased is experienced triggers concern about the spiritual situation of the deceased. This concern is reinforced by the knowledge that the death was not a good death, such as no funeral took place. The deceased can be reborn more easily if a dignified death was experienced and a proper mourning ritual. This was often not the case at the time of the Pol Pot regime.

The problematic spiritual status of the deceased, inferred from dreams, raises concerns that one's physical and spiritual health is threatened. This is especially in connection with 'calling – the soul – dreams.' These fears trigger crying and somatic symptoms. The PTSD is activated. In addition, the pain of the deceased is remembered, which in turn triggers renewed crying and somatic symptoms. PTSD stimulates the memory of the deceased in waking, and this again stimulates more disturbing dreams. These disturbing dreams require families to meet to discuss the spiritual situation of the deceased and to order special offerings. The physical pain experienced from the memories of the deceased's pain can be relieved through a body-based therapy called 'Coining,' an ancient method in Asia to rid the body of heat that warms the body, allowing one to experience a form of connectedness. The Coining procedure – massaging skin through a hard object – causes linear streaks and gives the impression that the flow of energy is restored (Hinton et al., 2013, p. 21).

In different cultures people deal differently with death and with the deceased in dreams. This should be kept in mind when we work with people from different cultures.

Back to our culture

Dreams in which the deceased appears in the 'best age,' healthy, vital, sometimes young, this is also a typical dream (Black et al., 2016) that pleases the mourners. They take them as a sign that the deceased is well. For psychotherapists, they are more the expression of having succeeded in integrating the deceased in a good way into the inner world, adapting one's life to the loss.

Dream

A 50-year-old man who had lost his partner in a car accident, and who initially had a very hard time coping with the new life situation, dreamed after two years of therapy:

> I dreamed about Karin [partner] again. This time she looked quite healthy, was full of energy. She was wearing the suede jacket that she always liked so much and that looked so good on her. With her was our architect and the two of them apparently had plans, they were going to add a new room to our house. It was a pleasant, stimulating atmosphere. I didn't have anything to do with them directly, but what they were planning was for me, I felt it acutely, and it vitalized me.

It was important to the dreamer that his wife now appeared 'quite healthy' in the dream for the first time. For him it was an indication that he can now also think of her in joyful melancholy, planning a house extension, so that he has apparently passed the mourning process – as far as that is possible – to some extent – that his living space can even be enlarged. He has already been surprised about the fact that his wife, although deceased, nevertheless appears present, virtually pointing into the future in the dream.

Conclusion: deceased in dreams – where are the dead?

In the process of mourning, dreams with the deceased are consolation and signposts for the psychological confrontation with the loss, indications of what is significant at this particular time. The mourning process is not a straightforward developmental process, and dreams can indicate which issues are emotionally important now.

Even when we are no longer in the process of mourning, we dream of deceased people who are amazingly alive in the dream. We meet long-dead grandparents in dreams, and we realize upon awakening – sometimes already in dreams – that we are now older than they were at the time of their death. And sometimes we dream of people who died centuries ago. So once Spinoza greeted me in a dream and reminded me not to forget the *Laetitia* (joy, excitement).

The dreams with the deceased remain mysterious, even if we understand these dreams on the subjective level, and the figures are seen as belonging to our inner life. The theory that what we deal with in our waking life influences our fantasies and imaginations, and ultimately our dreams, also makes sense. The more we occupy ourselves with these deceased people, the more likely they are to appear in our dreams as well.

And yet, the emotional quality of these dreams with the deceased remains a special one and can often grip us anew, making us realize that the deceased are always with us as well, and some seem quite alive, inspiring us. Let's think of Mozart, for example!

References

Black, J., Belicki, K., et al. (2020). *Internalized Versus Externalized Continuing Bonds: Relations to Grief, Trauma, Attachment, Openness to Experience, and Posttraumatic Growth*. Death Studies. DOI: 10.1080/07481187.2020.1737274.

Black, J., DeCicco, T. and Seeley, C., et al. (2016). Dreams of the Deceased: Can Themes Be Reliably Coded? *International Journal of Dream Research*, 9(2).

Black, J., Murkar, A., et al. (2014). Examining the Healing Process Trough Dreams in Bereavement. *Sleep and Hypnosis*, 16, pp. 1–2.

Calhoun, L.G. and Tedeschi, R.G. (2006). The Foundations of Posttraumatic Growth: An Expanded Framework. In Calhoun, L.G. and Tedeschi, R.G. (eds.), *Handbook of Posttraumatic Growth*. Mahwah, NJ: Erlbaum, pp. 1–23.

Garfield, P. (1996). Dreams in Bereavement. In Barrett, D. (ed.), *Trauma and Dreams*. Cambridge, MA: Harvard University Press, pp. 186–211.

Hinton, D.E., Peou, S., Joshi, S., Nickerson, A. and Simon, N. (2013). Normal Grief and Complicated Bereavement among Traumatized Cambodian Refugees: Cultural Context and the Central Role of Dreams of the Dead. *Culture, Medicine and Psychiatry*, 37(3) (September), pp. 427–464. DOI: 10.1007/s11013-013-9324-0.

Jung, C.G. (1928). The Psychological Foundations of Belief in Spirits. In *Collected Works, Vol. 8. The Structure and Dynamics of the Psyche* (2nd ed.). London: Routledge and Kegan Paul, 1991.

Kast, V. (1982/2013). *Trauern. Phasen und Chancen des psychischen Prozesses*. Freiburg: Kreuz in Herder.

Kast, V. (1986). *The Nature of Loving. Patterns of Human Relationship*. Wilmette: Chiron Publications.

Kast, V. (1988). *A Time to Mourn*. Einsiedeln: Daimon.

Kast, V. (2019). *Träumend imaginieren. Einblicke in die Traumwerkstatt*. Göttingen: Vandenhoeck & Ruprecht.

Owczarski, W. (2021). Dreams in Bereavement: Case Study. *International Journal of Dream Research*, Band 14, Nr. 1.

Von Franz, M.L. (1984). *Traum und Tod*. München: Kösel, p. 149.

Chapter 11

Immortality, mourning and ritual

Susan E. Schwartz

Introduction

Jung addressed those living against themself as 'needing to step into the consuming fire of immortality, in order to transform into what [one] truly is' (1950, para, 221). The impact of the word 'immortality' and its meaning unfold personally and collectively with issues pertinent to us all. This word came unexpectedly as an auditory experience to a woman I will call Ester, who had little background or familiarity with anything religious or spiritual. She was at a crisis without knowing how to make sense of what happened to her. Sadly, she said, 'I need more human parts as these are not developed in a relational way inside myself from early in life.'

From childhood, so many aspects were not encouraged by parents for this highly intelligent girl, including the areas of education, the spiritual, intellectual or aesthetic. In myriad ways, the early creation of the self was inundated with environmental failures and distorted early mirroring (Schwartz-Salant, 1982, p. 48). The quest for herself began as an isolated child, taking herself to church on her own, looking for something.

This discussion will explore the concepts in Jungian analytical psychology of the transcendent function, the alchemical stage of the nigredo, and the use of ritual in the processes for unwrapping the psyche. This includes the death and rebirth cycles arising from the unconscious to consciousness and addressing the dead and dissociated parts of the psyche. The purpose of alchemy is to liberate the whole individual which is hidden in the darkness, threatened by the rational and correct conduct of life, consequently experiencing themselves as hindered and on the wrong path (paraphrased from Jung, 1954, para. 433). These topics are generally ignored when the culture encourages a person to go on rather than mourn, reflect, and take the time to grieve. The unprocessed material lays in the conscious and unconscious waiting for attention and transformation.

The word 'immortality'

For many years, the word 'immortality' haunted Ester. It kept on requiring her tenacious regard, propelling the inward search as she was suffering from lack of

DOI: 10.4324/9781003313304-17

meaning. She began reading Jung and entered Jungian analysis, but there was more. Although she did not initially understand where this word came from or the reasons, it instigated a lifelong quest for herself. The beginning of Jungian work and the persistence of 'immortality' unfolded its symbolic nuances through a long analysis involving the analytical formal and informal rituals, recognizing grief and loss, as well as renewal.

Ester is an example of what happens when the ego suddenly encounters the numinous or transpersonal dimensions of the psyche. As in the 'Ode: Intimations of Immortality from Recollections of Early Childhood,' a poem written by William Wordsworth (1815), a person jaded by experience turns from the bucolic to perceive the world as it really is. In this process and through analytical psychology, the reflections in image, dream and symbolic messages from the unconscious help restore the personality. For Ester, this was spurred on by the word 'immortality' recognized by her as the transcendent function.

The indelible traces, traumatic blanks and distortions in the individual and collective unconscious occur personally and culturally in unending cycles of transformation occurring through death and rebirth. The word immortality and the surprise it set up for Ester created the imperative to explore what was previously unquestioned. As she described,

> I'm thinking of my unconscious helping, assisting me . . . an inner part is infinitely connected to the same thing spoken of as God . . . some searching has been going on and it is what has been the focus of my living.

Julia Kristeva, French psychoanalyst, stated, 'I am forced to recognize my own mortality, yet unable to do so at the same time, thus, I must repel it, reject it, abject it' (Kristeva, 1982, p. 13). Her concept of abjection is a means for establishing boundary and identity, a separation to connect and establish the parameters of self. Ester dreamt there are these parts inside of a body part place – the place is a container place, and the parts need to be in a certain way. I think all are a shade of brown and then they are swapped out somehow and the container has another content or colour, perhaps blue or grey. Her associations were the containers representing her inside that were able to provide safety. These were sparse associations as if she was disallowed to venture into more detail. In fact, the events preceding her hearing the word 'immortality' were about death, mourning, grief and how to integrate this information against the denial imposed culturally and socially.

The word came to Ester after an abortion, an important event for many women and usually unable to be mourned, given no ritual space and kept secret. The lack of death rituals forced the energy towards finding herself for acquiring the meanings from this event. At the time, Ester felt lost, wandering in a wasteland, and thought she was devoid of spirit or value as she considered the abortion both the right and the wrong action. The abortion experience is a collective and feminine experience of loss, often associated with physical and psychological danger, and has been contested through the ages. In fact, many are shunned having made this choice, and there is no place for the necessary psychological attention to loss and renewal. Instead, women are often made numb emotionally, some damaged physically, making the restoration of self even more a necessity but also very difficult. They shoulder the tragedy of the ones who are unforgiven, unblessed, punished and prohibited, keeping them as outsiders in all cultures.

An abortion is personal and is both physically and psychologically life changing from the experience of death within one's body and then the return to life. Symbolically for Ester, the abortion meant time stopped yet remained existent in her memory. Her soul needs to return from the land of the dead, to recover the vision of herself. The passage is through grief and loss in a form of ethical reflection taking place at the threshold of the psychological and social worlds. Mourning operates transitionally, providing a liminal space from what was to what will be. The various types of mourning observed personally and cross-culturally are to satisfy one's spiritual longings to find meaning and purpose. This is where the analytic process is significant, especially as the rituals for mourning the abortion process are without place socially and culturally.

Psychologically, the rituals around transitional events assisting with death are also for rebirth, containers of comfort for amassing the ability to go on. The rituals within grief are rites of passage between the loss and the eventual return to the routines of life. However, Ester, like so many women, had nowhere to mourn; all was secret and hidden, typical of abortions. Solace and comfort deprived locks the energy within, emerging for Ester in the word 'immortality' when she was in a rather altered state. The psychological demand is for developing self-awareness and the strength of character for return to oneself but changed.

Prompted by the word 'immortality,' its initially confusing message drew Ester inward to dreams and to recall childhood memories composed mostly of lack and neglect. Ester dreamt there is some type of sorting of the inside belongings of this little girl in her container-like part. (This was like the previous dream.) She said in the dream, I am there and know about the process. In discussing the dream, she commented,

> What must be addressed is a death of the way I've carried primary relationships, the early ones, in myself . . . I've adjusted to living as though it had its flaws but needed to be managed. Now there is recognition of death needed, not managed but replaced with insights.

In other words, rather than being trapped in the deadly old story, there can be growth through the current insights.

The word 'immortality' for Ester was enunciated by an unfamiliar voice and conveyed power and impact including physiological responses. The word immortal contains the emotions of loss, life, death, all needing recognition to amass Ester's vital energy. 'The more extreme traumatically engendered condition is that in which any capacity to represent self-experience is ruptured: a state of paralysis in which even the blank impress is lost within a void' (Connolly, 2011, p. 5). Ester had been living within a silent cocoon with no place for response. One part of her functioned in life and another was secretly with the un-mourned process laying within. Memories of previous death images, traumas, and loss were present from her distant childhood. She never imagined they would emerge or dismantle her carefully constructed personality structure. These memories were painful but remained 'immortal' in her psyche, and were the keys for release from the childhood emotional isolation and traumatic wounding.

The experience of 'I' and feeling real is constructed from a multitude of unconscious mechanisms and processes. Donald Winnicott, British psychoanalyst in the twentieth century (1971, pp. 28–29), described the adaptation of the false self that Ester had to adopt as she long ago put the real one under wraps to protect. Unfortunately, the shell over the real becomes hardened, and one can become lost. Ester narrated a story of personal and collective history composed of her secret vicissitudes based on inner distress and psychological confusion. One's soul feels wrecked from within, forming a swarm of instability and pain of existence. For Ester, the word 'immortality' would not let her leave the material unattended. It was calling her to find the courage to be herself.

Abortion for women lacks the opportunity for the mourning process and rituals to mark the unborn foetus. So many women have experienced a variety of difficulties, remaining shut in shame, some in self-rejection, some in just ignoring the effects, as if the body and psyche do not need to mourn this necessary ending. Psychological confusion continues when rituals around death for moving into life are unsanctioned and culturally negated. However, the grief and loss are both private and public. As the psyche and its wounds are addressed with personal and collective rituals, one returns to energic functioning and rebirth of the self.

Ritual

Immortality implies an ongoing quest, while rituals help cope with the finality of death and emptiness, laying pathways to the unknown future. Rituals, whether in dream themes, objects or ceremonies, mark the many stages of mourning. They facilitate the work of healing, dealing with the paradoxes, despair, and disillusionment of what was and now has died.

Ritual is a unifying process including the physical senses and usually involves participation with others. The main intent is to cause change within the mind and life of the person. Along with personal history, ritual reflects the collective history, accompanied by images gathered through the ages, binding people to each other and to their values. The symbols apparent in all rituals are part of what induce change and are displayed and ministered to facilitate the intended effect. The archetypes of the collective unconscious are stirred by rituals and similarly bring altering of consciousness with their emotional imagery, relating to the survival and life renewal for the person. The contemplation on these images is accompanied by the emotionality of participants leading to transformation and renewal.

Myth and ritual are the vehicles for the symbols of eternal return, signifying a sacred time and imbuing existence with value. 'In the homogeneous and infinite expanse, in which no point of reference is possible and hence no orientation is established, the Hierophany or appearance of the Sacred reveals an absolute fixed point, a center' (Eliade, 1961, p. 21). The current scarcity of these rituals and symbols may be part of the restlessness, apathy, alienation and general boredom many modern people experience. Without ritual, life can seem flat and devoid of rhythm and texture.

Rituals are enacted for many reasons – to remove unwanted influences, utilize special procedures and arouse spontaneous responses aimed to produce a change in feeling. Essentially, it means accessing a higher and altered level of consciousness. The resultant interaction between mind and body occurs in a complementary and synchronous manner. Physical and psychological features are part of the rituals driving this universal aspect of human behaviour, bringing union with the higher self.

Parallels appear in the mystery religions. An example is the ritual of imbibing the soma drink from the moon tree so one gains the ability to transcend death. This represents the gift of immortality and the power to create from what was previously unavailable (Harding, 1990, p. 237). The ritual of the soma drink had the power to put the worshipper in touch with the eternal, immoveable reality of the self. Associated with immortality, rebirth, inspiration or ecstasy (ibid., p. 230) the participants partake symbolically of the ever-renewing life of the moon (ibid., p. 236). Likewise, Ester had to accept her emotions and instincts through the voice of her inner daemon saying the word 'immortality.' She gradually became acquainted with the ultimate reality of her own nature and through it her depths and limits.

Jung stated (1976, Letters, vol. 2, pp. 208–210),

> the rite is a symbolic act, giving expression to the archetypal expectation of the unconscious . . . this means biological life has a numinous character portrayed in life epochs including death . . . it is a question wanting an answer, need that should be satisfied by a solemn act with words and gestures of an archetypal and symbolic nature . . . rites give satisfaction to the collective and numinous aspects of the moment beyond their purely personal significance.

The numinous brings direct contact with the divine and is also revealed through dreams and visions.

There is coherent and meaningful unity within the diversity of religions, culture and histories. The various worldwide myths suggest all human beings take part in the powerful socializations imposed by the sacred and delineate broad outlines of what constitutes meaningful human experience. 'With each periodical [ritual] festival, the participants find the same sacred time – the same that had been manifested in the festival of the previous year or in the festival of a century earlier' (Eliade, 1961, p. 69). Bringing people back to the mythical age returns time to its circular nature.

Meaning is forged through a system of beliefs and practices. Through the process of individuation, the masks of the self are stripped away to uncover the true self. This gives a sense of our individual and cultural significance and enhances psychological health. Rituals hold us together while the psyche becomes unravelled for returning to our original selves. Ritual is part of what gives meaning and takes us out of the mundane.

Ester was led one step at a time inward with the word 'immortality.' It began with the abortion, a singular experience having little to do with the man involved, as her feelings were mostly unshared. No doubt this was exacerbated, like it is for many women with no ritual to mourn, separate or grow from this event. It was just 'taken care of,' and although he was supportive, she needed to leave that life. Yet, it remained present in her memory and body, as the un-mourned and ungrieved.

The word 'immortal' led us analytically back to her beginnings to find meaning from what was an emotionally bereft and traumatizing childhood environment. No one listened to her; home was without peace, and her inner life ignored with hardly any personal depth or intimacy. The various layers of parental emotional and/or physical absence produced the 'absence of memory, absence in the mind, absence of contact, absence of feeling [and this becomes] the substratum of what is real' (Kohon, 1999, p. 8). The introverted attitude was natural to Ester, but she basically was terribly alone, her inner life enclosed. The chaos at home under the guise of order could not cover the rampant emotional disorder.

The movement backwards into psychological regression also was a forward movement into engagement with life. As Jung commented, 'The production of unconscious compensations is a spontaneous process; the conscious realization is a method. The function is called "transcendent" because it facilitates the transition from one psychic condition to another by means of the mutual confrontation of opposites' (Jung, 1953, para. 780). This changes a person, opens them to new levels of being, and helps arrive at a resolution of the conflicts formerly dividing the self.

Nigredo

The nigredo, the 'blackening' of consciousness, marks death, the prima materia, or black earth, the basic matter of the psyche, the darkness of beginnings. This mysterious substance contains the seeds of the alchemical goal, the lapis. The death and decay are inherent in the process for renewal. American writer F. Scott Fitzgerald commented on this as 'the ability to hold two opposing ideas in mind at the same time and still retain the ability to function. One should, for example, be able to see that things are hopeless yet be determined to make them otherwise' (Fitzgerald, 1945, p. 69).

This is a metaphor of the analytical journey Ester was taking into a darkness she had formerly denied but could no longer. Death emanated in Ester's family with picture books of terrorism on the front table filled with gruesome pictures, exacerbated by the daily traumas. There was no emotional peace or safety.

The nigredo stage is also referred to as the putrefaction and is the stage of confession or catharsis with the burning away of the dross and getting to the essence. The Jungian analytical process recognizes this as the darkest of times instigating the psychological descent inwards. The planet Saturn rules the nigredo and symbolizes the father or the old way, heavy, limiting, rule oriented, the law and a symbol of death. The nigredo is a time when the prima materia or basic material begins to decompose and rot. On both the physical and psycho-spiritual levels, it contains the lesser alchemical phases of burning and coming apart of calcinatio and dissolutio. This is the time when our spirit most deeply feels the anguish of separation from former assumptions and illusions.

We are letting go both within and outside what is false, inauthentic and not in alignment with who we are. This accesses the truths existing on a soul level, beyond the ego and its illusions about who we should be. It is a process made more difficult by the resistance and defences against change. Many people remain unwilling to accept the formerly known is over. Few of us are quick to grasp the new life waiting for us. It will require letting go of the limited vision of existence to which we desperately cling. When we become willing to surrender, the alchemical process truly begins. When we are willing to die, we can be reborn.

This is a time of deep introspection, articulating a nuanced description of the transformation process moving through depression, darkness and impasse. Jung's notion of the shadow explicates the importance of turning toward darkness as a challenge and complement to consciousness. Facing the shadow requires that we come to terms with the repulsive, unacceptable, and rejected parts of ourselves, as well as approach our yet unknown and unrealized potentials. Linking the darkness of the shadow with the light of consciousness paves the way for the paradoxical play of opposites, or the mysterium coniunctionis Jung perceived at the core of the alchemical vision.

This stage usually manifests when the question of meaning or purpose becomes central for the individual, triggered by feelings of dissatisfaction, unhappiness, frustration. The blackening of the nigredo is about depression, the melancholia, the initial stage causing one to slow down and examine life. In Jungian terms, this alchemical first stage includes recognizing and integrating the shadow. Individuation is the process by which we move towards unifying the opposites, recognizing the resultant transcendence and bringing into consciousness the Self. It is a redemptive process of recovering spirit, soul or Self from the unconscious. In analytical psychology the reflection in image, dream and symbolic messages from the unconscious helps restore the personality. For Ester, this was spurred on by the word 'immortality' as the auditory push from the transcendent function.

Transcendent function

This concept was introduced in Jung's 1916 essay on the topic, marking his break with Freud as Jung determined the transcendent function was guiding the psyche towards individuation. The transcendent function bridges the border between self and other, psyche and body. The word 'function' derives from the Latin verb *fungere*, to perform. 'Transcend' is a compound of two Latin words, the prefix *trans*, 'beyond, across,' and the verb *scandere*, 'to climb.' When something transcends, it goes above, beyond or below. This is an active confrontation between conscious and unconscious, resulting in the emergence of new symbolic forms. These transcend the internal conflicts and lead to increasing psychic wholeness. As Ester explained, she was in conflict when the word 'immortality' emerged. It was a psychic experience, when the energy of the living seems to follow the dead; when within the psyche, there is tension between one's desire for inertia and desire for re-engagement and life (Ulanov, 2008, p. 430). The rebirth in ego consciousness evolves from the deadened aspects of the psyche emerging and leading her venture into the unknown.

Dreams, complexes and dissociations of the psyche reveal the transcendent function in therapeutic work. The unconscious memories form an estranged and melancholic language, a crucible of mourning and for healing. Internal dislocation and division derive from personal, cultural, and intergenerational wounds, including the unshed mourning. The weight of unresolvable despondency keeps one emotionally separated from oneself. With a ritual, a funeral, a celebration of life, mourning gains a location on the map of grief and growth.

Ester comes to therapy at a loss about what to do, what to feel, what to think. What is her purpose? The therapeutic work consists neither of solely releasing nor repressing, but of holding and working with the psychological contents to uncover the internal and external complexes, challenges and blockages. Through therapy, she will make conscious these issues appearing in dreams, thoughts and feelings affecting relationships with self and others. The aim is also to elicit from the unconscious meaning relating to her future attitudes. The unconscious comes to consciousness through the transcendent function, appearing with symbol formation for regulation and balancing of the psyche with new attitudes. 'The self is supported in its development through the symbolic nature of the transcendent function so the creative resources residing in the unconscious become accessible' (Solomon, 2007, p. 244).

Some basic characteristics of the transcendent function are the following: it is composed of not new but unknown contents; it reveals the counter position in the unconscious; and it includes the acknowledgement of the risk of dissociation from unconscious contents. Analysis can bring these to awareness and free the psyche with the emerging readjustment of the psychological contents.

Jungian analytical therapy is a process to reconstruct and assemble the personality fragments and make sense of them. It provides the experiences to explore subjectivity and imagination. Jung's view of psychic dissociability presupposes an integral psyche, the self falls apart in a kind of regression, not as a defence, but because of deficiency. Regression is not the illness, because within it is the inherent impulse toward a unitary psyche. Because of this impulse, a pathologically disintegrated psyche spontaneously attempts to reintegrate. Regression reactivates this impulse. The challenge for the therapist is to assist in finding the yet-unknown aspects facilitated by dreams, the therapeutic relationship and other life events.

Becoming oneself involves the capacity of the mind to process the separation and mourn what was lost (Cavalli, 2014, p. 187). Holding the tension of the opposites in the analytic relational encounter brings participants face to face with their fantasies and tragedies. This includes the analyst's capacity to hold the patient's narrative, bridging culture and time and creating links for self and other. As the personality seeks self-regulation, the analytic process collects the dissociated fragments, the solitude wrapped in withdrawal, and brings it into relationship.

Internally, a person might have no room for other thoughts or space for interpretations. All seems noisy, intrusive and, like Ester, perhaps feeling overrun as she experienced previously in the family. Rather than this being an impediment, it exposes the impasse and the dissociated elements in the psyche. A person often does not realize how much these elements control freedom of expression, confidence, and ease in being. Here lay the uncomfortable gaps between self and others, the idealizations, the need for defence, all emerging in the therapeutic relationship.

Jung addressed the dissociation originating from traumatic experiences showing up in the complex. He stated,

> The essential factor is the dissociation of the psyche and how to integrate the dissociation . . . that a traumatic complex brings about dissociation . . . that the main therapeutic problem is not abreaction but how to integrate the dissociation . . . possesses the quality of psychic autonomy . . . to reintegrate the autonomous complex . . . by living the traumatic situation over again, once or repeatedly.
>
> (Jung, 1928, paras. 262–268)

These natural processes derive from a matrix based on the earliest relationships re-enacted in psychological treatment. Likewise, the childhood mis-attunements absorbed Ester's psyche and became preserved in a melancholic and invisible interior space. The longing to which they are connected comes forth in the therapeutic process of recovering what has been un-mourned.

The therapeutic process promotes the kind of psychic activity requiring a tolerance for contradiction and holding the energy pulling in many directions. This requires conversing and reconciling with the unconscious and the new attitudes not easily managed or accepted. The varied positions in the unconscious bring the psyche forward, out of the polarization and oppositional states, and this enables the process of individuation (Solomon, 1998, p. 232).

The transcendent function operates between patient and therapist, and out of this space symbols emerge as communicative gestures from the unconscious to conscious. The transition from one psychic condition to another brings the psyche from oppositional defensive states to symbol formation. Bridging the gap between conscious and unconscious, the transcendent function involves conflict and collaboration from which the symbols arise. Symbols can be described as a feature and function of the therapeutic third, a jointly created unconscious life from the flow between the therapeutic pair (Colman, JAP, 2010). Symbols transport us beyond the expressible, launching us past the limitations of language into inexplicable territory. From the energy released and the conflicts aroused, discontent and stress are re-experienced for new emotions, reactions and thoughts to emerge. This is part of the rebirth from the recognition of death assisted by the rituals for mourning.

The paradoxes of the psyche with its principle of synthesis and balance bring forth the submerged personality parts. Therapy explores the loss and wounding of all kinds, internal and external, acute and cumulative, personal and collective. The unconscious becomes activated by intent, fear, hope or any strong emotion. From this emotional process, the transcendent function forms. Ester repeatedly noted being helped by the transcendent function first in supplying the word 'immortality' and then in keeping her on the path. Jung described, 'From the activity of the unconscious there now emerges a new content, constellated by thesis and antithesis in equal measure and standing in complementary relation to both' (Jung, 1949, para. 825). Again, pain and resistance accompany breaking from the old, even as the psyche steps towards movement and renewal. The process requires gathering the pain receded into the unconscious and bringing it to consciousness, aided by the grief and mourning.

This depends on the ego's ability to hold the clash of what seems like opposing forces while keeping them in dynamic interplay. This occurs both within the person and within the therapeutic couple. About this, Jung described,

> The shuttling to and fro of arguments and affects between conscious and unconscious represents the transcendent function of opposites. The confrontation of the two positions generates a tension charged with energy and creates a living, third thing . . . a living birth that leads to a new level of being, a new situation. As long as these are kept apart – naturally for the purpose of avoiding conflict – they do not function and remain inert.
>
> (Jung, 1958, para. 189)

Jungian analysis, through recognizing the rituals and symbols of the death and rebirth cycles, provides the expression of desires formerly lost, frustrated or abandoned. The process for forging self-discovery and soul repair arises in the tension from the opposites within. We are confronted with the gap between the subject and its outline in the mirror, the symbol and the symbolized. If the tension can be sustained without succumbing to the urge to identify with one side or the other, the third and completely unexpected image unites the two in a creative new way. 'The psyche accomplishes its transformation through the creation of symbols which are capable of bringing together opposing aspects of the self' (Solomon, 1998, p. 227). Symbols are the impersonal metaphors, arising from convention, myth and cultural artefacts. They make ritual a medium of communication, revealing our inherent intersubjectivity and our need to connect to more beyond our personal being.

Jung contended,

> We need the coldness of death to see clearly. Life wants to live and to die, to begin and to end. You are not forced to live eternally, but can also die, since

there is a will in you for both. Life and death must strike a balance in your existence. . . . Therefore I behold death, since it teaches me how to live . . . Without
death, life would be meaningless, since the long-lasting rises again and denies
its own meaning. To be, and to enjoy your being, you need death, and limitation
enables you to fulfil your being.

(Jung, 2009, pp. 266–277)

The emotional wounds Ester suffered as an adult replicated events in childhood
formerly disremembered. She described childhood with a mother poorly attuned
to her, unable to empathize accurately with her internal experiences. The mother
was absent from the impress of emotion – a surface mother, not a connected one.
Mother was an uncanny absence, more than mere coldness, and Ester had no recall
of affection in a childhood devoid of psychic articulation. Unable to get close
enough or feel securely accepted, she did not know how to mother herself, be
soothing or comforting. Alone and telling no one, her feelings were stored in the
body and psyche as unassimilated material. In addition, father was forbidding, and
no one to get close to as that would be dangerous. There was nothing spiritual or
sacred in the harsh and empty environment.

The process of Jungian analytical therapy became her container for suffering
and facing the bleakness of her childhood. The rituals absent earlier evolved in the
analysis as she explored the netherworld of her psyche. The transference and the
setting created the space to feel and own the previously repressed, the melancholy
and the shock. Because they are immortal and occur throughout time, mourning
and its rituals allow life to return. This became her task, reflecting the archetypal
continuation of existence.

Sense of loss

The verb 'to lose' has its taproot sunk in sorrow; it is related to the 'lorn' in 'for-
lorn.' It comes from an Old English word meaning to perish, which comes from an
even older word meaning to separate or cut apart. When psychic growth is halted,
one cannot separate from or understand the traumas, until they are recognized. As
Rilke said, 'the dark interval continual transformations of the beloved visible and
tangible into the invisible vibration and excitation of our own nature, that new
frequencies of vibration are introduced into the vibrating spheres of the universe'
(Rilke, 2013, p. 90). For Ester, the internal and external situations were presenting material she could not formerly decode. This inability became a protective
mechanism like an emotional retreat. Remembering means differentiation and can
generate anxiety with the fear of fragmentation and loss of the imaginary unity. For
Ester, the past needed to be articulated, past time explored, so she could open to
current psychic life and emerge from its frozen impasse.

Ester did not realize she was paralyzed by time, walled off from the flow of life to
make sure there were no traumatic disruptions. She avoided focus on mourning and
grief, while the rituals in the analytic process reflected the immortal and ongoing
nature of it all. The separation and loss reach down into the deepest psychic regions

and needs to ritualize the past death, loss, grief and suffering so one becomes free to grow.

Jung stated,

> the same physiological processes that have been man's for hundreds of thousands of years still endure, instilling into our inmost hearts this profound intuition of the 'eternal' continuity of the living. But the self, as an inclusive term that embraces our whole living organism, not only contains the deposit and totality of all past life, but is also a point of departure, the fertile soil from which all future life will spring . . . the idea of immortality follows legitimately from these psychological premises.
>
> (Jung, 1953, para. 303)

In the process new birth and fertility are created, as the continual round of life is immortal. Psyche requires demise. The idea of the unconscious self, the unrealized latent self is a type of inner dead self, needing birth or resurrection through consciousness to come alive. The task is to make sense of the repressed and die to the old.

Clinging to fantasies exert a maniacal force and both the internal and external worlds become impoverished and lack reality. There is catastrophe when one cannot play with the fantasies and reconsider the past. Suspended in time, something inside is holding its breath. Grieving affects the necessary separation from what must die, yet it can be hard to see the trajectory or the way out. There is also quiet mourning, silent mourning and solo mourning, but they are too often the plight of those having abortions and absent the rituals for healing.

The word 'immortality' and the power it set up for Ester created the imperative to explore all she had not previously questioned to find her individual self. 'Immortality' offered Ester the opportunity of possible transformation of consciousness to embrace a life lived productively and meaningfully. It was a way in which the experience of what could not be born would help her live on, resolve the conflict and strengthen love for herself. Her analysis was the exploration of the experience of death and loss, including its rituals for the initiation of psyche into itself.

The numinous transcendent reality encounters with the sacred, defying logical understanding, were contained within the word 'immortality.' Ester reflected about this same word referencing the biblical tree of life in the Garden of Eden, where the suffering of expulsion, psychological death and rebirth was painful but ultimately meaningful. From initiation rites a feeling of immortality and life gains new perspective. The ordeals are designed to push the person to their limits and symbolize death and rebirth bringing release from the coma of unconsciousness (Harding, 1990, pp. 210–211).

A paradox of grief is that it's an occasion for both community and isolation. While the experience of loss is innately personal, it can also catalyse the desire for connection to self and others. We are wired for the communal, and the suffering is a vehicle for grieving deaths not properly mourned.

Contradiction

One cannot separate from or understand the traumas until they are recognized. Ester was confronted with entering another world where the issues are beyond her own, pointing to where she had not been looking. This can be called an aporia and references Jacques Derrida, French philosopher of the mid-twentieth century. It is an impasse, a state of paralysis, where we are lost in how to move through some place, set of ideas, etc. Aporia's best definition in Greek is 'difficulty.' Aporia is a term in the philosophical tradition indicating an insurmountable contradiction, which ends in an insoluble conflict between *poros*, meaning 'way,' and *a poros*, meaning 'lack of way.' Derrida perceived aporia as a paradoxical term whose teaching is to block the very ability to move between boundaries, to define, to formulate. Aporia is a blind spot blocking the field of vision. Derrida said,

> We are obligated – this is a kind of duty – to give oneself up to the impossible decision, while taking account of rules and law. . . . A decision that did not go through the ordeal of the undecidable would not be a free decision, it would only be the programmable application or unfolding of a calculable process.
>
> (Cornell et al., 1992, p. 24)

The death and rebirth cycle of the ego is symbolic of the process taking place not in the world but in the mind, a temporary death of the ego and its re-emergence or rebirth from the unconscious. This expresses a new potential, a new manifestation of life, a new fruitfulness that is created (Jung, 1949, para. 279). This is part of the constantly repeated experience of humanity.

Immortality was the opening of the psychological door for Ester. To come to terms with herself as an individual, she could not forget the dead, the old life and the losses. Denial and repression would work against her psyche. The journey inward is also outward, and there is permeability between death and life (Hillman and Shamdasani, 2013, p. 25). The cycle is never complete, and we let go to re-emerge, or else one becomes trapped by clinging to no longer viable ways of being. 'What we take to be our individuation, or our quest is taking up the unredeemed dead' (Hillman and Shamdasani, 2013, p. 85).

This has been made complex as the rituals around abortion are not present. Making meaning and finding communal support have become an interior process and whispered in secret among women who understand. Loss and devastation, shock, trauma, the unnamed or not discussed become solipsistic, wrapped in its own boundaries, and the self often withdrawn. Regarding the conception of what is morally binding, Judith Butler commented,

> it does not proceed from my autonomy or my reflexivity. It comes to me unbidden, unexpected, unplanned. In fact, it tends to ruin my plans, and if my plans are ruined, that may well be the sign that something is morally binding upon me.
>
> (Butler, 2006, p. 130)

Whether we are willing to develop the ethic-political imagination to deal fruitfully with the challenges of ensuring life-sustaining material, social and political conditions in our precarious world has been fraught with controversy. In the midst is the individual trying to find the meaning and the psychological awareness required by life-changing events, like abortion.

Conclusion

The word 'immortality' was Ester's initiation into herself. 'The urge to immortality is not a simple reflex of the death-anxiety but a reaching out by one's whole being toward life. Perhaps this natural expansion of the creature alone can explain why transference is such a universal passion' (Becker, 1973, pp. 152–153). Numinous personal experience, transcendent reality, meaningful encounters with the sacred often defy logical understanding. Conscious acts make something happen or seek to create a new reality. Identity before and after has changed as its previous formation becomes uprooted.

Ester's word immortality held many meanings. The sacred, something she had not experienced from young, exists outside any specific era and outside normal time. There is profane space, and there is space where

> the Sacred manifests itself; unlike profane space, sacred space has a sense of direction. Thus, human fulfilment does not lie in returning to a sacred time, but in escaping from time altogether. This is like the philosophical concept of eternal return in an endless cosmic cycle.
>
> (Eliade, 1961, p. 109)

William Wordsworth in his poem 'Ode: Intimations of Immortality' (1815), referenced this cycle and the emerging from suffering as: 'We will grieve not, rather find/Strength in what remains behind;/. . . In the soothing thoughts that spring/Out of human suffering.' From the experience of returning to self, finding meaning and purpose beyond what she ever imagined, Ester felt inner value and joy. She tapped into wells of sagacity she previously didn't know she possessed. This included revelation of the life within, and discovering her inner compass, Ester was now able to embody her world.

References

Becker, E. (1973). *The Denial of Death*. New York: Simon & Schuster.

Butler, J. (2006). *Precarious Life: The Powers of Mourning and Violence*. New York: Verso.

Cavalli, A. (2014). Clinging, Gripping Holding, Containment: Reflection on a Survival Reflex ad the Development of a Capacity to Separate. *Journal of Analytical Psychology*, 59, pp. 548–565.

Colman, W. (2010). Mourning and the Symbolic Process. *Journal of Analytical Psychology*, 55, pp. 275–297.

Connolly, A. (2011). Healing the Wounds of our Fathers: Intergenerational Trauma, Memory, Symbolization and Narrative. *Journal of Analytical Psychology*, 56(5), pp. 607–626.

Cornell, D., Rosenfeld, M. and Carlton, D. (eds.) (1992). *Deconstruction and the Possibility of Justice*. London: Routledge.

Eliade, M. (1961). *The Sacred and the Profane: The Nature of Religion* (Trask, Willard R. Trans.). New York: Harper Torchbooks.

Fitzgerald, F.S. (1945). The Crack-Up. In Wilson, E. (ed.), *The Crack-Up*. New York: New Directions reprint ed., 2009.

Harding, E. (1990). *Women's Mysteries Ancient and Modern*. Boston: Shambhala.

Hillman, J. and Shamdasani, S. (2013). *Lament of the Dead*. New York: W.W. Norton & Company.

Jung, C.G. (1928). The Therapeutic Value of Abreaction. In *Collected Works, Vol. 16. The Practice of Psychotherapy* (2nd ed.). Princeton, NJ: Princeton University Press.

Jung, C.G. (1949). Definitions. In *Collected Works, Vol. 6, Psychological Types* (2nd ed.). Princeton, NJ: Princeton University Press.

Jung, C.G. (1950). Concerning Rebirth. In *Collected Works, Vol. 9i, The Archetypes and the Collective Unconscious* (2nd ed.). Princeton: Princeton University Press, 1968.

Jung, C.G. (1953). The Tibetan Book of the Great Liberation. In *Collected Works, Vol. 11. Psychology and Religion* (2nd ed.). Princeton: Princeton University Press, 1969.

Jung, C.G. (1954). The Philosopher's Tree. In *Collected Works, Vol. 13, Alchemical Studies* (2nd ed.). Princeton: Princeton University Press.

Jung, C.G. (1958). The Transcendent Function. In *Collected Works, Vol. 8. The Structure and Dynamics of the Psyche* (2nd ed.). Princeton: Princeton University Press.

Jung, C.G. (1976). *Letters Vol. 2: 1951–1961*. Princeton: Princeton University Press.

Jung, C.G. (2009). *The Red Book, a Reader's Edition*. New York: W.W. Norton & Company.

Kohon, G. (ed). (1999). *The Dead Mother: The Work of Andre Green*. London and New York: Routledge.

Kristeva, J. (1982). *Powers of Horror: An Essay on Abjection* (Roudiez, Leon S. Trans.). New York: Columbia University Press.

Rilke, R.-M. (2013). *The Dark Interval. Letters on Loss, Grief and Transformation* (Baer, U. Ed.). New York: Modern Library.

Schwartz-Salant, N. (1982). *Narcissism and Character Transformation: The Psychology of Narcissistic Character Disorders*. Toronto: Inner City Books.

Solomon, H. (1998). Love: Paradox of Self and Other. *British Journal of Psychotherapy*, 14(3), pp. 271–283.

Solomon, H. (2007). *The Self in Transformation*. London: Karnac.

Ulanov, A. (2008). Transference, The Transcendent Function, and Transcendence. *Journal of Analytical Psychology*, 42(1), pp. 119–138.

Winnicott, D.W. (1971). *Playing and Reality*. London: Tavistock.

Wordsworth, W. (1815). Ode: Intimations of Immortality. In *The Project Gutenberg Ebook of Poems in Two Volumes*. Ebook #:8824. www.gutenberg.org/cache/epub/8824/pg8824.html.

Part VI

Towards an archetypal ontology of death

Chapter 12

The seduction of immortality

Jung, Heidegger and Hegel on death

Jon Mills

Introduction

The ontology of death is universal, hence archetypal. Nowhere do we witness any organic creature escape its talons. Analytical psychology has had an intimate relation to death for the simple fact that it contemplates the soul, the numinous and an afterlife. From Hegel to Heidegger, Freud and Jung, death was an existential force that sustained and transformed life, the positive significance of the negative. Rather than merely a destructive phenomenon, death informs Being, the power of nothingness that dialectically drives life. In this chapter, I will introduce the notion of what I call the *omega principle*, the psychological orientation and trajectory of our being towards death, what we may say is a universal preoccupation and recapitulation of the collective unconscious that subsumes our personal relation to death, an eternal return of the objective psyche constellated as *esse in anima*.

The philosophy of death

No words can placate, intellectualize or rationalize away our private encounter with death, for life hangs by a hair (*de pilo pendet*). Despite the impersonality of death and our brute rational acceptance of the implacability of finitude, logos cannot prevent the inevitable. Although there is an inherent teleology to both life and death, death becomes our final aim and destiny. In the sombre words of Quintilian, everything that is born passes away (*deficit omne quod nascitur*).

The fantasy of a return goes back to the ancients. The Primordial cosmic unity, the Neoplatonic One, the myth of the eternal return, the *eschaton* – all have to do with the fantasy of a return to origins. The return fantasy has metaphysically and symbolically conditioned culture since the time of civilization, such as in the need for a cosmogonic ordering principle, Godhead or eternity, like the view that the cosmos has always been infinite (*Ananta*) and uncaused, such as in the Vedic tradition or its permutation as the *Ein Sof* in Kabbalah. And for the Neoplatonists, all that exists – the many – is contingent upon the one as an unconditioned unity that conditions all unity (*Enneads*, V.3[49].15.12–14). Here One is a unity of singularity that conditions all being. Singularity as unitarity is the essence of anything

DOI: 10.4324/9781003313304-19

that exists, as the existence of all things is being. Yet the One is indivisible and is the original cause of being. There is no division, no separation, no difference within pure identity. It embraces a simplicity thesis of the rudimentary presence of identity where everything is collapsed into solitariness. The solitary is also further intimately connected to the notion of nothingness as 'that which is not one (*oude hen*)' (Plato, 1961, *Republic*, 478b), which Plotinus (1966) espouses (*Enneads*, V.2[11].1.1). Only one exists or it is nothing (*ouden*). So we either return to One or have never left it. Symbiosis, the merger fantasy, a return to a tensionless state – all presuppose a cosmogony of holism, a participatory metaphysics with divinity, a heavenly Eden or its equivalent in other religions, and peace, hence death (tensionlessness).

Jung on death

The Chilean diplomat and writer Miguel Serrano, who had travelled widely in India studying yoga, and who had close friendships with Jung and the poet Hermann Hesse towards the end of their lives, visited Jung less than one month before his death at his house in Küsnacht. In his interview with Jung in his study, he describes how 'Jung was seated beside the window, dressed in a Japanese ceremonial gown, so that in the light of the late afternoon he looked like a magician or a priest of some ancient cult' (Serrano, 1961, p. 465). After giving him a gift, Serrano said that he had just come from visiting Hesse where they had talked about death.

> I asked Hesse whether it was important to know if there was something beyond death. Hesse had said that he thought not, that he thought that death was probably like entering the collective unconscious, falling into it, perhaps.

Jung replied:

> Your question was badly put. It would be better phrased in this way: Is there any reason to believe that there is life after death?

"And is there?" responded Serrano.

> Were it possible for the mind to function at the margin of the brain, it would be incorruptible.

"Is such a thing possible?"

> Parapsychological phenomena suggest that it is. I myself have experienced certain things which also indicate it. Once I was gravely ill, almost in a coma. Everybody thought that I was suffering terribly, but in fact, I was experiencing something extremely pleasant. I seemed to be floating over my body, far above

it. Then after my father died, I saw him several times. Of course that does not mean that he in fact appeared. His appearances may have been entirely subjective phenomena on my part.

(p. 466)

Jung was referring to his space dream he reported in *Memories, Dreams, Reflections* (Jung, 1961, p. 289) after he suffered a heart attack and had a near death experience where he had the most profound sense of euphoria merging with the cosmos. Serrano continued,

But isn't it possible that all these things are in fact external and objective, and not merely something which happens in the mind? Hesse talks about the Collective Unconscious as if it existed externally, and he considers that death may merely be a *falling* into that state.

(p. 466, emphasis in original)

In a lecture Jung (1958) gave at the Basel Psychology Club, he was asked whether or not we can assume that individual consciousness continues after death. Although he replied that we can never know that, he offered 'an opinion about it with the help of the unconscious,' for 'the unconscious obliges and produces dreams which point to a continuation of life after death' (p. 377). Jung had reported dreams and several experiences of psychic phenomena including 'telepathic precognitions of death' (*CW*, 8, § 830, p. 430) associated with people who died or were about to die that point toward an afterlife (Harding, 1948, pp. 180–185). But in his famous *Face to Face* (Freeman, 1959) interview with John Freeman for BBC television, Jung questions if death really is an end because the psyche, he asserts, is not confined to space and time, nor is it 'subjected to those laws,' hence pointing towards a psychical existence beyond the material world as a 'continuation of life' (p. 437). Elsewhere, on several occasions (*CW*, 8, § 440, p. 231; § 837, p. 434; § 855, p. 445–446; § 948, p. 506), Jung had speculated that the psyche was subject to its own laws beyond quantum mechanics that suggests a possible transcendence of spacetime due to its relative 'trans-spatial and trans-temporal nature' (*CW*, 8, § 813, p. 413) confirmed through parapsychological experience such as telepathic phenomena and synchronicity. Jung (1934) writes:

The fact that we are totally unable to imagine a form of existence without space and time by no means proves that such an existence is in itself impossible. And therefore, just as we cannot draw, from an appearance of space-timelessness, any absolute conclusion about a space-timeless form of existence, so we are not entitled to conclude from the apparent space-time quality of our perception that there is no form of existence *without* space and time. It is not only permissible to doubt the absolute validity of space-time perception; it is, in view of the available facts, even imperative to do so. The hypothetical possibility that the psyche touches on a form of existence outside space and time presents a scientific question-mark that merits serious consideration for a long time to come.

(*CW*, 8, § 814, p. 414, emphasis in original)

Here Jung is careful to acknowledge our empirical experience of perception and the reality of the external world, only that we cannot make absolute or definitive claims that *that's all there is*. Here he employs an epistemological scepticism or hermeneutics of suspicion towards absolute claims to truth and knowledge *as such*. A scientific worldview, on the contrary, is confined by its observations and the need to confirm, verify and/or disqualify hypotheses based on refutation of conjectures, which is constrained, by definition, in its methodology of analysing appearances of the world. That which does not appear falls outside of its purview, notwithstanding contemporary developments in particle physics and field theory not known during Jung's time that the universe remains largely hidden as dark matter-energy, itself a problematic conjecture. Jung continues:

The nature of the psyche reaches into obscurities far beyond the scope of our understanding . . . If, therefore, from the needs of his own heart or in accordance with the ancient lessons of human wisdom, or out of respect for the psychological fact that 'telepathic' perceptions occur, anyone should draw the conclusion that the psyche, in its deepest reaches, participates in a form of existence beyond space and time, and thus partakes of what is inadequately and symbolically described as 'eternity.'

(*CW*, 8, § 815, p. 414)

Just as Freud proclaimed the unconscious to be 'timeless,' hence eternal, and as an assemblage of archaic or ancestral 'inheritance of memory-traces of what our forefathers experienced, quite independently of direct communication and of the influence of education,' where he further echoes Jung's thesis that 'the content of the unconscious is collective, a general possession of mankind' (Freud, 1939, pp. 127, 170), Jung believes the amalgam of experiences from collective humanity existing universally and from time immemorial speak to another dimension of reality or form of existence based on paranormal encounters and intuitions of the psyche. And yet he inserts a clever disclaimer: Whether we can know if these hypotheses are absolute truths or not can never be determined, for they are epistemically occluded.

In an interview with the English journalist Gordon Young (1960) just before Jung's 85th birthday, Jung states, 'it is just as legitimate to believe in life after death as it is to doubt it' (p. 448). Jung sometimes referred to the land of the dead as possibly being the unconscious and that the 'beyond is the unconscious' (*CW*, 10 § 698, p. 368). Elsewhere he refers to death as 'beyond consciousness' (*CW*, 7 § 302, p. 191). In analysing dreams of his patients, Jung also interpreted death dreams and symbolism as premonitions, collective dominants or archetypes, synchronistic phenomena, and once described a patient who died two years after having a cosmic

vision, which Jung applied to 'death as a final realization of wholeness' (*CW*, 10 §
698, p. 369).

The fear of death is a form of unconscious communication, of an impending
event that is to come, where 'the conscious separates from the unconscious alto-
gether' (*CW*, 18, § 239, p. 107). But Jung often intimated an immortality the soul
tries to achieve. In a memorial for Jerome Schloss that he gave in 1927 at the Analytical Psychology Club of New York, Jung tells us:

> When we penetrate the depths of the soul and when we try to understand its
> mysterious life, we shall discern that death is not a meaningless end, the mere
> vanishing into nothingness – it is an accomplishment, a ripe fruit on the tree of
> life. Nor is death an abrupt extinction, but a goal that has been unconsciously
> lived and worked for during half a lifetime.
>
> (*CW*, 18 § 1706, p. 757)

Here Jung amplifies on Horace where death is the ultimate goal of things (*mors
ultima linea rerum est*) and culmination of a lived life, that goal being 'a state of
rest' (*CW*, 8, § 798, p. 405). But his equally interesting and valid insight is that
death has been unconsciously prepared in the latter half of a person's life (also see
CW, 13 § 68, p. 46). In other words, the psyche unconsciously prepares for death:
anyone who has witnessed a dying person who has not contemplated their own end
becomes distraught and fights having to die. Those who have, more easily grow
into its acceptance, inevitability and desire for peace. There also is a making peace
with one's life in dying, an easing into, a celebration or gratitude for what one was
fortunate to have had and experienced.

Jung continues to acknowledge this 'secret work' the soul unconsciously under-
takes to prepare for death, which may be said to be the preoccupation of all religions, cults and mystical traditions exemplified by the customs, rituals and as
annotated in the wisdom literature that has been passed down over the aeons in, as
we may call, 'getting ready for the departure' (*CW*, 18 § 1707, p. 757). He evokes
the image of the four-pedalled flower – the four seasons of a man's life – as a symbol of 'immortal light.' Even if we are unaware of its unconscious operations, the
psyche nevertheless does its own underground death-work towards preparation and
purification. Of course, Jung was aware of Freud's (1920) celebrated text *Beyond
the Pleasure Principle* where the aim of all life is a return to origins, where death-
work is an unconscious preparation for endings only on the condition that it is
achieved through circuitous means. But Jung is reaching for immortality, or at least
an afterlife of some kind he thinks the psyche strives to achieve. He tells us: 'As a
doctor, I make every effort to strengthen the belief in immortality, especially with
older patients when such questions come threateningly close. For, seen in correct
psychological perspective, death is not an end but a goal' (*CW*, 13 § 68, p. 46). The
unconscious spoke to Schloss, who, Jung describes, 'beheld the vision of his own
sarcophagus from which his living soul arose' (*CW*, 18 § 1708, p. 757). Here death
becomes the sublation – hence, transcendence – of soul.

In Jung's (1934) essay 'The Soul and Death,' he takes up Freud's observations that life is an 'initial disturbance of a perpetual state of rest which forever attempts to re-establish itself' (*CW*, 8, § 798, p. 406). Following Aristotle's notion of teleology, Jung views the soul awaking as life that was disrupted from its initial quiescent nature of rest, which arises and then returns to its original condition of repose. The notion of the soul awakening from its initial slumber as rupture is also the very developmental scheme Hegel (1978, *EG* §§ 391–411) uses when describing how the psyche first manifests itself as embodied desire that is constellated in the form of its immediate sentient nature dialectically mediated from its original unconscious unity (Mills, 2000, 2010). And once psyche erupts into life, it must follow its natural course of being predisposed to reach its goal and to satisfy its aim, the fulfilment of its own becoming.

In youth we are oriented toward the future, and in old age we must embrace our destiny as life careens and merges with death. And for Jung, as we grow older, we remain vitally alive only on the condition that we die with life (*CW*, 8, § 800, p. 407). This is why the neurotic fear of life is in the service of avoiding death, and the neurotic fear of death is to refuse to accept the fulfilment of life. Clinging to the past eviscerates the present as a repudiation to live evocatively towards the horizon of death, which is incumbent upon us to accept meaningfully and with dignity in actualizing its truth. Hence the goal of death is to live a fulfilled and meaningful life that reaches its pinnacle as the complete unfolding of our uniquely subjective natures as existential providence, the aim and purpose of individuation. But Jung asks us a profound question: 'What is attained with death?'

It goes without saying that the psyche pines for and seeks reassurance in a continuance beyond the confines of our material embodiment, for we as humanity would never have invented the greatest living religions as complicated systems for the preparation of death where 'the meaning of existence is contemplated in its end' (*CW*, 8, § 804, p. 408). In Jung's signature use of typical epistemological and metaphysical stipulations that we can never know if anything lies after the end, and hence we have no rational grounds to posit an afterlife, he does turn towards the collective unconscious as the reservoir and revelation of archetypal symbols that arise from the same unconscious 'spirit' (*Geist*) that informs the phylogenesis of humankind. His argument shifts to the psychological language of the psyche as being in soul (*esse in anima*) that has the potentiality to be atemporal and aspatial in so far as collective or universal mind is not experientially bound to the confines of finite individual existence. Here is where the collective psyche adds currency to the hypothesis of a continuity of psychic existence that informs the ontological undergirding of a transpersonal unconscious cosmos that becomes the ground of all psychic manifestations, hence a world soul (*anima mundi*).

But this argument rests on the conviction that the collective or objective psyche takes precedence over the subjective souls of individuals that is conditioned by and gives rise to personal subjectivity. So, we may merge with or return to a collective cosmos – the *unus mundus*, but there is no guarantee this is particularized or constellated in any way on the concrete level of lived psychological experience, only merely an empty formalism, the parameters of which we do not need to critique here (cf. Mills, 2019). While this does not mean that death is simply a 'meaningless cessation,' it also affords us no guarantee or solace that there is anything that lies after the end. But it does hold an aporic message: If death is the fulfilment of life's goal that renders it meaningful in the truest sense, this means that we *have* to die in order to give life its truest meaning. This is why preparing for death is an existential necessity no one can escape in good faith, for it entails the reflective self-consciousness to *act*, that is, of agentically actualizing and truly living a good life in relation to our being towards death.

Being towards death

In Division Two of *Being and Time*, Heidegger sets out to investigate what is generally considered to be one of the most philosophically nuanced analyses of death. Heidegger (1927) initially asks whether we can obtain an ontologically adequate conception of death as an exisentiell question belonging to the character of Dasein or the human subject as being in the world. As Being-at-an-end (*Zu-Ende-sein*) in death (¶ 45, 234, p. 277), we must face the exisentiell nature of our lived experience as a particular understanding of ourselves. The peculiar relation we have is only as Being towards death (*Sein zum Tode*), which is a form of authentic relatedness to one's inexistence that is to come. Because existence by definition is incomplete, only the actuality of death may be complete, hence total, final or whole. But any gain in becoming whole comes at the loss of Being. This is why we are condemned to lack.

Heidegger tells us that 'Dasein must, as itself, *become* – that is to say, *be* – what it is not yet" (¶ 48, 243, p. 287, emphasis in original). Because the denial of death underlies an unconscious anxiety we'd rather not focus on, the demands of living an authentic life beckons the brute need to ponder and reflect on death as a value that informs our concrete existence that will come to an end; and this aspect of our ontological thrownness should become a moral impetus to improve our lives through genuine comportment, what Heidegger calls the still inner voice of conscience. It is worth noting that Freud (1916) also reflected on the nature of transience as giving life more beauty and worth long before Heidegger's reflections, a value that prioritizes the nature of temporal lived experience. Unlike Jung, the value of life therefore lies in the realization that it is temporary, which summons our own-most authentic potentiality-for-Being-a-whole as the very meaning of its Being as care, a caring that extends to all of our activities. To care is that something matters now. In other words, to be is to care as a primordial relation to temporality. Death is the end of time, the end of agency, hence no longer Being-there (*Nicht-mehr-da-sein*) as Dasein.

Death looms as the impending 'not-yet' we are thrown towards as part of our existential condition, the ontology of the not – where negation suffuses the very fabric of our essential Being. Ending, stopping, perishing, exiting, being used-up, passing-over-into, finishing, expiring, demising – all are euphemisms and signifiers of the *no more*. Death as the phenomenon of life is the privative relation to our lived encounters even though we don't know what death is like: epistemic erasure (~~know~~) No! – the barring of subjectivity, the foreclosure of Being.

For Heidegger, 'Death is a way to be, which Dasein takes over as soon as it is' (¶ 48, 245, p. 289). Here death becomes a negative totality with a positive valence, for nonbeing is predisposed in any discourse on living. This finishedness, this disappearing we face, that which is outstanding, becomes a basic state of being human, which saturates the fundamental characteristics of our Being in the world: (1) *existence* as Being 'ahead-of-itself,' (2) *facticity* as 'Being-already-in' and (3) *falling* as 'Being-alongside' everyday entities within the world (¶ 50, 250, p. 293). Being towards the end as the phenomenology of the not-yet is a basic comportment of who we are as that which is distinctively impending, stands before, and is there-with-us. The question therefore becomes: How do we live and understand our impending death? It is only in our own-most potentiality for Being as a solitary mode of authentic self-relatedness that we can ever come to offer an adequate answer, the task of individuation.

The Ωmega principle

Heidegger (1927) insists that 'the topic of a "metaphysic of death" lies outside the domain of an existential analysis of death' (¶ 49, 248, p. 292), but I must demur. Can we posit a destructive element to the collective or universal psyche – that which we all participate in based on a common essence relegated to human nature – that mirrors the destructive forces we observe in the physical world on a cosmic plane or a transpersonal netherworld? I have something more in mind than Freud's concept of the death drive or Jung's notion of a universal Shadow. What if everything revolves around Endings? The end is recapitulation, eternal repetition, an infinite finitude reimposed on a metaphysical level that saturates all Being. From nonconsciousness (nothingness) we emerge only to unconsciously resume, hence restore as reappearance of our nascent beginning. Nothingness saturates existence in order for nothing to exist forever. In other words, Nothingness conditions Being.

What *is* is always in relation to what it is *not*. Negation governs the ontological structure of being and becoming, for the ceasing to be or become is its ontological inverse, the recapitualization of its original essence as a return to nothing, the erasure of Being itself. We have no real permanence, no comfort or ontological security, for everything is transient and decays – from dust to dust. We have our moments of lived experience, such as pleasure, satisfaction and enjoyment (*jouissance*), as we do suffer (*pathos*), but it all comes to an end in our finite lives. This depressing antidote is fraught by the defensive (hence wishful) posit of a futurity without ending – an afterlife or eternal life, the seduction of immortality as a transcendental illusion that provides some reprieve from the austerity of the hopelessness of eluding death. We do not want to face this predetermined ontological thrownness – the certainty of nonbeing we are destined to embrace with or without consent. That is why psychic activity is in the service of displacement: we all want to escape from death even if by suicide. By replacing inexistence through allusion to some other extant object or realm, substituting or transferring it onto something else, as it were, we are constantly reinforcing the primacy of the negative.

But can we go further? What if nothingness is existence? That Being is literally No-Thing? Everything is timeless (eternal) process within a sea of beings (or entities) that are temporally curtailed in their being. The cosmological One, the Whole, the Absolute is really a series of *perishings* (of objects and subjects) merging with its origins as nonconsciousness, nonbeing or nothingness. We know nothing of where we come from, only that we find ourselves here and will expire. This is not the same question as the empirical biological explanation of birth from a reproductive organism. It is about the equiprimordiality of existence born/e from the *via negativa*, the ontology of the *not*.

The end is ontologically imbued from the start, what we might call the *omega principle*, the spiral that begins and ends as a return to itself as interiorized negativity. We are governed by it the moment we are born and are causally destined to return to nothingness. Unlike Parmenides and Lucretius who say that from nothing comes nothing (οὐδὲν ἐξ οὐδενός), because everything is teleologically oriented to die, to perish, to be expunged from existence, and yet this is the cycle of existence, this places nothingness at the centre of being. 'I am nothing, I have no self, I have no permanence, I am merely a mirage of attachments to perceptions and ideas that are temporary and ephemeral' says the Buddhist sage, referring to the illusion of being: the *void* – nothing – is the absolute ontological principle. Here I am merely a facsimile or hologram of existence, not a real entity, but rather an epiphenomenon of the pervasive inter-dispersement of the negative. In effect, I will return to where I come. It is only this flickering moment that will soon fade into nonbeing.

Bioscience confirms that we are dying the minute we are born, that cells are deteriorating as we grow and that we are all headed for a gurney with a toe-tag. Here death saturates life. It telegraphs the inevitable when we cast eyes on an old person, when we look at ourselves in the mirror. When we encounter death for the first time as a child, we are told that person is no longer alive and hence no longer exists. They simply vanished. And we know intuitively in our interior that the end is causally determined and it's just a matter of time before it's my turn. This produces such existential anxiety for the masses that we have the need to invent God (Mills, 2017), to mollify the worries of small children with transcendental promises of heaven, and placate social collectives through the advent of religion. But we die all the same. Even an imbecile knows there is a brute terminus imposed upon us against our will.

The omega principle acts within the organism as negative interiority, within our social collectives as privation, aggression and destructiveness, is embedded within the concept of world as deterioration and regeneration, and in the cosmos itself as the ontological necessity of entropy. Why? Because reality is process and is never static, an eternal series of passing away out of and returning to nothingness. And because we lack – the primal presence of absence that can never be satiated or fulfilled, we are always metaphysically emersed in nonbeing.

Being and nothing are the same

In the *Science of Logic*, Hegel (1812//1831/1969) traces the logical progression of cognition as pure reason, as pure thought thinking about itself and its operations as the coming into being of pure self-consciousness. What Hegel does is unlike no other philosopher: he makes thinking as objective logic the proper domain of metaphysics (see *SL*, p. 63; *Encyclopaedic Logic*, A. §§ 26–36), a self-governing formal system of the dialectical unfolding of truth as the ontology of pure interiority. As the science of thinking in general, logic confronts its inner forms as 'the formal conditions of genuine cognition,' the realm of truth 'as it is without veil, self-contained and complete in-itself (*an und für sich selbst*)' (*SL*, pp. 44, 50). In other words, Logic is the truth unveiled, the science of encountering and mediating contradictions and reasoning a unity through oppositions. At first 'unconscious of the antithesis of thinking within and against itself' (Hegel, 1817/1827/1830/1991, *EL* § 26, p. 65), it is through the force of the negative as pure interiority that we come to realize the dialectic in all its shapes.

In Hegel's famous treatment of the categories of Being and Nothingness, thought is first identical with itself as *pure being*, 'without any further determination' – it is merely an indeterminate immediacy as an undivided simple unity. It is pure emptiness or *nothingness*. Because there is no differentiation in itself, no determinativeness, there is nothing to be found or intuited other than itself in its purity. There is no content, only the *is*ness of vacuum, of absence, of lack. Being as the indeterminate immediate is therefore Nothing, 'neither more nor less than *nothing*' (*SL* § A. p. 82).

Nothing is *pure nothing*, equal to itself, completely empty and devoid of any content or determinations, 'undifferentiated in itself' – the same formal emptiness as pure being. Hegel elaborates:

> In so far as intuiting or thinking can be mentioned here, it counts as a distinction whether something or *nothing* is intuited or thought. To intuit or think nothing has, therefore, a meaning; both are distinguished and thus nothing *is* (exists) in our intuiting or thinking.
>
> (*SL* § B. p. 82, italics in original)

Notice that when 'nothing' is thought, it exists. The concept confers a determinate reality we experience in actuality as the interiority of our being. Because the same determination is the absence of determination in pure being and pure nothing, this allows Hegel to make the claim that being and nothing 'are the same.' Being does not pass over into nothing, but has *passed* over, just like nothing has passed over into being. In this sense they are identical and undistinguished from one another, yet paradoxically they are absolutely distinct categories that are inseparable and unseparated as each vanishes into its opposite. This immediate vanishing into each other then constitutes a greater movement of *becoming* other to itself, a movement in which both are distinguished, yet a difference that immediately resolves itself through mediating a unity through mutual opposition (*SL* § C. p. 82–83).

It is only when this unity of being as coming-to-be and nothing as ceasing-to-be unite within their mutual opposition as vanishing moments into each other do they find themselves as *becoming*. But as Hegel informs us, the distinction between being and nothing are self-contradictory: because the determinations of thought united within itself are opposed, the union between them remains destabilized yet fused as sublated or assimilated (*aufgehoben*) moments of the other. That is why Hegel says this unity between being and nothing as *moments* form a mediated oneness (*SL* § 3. p. 106). Hence, being and nothing come to be what they already are, the process of their own becoming expressed as the one-sided immediacy of differentially determined movements from and through their undifferentiated unity as pure relation. But this unity is not a static one: difference is merely a *transition* – hence transient – distinguished and maintained by reference to the process of thought itself.

If we think of nothingness as integral to being, as inseparable in its upmost abstract relation to existence that is still concretized, then being cannot exist without nothing. The omega principle is the beginning: Being comes from Nothing as nothing flows from being, the rotary motion of which all derives and returns. We can only posit ourselves in relation to what we are not. In the Sartrean formula: I am in the mode of being what I am not. The doubling of the negative is the ground of existence. Negation underlies everything that *is*. Here death becomes life.

Coda

Death has such a profound significance for and interdependence with life that we may conclude that the two forces embody an ontological dialectical unit that inform each other throughout our existence. If life involves a preparation for death, and death provides a sort of punctuation to and meaning for life, then the psychological implications of death and nothingness are imbricated in life itself. I personally see no overarching purpose or disambiguation we can assign to death other than the meanings we generate for ourselves. Just like our birth and our miraculous, astronomical thrownness into a life-supporting universe, it merely happens. Having said that, we may nevertheless say that life is teleologically oriented to die.

Even if we grant death the final cause of existence, understanding does not take away from the human angst it generates. Here death should be respected as an incentive to live life while you can, as banal as that sounds, and this means to maximize the cultivation and incorporation of experience. In our being toward passing, namely, the here-and-now presence of our felt-relation to a future ending, comes the realization that our time here on earth is precious, for death is the end of becoming.

If the aim of all life is death, then we are all preparing for rest, a tensionless state where we no longer feel anxiety and suffer, the culmination and fulfilment of life. God was invented to extinguish our suffering. Here there is no difference: death is the terminus of pain. In other words, death is eternal peace, the end to all negativity and conflict, the cessation of our *pathos*. From nothingness we emerge, and into nothingness we return. Here we may say that death is becoming unconscious, or in Hesse's and Heidegger's words, 'falling' into that state of the timeless-eternal collective, *ab origine*.

Note

A small portion of this paper was delivered as a Plenary Address titled 'The Black Foe: Being Toward Death' at the XXII International Congress of Analytical Psychology (IAAP) Buenos Aires, Argentina, September, 2, 2022.

References

Freeman, John. (1959). The 'Face to Face' Interview. In *C.G. Jung Speaking: Interviews and Encounters*. Princeton: Princeton University Press, pp. 424–439.

Freud, S. (1916 [1915]). On Transience. In *Standard Edition*, Vol. 14. London: Hogarth Press, pp. 303–307.

Freud, S. (1920). *Beyond the Pleasure Principle*. *Standard Edition*, Vol. 18. London: Hogarth Press.

Freud, S. (1939). *Moses and Monotheism* (Jones, K. Trans.). New York: Vintage.

Harding, Esther. (1948). pp.180–185. From Ester Harding's Notebooks: 1960. In McGuire, W. and Hull, R.F.C. (eds.), *C.G. Jung Speaking: Interviews and Encounters*. Princeton: Princeton University Press, pp. 440–442.

Hegel, G.W.F. (1812/1831/1969). *Science of Logic* (Miller, A.V. Trans.). London: George Allen & Unwin LTD.

Hegel, G.W.F. (1817/1827/1830/1991). *The Encyclopaedia Logic, Vol. 1 of the Encyclopaedia of the Philosophical Sciences* (Geraets, T.F., Suchting, W.A. and Harris, H.S. Trans.). Indianapolis: Hackett Publishing Company, Inc.

Hegel, G.W.F. (1978). *Hegel's Philosophy of Subjective Spirit, Vol.1: Introductions, Vol.2: Anthropology, Vol.3: Phenomenology and Psychology* (Petry, M.J. Ed.). Dordrecht, Holland: D. Reidel Publishing Company.

Heidegger, Martin. (1927). *Being and Time*. San Francisco: Harper.

Jung, C.G. (1916). The Relation between the Ego and the Unconscious. *CW*, 7, pp. 123–244.

Jung, C.G. (1929). Commentary on 'The Secret of the Golden Flower.' *CW*, 13, pp. 1–56.

Jung, C.G. (1934). The Soul and Death. *CW*, 8, pp. 404–415.

Jung, C.G. (1935). The Tavistock Lectures. *CW*, 18, pp. 1–182.

Jung, C.G. (1952). Synchronicity: An Acausal Connecting Principle. *CW*, 8, pp. 417–532.

Jung, C.G. (1954). On the Nature of the Psyche. *CW*, 8, pp. 159–236.

Jung, C.G. (1955). Memorial to J.S. *CW*, 18, pp. 757–758.

Jung, C.G. (1958). At the Basel Psychology Club. In McGuire, W. and Hull, R.F.C. (eds.), *C.G. Jung Speaking: Interviews and Encounters*. Princeton: Princeton University Press, pp. 370–391.

Jung, C.G. (1959). Flying Saucers: A Modern Myth of Things Seen in the Skies. *CW*, 10, pp. 309–433.

Jung, C.G. (1961). *Memories, Dreams, Reflections*. New York: Vintage Books.

Mills, Jon. (2000). Dialectical Psychoanalysis: Toward Process Psychology. *Psychoanalysis and Contemporary Thought*, 23(3), pp. 20–54.

Mills, Jon. (2010). *Origins: On the Genesis of Psychic Reality*. Montreal: McGill-Queens University Press.

Mills, Jon. (2017). *Inventing God: Psychology of Belief and the Rise of Secular Spirituality*. London: Routledge.

Mills, Jon. (2019). The Myth of the Collective Unconscious. *Journal of the History of the Behavioral Sciences* (55), pp. 40–53.

Plato. (1961). Republic. In Hamilton, E. and Cairns, H. (eds.), *The Collected Dialogues of Plato*. Princeton: Princeton University Press, pp. 575–844.

Plotinus. (1966). *Enneads* (Armstrong, A.H. Trans. & Comm.). Cambridge, MA: Harvard University Press.

Serrano, Miguel. (1961). Talks with Miguel Serrano: 1961. In McGuire, W. and Hull, R.F.C. (eds.), *C.G. Jung Speaking: Interviews and Encounters*. Princeton: Princeton University Press, pp. 462–469.

Young, Gordon. (1960). The Art of Living. In McGuire, W. and Hull, R.F.C. (eds.), *C.G. Jung Speaking: Interviews and Encounters*. Princeton: Princeton University Press, pp. 443–452.

Chapter 13

Destiny and personal myth

Archetypal constellations of the soul

Vicente L. de Moura

Introduction

Destiny and Fate are words usually related to important events in life, and for this chapter the differentiation of these two words is important. Destiny comes from the Latin word *destinare*, and it means 'to set apart, to appoint; preordain, to intend' (Hawkins and Allen, 1991). Fate comes from the Latin *fatum* that means 'a power regarded as predetermining events unalterably; or the future regarded as determined by this force' (Hawkins and Allen, 1991). Therefore, the main difference between destiny and fate is that destiny relates to an intention or a goal; while fate relates to something that will happen to you and cannot be changed. In other words, fate happens to you, while destiny you should strive to achieve. It is my goal in this chapter to present a concept which may be applied in Jungian psychotherapy and analysis.

Jung did not give a definition for these terms, although in many passages he pointed to some alien influence on his clients, which had an enormous impact on them and sometimes changed their lives. Usually, these events cannot be known beforehand, and the person feels impotent in front of them. He wrote in *Two Essays in Analytical Psychology*:

> But we know that there is no human foresight or wisdom that can prescribe direction to our life, expect for small stretches of the way.
>
> (Jung, 1942, para. 72)

The future is something beyond human knowledge and beyond human will. It is not possible to control, and it happens independently of will. What is left is how the person copes (or not) with the situation. In his paradoxical style, Jung writes:

> The plenitude of life is governed by law, and yet not governed by law, rational and yet irrational.
>
> (Jung, 1942, para. 72)

How one evaluates the event depends on the situation itself, his/her moral values, and the attitude of the person. Not rarely the meaning of the situation can turn into

DOI: 10.4324/9781003313304-20

its opposite, i.e., what was good yesterday may be evil today, and vice versa. Meaning is given by how one assimilates it.

Renos Papadopoulos explained the meaning of the word *Pathos* in a lecture named 'The Poetic of Pathos.'[1] Possible definitions for the term *Pathos* (πα'θος) are 'that which happens to a person or thing; what one has experienced (good or bad)' (Linddell and Scott, 1977, p. 1285). To cope with *Pathos*, one needs to use *Logos*. Some possible definitions of *Logos* (λο'γος) are 'esteem, consideration, value put on a person or thing,' but also 'relation, correspondence, proportion; explanation, thesis, hypothesis, reason, mentally conceived,' and, finally, 'embraced by thought with reflection' (Linddell and Scott, 1977, p. 1057). In this sense, whatever happens has neither good or evil connotation, and its meaning will be given by *Logos*, i.e., what happens must be embraced by one's thought with reflection, and this process will put a value on the event.

Many have the tendency to understand important happenings as something divine or demonic, and inside Jungian psychology, it may be understood relating it to the influence of the complexes. Jung gave an example, commenting on a case of a woman who was ruled by her father-complex:

If ever we are disposed to see some demonic power at work controlling mortal destiny surely we can see it here in these melancholic, silent tragedies working themselves out, slowly and agonizingly, in the sick souls of our neurotics.

(1949, para. 727)

In the same passage, Jung wrote:

If we normal people examine our lives, we too perceive how a mighty hand guides us without fail to our destiny, and not always is this hand a kindly one. Often we call it the hand of God or of the Devil.

(1949, para. 727)

Although we are unaware of it, the impact of the complexes is present in different parts of human life, in every meaningful decision, relationship and event. Jung wrote:

Man knows only a small part of his psyche [. . .]. The causal factors determining his psychic existence reside largely in unconscious process outside consciousness, and in the same way *there are final factors at work in him* which likewise originate in the unconscious.

(1930, para. 253, my italics)

However, relating to the complexes requires introspection, and most people have lost contact with the world within, with the symbolic life and its meaning. Often one believes he/she controls life and that he/she can rule the future. But the illusion of control comes to an end when fateful things happen. In this cases, unconscious contents floods and mesmerises the ego and, according to Jung, the ego may react in four different ways:

> But once the unconscious contents break through consciousness, filling it with their uncanny power of conviction, the questions arise of how the individual will react. Will he be overpowered by the contents? Will he credulously accept them or will he reject them? (I am disregarding the ideal reaction, namely critical understanding).
>
> (1930, para. 254)

One may think the way Papadopoulos put it: *to use Logos to connect with Pathos*. In other words: one does not have control over what happens, but one can relate to it through meaning. However, if this connection cannot be found, one may become neurotic or live a meaningless life.

We find examples about destiny in religious traditions, what one may consider as an archetypal background. What follows are four different approaches: the fate given by the gods in Greek mythology, God's grace in Calvin's predestination, the fate written by God in Islam and how it depends on our Karma in Buddhism.

Fate in Greek mythology – the Moirai

In the *Encyclopaedia of Religion, Fatum* is defined as something spoken, a prophetic declaration, an oracle, a divine determination (1987, p. 290). In Greek mythology, the gods ruled the world and enjoyed divine bliss. They had heroes or children and helped them in their worldly life. But even the gods could not change their fate given by the three Moirai at birth. Meunier gave the following description of the Moirai:

> They live not so far from the Hours, in a bronze palace. On the walls of this palace, they write the human destinies, as they mark out the movement that the stars should follow. Nothing could erase what they had written. They sit on a shining light throne, dressed in white clothes covered by stars, with flowers and wool on their heads. The three Goddesses spin the days of the mortals, giving them their destiny. The youngest, Clotho, holds the spindle and spin; Lachesis turns the spindle and selects the thread, giving to each man his fortune; Atropos finally cuts the thread giving the measure of his life, and with it she determines the moment of death.
>
> (Meunier, 1989, p. 5)

The roots of their names reveal the function of each one of Moirai: Clotho comes from the Greek verb *klóthein* that means to spin; she is the one who elaborates the development of one's life. Lachesis comes from the verb *lankhanein* that means to distribute, to draw, and therefore she is the one who distributes the good and evil events in one's life. Finally, Atropos comes from the verb *trepein* which means to turn away, and in this sense she is the one who does not turn away in her decision and gives the length of one's life – his death (Brandão, 1986, p. 231).

The most interesting aspect of the Moirai appeared once analysing the relationship between their writings and the will of the gods. Even Zeus respected the writings of the Moirai and, if he tried to change them, other gods and goddesses would do the same, and the balance of the world would be lost. W. Otto cited one passage in the *Iliad*, where we observe this dynamic clearly:

> Zeus knows that Hector is near death and the only thing he can do for him is to allow his glory to blaze once more before his extinction. But at the moment of decision the great god is filled with sorrow because the irreproachable hero, who was always meticulous in discharging his obligations to his godhead, must now be delivered to death. He asks the other gods whether he might not even now save Hector, and Athena replies: 'What mean you? Would you pluck this mortal whose doom has long been decreed out of the jaws of death? Do as you will, but we others shall not be of a mind with you! Then Zeus reassures his daughter: I did not speak in full earnest! Now fate takes its course.
>
> (Otto, 1978, p. 266)

Meunier explained the power of the Moirai as if they were a functional principle, in terms of acting agent, and it would come from pre-Homeric religions (Meunier, 1989, p. 230). The figures of the Moirai were the personification of a kind of force, a law which kept the balance between the will of the gods and the events in human life. They gradually emerged out of an ancient impersonal force into the personification as the goddesses of fate. In the example just presented, Zeus could have changed the fate of his son, but he did not dare, because it would have been against the natural order of the events, and the result would have been chaos.

Destiny in Christianity – the concept of predestination

Destiny in religious traditions is not the same as in Greek mythology. The Latin word *Praedestinatio* derives from the creation of an abstract noun, from the translation of the Greek word *proorizo*, which refers to deciding or setting limits on something beforehand (*Encyclopaedia of Religion*, p. 423).

The destiny of the soul has been discussed through the centuries in the Christian church, and the concept of predestination is one very polemic theme, full of contradictions. In Pauline literature, predestination and the salvation of the soul 'results from the divine initiative and is grounded in grace, so that no one may boast of being saved by his own efforts' (*Encyclopaedia of Religion*, p. 423). Later, Augustine affirms that:

> God predestined salvation some out of the mass of sinners, passing by the rest and thus leaving them to just condemnation for the sins they willingly committed.
>
> (*Encyclopaedia of Religion*, p. 423)

In the year 421 (AD) Augustine described what is called the double predestination, in which God not only predestined some to salvation but condemned the rest to damnation. The council of Orange (529 AD) elevated Augustine's ideas to dogma, but in the Middle Ages the council of Trent (1547 AD) relativised it with the following position:

> (God disposes people) through his quickening and assisting grace, to convert themselves to their own justification, by freely assenting to and cooperating with the 'grace,' but certitude about being among the predestined came only when the salvation was complete for those who persevered to the end.
>
> (*Encyclopaedia of Religion*, p. 427)

During the Reformation, however, the concept of predestination and free will took different interpretations. The position of the Church conflicted with the reformers and Calvin and Luther adopted Augustine's position on predestination. Luther said:

> The predestination or eternal election of God extends only to the good and beloved children of God, and this is the only cause of their salvation.
>
> (*Encyclopaedia of Religion*, p. 428)

Jung analysed in *Answer to Job* the concept of predestination and declared that it is difficult to understand its meaning in connection with the message of the gospels. Jung wrote:

> But taken psychologically, as a mean to achieving a definite effect, it can readily be understood that these allusions to predestination give one a feeling of distinction. . . . one feels lifted beyond the transitoriness and meaninglessness of ordinary human existence and transported to a new state of dignity and importance . . . In this sense man is brought nearer to God, and this is in entire accord with the meaning of the message in the gospels.
>
> (1952a, para. 646)

Therefore, psychologically one's feeling of been special in God's eyes (elected) and that one has something purposeful to come (salvation), elevates him/her from others and gives a feeling of distinction and meaningfulness in life.

Fatalism in Islamic faith – Maktub

To understand the concept of Fate in Islamic tradition is necessary to refer to pre-Islamic Arabia, where the basis of the development of concept comes from. The poetry of that time shows the belief that much of human life, especially misfortune, is determined by time (*Ajal*) a natural factor belonging to the situation. *Ajal* means one's term, or 'the date of his death was determined or predetermined. If he was destined to die on a certain day, he would die then, no matter what he did' (*Encyclopaedia of Religion*, p. 429).

Fate was identified with time, an idea that can be found in ancient Iran, in Zoroastrianism and in a period called Zurvanism. This idea was present when Mohammed wrote the Qur'an and ideas about time and fate from the pre-Islamic time can be found in the Qur'an, for instance: 'There is only our present life, we die and we live, and time (*dahr*) alone destroys us' (Suran 45:24).

But while in the pre-Islamic world time is sometimes personalised and mythologised, in the Qur'an it is God who fixes the *Ajal* (time) and knows it beforehand. 'He is the one who created you from clay, and then fixed an *Ajal*' (Surah 6:2).

In the same terms that Jung explained predestination in Christian tradition, one may understand psychologically this idea analysing life conditions in the desert. Life and death are a close reality in such a condition, and one never knows if he/she would survive or not: a wrong route could cost money and lives; a mirage could lead to a catastrophe; or thieves could be waiting on the path, etc. In such situations, anxiety could paralyse the person who confronts these life conditions. But all these difficulties and dangers would not be a problem if one believes that one's destiny is in the hands of God. He knew the destinies, and He controlled what would happen. The person would die when, and only when, the time had come. In Islamic tradition there is a passage which describes how only God knows your destiny and wrote it down. There is a passage where Mohammed said:

> The first thing God created was the pen, then He said to it – write all that will happen until the Last Day!
>
> (*Encyclopaedia of Religion*, p. 431)

This passage is expressed by an Arabic saying, 'is written down,' *Maktub*. One may recognise the background for a fatalistic view of the world in this sentence. If everything is already written, one can do nothing to change it.

But it is important to note that the Nomads in the pre-Islamic tradition also believed that it was the outcome of human actions which was determined, but not the actions themselves. In other words, one should deal with the vicissitudes and sufferings of life, and one is still responsible for his acts. John Bowker, analysing the meaning of suffering in Islam, wrote:

> Although the Islamic attitude to suffering has at certain times and in certain individuals become fatalistic, that is a perversion of Islam, and not its true expression, and the Quran militates against such an attitude.
>
> (Bowker, 1970, p. 116)

One may conclude that in Islamic faith God is omniscient and knows the outcome of human actions, but what one still has responsibility for one's acts and is still responsible for them? The fatalistic interpretation concerning one's own destiny is a misinterpretation of God's will.

Destiny in Buddhism – Karma

The concept of Karma is one of the basic concepts in Eastern religions and has an impact even in the Western world. Karma in Sanskrit comes from the verbal root *Kri*, meaning to act, to do, to bring about; and here the idea is that one engenders something by doing something, or, in other words, one creates by acting (Humphreys, 1944, p. 11).

There are different connotations applied to this term. In the *Encyclopaedia of Religions* (pp. 262–265) one finds a description of the evolution of this term, which can be summarised as follows:

- In the *Vedic Mantrasamhitas* (1200 BC), the gods could be pleased by rituals. *Karma* was known as the sacerdotal performance, the ritual undertaken to achieve a particular end, and the action could be accepted or not by the gods.
- The concept changes later among the *Purva Mimamsa* philosophers (900 BC); if the priest did the action in the right way, the gods must attend what was asked, i.e., the performance of the priest controlled the gods. Karma in this sense was an impersonal metaphysical system of cause and effect, in which an action brought an automatic response.
- In the *Upanishads* (800 BC), every action, not only those performed in the ritual, lead to consequences. Therefore, the idea that one's worldly situation and personality was determined by one's desires, in other words, desiring affected one will, and led to act in a certain way. At the end, one's actions brought the proportionate and consequent result. One's actual life condition would be the result of past lives, and actions today engender the future lives through rebirth. This circle of life and death was named *Samsara*, and the liberation of this process could be attained through enlightenment and through the intervention of a supreme deity.
- For classical yoga, Karma involves what might be called a substance, that lead the soul from one body to another as it moved from birth to birth. In this view, Karma was like a seed that will mature either in one's present life, or, if not fully ripened, in another lifetime. What inhibits the ripening of the seed are the *Klesas*, i.e., personal afflictions or ignorance, egoism, hatred and the will to live. The function of the yoga was to eliminate the *Klesas*.
- The *Ayurveda* traditions mentioned Karma as a material entity, of a sort that can be passed from one generation to another, and it is an important factor in medical aetiologies and in fertility techniques.
- In the doctrine of *Jainism Jiva*, there is a pure, colourless and crystalline substance, which lies inside all living things and is by nature blissful and intelligent. But a kind of subtle dust or stained liquid, that has existed since time immemorial, adheres to the *Jiva* and defines the conditions and circumstances of one's rebirth. This blurry, coloured substance is named Karma. Every act of unintentional violence, however, burdens the *Jiva* with the stain of Karma. To get rid of one's Karma demands asceticism and complete unwillingness to kill or to injure any living creatures.

• In the *Bhagavadgita*, the idea was presented that one should perform actions that are obligatory according to one's position in society. The better one performs his/her duties, the purer the results. One's actions should be dedicated to *Krsna* (god), and, through them, the liberation of the Karma would be possible.

These were ideas known by Siddhartha Gautama Sakyas, alias, Buddha, and with them in mind it is possible to apprehend the development of the concept of Karma in Buddhism.

Budh in Sanskrit means both: to wake up and to know. In that sense Buddha means 'the enlightened One,' or 'the awakened One' (*Encyclopaedia of Religion*, p. 80). But to understand the connotation of Karma in Buddhism, one needs to know two more concepts, *Nirvana* and *Annata*, because they differentiate Buddhism from other religious traditions in this chapter. Concerning the concept of *Nirvana*, which etymologically means 'to blow out' or 'to extinguish,' Smith wrote:

> Nirvana is the highest destiny of the human spirit, and its literal meaning is extinction, but we must be precise as to what is to be extinguished. It is the boundaries of the finite self. It does not follow that what is left will be nothing. Negatively, nirvana is the state in which the faggots of private desire have been completely consumed and everything that restricts the boundless life has died. Affirmatively, it is that boundless life itself.
>
> (Smith, 1991, p. 113)

But is Nirvana God? In Buddhism there is no concept of a Godhead. There is no supreme Being with a personality, a personal creator. In this sense, Buddhism is an atheistic religion.

Concerning the concept of *Annata*, the term means 'no soul.' Buddha refuted the existence of one spiritual substance which, in accord with the dualistic outlook of Hinduism, retained its separateness throughout eternity. Buddha explained the concept of reincarnation, also important in the concept of Karma, with the simile of a flame passing from one candle to another.

> As it is difficult to think of the flame on the final candle as being the original flame, the connection would seem to be a causal one, in which influence was transmitted by chain reaction but without a perduring substance.
>
> (Smith, 1991, p. 115)

With these concepts in mind, it is possible to understand the definition summarised by Smith for Karma in Buddhism:

> (1) There is a chain of causation threading each life to those that have led up to it, and to those that will follow. Each life is in its present condition because of the way the lives that led up to it were lived. (2) Throughout this causal

sequence the will remains free. The lawfulness of things makes the present state the product of prior acts, but within the present the will is influenced but not controlled. People remain at liberty to shape their destinies. (3) The two preceding points affirm the causal connectedness of life, but they do not entail that a substance of some sort be transmitted. Ideas, impressions, feelings, streams of consciousness, present moments – these are all that we find, no spiritual substrate.

(Smith, 1991, pp. 115–116)

It is important to note the major difference between Karma in Buddhism and destiny in Christian and Islamic traditions: in Buddhism there is not the will of God, neither a soul to be saved and the way one acts towards his/her desires, thoughts, and experiences (past lives), has consequences for one's destiny (Karma).

This life and afterlife

From the material presented earlier, one concludes that for these religious traditions there is an existence after death. We may resume their imaginary of immortality of the soul and its destiny after death as follows:

In the Christian tradition we find the idea of Eternal life, a perfect eternal life, sharing in glory and bliss. For the Christian believers, after the final judgement, they will resurrect from the dead in an eternal life: *There is one glory of the sun, and another glory of the moon, and another glory of the stars; for star differs from star in glory. So it is with the resurrection of the dead* (1 Corinthians 15:41–42). For those who do not live accordingly to the faith, there will be an eternal punishment (Matthew 25:46) for the opposing of to eternal life is not earthly life but eternal death.

Also, in the Islamic faith, those who make good deeds in their life will enter paradise, where there is no suffering or illnesses. But those who perform evil deeds and those who are non-believers will go to hell, living eternally physical and spiritual suffering, although Allah may forgive those who regret their actions and have performed good deeds during their life. In the Qur'an is written:

Of the good that they do nothing will be rejected of them; for Allah knoweth well those that do right. Those who reject faith – neither their possessions nor their (numerous) progeny will avail them aught against Allah; they will be companions of the fire, dwelling therein forever.

(Qur'an 3:115–1:116)

Concerning Buddhist afterlife beliefs, it is mainly related to the concept of reincarnation and, after death, either one will be reborn into another being or one will reach nirvana, the awakening achieve by Buddha, where there is no suffering. Death, therefore, is not the end, but part of a process, in which the next reincarnation will depend on his deeds on the previous life.

Finally, in Greek mythology, after death the soul leaves the body and goes to the underworld, the world of Hades, where one is only a shade of his/her former existence, a world of misery and gloominess. Paradoxically, this imaginary led some to live intensely, because one's lifetime was the only time when one may feel joy.

Important Jungian concepts related to destiny and fate

Powerful events, which some relate to the influence of divine or demonic powers in one's life, indicate situations that have profound impact in one's life, and it does not matter if the event in intrapsychic (like a realisation of something crucial) or an external happening. A term used to define such events is the term *Numinous*, and it is important to know the connection of this term with Jung's understanding of the term *Religion*.

> Religion, as the Latin word denotes, is a careful and scrupulous observation of what Rudolf Otto aptly termed the *numinosum*, that is, a dynamic agency or the effect not caused by an arbitrary act of will. On the contrary, it seizes and controls the human subject, who always is rather its victim that its creator. The *numinosum* – whatever its cause may be – is an experience of the subject independent of his will.
>
> (1957, para. 6)

and further he wrote:

> We might say, then, that the term 'religion' designates the attitude peculiar to a consciousness which has been changed by the experience of the *Numinosum*.
>
> (1957, para. 9)

Jung used the term coined by Rudolf Otto in his book *The Idea of the Holy*. In his book Otto proposed the term *Numinous*, because he affirmed that the word 'holy' or 'sacred' was contaminated with the idea of 'completely good,' which is a moral judgement, and that was not the original meaning of the word 'holy.' He writes:

> But this common usage of the term (holy) is inaccurate. It is true that all this moral significance is contained in the word 'holy,' but it includes in addition – as even we cannot but feel – a clear overplus of meaning, and this is now our task to isolate. Nor is this merely a later or acquired meaning; rather, 'holy' or at least the equivalent words in Latin and Greek, in Semitic and other ancient languages, denotes first and foremost *only* this overplus: if the ethical element was present at all. At any rate it was not original and never constituted the whole meaning of the word. . . . It would be useful, at least for the temporary purpose of the investigation, to invent a special term to stand for 'the holy' *minus* its moral factor or moment, and, as we can now add, minus its 'rational' aspect altogether.
>
> (Otto R., 1946, p. 6, the italics are in the original)

Otto meant numinous in the sense of 'holy,' but above and beyond the meaning of goodness. He wrote:

> I shall speak then of a unique 'numinous' category of value and of a definitely 'numinous' state of mind, which is always found wherever the category is applied. This mental state is perfectly *sui generis* and irreducible to any other; and therefore, like every absolute and primary and elementary datum, while it admits being discussed, it cannot be strictly defined.
>
> (Otto R., 1946, p. 7)

To help someone to understand the term, Otto suggested that one must not just think about but experience.

> He must be guided and led on by consideration and discussion of the matter through the ways of his own mind, until he reaches the point at which 'the numinous' in him perforce begins to stir, to start into life and into consciousness. . . . In other words our *X* (experience) cannot, strictly speaking, be taught, it can only be evoked, awakened in the mind; as everything that comes 'of the spirit' must be awakened.
>
> (Otto R., 1946, p. 7)

Otto wrote further in this experience that one would realise being a creation, therefore a creature consciousness or creature feeling:

> It is the emotion of a creature, abased and overwhelmed by its own nothingness in contrast to that which is supreme above all creatures.
>
> (Otto R., 1946, p. 10)

and he added:

> All that this new term, creature feeling, can express, is the note of self-abasement into nothingness before an overpowering, absolute might of some kind; whereas everything turns upon the *character* of this overpowering might, a character which cannot be expressed verbally, and can only be suggested indirectly through the tone and content of a man's feeling response to it. And this response must be directly experienced in oneself to be understood.
>
> (Otto R., 1946, p. 10, emphasis in original)

Further, Otto used the term 'Mysterium tremendum' to express this 'who or what' that goes beyond conception or understanding. He described some characteristics of the numinous experience: the element of 'Awefulness' (fear, reverence); the element of 'Overpoweringness' (being reduced to nothing – the creature-consciousness) and the element of 'energy' or 'urgency' (the vitality, passion and movement)

It is important to notice that these are exactly elements present when one feels the 'blow of destiny' or meets 'his fate.' In such situations consciousness meets something that cannot apprehend, the 'completely other' or 'the mystery of life' and with it comes an element of fascination. Otto wrote:

> These two qualities, the daunting and the fascinating, now combine in a strange harmony of contrasts, and the resulting dual character of the numinous consciousness, to which the entire religious development bears witness, . . . is at once the strangest and the most noteworthy phenomenon in the whole history of religion.
>
> (Otto R., 1946, p. 31)

Otto's work is very important to understand Jung's use of the term Numinous and Jung's comprehension of Religion. If one compares the similarities, concerning the concept of the Numinous in Jung's and Otto's writings, one finds the following: both referred to something impersonal, in the sense that can be seen in the ancient religions; both see the ambivalence and the antimony of the Mysterium, that there is something irrational about it. They do not accept the idea of God as the *summun bonum*, and both understand that the realisation of this term relates to living experience.

Summarising, one might say that when someone is confronted with a tremendous emotional experience, he/she will be probably transformed. The reaction of the ego will depend on its characteristics, its strength and its ability to deal with such happenings and give meaning to it.

Jung and synchronicity

Besides the term *numinous*, another of Jung's concept is important in this context, namely, *synchronicity*. He postulated the concept of synchronicity as an acausal principle connecting two or more simultaneous events, where meaning was the linking factor. He wrote:

> Instead of simultaneity we could also use the concept of a meaningful coincidence of two or more events, where something other than the probability of chance is involved.
>
> (1952c, para. 969)

Jung described how some apparently random events had profound impact in the development of some of his cases and mentioned that these events seemed to be outside chance or without causal motives. As example he mentioned the beetle that flew inside the room after his patient dreamed of a scarab.[2] Jung named three categories for the phenomena:

1 The coincidence of a psychic state in the observer with a simultaneous, objective, external event that corresponds to the psychic state or content, where there is no evidence of a causal connection between the psychic state and the external event, and where, considering the psychic relativity of space and time, such a connection is not even conceivable.
2 The coincidence of a psychic state with a corresponding (more or less simultaneous) external event taking place outside the observer's field of perception, i.e., at a distance, and only verifiable afterward.
3 The coincidence of a psychic state with a corresponding, not yet existing future event that is distant in time and can likewise only be verified afterwards (1952b, para. 984).

For the corroboration of his ideas, Jung referred to Rhine's experiments in Telepathy, Clairvoyance and Psychokinesis which showed impressive numbers that seemed to prove the existence of the PSY factors, even though Rhine experiments were under severe criticism due to methodological mistakes. In Rhine's experiment and in Jung's categories there is a common point that seems to have an influence on the results: the psychic state of the subject. One's interest and affects could be considered one important factor connecting the occurrence of the synchronistic phenomena.

Searching historical support for his postulation, Jung mentioned alchemists like Avicena and Albertus Magnus, who knew about such events and emotional conditions. The previous passage was referred to regarding the influence of strong emotions and the occurrence of synchronistic events:

When therefore the human soul of a man falls into great excess of passion, it can be proved by experiment that it (the excess) binds things (magically) and alters them in the way it wants.

(1952c, para. 859)

The impact caused by such event has a numinous character which, according to Jung, may indicate that the event was due to the constellation of an archetype, and from its numinosity comes the aspect of 'Awe.' Jung wrote:

The numinosity of a series of chance happenings grows in proportion to the number of its terms. Unconscious – probably archetypal – contents are thereby constellated, which then give rise to the impression that the series has been 'caused' by these contents. Since we cannot conceive how this could be possible without recourse to positively magical categories, we generally let it go at the bare impression.

(1952c, para. 827 n)

The 'magical categories' that Jung referred to are related to the Alchemical concept of the *Unus Mundus*. By this concept is meant a unity between psyche and the external, material world, that would be one and the same thing. Psyche and matter would be then one and the same energy, but in different forms. Von Franz wrote:

> Synchronistic events thus seem to point towards a unitary aspect of existence which transcends our conscious grasp and which Jung has called *unus mundus*.
>
> (von Franz, 1992, p. 40)

The postulated connection between a psychic state and an external event would be the manifestation of some aspect that goes beyond psyche and external reality. Therefore, a synchronistic event would be the indication of the link between two apparently separated worlds.

There is an alchemical saying: 'What is within is also without.' One possible psychological meaning of this phrase would be that a complex inside the psyche can also be experienced outside in external reality. Jung's postulation, however, indicates that for him a synchronistic event could be more than an interpretation of meaning.

He related the connection between psychic and non-psychic events to the dual nature of the archetype, namely, its psychoid nature. By that Jung meant that the nature of the archetype goes beyond psyche, i.e., it is not only included in one's mind. The psychoid nature of the archetype postulates the possibility of an organisational factor outside the psyche.[3] Jung wrote:

> Synchronicity tells us about the nature of what I call the psychoid factor, i.e., the unconscious archetype (not its conscious representation). As the archetype has the tendency to gather suitable forms of expression round itself, its nature is best understood when one imitates and supports this tendency through amplification.
>
> (1955, para. 1208)

One may conclude that a synchronistic event works as a kind of amplification of a psychic content in the external world that gathers the events around a meaning constellated in the subject and with it (re-)organises his experience. For Jung, however, there is an element in human mind which regulates its functioning and the relation to external events, namely, the Self, a superior entity which rules over the entire psychic life.

Whitmont's ideas on the concept of destiny

Among Jungian authors, almost none approach the concept of Destiny. One exception is an article written by Edward Whitmont, presented at the Fourth International Congress for Analytical Psychology, in 1972, under the title 'The Destiny Concept in Psychotherapy.' He presented a working hypothesis where the events considered as causes of psychopathology, would be 'manifestations of a life pattern.' He wrote:

> In terms of what we know of the objective psyche, destiny does not imply an absolute determinism. We encounter it as what I would call a plan of unfoldment of a prepersonal yet individual pattern of intended wholeness which arises from the Self and which necessitates a cooperative attempt of realization in concrete life, of fulfilment within the limits of the ego's capacity. Thus, destiny or fate is the unfoldment of the Self archetype in time and space.
>
> (Whitmont, 1992, p. 185)

In his postulation there is a life pattern which exists before the individual does, and it is completed in an individual way. Traumatic events in one's life would be an actualisation of a life pattern and events in childhood would be not necessarily the result of an accident or of bad luck, but the beginning of the manifestation of this pattern. The reason for these manifestations is the following:

> Traumatic events of childhood . . . may perhaps be seen as essential landmarks in the actualisation of a pattern of wholeness, as the necessary 'suffering of the soul' which engenders present and future psychological advance.

> Our suffering as children or adults through disturbed relationship with parents and other close associates may be seen not merely as chance or misfortune but as a destined emotional impasse essential for the particular individual in the actualisation of his own pattern of wholeness.
>
> (Whitmont, 1992, p. 186)

Whitmont's ideas postulate that the conflict to be confronted is already arranged inside the life pattern, and life experiences before the conflict are preparatory steps for the future development. He wrote:

> What must be experienced at the age of sixty-six, could well necessitate and precipitate certain experiences at the age three or four.
>
> (Whitmont, 1992, p. 188)

One can conclude that in Whitmont's concept, the Self knows what is necessary for the development of the personality, like the author of the play who knows what he wants to present, and therefore the Self causes events and conflicts in the early phases of one's life, because these events are necessary for the future development that will come. Whitmont concluded:

> We may understand a play reductively in terms of its cause and effect sequence, but unless we can also comprehend the dramatic intent of the destined meaning

behind the particular sequences we are not really moved by the inner logic of its timing and consequently are not able or qualified to assist in the staging, in bringing out the essence of the particular drama.

(Whitmont, 1992, p. 189)

Destiny and personal myth

With these ideas in mind, I would like now to present tentatively a hypothesis for the concept of Destiny in psychotherapy using the background of Jungian psychology.

Destiny would be defined as the potential for psychic development observed in the inner arrangement of one's experiences (meaning), based on one or more constellated archetypes. The experience of meaning is usually related to objective circumstances by individual understanding, symbolic and emotionally apprehended by the person in synchronistic events.

The individual constellation of an archetypal pattern in one's psyche, resulting from the manifold influences in his life (like genetic factors, culture, ethnic group, religion, life events, etc.) could be called one's Personal Myth.

By it is not meant that every life event can be given a meaning, or that every tragedy is part of a big unknown plan given by the Self. The attempt to fit in every single life event into a concept would be an inflation, because the plenitude of life cannot be put inside a constructed framework. What is meant is that the experiences in the individual's life have the tendency to be fitted into one's inherent inner pattern of meaning. This inherent pattern tends to relate with what happens, using one's own constellated meaning potential. If the ego can relate to the event and take it carefully into consideration (Jung's religious attitude), it will be able to relate with the event in a way which may bring an increase of consciousness in one's life.

Pathos, that which happens, is neutral, and the greatest impact on the individual will be result of the meaning that one's psyche gives to the event, i.e., the difference is how the ego relates to what the world (outside and inside) brings to it.

If the ego tries to suppress the content, in other words, consciously using the will to avoid contact with the content, it will cost psychic energy; therefore, the event would still have influence in the conscious life. It is as if the complex touched by the event would work like the riddle of the Sphinx: Decipher me or I will eat you! i.e., 'find the meaning or I will consume you.'

One may propose tentatively a psychological differentiation between the ideas of Fate and Destiny. As mentioned earlier, the connotation of Fate has something that cannot be changed, like a future event regarded as unchangeable, while Destiny has the connotation of an achievement.

If the ego attitude is negative and constellated complex is accepted without criticism or rejected, the complex may act inside the psyche like one's fate, because it becomes something unchangeable. The psychic economy would be ruled by the complex; therefore, the individual would be caught in its devouring aspect.

But if the ego attitude towards it is one of critical understanding, in other words, if the conscious attitude confronts the meaning given by the complex, the acceptance of the challenge may activate the spiritual potential of an archetypal pattern, engendering transformation. In this sense, one will be transforming one's Fate in one's Destiny. Jung wrote that the neurotic person is the person who does not have *Amor fati* – the one who does not love his own fate. Summarising: you conquer your fate by accepting it and transforming it into your destiny.

It relates to the question of suffering. On the one hand, suffering caused by some events in life may lead the person to relate carefully with the aspects involved with it. On the other hand, however, if one does not digest the event, if one does not use his Logos to relate to the occurrence, suffering will be meaningless, empty suffering. In other words, suffering without meaning is damnation, while suffering with meaning is redemption.

The question of the meaning in suffering seems to be based on the capacity of healing that comes from the unconscious when the connection with deeper spheres of the psyche is activated. If the conscious mind can assimilate a deeper meaning, a new symbolic pattern will be added to the conscious situation.

The function of one's suffering seems to relate to the possibility of elevating the level of individual consciousness through experience. The value given to the event and the way it is digested seems to be able to transform its meaning, creating a living connection between the conscious mind and the potentiality present in an archetypal constellation. Meaning would be felt in the emotional connection established between what one has lived and the depths of one's own psyche.

Intra-psychically, the introspection usually caused by suffering – i.e., the dynamic of the libido in the process – would activate the archetypal patterns present in one's psyche. The libido flowing inwards may activate images, feelings and potentials present in the archetypal world, and with them, it would allow healing processes through a meaningful connection, if the conscious mind is able to relate with it.

But this connection is not made automatically; one needs to do it consciously and recognise the deeper realm that symbolic redemption may bring to one's suffering. This requires the right attitude and a connection with the inner world. The ability to develop a symbolic life seems to be the way to deal with sufferings caused by what one would call his or her fate.

The events in life that cause joy and happiness have a similar effect but are easier to relate to. Usually, the person considers such occurrences as luck or merit, and takes them as a result of one's own work, the payment for one's effort. That may be true, because the conscious will is focused on achievement. This positive result could be linked to the concept of Destiny as well because goals are constellated in the individual. No one can choose what will fascinate him or her, it just happens. One is caught in the fascination of the goal to be achieved.

This aspect points to the concept that I called *Personal Myth*. In this hypothesis the pattern of meaning in one's life engenders goals, and with it guides one's conscious attitude towards them. This fascination is not chosen but happens to the person.

One may use a metaphor to understand this idea: the image of a prairie with uncountable seeds spread all over it. The diverse conditions of the field, the soil, the amount of rain, the strength of the wind or the amount of water available may facilitate the development of some seeds and block others. As time goes by, the prairie will achieve its unique characteristic. It can develop into a forest, a field of flowers or a desert, but it will be the result of many aspects that were present as potential in the beginning. One may ask, what would be the role of the ego-consciousness in this metaphor? It would be the gardener, whose work may make the prairie produce fruits or not, may make it beautiful or not, once realising the potential present in the seeds over the earth.

Concluding remarks

Sometimes life offers a challenge, in a dream, in a fascination, in a goal to be achieved, which comes from the deepest part of one's soul. It works like a call, a magnet which attracts one's attention, and does not let it rest. Usually, one is unconscious of its source and does not think but feels it. Such fascination demands attention and focus on one's perception of it.

The voice of the personal myth is in this call, a call from the soul which should not be ignored. But by that I do not mean *achieving* the goal; *the journey towards it* is one's personal myth.

Not living one's personal myth means losing contact with one's own soul. Life will tend to become boring and meaningless. One may have everything that she/he wants, but probably not what one's psychic life really needed. At this point the occurrence of a neurosis can be a sign that one is living far away from his internal pattern, and illness could be understood as the attempt of the psyche to question the conscious attitude. I would like to conclude with Jung's comment:

> If you fulfil the pattern that is peculiar to yourself, you have loved yourself, you have accumulated and have abundance, you bestow virtue then because you have lustre. You radiate; from your abundance something overflows. But if you hate and despise yourself – if you have not accepted your pattern – then there are hungry animals (prowling cats and other beasts and vermin) in your constitution which get at your neighbours like flies in order to satisfy the appetites which you have failed to satisfy. Therefore, Nietzsche says to those people who have not fulfilled their individual pattern that the bestowing soul is lacking. There is no radiation, no real warmth; there is hunger and secret stealing. . . . You see, that degenerate sense which says 'all for myself' is unfulfilled destiny.
>
> (Jarrett, 1998, p. 185)

Notes

1 Private notes of the lecture 'The Poetic of Pathos' by Renos Papadoupoulos SS 1994, C.G. Jung Institute Zürich
2 For more details, see de Moura (2019).
3 Jung presented the idea of a second psychic system, a kind of 'super consciousness,' co-existing with ego-consciousness – CW 8 par 369.

References

Bowker, J. (1970). *Problems of Suffering in Religions of the World*. Cambridge: Cambridge University Press.

Brandão, J. (1986). *Mitologia Grega – Vol. 1* (my translation). Rio de Janeiro: Vozes

de Moura, V. L. (2019). *Two Cases from Jung's Clinical Practice*. London: Routledge.

The Encyclopaedia of Religion (1987). New York: Macmillan.

Hawkins, J.M. and Allen, R. (1991). *The Oxford Encyclopaedic Dictionary*. Oxford and Clarendon Press.

Humphreys, C. (1944). *Karma and Rebirth*. London: Albemarle Street W.

Jarrett, J. (ed.) (1998). *Jung's Seminar on Nietzsche's Zarathustra*. Princeton, NJ: Princeton University Press.

Jung, C.G. (1930). The Alchemical Interpretation of the Fish. In *Collected Works, Vol. 9ii, Aion, Researches into the Phenomenology of the Self* (2nd ed.). London: Routledge and Kegan Paul, 1989.

Jung, C.G. (1942). The Problem of the Attitude Type. In *Collected Works, Vol. 7, Two Essays on Analytical Psychology* (2nd ed.). London: Routledge and Kegan Paul, 1990.

Jung, C.G. (1949). The Father in the Destiny of the Individual. In *Collected Works, Vol. 4, Freud and Psychoanalysis* (2nd ed.). London: Routledge and Kegan Paul, 1993.

Jung, C.G. (1952a). Answer to Job. In *Collected Works, Vol. 11, Psychology and Religion* (2nd ed). London: Routledge and Kegan Paul, 1991.

Jung, C.G. (1952b). On Synchronicity. In *Collected Works, Vol. 8. The Structure and Dynamics of the Psyche* (2nd ed.). London: Routledge and Kegan Paul, 1991.

Jung, C.G. (1952c). Synchronicity: An Acausal Connecting Principle. In *Collected Works, Vol. 8, The Structure and Dynamics of the Psyche* (2nd ed.). London: Routledge and Kegan Paul, 1991.

Jung, C.G. (1955). Letters on Synchronicity. In *Collected Works, Vol. 18. The Symbolic Life* (2nd ed). London: Routledge and Kegan Paul, 1993.

Jung, C.G. (1957). Psychology and Religion. In *Collected Works, Vol. 11. Psychology and Religion* (2nd ed.). London: Routledge and Kegan Paul, 1991.

Linddell, G.H. and Scott, R.A. (1977). *A Greek-English Lexicon*. Oxford: Oxford University Press.

Meunier, M. (1989). *Nova Mitologia Clássica* (my translation). São Paulo: Ibrasa.

Otto, R. (1946). *The Idea of the Holy*. London: Oxford University Press.

Otto, W.F. (1978). *The Homeric Gods*. New York: Octagon Books.

Smith, H. (1991). *The World's Religions*. London and New York: Harper Collins.

von Franz, M.L. (1992). *Psyche and Matter*. Boston and London: Shambala.

Whitmont, E. (1992). The Destiny Concept in Psychotherapy. In Wheelwright, J. (ed.), *The Analytical Process: Aims, Analysis and Training*. New York: G.P. Putnam & Sons.

Part VII

Psycho-social dimensions of grief and the mourning process

Chapter 14

Opening the eyes to invisible people

Idalina Souza

Introduction

During the first three to four years of the Covid pandemic, the number of vulnerable homeless people in Brazil has grown to an alarming degree. The pandemic has increased the suffering of the poor to a tragic level where their plight can no longer be ignored. Disparities of wealth and access to social services have become glaringly apparent. Homeless people have been exposed to violence, hunger, disease, fear, rain and cold weather. Kardec (2006) has expressed how a person's worth is diminished if she/he has to beg for charity. He adds that a society based on justice must offer the weaker person a life without humiliation. For the homeless, there is no place to shower, go to the toilet or drink fresh water, as some water is polluted. The vulnerability and precariousness of their existence include hunger, lack of housing and infrastructure, difficulties obtaining essential documents, medical care, medication and, mainly, enough attention to their plight. Vulnerability is usually defined by its semantic meaning, derived from the Latin *vulnus*, which means wound. Thus, this vulnerable population suffers in several different areas from the physical dimension relative to their social status. Personal and social vulnerability is certainly a fault of public policies. The people and families who live on the streets, however, have no interest in politics and political parties because most do not have the valid documentation to promote their identity to be able to vote in the first place. Therefore, they live like invisible entities, offering repulsion and fear while threatening families and communities near their homes. Authorities, theoretically responsible for the lives of the citizens, despise these human beings for their failure to promote equity, security and dignity.

Some perverse opinions, without any scientific research basis, have pointed out that Covid contamination would be less severe for homeless people and they thus became the uncounted, invisible victims of COVID-19. Margot Kushel (2021), a professor of medicine who directs the Center for Vulnerable Populations at the University of California, San Francisco, said that she didn't accept the narrative that Covid has not adversely affected homeless people. In Brazil, some health authorities wanted to ignore the sick Covid homeless people and avoided revealing

DOI: 10.4324/9781003313304-22

the true causes of their deaths. Most of the Covid victims were buried as paupers, without status value.

Historical dimensions

Jungian analyst Walter Boechat (2012, p. 34) reports how the history of Brazil has been an encounter between different peoples and races since its discovery in 1500 by the Iberian Portuguese. From that time, the first male settlers had sexual relationships with indigenous women and had offspring with them, so the first mother of all Brazilians was *the great Indian mother*. Boechat contests the notion of a 'racial democracy' coined by sociologist Freyre; instead, there is strong evidence of racial prejudice attached to skin colour, representing one of Brazil's most important cultural complexes. The identity of the new nation of Brazil was the product of interbreeding between white Portuguese and the indigenous population. Their offspring, the Mestizos, integrated both ethnicities, but it was not a peaceful co-existence as the Portuguese tried to enslave the indigenous people for labour. Many died or fled to the interior of the Amazon Forest to avoid the cruelty and diseases brought by the Portuguese. As Feldman (2012, pp. 111–113) notes, the indigenous people were treated as alien 'others' with the view that Brazil had to be conquered, integrated and subjugated under mother Portugal and Catholicism as soon as possible and hopefully at a profit. Indigenous people were viewed as primitive subhumans lacking a soul.

Colonial discourse (cf. Gambini, 2000) shows that indigenous Brazilians were conceptualized as exotic (sexual) and pathological (cannibalistic), the disavowed 'other' of the colonizing Portuguese. The image of the sadistic enslaver and the suffering enslaved person has solidified itself within the stratified system of Brazilian society. Early colonial times in Brazil also marked the beginning of human trafficking, where Africans were captured and brutally shipped to Brazil to work in sugar cane plantations and gold mines. The importation of enslaved Black people began at the end of the 16th century and ended in 1895. To survive, Africans clung to their indigenous beliefs with the widespread Afro-Brazilian religion called *Candomble*, which includes African and Christian gods to protect Black identity in the new world. Racism as a cultural complex continues to influence society through its sadistic class system. Low wages and lack of opportunities with a concentration of wealth among a small proportion of the 'white' population with a substantial prejudice against the 'weakest' classes are influenced by ethnic discrimination since the Blacks and Mestizos have great difficulty achieving better living standards. The prevalent cross-breeding in Brazilian history is a major factor of its social makeup. Although Mulattos and Mestizos have participated with significant success in Brazilian culture, their contribution is often devalued. Despite claims that Brazil has a 'racial democracy' or claims that it has a benign 'cordial racism' (cf. Boechat, 2012), racism still appears in disguise as a collective shadow and goes hand in hand with social class prejudice. An affable 'cordial persona' can just as efficiently function as a disguise for violence, rejection and superiority, closing its doors to equality in jobs and education for Blacks, Mulattos and indigenous Brazilians.

The roots of poverty in Brazil

Studies of Brazilian history show how poverty and low self-esteem were established from the beginning. When Portuguese migrators came to the continent, they were interested only in the resources the new land could offer. They were predators, not interested in the welfare of the indigenous population. The women were raped, became pregnant and abandoned with their mixed-race children being born in the forest without their fathers. Many of these children were rejected by their tribes and then murdered. In my opinion, the invasion of the white European brought several disasters to the New World, such as diseases, for example, influenza, syphilis, gonorrhoea, smallpox, measles and alcoholism, among others.

Since that time, Brazilian people have constituted a second-class, devalued race, not considered a sovereign people but as a European colony by colonists who were intent on exploring new territory. Brazil was not cared for but exploited, despoiled of its resources and, sadly, of its vast potential. This situation has lasted for centuries without any solution or modification. With the introduction of slavery in the 1530s, the Portuguese colonists implanted the bases of slavery to meet the demand of Portuguese farmers for agricultural labour. Such a process happened, firstly, with the enslavement of the indigenous population and then substituted by Africans brought by the slave trade.

Slavery, as a cruel and perverse institution, has been experienced for over 130 years after the Áurea Law abolished it. The violence and the discrimination suffered by Black people are the direct reflection of a country that built itself on normalizing prejudice and violence against this group. However, it is vital to remember that the indigenous Indians were made slaves as well by the Portuguese and that their slavery has perpetuated prejudices and violence against them.

Brazil was the last country on the American continent to abolish slavery. The Áurea Law, signed by Isabel Princess, was meant to end that misery. However, the Áurea Law was not a benevolent act by the monarchy but the result of the Brazilian people who forced the princess's hand. The Eusébio de Queirós decree prohibited Black traffic in 1850. As the abolitionist movement became more vigorous, several associations defended the cause and emerged in the country with different ways to fight against slavery. Lawyers defended the enslaved people against their owners; newspapers published articles supporting abolition, and ordinary people harboured slaves who had escaped. However, the formerly enslaved people increasingly suffered because of the prejudices still against them, and because they had no money, job or a place to live. Homeless people thus came into existence. Throughout its history, Brazil has existed with much of its population in deep poverty. The tendency is tragically increasing, with the poor excluded from minimal financial resources, but also health care, schooling, adequate food and the rights that guarantee citizenship status (Silva et al., 2022).

Valladares (1991, p. 93) affirms that poverty was recognized as a social issue only from the 1950s to 1960s because a society based on an agrarian-export economy moved towards a more modern, urban-industrial type. Industrialization conditioned a process of population expansion in large urban centres due to the rural exodus from the countryside to the city looking for employment and housing which accelerated growth and disorganized urban areas, especially in locations where the industrial development was more dynamic. Moreover, according to Valladares, in the Brazilian case, this economic expansion, associated with the impoverishment and disruption of the labour market, developed without the concern of a social care state system to minimize the impact and be capable of promoting social development. Thus, there has been a general worsening of living conditions in cities resulting from the inability to meet the basic needs of an ever-increasing population. An informal work sector consequently developed without the guarantee of human rights.

The urban space

It was only during the 1990s, according to Pereira et al. (2006), that poverty in Brazil became part of the public agenda, gaining visibility as an object of general interest since it represents a problem to be solved in a democracy under the suspicion of constituting a threat to the very stability of re-democratization. Fabiana Lemos Sant'Ana (2019) affirms that the city is a landmark in consolidating capitalism; in that sense, it expresses its inequalities within urban space. In Brazil, its disorderly consolidation presents numerous contradictions and processes of exclusion of a large part of the population. The country that historically bills itself as a nation amidst significant differences (racial, cultural and social) in the urban space denounces disparities and hegemonic interests. Housing and the occupation of space show these differences. The processes of formation of the Brazilian territory and the growth of cities reflect the present reality. And it is in this space, the urban city, where we encounter the contradictions of capitalist production, as Lefebvre (1999) points out, and where the broader, more complex reproduction cycles are realized. (p. 171). Because of the historical growth process of Brazilian cities, urban growth, actions and responsibility of the Brazilian state are also related. In this scenario, we have embedded differentiated strategies related to its population, class relations and race in its history, stamping different realities within the urban space. In this context, we highlight the emergence of *favelas*, mainly Rio de Janeiro favelas, which correspond to this period of housing crisis addressed by Silva (2005, p. 37), and which, for the author, gains visibility between 1930 and 1940 as a national "housing problem," a clear projection of the reality of Rio de Janeiro as the republic's capital as a mirror for the whole country.

Thus, a bibliographical review aims to understand the space occupied by the Black population in Brazilian cities, mainly in Rio de Janeiro, and emphasizes the racial question in an attempt to know the uses, appropriations and inequalities. From the formation of quilombos to the transmutation to slums and favelas, as Campos (2012) presents, we highlight the incessant struggle for citizenship. The time of slavery criminalized spaces always subject to a hegemonic order, which remains to the present day. We show, mainly from Black authors, quilombolas and slum dwellers, the contradictions and hierarchies of an unjust society where citizenship rights are selective and restricted. From these studies, we conclude how homelessness developed and how poverty became a tragic reality, bringing to the streets, men, women and children who are invisible to others and to the authorities.

The homeless

The conflicts that appear in the interrelations between the homeless population and the other city inhabitants of the city show that the individual is blamed for their extreme poverty. They are highly vulnerable, abandoned and not seen. Sotero (2011) argues that this group is exposed and perceived as the fault of public policies designed to promote equity and targeted to suppress historical distortions. The conflicts that appear in interrelations between the street population and the other inhabitants of the city show that they are facing the barrier imposed by their life history; they also need to meet the prejudice, which not only diminishes their self-esteem, but interferes with social interaction situations, becoming another hindrance in constructing their citizenship.

The Universal Declaration on Bioethics and Human Rights (UNESCO, 2005) propose that *individuals and groups especially vulnerable should be protected, and these individuals' integrity should be respected.* Therefore, one expects that public policies would provide visibility and solutions to the problems experienced by the homeless and stimulate actions to correct their plight. Júlio Lancelloti (2022), the humanistic Brazilian priest, affirms that all the homeless and poor people from ancient times until now are the mirror of deep personal characteristics, marked by indifference and selfishness. Lancelloti agrees with Chrysostom (2018) that all unfair distribution of wealth is perverse and must be denounced. Necessary attention and discernment are urgent for the transformation of societal inequality. Governments must protect and take care of their citizens, avoiding misery, diseases, and hunger by giving them healthcare, education and comfort. That should be the government's most essential function (cf. Lima, 2022 on education). The difficulty of implementing social change is integrating the shadow projection of the homeless as *homo sacer* and deserving of social justice.

Homo sacer as the 'shadow' of the collective unconscious

The *homo sacer* was an archaic figure of Roman Law who, because of the extreme exposure to violence and political and social vulnerability, dwelt in the non-being zone. In the Old Roman time, when an individual was proclaimed *sacer*, s/he was excluded from all rights and, consequently, from the public and religious life of the city. The *sacer* condition showed a paradox: their life had to be kept in the position of a dead-alive one, exposed to the ignomínia, but neither dead nor utilized in sacrificial rituals. However, anyone could kill him/her without any legal responsibility or ramifications for that murder. The *homo sacer* became a human body completely exposed to death, a life abandoned by law, including being dumped in an anomie zone. The *homo sacer* was a murdered life, an invisible taboo to the community's political values and religiosity. They were human lives abandoned to death.

Agamben (1998) vividly expands on the concept of *homo sacer* by analysing biopolitics in the context where ethics has lost its previous religious, metaphysical and cultural grounding. Agamben defines the *homo sacer* as a person who can be killed but not sacrificed, a paradox he sees as operative in the status of the modern individual living in a system that exerts control over the collective naked lives of all individuals. There is a distinction between the philosophic *sacer*, a white European man, and the Brazilian, São Paulo, who is younger, poor and Black as the *homo sacer Brasilis*, who suffers the deathly, ghostly experience of ancestral structural racism, equally evident in the mishandling and abuse of Black people in the United States and the United Kingdom. Geopolitics shows that suffering is widespread in most countries that are not concerned about the welfare of all their citizens but only with their political and material power, based on the exclusion of shadow others.

This phenomenon was most evident in Germany's antisemitic treatment of German Jews during the Third Reich. Jews became invisible as shadow, filthy, contaminated people with no right to exist because they did not conform to the white, ascetic, pure Aryan image. Their shouts were ignored, their tears were dried and bloody and their hands were empty. Nobody was interested in their fate. They had become vermin, pests and cultural degenerates who must be exterminated. Descriptions of Jews as 'rats' that spread diseases are designed as mechanisms of dehumanization to take away their human rights and deny them access to humanness. Recent research into dehumanization (Hodson et al., 2014, pp. 88–105) shows that dehumanizing metaphors typically communicate that an excluded outsider group is unlikeable, lower in ability and morals either as subhuman or inhuman, making ignorance of their inhumane expulsion easier, irrespective of their actual worth.

Rene Girard similarly discusses the correlation between violence and sacredness (1988, p. 29). Specific individuals as anomalies or monstrosities of nature which cause impurities and contagion are singled for sacrifice to restore a cohesive balance within the collective structure. Violating the miscegenation taboo of interbreeding between ethnic groups would be one such example. Biracial or multiracial people have no proper place. Dark colours emanating from the margin (skin) are hazardous, linking blackness with fear of unknown 'shadow' aspects of dirt that cannot be washed away and is associated with chaos and death. Such blackness has supposedly travelled from the inside to the outside and can be classified as 'outsider dirt.' Miscegenation operates to facilitate certain combinations of racial mixing while contradicting the fantasy of racial purity. It constructs racial categories, regulates sex and organises kinship to determine legitimacy, descent and inheritance. Biracial or multiracial people who have crossed over the margin/border that structures experience and self-cohesion fall into an in-between state of two or more cultures. Their sense of identity becomes sinister, unstable and uncanny to themselves (cf. Bergner, 2005. p. 65).

Images of dissociative defences in street art (graffiti images) in São Paulo show how unintegrated affect generated by intergenerational trauma threatens the experience of self-cohesion and self-continuity. Jungian analyst Wahba (2012, pp. 75–107) movingly illustrates how these images reveal the suffering and dehumanization of the subject and also portray isolated parts of the body. Negative emotions are shown through freezing and numbing shots as if communication itself is precarious, with words locked inside or imaged through gaping mouths with teeth grinding open up into bottomless wells starved of psychic and physical nurture. Figure 7 in Wahba (2012, p. 87) shows the state of shock in daily city life where aggression is disconnected from feeling. Wahba (2012, p. 87) poignantly states: 'With no sense for life, death loses its existential significance, tragedy becomes trivial and heroic death disappears, leaving in its place tedium and the indifference of destiny.'

Depositions from homeless people

A   G.B. He doesn't know how old he is. He sat down on the bus stop stairs. He was happy because he received two bags full of groceries as wages; he says he is afraid of becoming sick with Covid. He doesn't want to die. He picks recycled materials on the streets. He feels he is destitute and has nothing in this life.

B   B.F. He was 27 years old. He was in the bus station with dirty clothes. He has no profession. Sometimes, he works as a bricklayer. He was married years ago but has lived on the streets for seven years. He is scared of dying alone on the streets.

C   G.C.P.B. He sat down under a tree and unrolled several dirty and smelly blankets. He had backpacks with clean clothes he had earned. Someone gave him food. He came initially from Ceará, in the north of Brazil. He was previously able to work cooking barbecues, and he was an excellent cook, but he began to drink. He says nobody trusts him as if he were not expected to live. Some days he has food, some days nobody gives him anything and some people give him blankets. He says that he dreams. One dream is a nightmare when somebody stabs him in the back. He comes and goes, day and night. He says he has nothing, but sometimes, he thinks he has the whole city to himself.

D   A.C.A. He had no possessions, only a bag with some biscuits. He wanders around the city. His father and mother died when he was eight years old, and he is alone. He has already worked as a bricklayer in sugar cane agriculture camps. But alcohol and drugs have destroyed him.

E   J.A.S. He came closer to me because of the sandwiches on offer. He was hungry. He had clean clothes and some more in a suitcase. He has lived on the streets for ten years. He sleeps under a roof close to the bus station. He worked with a truck for several years, but after leaving his wife, he became lost. He says he is afraid of everything and everybody.

Integrating 'shadow' as part of the individuation process

Jung (1954) defines individuation as the archetypal process that asks, who am I beneath all my social roles and responsibilities? To move towards the integrative goal of the psyche, it is necessary to integrate the 'shadow' to transform the psyche into humanness without projecting the unwanted parts of oneself onto others as the 'outsider.' It is often easier to love pets, defend ecology and worry about climate change than to care about people suffering from poverty, starvation, disease and homelessness. Why do most of us remove ourselves from human suffering, even if we know that the transformation of the psyche is impossible without loving and accepting each other?

Jung (1949) emphasizes that the development of the human soul deals with integrating the complexes, the shadow and the awakening of a sense of ethics towards the other. It is generally the process by which individuals are formed and differentiated from general collective psychology. Any serious check to individuality is artificial stunting, and stunted individuals in any social group cannot preserve their internal cohesion and positive collective values. Individuation is opposed to the collective norm but not directly antagonistic towards it, only differently orientated, being closely associated with the transcendent function that creates individual lines of development which could not be reached by adapting to the collective norm (Jung, 1949, paras. 757–762). This means reforming public policies is the second step, which comes after the plight of the excluded has been felt by the individual. Strong movements focusing on the necessity of care on different fronts in more diverse groups of psychologists, physicians, social workers, teachers, lawyers and nurses will be strong enough to produce socio-economic change, but only when each person has suffered deep inside themselves the vulnerability of the discarded homeless people as if s/he were oneself.

Social change and a new ethic

An excellent personification of the individuation process is Eduardo Moreira, a Brazilian engineer who lived through difficult times of inner suffering and anxiety and decided to go deeper into the issues of inequality (UNESCO, 2005). He chose to fight for a fairer Brazil using Saint John Chrysostom's (2018) compilation of sermons about richness and poverty. John Chrysostom died in 407 CE. His speeches are still pertinent and linked to the current situation in Brazil, as well as worldwide. The poor in Brazilian society have suffered enormously from the negativity of the authorities and citizens in general. Chrysostom (2018) argued that ordinary people as citizens could ask for help and find solutions for poor people. Still, paradoxically, most do not help, ignore proposals of service and continue being absorbed in their vested interests, ignoring signs of any solution. What is relevant is that insensitivity, non-compassion, hate and prejudice are still part of the human psyche. Therefore, it is essential to bring to consciousness the inner content of aspects of the psyche: malignancy, turpitude and perversity. Thus, a deep education toward the essence of humanity comes first; then, society will move closer to benevolence and compassion, independent of politics and vested interest.

Júlio Lancelloti (2022), the humanistic Brazilian priest, affirms that all the homeless and poor people from ancient times are the mirrors of the deep soul marked by indifference and selfishness. He agrees with Chrysostom (2018) that all unfair distribution of wealth is perverse and must be denounced. Attention and discernment are urgently necessary for the transformation of actual reality. That means the authorities must protect and take care of all its citizens, avoiding misery, diseases, and hunger and giving them medical health insurance, schools and comfort. That is genuinely urgent, and the government's most essential mission.

Neumann and Jung on 'shadow' phenomenology

Erich Neumann (1990) highlights that new ethics demand responsibility and must be accepted as unconscious processes are derived from the problematic psychological situation of modern man as an individual. Even in terms of the collective, however, the same problem is thrusting its way into the foreground, since no elite can impose its ethic on the masses without bringing upon itself the resultant catastrophe. He affirms that in modern man, the process of collectivization and its polar opposite, individualization, has led to differences in ethical levels, and this, in turn, has resulted in such an intensification of psychic tension in both individual and collective that this whole situation requires for its solution a new development of consciousness, thus, a new ethic.

For Neumann (1990), the partial ethic is individualistic since it accepts no responsibility for the unconscious reactions of the group or the collective. As a person individuates, s/he gains a clearer sense of self and the purpose of the others around them. Thus, as much as the individual becomes sensitive and caring to the pain of humanity, so the unconscious can support this development. Those who sincerely wish to live in harmony with the 'other,' side by side in equity, s/he automatically works hard to eliminate selfishness, antipathy, cruelty and domination.

Equally, Neumann (1990) stresses that the new ethic must be installed within the contemporary psyche. It demands that the efforts come from the unconscious, derived from the problematic psychological situation of modern man as an individual. To reach this level of humanity, 're-collectivization' and its polar opposite, individualization, have to lead to significant differences in the ethical level, and this, in turn, has resulted from such an intensification of psychic tension in both individual and collective that this situation now requires a solution that promotes a new development of consciousness and a new ethic. We ask the following questions: how is it possible to live in comfortable houses when men, women and children don't have any protection from storms, snow and floods? How can we eat a good lunch or dinner, look outside and see someone asking for something minimal to eat? How can we be happy buying a warm overcoat when someone doesn't have basic clothing? How can one take a comfortable warm shower when someone has not taken a bath for weeks? How can we visit a competent physician to care for our health when people die on the streets alone without assistance? Who are the ordinary people, and not the authorities, to interfere in the situation? They are the ones who can change their concept of humanity, going beyond their own lives and searching for ones which are suitable for others, too.

I agree with Neumann (1990) and Jung (1957) that the psychic development of modern humans begins with the moral problem and their reorientation, which is brought about through the acceptance and assimilation of the 'shadow' and the transformation of the persona. Neumann emphasized that 'the moral problem raised by depth psychology is most clearly formulated by the concept of the shadow personality.' Accepting one's self as including a dark aspect is a solution that brings unconsciousness of the problem to an end (Neumann, 1990, p. 143). Jung's analytical psychology shows a revolutionary faith in the creativity of the human psyche. The dark and ambiguous figure of the 'shadow' holds the key to developing a new wholeness and healing the split in humanity. Neumann interprets the 'shadow' as the guardian at the threshold who may appear first as the frightening devil who leads you into the depth of the unconscious. Jung (1957), like Neuman (1990), sees the shadow as the 'opposing will,' a necessary quality that promotes independent thinking, capable of making ethical decisions that promote change by opposing its authoritarian creator. Jung places himself on the side of humanity on the one hand, but equally, on the side of the shadow. as the alchemical Mercurius (Jung, 1957, para. 289). As Jung recognized, the zone of the 'shadow,' particularly the social shadow, as an outcast, and the confrontation with this figure must be fully experienced and assimilated for any true in-depth development that promotes social justice.

Social justice

Jung's thought (Jung, 1933) in the search for the soul is current, modern and prevalent in most countries worldwide. Jung realized that every step toward material progress, without compassion and love, would lead to catastrophe. Political ethics cannot differ from personal ones in daily life. It seems that we have been living in an intimation of the law that governs blind contingency, which Heraclitus called the rule of enantiodromia, or the conversion into the opposite. Perhaps the Covid pandemic, global conflict and unprecedented loss of life without mourning rituals and proper burials have disturbed the establishment and brought about new reflections about the disparities in the distribution of wealth and access to social justice. As John Chrysostom (2018) has reflected upon the nature of wealth, we ask ourselves in what manner does one possess the wealth of this world? And finally, what should one do with worldly wealth? Let us learn from this man not to call the rich lucky, nor the poor unfortunate. Instead, if we are the rich man, we are not the one who has collected many possessions, but the one who needs few possessions; and the poor man is not the one who has no control, but the one who has many desires. We ought to consider this the definition of poverty and wealth. So, if you see someone greedy for many things, you should consider him/her the poorest of all, even if s/he has acquired everyone's money. On the other hand, if you see someone with few needs, you should count her/him the richest of all, even if s/he has acquired nothing. Otherwise, there is poverty, the real one, as we know. So, what can the rich person, full of objective natural treasures, do, or must do?

In other words, how is the level of the individuation process of a post-modern person differ from the Jungian concept of individuation? Only the modern person, in our meaning of the term, who lives in the present-day consciousness, finds the way of life that corresponds to earlier levels appalling to him/her. The values and strivings of the past no longer interest him/her: s/he has become 'unhistorical' in the most profound sense, and has estranged him/herself from the masses who live entirely within the bounds of tradition. Indeed, s/he is thoroughly modern only when s/he has come to the very edge of existence, leaving behind all that has been discarded and outgrown and acknowledging that s/he stands before a void, out of which, however, new ideas may grow. The central thesis I defend is the universal individuation process of individual development together with the total movement of becoming integrated, and that both developmental processes come together.

Jung (1933) affirms that humanity does not exist for much of the time, but society has at least realized that every step toward material progress, without compassion and love, can lead to catastrophes. Until now, history's most prominent leaders have been mainly devoid of humanitarian values. They govern through vested personal interests as a reflection of their precarious, split inner world. Their unconscious contamination with cultural complexes, particularly concerning race, class and skin colour, results in the homeless on the streets being 'overlooked' as dirty, primitive 'shadow,' shameful aspects of themselves they wish to ignore, as not belonging to them.

Sotero (2011) states that in the case of the homeless population, who generally experience a lack of schooling, medical care, employment and money, the vulnerability inherent to the human condition is intensified and materialized. Then, in the generic and existential meaning extensive to humanity, one starts to identify this group as 'injured' and not as vulnerable, deserving of assistance.

Agreeing with Jung and Neumann almost without exception in their in-depth analysis of 'shadow' phenomenology, the psychic development of modern man begins with a moral problem. It can be resolved through the assimilation of the 'shadow' and the transformation of the persona. The social 'shadow,' embroiled in unconscious cultural complexes, prevents society from observing the problems, hurts, desperation and helplessness. And, in consequence, the crowd becomes blind to the ethical, feeling function. The invisible people don't exist. They are dirty, smell bad, are ugly, covered with scars, almost naked, and catch the eyes. But, as we do not feel responsible, we avoid seeing them, and they become invisible; they disappear in plain sight. We conclude that invisible victims do exist, and that the real injuries come from those who are blind and insensitive to their plight. The unique way to correct the situation is the transformation from the inside, focusing on compassion, benevolence and humanity. I conclude with Priest Lancelotti's (2022) paraphrased comments, which I think sums up the plight of the homeless in Brazil.

Priest Julio Lancelotti Speech

My connection with homeless people came before I became a priest in 1985. At that time, I tried to learn how to live close to them and understand their lives, sufferings, and hopes.

Nowadays, the number of these individuals increased significantly. Officially, they are thirty thousand people in São Paulo. The street population is not attractive because it is impoverished, ugly and dirty. Also, they carry difficult societal circumstances; some come from the jail system, most are migrants living far from their families, and many can have mental disturbances and are addicted to alcohol and drugs. They are pathologized as wrong, bad people and are strongly stigmatized. The connection to the homeless people is not an angelical one. It has conflicts, difficulties, challenges, misunderstands, and disputes to 'yes' and 'no' as in any ordinary human communication. To live with street people is to live with pain; privileged people think that street people should be humble, simple, thankful, and gentle. But they don't have love or happiness. They only have sadness, challenges and difficulties. Then, some people think that if they offer something, the street person has to accept, even when s/he doesn't like it. Some keep the food in their hands, but don't eat it. This means they are so alone, isolated from the ordinary people who don't talk to them and don't know their names. They are invisible and unheard even when they are in front of us. People are not what they show; we must catch and recognize their signs.

Last week, I received sweatshirts from a marketing campaign. I gave them away. The homeless were delighted when they realized that the clothes were new. They rarely receive something new.

Men and women have to use old, used underwear. Sometimes, they don't have toothpaste, brush, towels and soap. The street people are not as fake as plastic bags; everyone is not identical.

We can do several things to help them. Mainly, please, don't discriminate, don't feel prejudices, don't be against them, don't feel indifference, but also, don't idealize them: they are not angels nor demons. They are just human beings. Some days they are easygoing; some days not. They don't need only money as charity. They need to be considered just human beings. LGBTQI+, trans women, black people, older adults, and young people are human and must be looked at, cared for, and heard. It is more dangerous inside the National Congress and in the House of the Ministries than on the streets of our city. In São Paulo, we can do many things in the São Francisco Square Convivence Spaces oriented by São Francisco priests, who attend to one hundred people daily. In the church where I am, named Saint Miguel Arcanjo, the muslin group helps me. Also, the Candomblé and Umbanda groups, non-religious groups, come together to help.

I want to emphasize again that homeless people need a much more humanized, caring approach where the poor all have a place, voice, and food, where nobody is rejected, humiliated or banned.

Final considerations

I agree with Silva, A.C. et al. (2022) that poverty in Brazil developed throughout its history, mainly from a framework of extreme inequality, which developed a system of excluding and concentrating on socio-economic factors allied with the processes of industrialization and urbanization of cities, where people migrated in search of better living standards and employment. In this way, although the trajectory of poverty presents characteristics peculiar to each period of the country's history, it is notorious that in all of them, there is the predominance of impoverishment, precariousness and social exclusion of vast population contingents, which shows that society seems to have 'created a wall that becomes impassable' separating rich and poor, wealthy and destitute and, what is worse, under the appearance of normality. The Brazil 'shadow' is directly related to corruption and poverty. The roots are firmly grounded in the European invasion/colonization.

At present, more than 500 years later, the situation is still tragic, since poverty is a vital institution. Low self-esteem makes Brazilian people lower their heads to other cultures, devaluating the country's richness, culture, history and the main characteristic of kindness, charity and joy. The invisible people, dying and neglected on the streets, are the portrait of our 'shadow,' personifying what has to be hidden. Only when they are promoted and have the same rights and opportunities as everybody else will the 'shadow' come to light, and its potential become wealthy. On a societal level, working with the individuation process, it becomes impossible to keep closing our eyes toward the plight of the homeless. Being a Jungian analyst, it is a challenge to call to the attention of colleagues and Jungian societies to leave their praxis, turn to face the homeless in the streets and look into the eyes of sad, hungry, dirty, sick, humiliated people. But we need to do that, if we want Jungian psychology to include and serve everybody, democratically.

References

Agamben, G. (1998). *Homo Sacer: Sovereign Power and Bare Life*. Stanford, CA: Stanford University Press.

Bergner, G. (2005). *Taboo Subjects: Race, Sex and Psychoanalysis*. Minneapolis and London: University of Minnesota Press.

Boechat, W. (2012). Cordial Racism: Race as a Cultural Complex. In Amezaga, P., et al. (eds.), *Listening to Latin America, Exploring Cultural Complexes in Brazil, Chile, Columbia, Mexico, Uruguay, and Venezuela*. New Orleans, Louisiana: Spring Books, pp. 31–50.

Campos, A. (2012). *Do quilombo à favela. A produção do 'espaço criminalizado' no Rio de Janeiro* (5t ed.). Rio de Janeiro: Bertand Brasil.

Chrysostom, S.J. (2018). *On Wealth-Poverty*. Louisville: GLH Publishing.

Feldman, B. (2012). The Cultural Skin in Latin America. In Amezaga, P., et al. (eds.), *Listening to Latin America, Exploring Cultural complexes in Brazil, Chile, Columbia, Mexico, Uruguay, and Venezuela*. New Orleans, Louisiana: Spring Books, pp. 109–125.

Gambini, R. (2000). *Indian Mirror: The Making of the Brazilian Soul*. São Paulo: Axis Mundi.

Girard, R. (1988). *Violence and the Sacred*. London and New York: Continuum Press.

Hodson, G., Macinnis, C.A. and Costello, K. (2014). (Over)Valuing Humanness as an Aggravator of Intergroup Prejudices and Discrimination. In Bain, P.G., Vaes, J. and Leyens, J-P. (eds.), *Humanness and Dehumanisation*. New York and London: Routledge, pp. 86–110.

Jung, C.G. (1933). *Modern Man in Search of a Soul*. New York: Harvest.

Jung, C.G. (1949). Definitions (no 29, individuation). In *Collected Works, Vol. 6. Psychological Types* (2nd ed.). Princeton: Princeton University Press.

Jung, C.G. (1954). Archetypes of the Collective Unconscious. In *Collected Works, Vol. 9i, Archetypes and the Collective Unconscious* (2nd ed.). Princeton: Princeton University Press.

Jung, C.G. (1957). The Spirit Mercurius. In *Collected Works, Vol. 13. Alchemical Studies* (2nd ed.). Princeton: Princeton University Press.

Kardec, A. (2006). *The Spirits' Book* (3rd ed.). Brasília, DF: International Spiritist Council.

Kushel, M. (2021). [Acesso em: 10 de dezembro de 2022]. Disponível em: www.statnews.com/2021/03/11/the-uncounted-people-who-are-homeless-are-invisible-victims-of-covid-19/.

Lancelloti, J.R. (2022). *A Riqueza e a Pobreza – prefácio* (2nd ed.). Rio de Janeiro: Editora Paz e Terra.

Lefebvre, H.O. (1999). Capital e a Propriedade da Terra. In *A Cidade do Capital*. Rio de Janeiro: DPeA editora.

Lima, M.E. (2022). Junior A da SM. BRZEZINSKI I. Cidadania: sentidos e significados. XIII EDUCERE – Congresso Nacional de Educação, pp. 2481–2494. Curitiba-PR. [Acesso em 6 de dezembro de 2022]. Disponível em: https://educere.bruc.com.br/arquivo/pdf2017/24065_12317.pdf.

Neumann, E. (1990). *Depth Psychology and a New Ethic*. Shambhala: Reprint Edition.

Pereira, M.E.F.D., Guilhon, M.V. and Sousa, S.M.P.S. (2006). Pobreza e Justiça Social: eixos articulados dos programas de transferência de renda. *Revista Temporalis. Estado e política social: inflexões e desafios ao Serviço Social. Ano VI, nº12- julho a dezembro de*. Brasilia/DF.

Sant'Ana, F.L. (2019). O Negro Na Cidade: Quilombos, Favelas E Cidadania. *XIII Enanpege: A geografia Brasileira na Ciência-Mundo: produção, circulação e apropriação do conhecimento*. São Paulo, USP/BR. https://www.usp.org.

Silva, A.C., Bandeira, E.S.F. and Lopes, E.B. (2022). Pobreza No Brasil: Aspectos Conceituais e o Processo de Construção Histórica. [Acesso em: 08 de dezembro de 2022]. Disponível em: www.joinpp.ufma.br/jornadas/joinpp2011/CdVjornada/JORNADA_EIXO_2011/DESIGUALDADES_SOCIAIS_E_POBREZA/POBREZA_NO_BRASIL_ASPECTOS_CONCEITUAIS_E_O_PROCESSO_DE_CONSTRUCAO_HISTORICA.pdf.

Silva, M.L.P da. (2005). As transformações no Estado nacional e a cidade do Rio de Janeiro. In *Favelas Cariocas, 1930–1964*. Rio de Janeiro: Contraponto.

Sotero, M. (2011). *Vulnerabilidade e vulneração: população de rua, uma questão ética*. Rev bioét (Impr.). Brasilia (DF): University of New Brunswick Press.

UNESCO. (2005). *Universal Declaration on Bioethics and Human Rights*. Paris: UNESCO.

Valladares, L. (1991). Cem anos pensando a pobreza (urbana) no Brasil. In Boschi, Renato R. (Org.), *Corporativismo e desigualdade: a construção do espaço público no Brasil*. Rio de Janeiro: Rio Fundo, IUPERJ.

Wahba, L.V. (2012). Dao Paulo and the Cultural Complexes of the City: Seeing through Graffiti. In Amezaga, P., et al. (eds.), *Listening to Latin America, Exploring Cultural Complexes in Brazil, Chile, Columbia, Mexico, Uruguay, and Venezuela*. New Orleans, Louisiana: Spring Books, pp. 31–50.

Chapter 15

The Katako syndrome
Japan's problem with youth suicide

Hiroko Sakata and Cécile Buckenmeyer

Introduction

One afternoon, in a provincial town in Japan, a 17-year-old boy ('D') told his family that he was going for a walk. A day later, he was found dead, hanging from a tree, in a local park. He came from an unstable family environment, but at the time of his death, he was not thought to be at risk of committing suicide. He attended his school's opening ceremony at the beginning of the school year, two days before his death, and joined the class photograph. He didn't leave a suicide note, and there is no clear indication of what ultimately led him to take his own life. The park where he was found lies opposite his high school. Following his death, the teachers and school counsellors offered psychological support to all those who knew him. Sakata, one of the school counsellors, saw 20 of them in the days following his death, including some who have had suicidal thoughts themselves.

In this chapter, we wish to explain why the death of this young man is significant, socially, culturally, psychologically, spiritually and mythologically. We first introduce recent statistics about youth suicide in Japan and explain why it is seen as a major social problem. We also briefly present some traditional beliefs about death and the afterlife shared amongst the Japanese. Then, guided by Hayao Kawai's interpretation of Japanese mythology and the fairy tale *Katako*, we explore the imaginal which lies beneath youth suicide in Japan. Using a clinical vignette and a recently published manga, we highlight the archetypal themes that shape the inner life of young people who stand between life and death. This chapter is both an attempt to understand youth suicide and an attempt to describe a collective, unconscious process that takes place deep in the Japanese soul today.

Synchronistically, D died by suicide precisely at the time when we started working on this book chapter together. Although we didn't know him, we have held him in mind. We hope that our reflections can bring some insight, comfort and healing to those affected by youth suicide and somehow, bring peace to the departed souls.

DOI: 10.4324/9781003313304-23

Youth suicide in Japan

The overall number of suicides in Japan has declined in recent years to reach the lowest number on record in 2019 (just under 20,000).[1] But the number of suicides amongst Japanese children and young adults has dramatically increased since 2015. In 2020, 499 children in elementary, junior high and high school, committed suicide.[2] This was the highest number since records began in 1974, and 25% higher than the previous school year. The suicide ratio was 1.2 per 100,000 for those under 20 in 2006,[3] it more than doubled by 2018 and reached 3.1 in 2020.[4] Within 20 years, Japan's suicide rate for children, which was noticeably low, has become high compared to other G7 countries. There is no doubt that the COVID-19 pandemic has had an effect on young people's mental health, but the increase in youth suicides started before Covid, and as Covid restrictions were lifted, it continued to be high (473 in 2021).

An alarming aspect of youth suicide in Japan is that a third of the young people who took their own life in 2020 didn't express why they chose to do so.[5] In June 2021, the NHK broadcast a documentary on the impact of children suicides on their families.[6] The father of a boy who committed suicide in his early teens commented that his son had not shown any signs of being suicidal. He had been reluctant to go to school the morning of his suicide, but not in an unusual way for a junior high school pupil. He was active, enjoyed swimming and camping by the sea; he seemed to share openly his feelings with his parents. Three years after his death, his father is still unable to bury his son's ashes as he cannot understand what led his son to take his own life and what could have prevented him from doing so.

The anthropologist Ozawa-de Silva researched Japanese Internet suicide sites between 2003 and 2008 and offers an insight into the suicidal thoughts that people share on these online platforms. She notes that visitors commonly make comments to the effect that 'there is nothing wrong with my life, but I just don't know the reason to keep living' and 'it is not that I want to die, but I also don't want to live.' One person wrote, 'it is not that I really wanted to die. I just wanted to pause from living.' Visitors to these sites often express the lack of *ibasho* (literally, a place to be, a sense that they belong) and worry that other people could not accept them if they knew who they truly were, because they are not 'normal' (Ozawa-de Silva, 2008). According to Ozawa-de Silva,

> [the] social pressure they experience can become overpowering and lead to the wish to 'vanish' from the overburdening gaze of others.
>
> (Ozawa-de Silva, 2010)

This research highlights a lack of motivation – to live or to die – and a sense of disconnection from others; it helps understand why, if moved to commit suicide, some people don't want to (and perhaps cannot) explain their action; they experience a deep sense of isolation and an inability to share their feelings with anyone; they are desperate, but don't know how to ask for help. Following their deaths, parents, friends, teachers are left wondering 'Why?' and 'What could we have done to prevent it?' These unexplained deaths have a particular impact and meaning in Japan where, traditionally, the soul of the dead needs to be carefully accompanied into the afterlife.

Where does the soul go? Beliefs about death and the afterlife

The meaning of death and the afterlife in Japan cannot be conceived without grasping something of the complex and mysterious world of spirits. According to the worldview of Shinto and the form of Buddhism present in Japan,[7] the world is inhabited by a multitude of *reikon* (spirits). These are *kami* (best translated as gods or deities, but in fact very different from what is generally understood by these words), *tama* (souls), *rei* (spirits) and *mononoke* (ghosts) (Komatsu, 2018, p. 15). These *kami* and other spirits are rarely depicted but tend to be associated with a physical form, such as a stone, a tree, a mountain, a forest, an object and occasionally a person. The current emperor is thought to be a direct descendant of the sun goddess Amaterasu and, according to the Shinto priest Yamakage,

> since ancient times, Shinto has taught that the goal of human life is to 'become like a Kami' through the work of refining the personality and bringing out a clean and bright character. This work is understood to continue even after death.
>
> (2006, p. 149)

The boundary between spirits, people, places and objects is subtle in Japan. There is a dynamic relationship between the physical world (human and non-human, natural and man-made) and the world of spirits, including the spirit of the dead. In other words, the world of the dead is not entirely distinct from the world of the living:

> It has been widely believed in Japan that ancestral spirits exist in the invisible world, overlapping with physical reality and having intimate connection with people living in this world. In this unseen world, the ancestral spirits continue to work on their own purification.
>
> (Yamakage, 2006, p. 153)

This perspective about death and the afterlife is not only shared amongst Shinto priests and scholars but also is widely present in popular culture, including manga and animated films. The world of the living and the world of the dead are in constant interaction. Some spirits can be caught between these worlds, belonging to neither. According to the Shinto priest Yamakage:

> During the period of transition from this world to yukai, the hidden world of subtle energy, the spirit-soul is at its most vulnerable. It can be likened to a delicate butterfly, at the moment of emergence from its chrysalis.
>
> (2006, p. 157)

And,

> It should be noted that the spirit of the dead sometimes stays around in the early
> stages, but usually the spirit moves quickly into the other world.
>
> (2006, p. 163)

A peaceful death is more conducive to a smooth transition to the afterlife, in contrast to sudden, untimely or violent deaths. There is no traditional view that suicide
creates a difficult transition to the afterlife; suicide is not regarded as a sin in the
Christian sense of the word, but the manner of someone's death and their state
of mind when they die contribute to releasing uncleanliness or *kegare* (literally,
energy that withers or leaves, a potent, negative energy). For example, D's death
by hanging had an impact on many people: friends, family members, teachers, but
also passers-by and people working for emergency services. All these people and
the places where he died (the whole park) are exposed to *kegare*. They become
unclean and, traditionally, they would need to be thoroughly purified with water,
fire or light, according to Shinto practices.

Katako's suicide

Long before it became a major social issue, Hayao Kawai (1928–2007) was concerned about the problem of suicide in Japan. He was the first Japanese to train
as a Jungian analyst (in 1965) and became a highly influential figure in Japan and
beyond, especially known for his analysis of mythology and the Japanese psyche.
In 1985, he gave a lecture at the 54th Eranos Conference entitled 'Balancing the
Gods' in which he referred to the 'hidden gods' of Japanese mythology and specifically, to 'Hiruko, the abandoned god.' During his lecture, he introduced the
fairy tale *Katako*, the story of a young boy who commits suicide. We believe that
his analysis of this fairy tale, in conjunction with his account of Hiruko, can help
understand youth suicide in Japan today. Here is a summary of *Katako* based on the
version that Kawai used in Eranos:[8]

> Once upon a time, a man met Oni (a kind of devil) in the mountain. Oni asked
> him whether he liked mochi (rice cakes). The man jokingly answered that he
> liked them so much that he would trade his wife for some. Oni gave him lots
> of mochi, which the man happily ate. However, when he went home, he real-
> ized that Oni had taken him at his word and taken his wife in exchange. The
> man looked for his wife for ten years, until he finally realized that he had to
> go to the island of Oni to find her. On arrival, he met a ten-year old boy called
> Katako (half-child) who turned out to be the child of the man's wife and Oni.
> With the help of Katako, the couple were able go back to Japan and they took
> Katako with them. But in Japan, Katako was called 'Oniko' (child of Oni); he
> was rejected by the Japanese people. Finding it difficult to live there, he told his
> mother: 'If I die, cut the Oni part of my body into pieces, spit them out and leave
> them in front of the door. Then no Oni will be able to enter the house. If any

Oni dares to try, throw stones at his eyes.' After that, Katako climbed a tall tree and fell to his death. His mother grieved his death but did what he had asked her to do: when one day Oni came to their house, he shouted 'Japanese women are horrible. They spit out their own children's flesh!' Oni tried to break in, but the couple stopped him by throwing stones at his eyes.

The kind of devils called Oni bring destruction to the human realm; they can be described as a shadow image of humanity.[9] But, as all shadowy figures, they can also be tricksters, agents of transformation. Katako, half-Oni, half-child, held two deeply opposing worlds within himself and he belonged to neither of them. He wanted to be with his mother, but he didn't have an *ibasho* in Japan. He felt he had no choice but to kill himself.

After Katako's death, his mother 'spat out' pieces of his body. Eating people and sucking human blood is what Oni typically do in Japanese fairy tales, so one could say that Katako's mother behaved like an Oni. She tried to stop Oni coming into her house, but in the process, she became more like one.

In one version of the tale, Katako returned to his father's land, but in all others, the story ends with his suicide. Here is another example:

When Katako grew up, he couldn't help himself but eat people. So he asked his grandfather to kill him; otherwise, he would continue to eat people. The grandfather answered that he could never kill his own grandson, even if he was the child of Oni. Then Katako said 'It can't be helped. I will kill myself.' He went into the mountains and built a hut in the forest. He entered it and set it on fire. After Katako died in the fire, his ashes turn into mosquitos and leeches.

Katako wanted to be human and live among the Japanese, but he was animated by a powerful, Oni energy which he was not able to control. Unable to bear the tension within himself, he destroyed his body using fire (a powerful means of purifying *kegare* in the Shinto tradition), but he didn't completely vanish. In this version of the tale again, something of his Oni part stayed in Japan, not in his mother's behaviour, but in the form of mosquitos and leeches who suck blood like Oni.

According to Kawai, Oni's comment 'Japanese women are horrible. They spit out their own children's flesh!' indicates that the maternal side of the Japanese 'has a very cruel aspect; it rejects its own flesh and blood in order to protect itself from being invaded by strong masculinity' (1995, p. 97). Katako's Oni part contains 'strong masculinity' which challenges the 'maternal side' and is rejected. But across all versions of the tale, the birth of Katako blurs the divide between human and Oni; something of Oni survives in the human realm: Katako's mother eats his flesh, his ashes turn into leeches and mosquitoes.

In order to get a clearer insight into what Kawai means by the 'maternal side' and 'strong masculinity' – and therefore, to get an insight into what *Katako* might mean psychologically – we need to introduce Kawai's ideas about Japanese mythology, and in particular about an obscure *kami* called Hiruko.

The abandoned god, Hiruko

Kawai's in-depth analysis of the *Kojiki* and *Nihonshoki*, the two most ancient mythological texts, led him to identify what he called 'the Hollow Centre Structure of Japanese Mythology' (1995, p. 81). According to him,

> There is an aimless deity at the center, and the other deities form a harmonious wholeness. They are partly in conflict and have disputes with each other, but the whole is well balanced. There is no logical consistency but a sense of aesthetic harmony.
>
> (2003, p. 309, our translation)

This is in contrast with the Judeo-Christian mythology and many other world mythologies where one god is central and supreme:

> In Christianity, the center has the power to integrate all elements whereas in Japanese mythology the center has no power.
>
> (1995, p. 87)

Kawai also noticed that not all gods were contained within this hollow centre structure. Indeed, one god, Hiruko, was rejected from it shortly after his birth. Kawai thought that it was important to understand where Hiruko fitted within the Japanese pantheon and introduced his thoughts at Eranos.

Hiruko is a child of Izanami and Izanagi, the gods of creation. He is born as 'a limbless Leech Child' who struggled to survive because he could not stand on his feet, and so he was placed in a reed boat and set out to sea. Kawai believed that, like Moses and Perseus, Hiruko was rejected and set adrift on the water, but he was meant to return as a hero:

> The psychological significance of [Hiruko's] story is obvious: what was excluded from a system organised around a centre, gains power at the periphery and creates a new, different system. This is what defines a hero.
>
> (2003, p. 323, our translation)

The name 'Hiruko' gives some insight into what he represents – what was rejected, and what needs to return. Hiruko has two different spellings, with two very different meanings: it can mean Leech Child and also Noon Child. 'Leech' emphasizes the fact that he was 'limbless' and could not stand on his feet. 'Noon' suggests that he represents the male sun within the Japanese pantheon, a male counterpart to the powerful sun goddess Amaterasu, also known as Hirume (female sun).[10] Kawai thought that his presence as male sun was not compatible with the hollow centre structure:

> It was necessary for the Japanese pantheon to discard [the male sun/Hiruko] in order to maintain the stability of its hollow centre balanced structure. Japanese

mythology allows for the male-female pair of opposites, but the male aspect is always softened. . . . The male sun is too strong and willful, and would disrupt the balance of the hollow centre structure.

(1995, p. 91)

Both a leech and a solar god, Hiruko is weak and strong. He is watery, legless, but potentially, he is fiery, powerful and central, which makes him incompatible with the hollow centre structure. He has been rejected since time immemorial by the Japanese collective consciousness, but according to Kawai, it is the task of the Japanese people to find ways of engaging with him (2003, p. 330). At Eranos, he said:

The acceptance of the strong male, which the Japanese have rejected up to now, is the onus of the modern Japanese. In mythological terms the dilemma is to find a place in the Japanese pantheon for the male sun, Hiruko. This is an extremely difficult but necessary undertaking which confronts us today.

(1995, p. 92)

Hiruko and Katako in Japan today

The Eranos conference of 1985 is the first and last time Hayao Kawai presented in detail his thoughts about Hiruko, the abandoned god, and Katako, the abandoned half-child (Kawai, 2009, p. 228). In this lecture, Kawai hinted at a link between the two:

The transformation of Katako's ashes into leeches makes us realize . . . the secret relation between Katako and Hiruko. It dawned on me that the Oni in this story might be the offspring of the Leech Child, the carrier of strong masculinity.

(1995, p. 96)

Katako was rejected, and he committed suicide, but the appearance of leeches indicates that, through him, Hiruko was, in some form, able to return.

Kawai concluded his lecture by saying that 'many Katakos live among the Japanese people today' (1995, p. 97). He implied that there are people whom he called Katakos, who somehow facilitate the return of Hiruko in Japan today, people who engage in an 'extremely difficult but necessary undertaking' which involves challenging 'the maternal side' and supporting 'strong masculinity.'

We find Kawai's analysis compelling. Rooted in a careful study of Japanese mythology, it hints at the presence of mythological themes in the lives of modern Japanese people and can have important clinical applications. Some aspects of his formulation are problematic and have attracted criticism (Nakamura, 2013): Kawai associated the strong 'maternal side' with Japanese conformist society,[11] and 'strong masculinity' with a powerful new element,[12] but he has left unclear and open to interpretation what he meant by these words. Also, he has not illustrated who exactly these Katakos might be. Our intuition is that he may have consciously left these questions unanswered, in order for them to naturally evolve in the consciousness of the Japanese people. But we recognize that some answers must be provided for Kawai's analysis to be effectively applied psychologically, in a clinical setting.

In the second half of this chapter, we introduce those we believe are real-life Katakos. Using the expressions 'maternal side' and 'masculinity' cautiously, with quotation marks, we wish to offer our understanding of what, beyond these words, Kawai's analysis might mean, psychologically. Our hypothesis it that the tremendous psychological pain experienced by some young people in Japan is a sign of what he called 'the return of Hiruko' – a shift occurring in the depths of the Japanese soul. Using a clinical vignette and a popular manga, we describe how the themes and narratives of Hiruko and Katako permeate the inner lives of some Japanese people today.

A clinical vignette

Sakata, a Jungian analyst, clinical psychologist and licensed psychotherapist, works in educational settings from elementary school to university level. In recent years, she has met an increasing number of young people with suicidal thoughts. Miss K is a young woman she has worked with – someone we believe is a Katako.

K was an only child who had suicidal thoughts since she was in primary school and attempted suicide on several occasions when she was 15. Within a few months, she tried to hang herself and, twice, she tried to jump off the balcony of her parents' flat on the sixth floor. Her parents were luckily able to stop her in time and ensured that she didn't have access to dangerous household products and knives. As soon as her mother became aware of her daughter's suicidal impulses, she arranged for her to see a psychiatrist, who prescribed her antidepressants. K's teachers were also very responsive and recommended that she sees a school counsellor. K worked with Sakata for two years, meeting regularly, on average twice a month on the school premises. During these two years, K didn't actively try to take her own life, but she continued having suicidal thoughts. She was a studious, quiet and disciplined high school pupil, who had not developed meaningful friendships with peers since her suicide attempts.

Her father was a perfectionist and hard-working engineer, often working overtime and travelling away for work. He was a 'Showa man' (the Showa period lasted from 1926 to 1989), born at a time when Japanese men were expected to dedicate their life to their companies and help Japan achieve economic success. He had high standards for himself, but as he was socially isolated, he demeaned, criticized and bullied his family. He regularly insulted his wife, commenting that she was useless in front of their daughter.

K's mother had, like her father, left school at 18. She was a quiet, self-effacing housewife. For a time, she became suicidal herself, especially as her own mother blamed her for her daughter's difficulties. She once told K 'let's die together.' For her benefit as well as that of her daughter, Sakata introduced K's mother to a psychiatrist, who helped her become more stable and therefore better able to support her daughter.

K was an intelligent young woman, who could play Beethoven's piano sonatas and who aimed to join a prestigious university, but she didn't like going to school. She had at times thought of enrolling in a correspondence school to avoid having to meet anyone. She said that she wanted to become a civil servant, a profession where there is no gender pay gap. Above all, she was determined not to live the life of her mother. She sometimes had a fantasy of living a quiet, isolated life in the countryside or to become a nun in a Buddhist temple. She also had in mind, when she could afford, to go to Switzerland and seek assisted suicide because she didn't want to be part of a 'competitive society.'

Even when she was sick with anxiety, to the point of losing up to ten kilos and developing a fever, her father insisted that she went to school. She was aware that her feelings were denied, but she didn't know how to stand up for herself. At school, she hesitated to ask questions to her teachers when she needed help because 'it creates a bad atmosphere.' She knew that she wanted an *ibasho* (a sense that she belonged) but didn't know how to find her own voice. She didn't even have the space to find out who she was. In this context, daily experiences of self-denial were like small suicides, a negation of herself.

Three months after she started working with Sakata, K said 'I guess I'll just have to get along with people. Just accept life as it is. I'll just have to go on living like that.' And she shared a recurrent dream that she has had since she was in primary school:

I am trapped in a lift. My house is on the sixth floor [as in real life], but I'm on a different floor. There is a basement that looks like a public bath house or a warehouse. The lift goes to dozens of floors, even to the 23rd floor, but it doesn't stop at the sixth floor. What is frustrating is that, if I stop at the ninth floor, I can take the fire exit and walk, but I still can't get to my house.

The fact that K cannot go back to her house on the sixth floor captures the anxiety of not having an *ibasho*. Her dream is especially poignant when we know that she has tried to commit suicide by jumping off the balcony: her suicide attempt must have felt like the only way she could resolve her situation of being 'trapped in a lift' without ever being able to get back home.

The lift moves, but she doesn't control it; only from the ninth floor, she can walk up and down. The floors could be thought as her age and stages in her life. Until she was nine, she was not independent enough to choose the direction of her life; she was in an automatic lift. At nine, she became a Katako (he was ten when he was found on the island of Oni): able to walk, but still without an *ibasho*. Significantly, she needs to use the fire exit to find her way: it symbolically captures that she is in an emergency situation, that it is a matter of life or death. She is aware that the lift goes as high as the 23rd floor, but there is no mention of more floors above it. All being well, K would be 23 when graduating from university. She would then leave education and look for her way into life as a *shakaijin* (member of society). But in reality, she struggled to imagine what her life beyond 23 would look like: would she become a Buddhist nun, or commit suicide in Switzerland?

As Kawai wrote, 'the half-man [Katako] is always facing death. What they need is for their creative fantasies to be accepted' (Kawai, 1989, p. 260, our translation). K was symbolically standing on the balcony of her tall apartment building, facing death. Her creative fantasies were small threads that prevented her from falling: moments of realization, allowing her to delicately weave a new consciousness about herself, her future, the possibility of an *ibasho*. Here are some examples of such creative threads.

K had played the piano since she was in primary school, but she had stopped before she entered high school. Three months into the therapy process, she started playing again, for example, Beethoven's sonata No. 23 'Appassionata' (again, the number 23!). This piece is technically challenging and requires intense emotional expressiveness. When Sakata realized that K was able to play such complex pieces, she suggested that her father was perhaps criticizing her because he did not want to admit that his daughter was more capable than he was. K agreed. At the next session, K, who had been quiet and subdued, smiled when she entered the therapy room. Sakata was taken aback: K revealed for the first time a whole new aspect of her personality. From then on, she became more relatable, and even charming.

Around the same time, K shared that in the middle of the night, she obsessively watched the Japanese manga series *Jujutsu Kaisen* which is about a strange school where young sorcerers learn to destroy cursed spirits. K explained that when she went to school, it gave her comfort to think that she went to this school for sorcerers; it gave her the image of a way to survive. This series was so important for K, and it captures so well the inner world of a Katako, we believe it is worth exploring in some detail.

Jujutsu Kaisen 0

Jujutsu Kaisen is one of the most popular manga series of all time.[13] In the first book of the manga series, the main character is Yuta, a boy who is haunted by the spirit of his childhood friend, Rika. When they were both about 10 years old, Yuta and Rika had promised each other that they would get married, but shortly after, she died in a car accident. *Jujutsu Kaisen 0* is the story of how Yuta learns to control the power of Rika's spirit and destroy other cursed spirits. When Yuta is bullied, Rika becomes a ferocious force which punishes his bullies. And when Yuta has suicidal thoughts, he admits, 'I tried to kill myself. But Rika wouldn't let me.' The spirit of Rika protects him, but it hurts other people. Yuta gets desperate to the point that he doesn't want to hurt anybody anymore and decides not to go outside. He is then approached by a teacher at the Tokyo Prefectural Sorcery Technical School who tells him, 'The curse attached to you can help people depending on how it's used. Learn to control its power.' Yuta is introduced to the students at the school. They all have special powers, which they have learned to use effectively. When they first meet Yuta, they see a shy and polite young man (the person Yuta thinks he is), but they also see all around him a horrific monster, which is worm-like (no legs), with long muscular arms, nails and sharp teeth – the spirit of Rika. In the course of the story, Yuta learns about curses (which look like monsters of all kinds), and he trains with other students.

One day, when the lives of three people are threatened by one powerful curse, Yuta knows he needs to act. He has a moment of realization: 'I tried to run away and disappear, but I want to be with people, I want to be relied on by somebody. I want to believe that it's okay to keep living.' This leads him to accept his unique powers and to start exorcising. He learns to actively summon the spirit of Rika and work together with her.

Later in the story, Yuta realizes that he needs all the powers of Rika to kill 'the worst of all curse users': he sacrifices his life in exchange for her powers. After the battle, when Yuta willingly goes into death with Rika, the curse on him is suddenly lifted. He discovers that Rika was not cursing him after all: he cursed her because of his deep love for her, because he had refused to let her die. Once the curse is lifted, Rika's spirit is able to move on to the afterlife, and Yuta goes back to the school where he continues learning how to use his powers as a gifted sorcerer.

Jujutsu Kaisen shares many themes with the stories of Hiruko, Katako and K, indicating that they belong to the same archetypal field. Yuta's life changed when he was ten: his friend Rika died and he became 'cursed': Aged ten, he became a half-human, half-Oni Katako, made of a shy and polite boy on one side, and a ferocious cursed spirit on the other (see Figure 15.1) Interestingly, his Oni part, the spirit of

Figure 15.1 Yuta and his Oni part, the spirit of Rika

Figure 15.2 The spirit of Rika as a legless monster

Rika, looks like Hiruko: it is a legless leech with immense powers (see Figure 15.2). The tension between his two sides is unbearable for Yuta. He wants to kill himself, but something stops him. He wants to believe that 'it's okay to keep living,' but he is caught in a place without an *ibasho*, between life and death (K's lift).

The 'maternal side' in Japanese conformist society

The story of *Jujutsu Kaisen 0* might help us understand the power of what Kawai calls 'the maternal side' within the psyche of a young person like K. She is 'cursed' by her father's conformist attitude and continuous criticism, and by her mother's inability to stand up for herself. She is also 'cursed' by her own powers, an emerging awareness that she is more capable than her parents. These 'curses,' combined together, create a deeply oppressive situation, where the thought of being different from her parents is both attractive and overwhelming: she knows that she wants to be different from her mother, but she finds it difficult to imagine her future and even more difficult to have the confidence to say, 'this is who I am.'

The pressure to conform (an aspect of what Kawai called the 'maternal side') comes from her parents, but also her friends. Children who express their own feelings and aspirations can be cruelly ignored or bullied by their peers. They lose the confidence to voice their *honne* (honest opinion) and learn to superficially agree with others (*tatemae* in Japanese). As a result, they doubt that their thoughts and feelings have any value at all. K missed school for long periods of time, making it especially hard to join a friendship group. As a teenager, without the support of friends, she could not develop a meaningful image of who she was and could not healthily separate from her parents either.

Until she entered therapy, K didn't have the opportunity, at home or at school, to freely explore her own thoughts and feelings. In her imagination, she went to the Tokyo Prefectural Sorcery Technical School to conceive in her mind what it would be like to assert herself within a 'competitive society' (her words). It gave her an imaginary friendship group, within which she could learn to have her own voice and to 'destroy cursed spirits.'

Connectedness and suicide

Affiliation with others is at the core of many Japanese people's sense of themselves, arguably to a greater extent than for most people in Western countries. Kawai wrote that the Japanese form of ego 'has the premise of connection with others . . . [which is not] about the relationship of an independent ego to others . . . [but] a pervasive sort of connection that exists before the ego state' (1996, p. 112). He also wrote, 'in Japan, when you feel the existence of your connectedness with others, you can live,' but when there is a loss of connectedness, 'suicide will be attempted' (1996, p. 113). Ozawa-de Silva reached a similar conclusion:

> Currently, Japan is following the suicide prevention policies put forth by western nations and international organizations such as the WHO and the UN. However, these policies may not fully address the root causes that are driving individuals in Japan to existential suffering and the contemplation of suicide. One of these root causes appears to be a lack of affiliation and a strong felt need to affiliate.
>
> (2010, p. 414)

Katakos want to be with people but feel that they cannot be accepted. Their human part wants to be connected, but their Oni part triggers rejection, which makes it difficult for them to stay connected with others in the profound, pre-conscious way described by Kawai. Some Katakos like K have the strength to 'go on living like that,' despite their wish to 'vanish.' Some literally commit suicide, perhaps with the hope that it will resolve their internal conflict and help them return to a state of connectedness with others. In K's case, and probably many others, the words and actions that seem to express 'I want to die' are a cry for help, expressing how hard it is to go on living 'like that,' stuck in a lift, without an *ibasho*.

Within this context, the therapeutic relationship with a Katako is potentially life-saving, sustaining an experience of connectedness with others. It also creates a place where a form of death is encountered. Sakata's therapy process with K involved the acceptance of her creative fantasies in order to prevent a literal death, but it enabled a symbolic death, out of the pressures of a conformist society and into a new, imagined world, with a new form of connectedness with others. Something had to die for K to survive as a Katako: she had to die as a solely human being (as her parents' daughter) in order to live as a Katako who has an Oni part with all its powers and possibilities.

Oni and 'strong masculinity'

Another important feature of both Katako and Yuta to which we wish to draw attention is their relationship with Oni. In Japanese fairy tales, the task is traditionally to trick Oni and run away from him as quickly as possible (e.g. *The Laughter of Oni*). But, Katako cannot run away from his Oni part. Likewise, Yuta cannot 'vanish' into another world, because 'Rika would not let him.' 'Vanishing' is another typical theme in Japanese fairy tales (e.g. *A Flower Wife* or *Princess Kaguya*) where the main character completely 'vanishes' into another world or the afterlife. But Katako and Yuta cannot 'vanish.'

We believe that real-life Katakos cannot ignore their Oni part, and they cannot 'vanish,' either. Psychologically, they cannot reject an unknown, powerful Oni part of themselves which is emerging into consciousness. And even if some of them commit suicide, they cannot 'vanish': their death leaves *kegare*; their spirit is not free to go to the afterlife. Once they are a Katako, aware of their Oni part and of all its possibilities, they must wrestle between life and death until they find their *ibasho*.

For K, engaging with her Oni part is a process of discovering her own voice, her own powers, without losing her connectedness with others. Psychologically, it is a process of developing a new self-consciousness, of acknowledging her own thoughts, feelings and abilities; of breaking the 'curse' of peer pressure and conformity; of recognizing that she is not only the product of parental and social norms, but also her own creation. At a personal level, it is, in our view, a process of engaging with what Kawai called 'strong masculinity.'

A new vision

The tale of Katako may appeal to people beyond the Japanese shores, especially young people who struggle to form a clear sense of themselves, but it is uniquely Japanese; its images and narratives speak to the Japanese soul in a unique, intimate way. There are many Katakos like K in Japan today, who face death as they try to imagine a future for themselves. In addition to the question about their personal *ibasho* within Japanese society, these Katakos carry the burden of a collective task: finding a way to integrate Oni and allowing the return of Hiruko, at the cost of the age-old equilibrium of the hollow centre structure. Psychologically, they support the emergence of a new consciousness that shines its own light, however disruptive it may be. And in doing so, they participate in the emergence of a new mythical and spiritual structure, with a centre.

Through the inner struggles of Katakos across Japan, a new vision of the future is created. Some Katakos inevitably commit suicide, overwhelmed by the tension created by their two sides. It is our role as psychotherapists, school counsellors, parents and teachers to keep them alive. As stated by Kawai:

> There are many Katakos living amongst the Japanese today. I do not want them to commit suicide or go back to their father's land [i.e. Oni]. . . . The only path left is to keep them alive in Japan however difficult it may be. . . . I am certain that we have to keep these Katakos alive even though it is an enormously difficult task.
>
> (1995, p. 97)

As many more Japanese people, over generations, are likely to be Katakos, the nature of what we could call the Katako syndrome needs to be consciously engaged with. This includes developing a better understanding of the dynamics of friendship groups, the impact of social and parental expectations, the importance of young people's 'creative fantasies.' Above all, this may also require a shift in Japan's attitude towards its myths, beliefs and traditions.

Conclusion

The changes within Japanese society since the Meiji period (1868) and especially since the end of World War II are profound, but they have come at a great cost, spiritually. After the end of the Second World War, the Allies ordered a clear separation between 'the Shinto religion' (the Emperor, the shrines) and the state. The educational system was also revised, to protect people's freedom of religion. There are now many religious sects in Japan, but public schools do not offer any religious education at all. As a result, most people born after the war are not familiar with their own mythology.

Japanese people today are not necessarily aware of a 'hole' in their spiritual life, but compensatory dreams, products of their imagination and creative works like manga reveal the need for connection with the ancient myths and the world of spirits. In his last book, Kawai explains his personal experience:

> Japanese mythology has an unfortunate history of being interpreted and imposed on people by the military to serve their own purposes. Because of this

experience in my childhood [during World War II], I deeply disliked Japanese mythology. But to my surprise, I encountered Japanese mythology, when I studied in the U.S. and Switzerland, when I explored my inner world to become a Jungian analyst.

(2003, p. 333, our translation)

Japanese children and young adults who know little about the world of spirits and *kami* are unconsciously participating in the collective story of their people over millennia. As they wrestle with new archetypal forces emerging out of their unconscious, they need the help of existing, collective narratives to support them, guide them and, literally, keep them alive. Modern versions of the Japanese myths (like *Jujutsu Kaisen*) will naturally evolve out of the mind of young Katakos, but Japanese people need more opportunities to be in conscious relation with their myths to create an image of their future. As the mythologist Dumézil poignantly writes, 'a people without myths is already dead' (1970, p. 3).

Notes

1 The suicide rate in Japan, across all ages, was 12.2 per 100,000 in 2020, which is closer to the rates of other developed nations where it tends to be under 10.
2 www.mext.go.jp/content/20210625-mext_jidou01-000016243_001.pdf, retrieved in October 2022.
3 www.nippon.com/en/japan-data/h00572/child-suicides-at-highest-rate-ever-in-japan.html, retrieved in October 2022.
4 www.nippon.com/en/japan-data/h00857/, retrieved in October 2022.
5 www.nhk.jp/p/special/ts/2NY2QQLPM3/blog/bl/pneAjJR3gn/bp/p9Dr8MOm16/, retrieved in October 2022.
6 'We cannot let our youth choose death' (14 June 2021), www.nhk.jp/p/special/ts/2NY2QQLPM3/blog/bl/pneAjJR3gn/bp/p9Dr8MOm16/, retrieved in October 2022.
7 About this particular form of Buddhism, Kawai commented: 'After Buddhism was transmitted to Japan in the sixth century, it spread quickly. Among the general population, however, it was not well understood, as its doctrines, rules, and rituals were totally unfamiliar. Instead, Buddhism was received to the extent that it fused with Shinto, the indigenous animistic religion, and gradually it came to permeate daily life' (1996, p. 92).
8 His lecture, which took place in 1985, was published in 1995 as a chapter in the book *Dreams, Myths and Fairy Tales in Japan*. The first time Kawai wrote about *Katako* in Japanese was in *Sei to Shi no Setten*, published in 1989. The most comprehensive compilation of his ideas on this subject is available in his last book *Shinwa to Nihonjin no Kokoro*, published in 2003.
9 'You might say that in order to establish the concept of the human, Oni were created as our opposites' (Komatsu, 2018, p. 98).
10 Amaterasu is also known as O-hirume-no-muchi. Hirume literally means female sun.
11 'A conformist society that does not tolerate the existence of Katako because he is different, the attitude of parents who silently watch their own child commit suicide because they can't face social pressures, can these be linked to the superiority of the maternal side in the Japanese?' (1989, p. 255, our translation).
12 Kawai was vague about what he meant by 'strong masculinity': '[Hiruko] appears evil from the standpoint of the Moon God. At the same time, he may be regarded as a completely new element which could open a new way for the Japanese to proceed' (1995,

p. 91). He emphasised how Hiruko/'strong masculinity' was new, but he didn't define this 'new element.'

13   It is written and illustrated by a mysterious manga artist using the pen name of Gege Akutami (2018), who has received many awards but has never revealed their real name, or even their gender. An even more popular manga series called *Demon Slayer* is also written by an author who maintains anonymity in public. Koyoharu Gotouge (pen name) has written and illustrated the ninth best-selling manga series of all time, but very little is known about him. The main character in his manga, Tanjiro, is an adolescent boy, fighting Oni to save his young sister who has turned into an Oni. Like Yuta and Rika, Tanjiro and his sister are a pair, learning to master their powers and fighting together against Oni. Together, they are half-human, half-Oni – Katakos.

References

Akutami, G. (2018). *Jujutsu Kaisen 0*. Tokyo: Shueisha Inc.

Dumézil, G. (1970). *The Destiny of the Warrior*. Chicago: University of Chicago Press.

Kawai, H. (1989). *Sei to Shi no Setten*. Tokyo: Iwanami Shoten.

Kawai, H. (1995). *Dreams, Myths and Fairy Tales in Japan*. Einsiedeln: Daimon.

Kawai, H. (1996). *Buddhism and the Art of Psychotherapy*. College Station, TX: Texas A&M University Press.

Kawai, H. (2003). *Shinwa to Nihonjin no Kokoro*. Tokyo: Iwanami Shoten.

Kawai, T. (2009). *Nihon Shinwa to Kokoro no Kozo*. Tokyo: Iwanami Shoten.

Komatsu, K. (2018). *An Introduction to Yokai Culture*. Tokyo: Japan Publishing Industry Foundation for Culture.

Nakamura, K. (2013). Goddess Politics: Analytical Psychology and Japanese Myth. *Psychotherapy and Politics International*, 11(3), pp. 234–250.

Ozawa-de Silva, C. (2008). Too Lonely to Die Alone: Internet Suicide Pacts and Existential Suffering in Japan. *Culture, Medicine and Psychiatry*, 32, pp. 516–551.

Ozawa-de Silva, C. (2010). Shared Death: Self, Sociality and Internet Group Suicide in Japan. *Transcultural Psychiatry*, 47(3), pp. 392–418.

Yamakage, M. (2006). *The Essence of Shinto*. Tokyo: Kodansha International.

Index

Augustine 215–216
Áurea Law, Brazil 235
Australia 8, 55–56
Awe 170, 224
Awefulness 222
Awen 33, 36, 44
Azetec-Mexica roots 17
Azteca-Mexicana culture 90
Aztecs: Cochise as parent culture of 95n12; cosmology and religious worldview 20, 25–28; creator goddesses 90; funeral rites 21; mythology 19; Nahuatl language of 87; Tenochititlán 88

Bardo 101–105; Chikkai Bardo 105; *Chönyid Bardo* 105, 109; Sidpa Bardo 105, 109
Bardo Thödol (*Tibetan Book of the Dead*) 57, 102, 104–105, 109, 123
Bastian, Adolf 114
Baum, Frank L. 77–78
BBC: *Face to Face* 201
beaver 33, 38–39
bhava 111n9, 111n10
Bishop, Michael 71, 74–6, 77
Black people: in Brazil 234, 235, 236, 238, 244; enslavement of 234; as invisible people 6
Black Book (Jung) 85
Black Power Movement 23
boats: body of deceased placed in 56; ferry, as means of transportation for the dead 145; reed (Hiruko) 252; for souls 32; sacred 36; solar 31; sun god's 46
Book of Caverns (Egyptian) 45
Book of Durrow 57
Book of the Dead: Egyptian 41, 44, 46; Irish 10; Tibetan 57, 102, 104–105, 109, 123
Book of Kells 57, *58*
Britons, ancient 7, 32, 34, 40
Brown, P. 5
brown and indigenous peoples 6, 23–24, 26, 28
brownness 23–24
burial: collective 122; commemorative structures 6; COVID-19 and 124, 242; 'double burial' 138–140; excavations 7; first burials, Paleolithic 115–116; grounds 117, 120; mounds, Neolithic 55; mythological thinking associated with 118; primeval 114; ritualized 113; second

burial 140, 143; second burial, Japan 104; sites, Egyptian 55
burial rituals: cult of the dead 121; dangerous dead and 144, 146; Jungian dimensions to the mourning process of 1–11; mourning process, importance of 161–163, 242
burning: alchemical 188; of belongings of the deceased 138; of breasts 8; of lead, poured over coffins 43; of victims and their bones 45
Butler, Judith 194
Byung-Chul, H. 121

Caer: Golud 36, 37; Pedryvan 36; Pefryyan 37; Vedwit 36, 37; Wydyr 36, 37
Caernarfon 34
calcination and dissolution 188
Cambell, Joseph 113, 118
Cambodia: refugees from 178
Candomblé 234, 244
Catholic Church: All Saints' and All Souls' Day 18; beliefs 20; in Brazil 234; mass 85; in Mexico 90; rituals 18
cauldron: Ceridwen's 7, 21, 33–38, 45
cenotes 122
Ceridwen 7, 30–31, 33–38, 44–45, 47
Cervantes, Yreina 18
CG *see* complicated grief
chaos 24, 28, 31; Ceridwen and 35; Cythrawl as embodiment of 33; death/chaos versus life/logos 40, 43; dragon of 41; Hen Wen as pushing forth out of 47; Seth as personification of 43, 44, 47
Chavez, Cesar 23
Chicana culture 90; *see also* Anzaldúa
Chicano movement 17–18, 23, 27–28
Chicanx feminism 86; *see also* Anzaldúa; feminism
chrysalis 249
Chrysostom, John (Saint) 237, 240–242
chthonic gods 25
Cihuateteo 25
clairvoyance 224
climate and topography 7–8, 10, 30, 34, 47
climate change 240
Clotho 214
Coatlicue 25–26, 87, 88, 90
Cochise culture 95n12
commemoration and 150
compensation theory 23, 111n12, 187
complicated grief (CG) 139, 147–152, 179

For Product Safety Concerns and Information please contact our EU
representative GPSR@taylorandfrancis.com
Taylor & Francis Verlag GmbH, Kaufingerstraße 24, 80331 München, Germany

www.ingramcontent.com/pod-product-compliance
Lightning Source LLC
Chambersburg PA
CBHW050632280326
41932CB00015B/2612